Notes for Violists

Notes for Performers

Kyle Dzapo, Series Editor

Notes for Flutists
Kyle Dzapo

Notes for Clarinetists
Albert R. Rice

Notes for Violists

A Guide to the Repertoire

DAVID M. BYNOG

OXFORD
UNIVERSITY PRESS

Oxford University Press is a department of the University of Oxford. It furthers
the University's objective of excellence in research, scholarship, and education
by publishing worldwide. Oxford is a registered trade mark of Oxford University
Press in the UK and certain other countries.

Published in the United States of America by Oxford University Press
198 Madison Avenue, New York, NY 10016, United States of America.

© Oxford University Press 2021

Library of Congress Cataloging-in-Publication Data
Names: Bynog, David M., author.
Title: Notes for violists : a guide to the repertoire / David M. Bynog.
Description: New York : Oxford University Press, 2020. |
Series: Notes for performers series | Includes bibliographical references and index. |
Identifiers: LCCN 2020024088 (print) | LCCN 2020024089 (ebook) |
ISBN 9780190916107 (hardback) | ISBN 9780190916114 (paperback) |
ISBN 9780190916138 (epub)
Subjects: LCSH: Viola music—History and criticism. |
Viola music—Analysis, appreciation. | Concertos (Viola)—History and criticism. |
Concertos (Viola)—Analysis, appreciation. | Sonatas (Viola)—History and criticism. |
Sonatas (Viola)—Analysis, appreciation. | Viola and piano music—History and criticism. |
Viola and piano music—Analysis, appreciation.
Classification: LCC ML905 .B96 2020 (print) | LCC ML905 (ebook) |
DDC 781.2/73186—dc23
LC record available at https://lccn.loc.gov/2020024088
LC ebook record available at https://lccn.loc.gov/2020024089

3 5 7 9 8 6 4 2

Paperback printed by Marquis, Canada
Hardback printed by Bridgeport National Bindery, Inc., United States of America

For Paul, who endures

Contents

From the Series Editor

"Notes for Performers" is a series born of my desire to help musicians connect performance studies with pertinent aspects of scholarship. My favorite theory professor, John Buccheri (Northwestern University), used to say that to know a piece intuitively, technically, and intellectually is to *really* know a piece. While some may argue that one should simply "play from the heart," knowledge can be a powerful tool in strengthening or refining a performer's instincts. Additionally, when musicians are armed with knowledge, they can enhance their audiences' understanding of compositions. Having served as a pre-concert lecturer for the Chicago Symphony Orchestra for more than twenty years, I have had the satisfaction of helping audiences engage more fully with the music they are about to hear. I hope this series will encourage performers to offer written or spoken commentary to enhance their audiences' listening experiences.

While all musicians will gain insights from the books in the series, the writing is intended for undergraduate students, perhaps with a bit of professorial guidance. The selection of pieces is admittedly subjective. Each author is asked to identify the best-known compositions written for the instrument. It is my hope that instrumentalists will view each volume as a starting point for connecting performance studies with scholarship and that it will encourage them to explore other works in a similar fashion. Many more works are worthy of inclusion in each volume and, in time, perhaps second volumes may be added with additional compositions, including more recent works that have stood the test of time and become part of a given instrument's core repertoire.

There have long been helpful resources available to performers for learning about chamber, orchestral, and operatic works, but similar in-depth information to guide one's understanding of a given orchestral instrument's solo repertoire has thus far been noticeably absent from bookshelves. The goal of this series is to fill that open space on the shelf, and my goal as Oxford University Press's "Notes for Performers" editor is to contribute to the intellectual understanding necessary, as Dr. Buccheri would suggest, for a musician to *really* know a piece.

Kyle Dzapo
Professor of Music
Bradley University

Preface

Historically, the viola has been mistreated and misunderstood—the proverbial "middle child" that is overshadowed by its more popular siblings, the violin and cello. Given its unique characteristics, the viola's charms may not be readily apparent to the uninitiated. An acoustically imperfect instrument, the viola has no standardized size, resulting in a wide range of tonal qualities depending on the specific instrument. The viola's music is principally written in alto clef, which has deterred many individuals from learning the instrument and perplexed musical colleagues as they have attempted to decipher the viola's notes in a score. Yet for violists, the alto clef has become an emblem of pride, appropriately dubbed the "viola clef." And among orchestral instruments, the viola is unusual in that most of its performers started by learning to play a different instrument: the violin.

As someone who, atypically, started out playing the viola, I have spent many years attempting to understand this fascinating instrument. Not only the instrument itself but all aspects related to it, including its history, repertoire, performers, and critical reception. This book is intended to help violists better understand thirty-five key pieces of the repertoire with the goal of enriching performances. In addition to basic biographical information about each composer, I have attempted to provide as much practical source information about the origins and development of each work as possible. Detailed analyses, a major component of each book in the "Notes for Performers" series, are also included. Analysis can take many forms, and while my approach has been fairly traditional, I have attempted to tailor my approach to the specific work being discussed. In many instances, I have provided references to alternate analyses (typically in a note). Select chapters also include a list of sources to consult. I consider the analysis of each work not as an end but rather as a beginning. Readers will likely find the analysis portion most useful if they follow along with the score, but numerous charts are also provided to assist even if access to a score is not readily available. The musical snippets in the charts serve as a guide to the specific thematic areas; for space reasons, many tutti snippets have not been included. In most instances, the snippet corresponds to the beginning of the thematic area, but in some instances a later snippet has been selected, typically the viola's first significant entrance in that area.

In selecting the repertoire for this book, I first consulted several well-known sources: *Representative List of Viola Repertoire*, by Donald McInnes; *The Viola: Complete Guide for Teachers and Students*, by Henry Barrett; and

Playing and Teaching the Viola: A Comprehensive Guide to the Central Clef and Its Music, edited by Gregory Barnes. I next visited the websites of many violists, reviewing their repertoire lists. From these sources, I generated a list of fifty works that I then narrowed down to the thirty-five that are included in this book. In making the final selections, I attempted to cover as broad a spectrum as possible regarding time periods, nationalities of the composers, and instrumental combinations (including works for viola alone, viola and piano, and viola and orchestra). Since the "Notes for Performers" series is largely designed for students, I included works that many high school, undergraduate, and graduate students at every level are likely to encounter. Other books in the series have selected only one work by each composer, but given the prominent place that Paul Hindemith's music has in a violist's repertoire, I have selected two works by him: one sonata and one concerto.

Throughout the book, when specific pitches are referenced, they are notated using the following Helmholtz system:

$$c - b \qquad c^i - b^i \qquad c^{ii} - b^{ii} \qquad c^{iii} - b^{iii}$$

David M. Bynog
March 2020

Acknowledgments

Special thanks go to Hillary Herndon and Ed Klorman, who provided constructive feedback during the developmental stages of this book. Ed generously offered his expertise with other matters, not least of which was assisting with translations. I am grateful for additional translation assistance from Elena Artamonova, Robert Estep, Deborah Harter, Harald Krebs, Sharon Krebs, Alexandra Moellmann, Anna Shparberg, Liza Stepanova, and especially Paul Engle, who also transcribed many sources. I appreciate the willingness of Jacob Adams, Andrew Filmer, and Christopher Johnson to read through early drafts of individual chapters; their thoughtful comments were much appreciated. As always, I am grateful to Jeff Koffler for sharing his graphic design expertise. And I would like to extend my warm thanks to series editor Kyle Dzapo and Oxford University Press editor Suzanne Ryan for their guidance throughout the process.

I am indebted to many individuals who graciously provided me with materials: Janice Braun (Library Director and Special Collections Librarian, Milhaud Archivist, and Director, Center for the Book, F. W. Olin Library, Mills College), Rachel Heimovics Braun, Jeanette Casey (Music and Dance Librarian Head, Mills Music Library, University of Wisconsin–Madison), Beverly Chubat (Editor and Designer, Chicago Jewish Historical Society), Aaron Conitz (Development Assistant and Board Liaison, Kirkland Arts Center), Genevieve Coyle (Library Service Assistant, Manuscripts and Archives, Yale University), Amy Foster (Library Assistant, Royal Academy of Music), Janita Hall-Swadley, Deborah Hefling (Assistant Archivist, The Cleveland Orchestra), Andria Hoy (Archivist, The Cleveland Orchestra) Christopher Johnson, Myrna Layton and staff (Primrose International Viola Archive, Brigham Young University), Donald Maurice (Professor of Music, Victoria University of Wellington), Katja Riepl (Composer Manager, Concert Opera Media Division, Schott Music), Dr. Jürgen Schaarwächter (Max Reger Institute), Jordan Sprunger (Library/ Archives Assistant, Oscar Rennebohm Library, Edgewood College), Scott Vieira (Collection Development Coordinator, Fondren Library, Rice University), Frank Villella (Director, Rosenthal Archives of the Chicago Symphony Orchestra), Abigail Williams (Britten-Pears Foundation), and Anthony Zatorski (Client Liaison, Tarisio Fine Instruments and Bows).

A huge thanks to my principal viola teachers, who nurtured my love of the viola repertoire: Julia Davis, Jo Hix, Jerzy Kosmala, Csaba Erdélyi, and Roberto

Díaz. I am eternally grateful for the encouragement of my parents, Mark and Wanda Bynog, who have supported me throughout this project and all my musical endeavors. Lastly, I am grateful to my colleagues at Fondren Library, whose hard work and dedication enabled much of the research necessary for this book.

1

Johann Sebastian Bach: Brandenburg Concerto No. 6, BWV 1051

I.   [Allegro]
II. Adagio ma non tanto
III. Allegro

Date of Composition: by March 24, 1721

First Edition: Jean Sebastien Bach, *Sixième Concerto pour deux Altos, deux Violes da gamba, avec Violoncelle et Basse*, ed. S. W. Dehn, Leipzig: Au Bureau de Musique de C. F. Peters, [1852], Plate No. 3528 (Score); Plate No. 3529 (Parts)

Select Later Editions: J. S. Bach, *Brandenburgisches Konzert Nr. 6 B-Dur*, ed. Heinrich Besseler, Kassel: Bärenreiter, 2010 (© 1959), BA 5113 (Score and Parts); J. S. Bach, *Brandenburg Concerto No. 6 in B flat major*, New York: International Music, 1978 (© 1950), No. 312 (Piano Reduction)

Dedication: Dediées A Son Altesse Royalle Monseigneur Cretien Louis, Marggraf de Brandenbourg &c. &c. &c.

Orchestral Instrumentation: 2 viole da braccio, 2 viole da gamba, violoncello, violone e cembalo

Introduction

The Brandenburg Concertos show us the composer at his most cheerful and invigorating, and they are blessed with a tunefulness and rhythmic vitality which he rarely surpassed.

This is not to say that they pose no problems for the student and scholar (let alone the performer). Like every other major work by Bach, it seems, they raise questions which are difficult, and in some cases impossible, to answer—questions in response to which one can only offer, at best, plausible conjectures.[1]

Many violists believe that Bach saved the most "cheerful and invigorating" of his Six Brandenburg Concertos for last. But, with its unusual instrumentation, requiring two gambas, the Sixth Brandenburg Concerto has also proved the most challenging to program. Though the modern historical performance movement has helped matters, violists have also embraced alternative means of performing the work, often programming it in a version for two violas with piano or in mass viola ensembles.[2]

Bach's choice of instrumentation has also prompted many interesting questions among the scholarly community, including how to categorize the work: "Much ink has been wasted on attempts to determine, as with Concerto III, to which precise concerto subgenre it belongs," notes Michael Talbot.[3] Debates over whether the work should be considered a solo or ripieno concerto—or if it qualifies as a concerto at all—has undeniably consumed much ink. While Talbot remarks that "the work is certainly a concerto,"[4] David Ledbetter notes that "it is nonetheless well to consider Bach's actual title for the collection: "Six Concerts Avec plusieurs Instruments. . . . the French 'concert' had nothing of the formal connotations of the Italian 'concerto,' and meant simply a piece of chamber or ensemble music."[5] Peter Williams echoes this sentiment, suggesting that Bach's use of "the word *concerts* in the title-page indicates not *concertos* but *concerts* in the French sense, i.e. pieces for mixed consort."[6] Williams continues:

> No. 6 conforms exactly to the composer's term *concert* (it is a *consort à 5*), and its pairs of violas and gambas without violins were not unfamiliar in older German cantatas. They are therefore not a sign that this concerto was composed earlier than the others or that it was meant to represent the "archaic" or that it once had a quite different scoring.[7]

Williams alludes here to additional theories that have stemmed from the concerto's unusual instrumentation: theories related to its date of composition and Bach's possible borrowing from an earlier trio sonata for the work.[8] Bach's treatment of the violas (with their relatively complex parts) and gambas (with their relatively simple parts) has also given rise to theories regarding the sociological implications of the work.[9] For the most part, violists have not overly concerned themselves with these scholarly debates, preferring instead to revel in Bach's joyous music, from the first note until the last. And, indeed, the concerto's "last movement serves as a welcome reminder that, for all the problems and uncertainties with which the Brandenburg Concertos confront the modern scholar and performer, Bach intended them for the enjoyment of his patrons and his fellow musicians."[10]

Biographical Sketch

Born in Eisenach, Johann Sebastian Bach (1685–1750) was the last of Maria Elisabeth and Johann Ambrosius Bach's eight children. His father served as a court trumpeter and director of town music, having previously served as a violinist in Erfurt.[11] Little is known about Bach's earliest years, including details of his musical education, but his father presumably "taught him the rudiments of string playing."[12] Bach's mother died in the spring of 1694, and his father died less than a year later, leaving him an orphan. He went to live with his brother Johann Christoph, who was organist at the Michaeliskirche (St. Michael's Church) in Ohrdruf. It was under his brother's guidance that J. S. Bach "laid the foundations for his playing of the clavier."[13]

In March 1700, Bach traveled to Lüneburg to study at the Michaelisschule (St. Michael's School), where he received free tuition, room, and board as a singer in the select Mettenchor (Matins choir). While his duties in the choir would have kept him busy, Bach was also likely engaged as an instrumentalist on occasion at the school. Bach graduated in 1702 and obtained his first professional position as a court musician in Weimar starting in January 1703.[14] Later that August, he accepted a position as organist at the Neue Kirche in Arnstadt. He remained in Arnstadt until 1707, when he accepted a position as organist at St. Blasius in Mühlhausen. On October 17 of that year, he married Maria Barbara Bach; they would have seven children together, of whom four survived beyond infancy.

Bach left Mühlhausen in the summer of 1708 for a position as court organist and chamber musician to Duke Wilhelm Ernst in Weimar. A devout Lutheran, the duke was interested in the arts, and he greatly admired Bach's organ playing.[15] In 1714, Bach was promoted to the position of Konzertmeister at the court, but he was denied the position of Kapellmeister when it came open in 1716. Searching elsewhere, he obtained an appointment in August 1717 as Kapellmeister to Prince Leopold in Cöthen. Duke Wilhelm presumably refused Bach's initial request to leave and then had him imprisoned when Bach pressed the matter:

> On November 6, [1717], the quondam concertmeister and organist Bach was confined to the County Judge's place of detention for too stubbornly forcing the issue of his dismissal and finally on December 2 was freed from arrest with notice of his unfavorable discharge.[16]

Within days of his release, Bach was in Cöthen. His new employer, Prince Leopold, was himself a musician who played violin, harpsichord, and viola da gamba.[17] In 1720, Bach's wife died, and he married Anna Magdalena Wilcke the following year; the couple would have thirteen children together, of whom six survived beyond infancy. Bach remained in Cöthen until 1723, when he accepted a joint position as Kantor at the St. Thomasschule (St. Thomas School) and city music director in Leipzig. In this position, he was responsible for training students at St. Thomas, overseeing music at the city's four principal churches, and contributing to aspects of the city's musical life.[18] In 1729, he added duties as director of the city's *collegium musicum*, a "voluntary association of professional musicians and university students" that gave weekly public concerts.[19] He served as director of the group until the summer of 1737 and took up the position again from 1739 to 1741.

During his final years, Bach was plagued by eye troubles (cataracts). In late March and early April 1750, he underwent two unsuccessful operations by the visiting English oculist John Taylor. His health greatly deteriorated in the following months, and he died on July 28 after suffering a stroke.[20]

Bach's Brandenburg Concerto No. 6, BWV 1051

J. S. Bach possessed considerable skills as an instrumentalist; in addition to his status as a virtuoso keyboard player, he was also an adept violin and viola player, as attested to by his son C. P. E. Bach:

> As the greatest expert and judge of harmony, he liked best to play the viola, with appropriate loudness and softness. In his youth, and until the approach of old age, he played the violin cleanly and penetratingly, and thus kept the orchestra in better order than he could have done with the harpsichord. He understood to perfection the possibilities of all stringed instruments.[21]

Bach's perfect understanding of the viola's possibilities is evident in the Third and Sixth Brandenburg Concertos, which have solo parts for three and two violas respectively. Several of Bach's cantatas also have prominent parts for the viola, including *Gleichwie der Regen und Schnee vom Himmel fällt*, BWV 18 (1713–1715), originally scored for four violas, cello, bassoon, and continuo; and *Wo soll ich fliehen hin*, BWV 5 (1724), which has an impressive accompanying solo viola part in the tenor aria "Ergieße dich reichlich, du göttliche Quelle." And in 1996, a new entry was added to the viola repertoire in the form of the reconstructed Viola Concerto in E♭ Major by Bach.[22]

Bach dedicated his set of Six Brandenburg Concertos to Christian Ludwig, Margrave of Brandenburg, in a presentation copy dated March 24, 1721. However, "it is reasonable to assume that the Brandenburg Concertos were played by, and for the most part composed for, the orchestra at Cöthen."[23] The concertos were presumably composed over an extended period of time prior to 1721. Proposed dates for the sixth concerto have varied widely: Heinrich Besseler suggested that the sixth concerto was the earliest of the set, proposing a date of 1718.[24] Thurston Dart felt that the concerto was written earlier, probably during Bach's time in Weimar or even during his time in Arnstadt (1703–1707).[25] No evidence has yet surfaced that can pinpoint a date of composition, and "the fact remains that the only thing that can be said with certainty about the chronology of the Brandenburg Concertos is that they were all composed by March 1721, the date on Bach's autograph copy."[26] Readers interested in a broad overview of the concertos as a group should consult Malcolm Boyd's book *Bach: The Brandenburg Concertos*.[27] Many other sources also approach the concertos as a group, analyzing them according to diverse criteria, including the overall tonal plan and the number of instruments represented in each concerto.[28] The analysis that follows is restricted solely to the Sixth Brandenburg Concerto.

Following the rediscovery of Bach's autograph manuscript in 1849 by Siegfried Wilhelm Dehn, C. F. Peters began to individually issue the Brandenburg Concertos the following year. In the preface to the sixth concerto, Dehn wrote:

> For the performance of this concerto one really requires the viole da gamba parts to be played upon these instruments—a circumstance which offers many difficulties, since the viole da gamba has entirely gone out of use. A trial has shown, however, that the violoncello of today, of the smallest formation and feebly strung, may readily take the place of the viole da gamba, although, even so, one loses the soft and somewhat nasal tone of this instrument.[29]

Many subsequent performances and recordings of the work have substituted cellos for gambas, including the premiere recording of the complete set in 1936 by the Busch Chamber Players, directed by Adolf Busch.[30] The work has also frequently been performed (and occasionally recorded) in orchestral settings where the Viola I and Viola II parts have been played by the entire viola section (with multiple violas on each part).

As with G. P. Telemann's Viola Concerto in G Major (see chapter 31), ritornello form serves an integral function in Brandenburg Concerto No. 6:

> The importance of ritornello form to Bach's concertos cannot be overestimated. It is a pre-requisite of the 1st movement and an important unifying device in many Finales too. . . .
>
> The broadest definition of a ritornello is a passage which recurs at various points during a movement or complex of movements. In a concerto, the ritornello is that recurring tutti passage with which the movement begins and which lasts until the beginning of the first solo episode (e.g. bars 1–8 of the 1st movement of Brandenburg no. 2). While there is no problem in identifying

the first and last statements of the ritornello, the number and exact position of the middle statements is not always so sharply defined. This is especially true of Bach's concertos where one has to distinguish between structurally important ritornello statements and passing references to the opening tutti material.[31]

In the first movement of the Sixth Brandenburg Concerto, the ritornello form is fairly clear-cut (Chart 1.1).[32] Bach's manuscript does not list a tempo marking for this movement; many sources have selected Allegro as an appropriate tempo. The movement begins with the two solo violas playing in strict canon at the unison (separated by an eighth note) for the first fifteen measures. Ares Rolf notes that this canon, at an Allegro tempo, "is barely perceptible as such; rather, the impression emerges of an undulating texture."[33] Bach continues with imitative writing in the first episode at m. 17 with the cello introducing a new theme (Ex. 1.1) that is then passed among the other instruments. Alternating ritornello statements and episodes follow; for each of the ritornello statements, the two violas start off in canon at the unison separated by an eighth with Viola I leading each time except for Ritornello 5 at m. 86. Each of the episodes uses material from the first episode, and each begins with the same figure (see Ex. 1.1) except for Episode 4 at m. 80. Bach concludes the movement with a full restatement of the opening ritornello, which now starts in the middle of the measure at m. 114.

The second movement, Adagio ma non tanto, begins in E♭ major but, rather unusually, ends in a different key: G minor. Here, Bach eliminates the gambas, thinning out the texture and producing a more intimate atmosphere than in the outer movements. Scholars have variously described this movement as resembling a two-part fugue, a chaconne, and a passacaglia.[34] Five iterations of the opening ten-measure melody occur over the course of the movement (Chart 1.2). This melody consists of a subject and countersubject (Ex. 1.2), which is traded among instruments in a fugal fashion, though there are no true episodes. Bach sets this melody over a "quasi-ostinato" bass line--the feature that has drawn the comparisons to a passacaglia and chaconne.[35] For the second iteration of the melody (mm. 11–20), Bach shortens the statement by one measure

Example 1.1 Bach, Brandenburg Concerto No. 6, BWV 1051, movt. I, mm. 16–18, cello.

Zone	Thematic Areas/Snippet	Measures	Principal Tonal Areas/Function
Ritornello 1	Vla. 1	1–17	B-flat major
Episode 1	Vla. 1	17–25	B-flat major to F major
Ritornello 2	Vla. 1	25–28	F major to B-flat major
Episode 2	Vla. 1	28–46	B-flat major to C minor
Ritornello 3	Vla. 1	46–52	C minor
Episode 3	Vla. 1	52–73	C minor to G minor
Ritornello 4	Vla. 1	73–80	G minor
Episode 4	Vla. 1	80–86	G minor to E-flat major
Ritornello 5	Vla. 2	86–91	E-flat major
Episode 5	Vla. 1	91–114	E-flat major to B-flat major
Ritornello 6	Vla. 1	114–30	B-flat major

Chart 1.1 Bach, Brandenburg Concerto No. 6, BWV 1051: Structural analysis, first movement, [Allegro].

Example 1.2 Bach, Brandenburg Concerto No. 6, BWV 1051, movt. II, mm. 1–7, viola II.

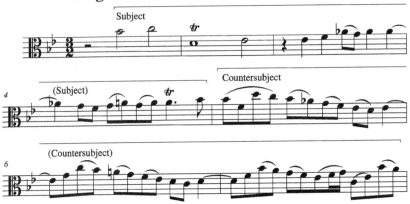

(eliminating the fourth measure), but the following two statements return to the ten-measure pattern of the first iteration. In mm. 40–43, the cello and continuo make two attempts to start the fifth fugal statement, finally getting things right in m. 44. Bach retains the fifth statement's key of G minor in the coda (mm. 54–62), ending the movement with a Phrygian cadence.

In the final Allegro, "elements of ritornello, 'da capo,' and rondo form are all combined within a single movement."[36] The ritornello form in this movement is less clearly defined compared to the first, given the similarity of material in several episodes to that from the ritornellos. Nonetheless, Boyd notes that "the ritornellos remain easily identified by the merging into unison of the violas,"[37] and the analysis here follows this approach (Chart 1.3).[38]

After the gigue-like opening ritornello (mm. 1–8), the two violas engage in playful dialogue to start the first episode (mm. 9–12), which "is merely a variant of the original tutti material."[39] Following a short ritornello (mm. 13–14), the two instruments trade roles for a reprise of the first episode, now in F major (mm. 15–18). The third episode (mm. 23–27) features an imitative passage in the violas, and the cello figures prominently in this and the following episode (mm. 28–33). Back-to-back ritornellos, including a restatement of the opening ritornello (mm. 38–45), close out the first (A) section. Bach explores the minor mode in the middle (B) section, giving the violas and cello virtuosic sixteenth-note passages that are punctuated by short ritornello statements. A da capo at the end of m. 65 takes us back to the beginning for a repeat of the opening section and a joyous conclusion to the movement.

Zone	Thematic Areas/Snippet	Measures	Principal Tonal Areas/Function
Statement 1	Vla. 2	1–11	E-flat major to B-flat major
Statement 2	Vla. 2	11–20	B-flat major to E-flat major
Statement 3	Vla. 1	20–30	E-flat major to F minor
Statement 4		30–44	
	Unit 1.1 — Vla. 2	30–40	F minor to A-flat major
	Unit 1.2 — Vc.	40–43	A-flat major; C minor
Statement 5	Vc.	44–54	G minor
Coda	Vc.	54–62	G minor; ending on D major

Chart 1.2 Bach, Brandenburg Concerto No. 6, BWV 1051: Structural analysis, second movement, Adagio ma non tanto.

A scarce example of a concertante work for viola from the Baroque period, Bach's Brandenburg Concerto No. 6 serves as an important landmark in the viola's development as a solo instrument. Beloved by violists, it is also widely admired by scholars, who recognize the historical and musical significance of the work:

In the absence of the despotic violin in No. 6, the two violas have the rare chance to crown the musical texture: at the opening of the concerto the violas revel in canon above the low, lush homophony of the lower strings. What one might describe as the democratization of the orchestra, achieved not only by according instruments unusual roles but also by destabilizing formal boundaries, is one of Bach's major contributions as a concerto composer.[40]

	Zone	Thematic Areas/Snippet	Measures	Principal Tonal Areas/Function
A	Ritornello 1	*Vla. 1 & 2*	1–8	B-flat major
	Episode 1	*Vla. 1*	9–12	B-flat major to F major
	Ritornello 2	*Vla. 1*	13–14	F major
	Episode 2	*Vla. 2*	15–18	F major to C major
	Ritornello 3	*Vla. 2*	19–22	F major
	Episode 3	*Vla. 2*	23–27	Sequential
	Ritornello 4	*Vla. 1 & 2*	27	F major
	Episode 4	*Vla. 2*	28–33	F major to B-flat major
	Ritornello 5	*Vla. 1 & 2*	34–37	B-flat major
	Ritornello 6	Same as Ritornello 1	38–45	B-flat major
B	Episode 5	*Vla. 1*	46–51	G minor
	Ritornello 7	*Vla. 1*	52–53	G minor
	Episode 6	*Vla. 1*	54–63	G minor to D minor
	Ritornello 8	*Vla. 2*	64–65	D minor
	Da Capo		1–45 (66–110)	

Chart 1.3 Bach, Brandenburg Concerto No. 6, BWV 1051: Structural analysis, third movement, Allegro.

Dig Deeper into Bach's Brandenburg Concerto No. 6

Readers interested in learning more about the Sixth Brandenburg Concerto are referred to the following sources:

Boyd, Malcolm. *Bach: The Brandenburg Concertos.* Cambridge: Cambridge University Press, 1993.

Rolf, Ares. *J. S. Bach: Das sechste Brandenburgische Konzert; Besetzung, Analyse, Entstehung.* Dortmund, Germany: Klangfarben Musikverlag, 2002.

2

Béla Bartók: Concerto for Viola and Orchestra, Sz. 120 (BB 128)

I.   Moderato — Lento parlando
II. Adagio religioso — Allegretto
III. Allegro vivace

Date of Composition: 1945

First Edition: Béla Bartók, *Concerto for Viola and Orchestra*, Op. posth., Prepared for publication from the composer's original manuscript by Tibor Serly, Viola Part ed. William Primrose, London: Boosey & Hawkes, 1949, Plate No. B. & H. 16854 (Piano Reduction); Bela Bartok, *Concerto for Viola and Orchestra*, Op. Posth., Prepared for publication from the composer's original manuscript by Tibor Serly, London: Boosey & Hawkes, 1950, Plate No. B. & H. 16953 (Pocket Score)

Select Later Editions: Béla Bartók, *Viola Concerto*, Revised version by Nelson Dellamaggiore and Peter Bartók, London: Boosey & Hawkes, 1995, 9649 (Score); 9854 (Piano Reduction); Béla Bartók, *Viola Concerto*, critical restoration and orchestration by Csaba Erdélyi, Wellington, NZ: Promethean Editions, 2004, PE065 (Score); PE066 (Piano Reduction)

Date/Place of First Public Performance: December 2, 1949, William Primrose (viola), Minneapolis Symphony Orchestra, Antal Doráti (conductor), Cyrus Northrop Memorial Auditorium, Minneapolis, MN

Orchestral Instrumentation (Serly Edition): Solo viola, piccolo, 2 flutes, 2 oboes, 2 clarinets in B♭, 2 bassoons, 3 horns in F, 3 trumpets in B♭, 2 trombones, tuba, timpani, percussion (side drum, bass drum, large cymbals, small cymbals), strings

Orchestral Instrumentation (Revised Version by Dellamaggiore and Bartók): Solo viola, piccolo, 2 flutes, 2 oboes (second also English horn), 2 clarinets in B♭, 2 bassoons (second also double bassoon), 4 horns in F, 3 trumpets in B♭, tenor trombone, bass trombone, tuba, timpani, percussion (triangle, side drum, bass drum, large cymbals), strings

Orchestral Instrumentation (2004 Erdélyi Restoration): Solo viola, piccolo, 2 flutes, 2 oboes, 2 clarinets in B♭ (second also bass clarinet), 2 bassoons, 4 horns in

F, 3 trumpets in B♭, trombone, bass trombone, tuba, timpani, percussion (snare drum, bass drum, piatti, suspended cymbal, pocket knife), strings

Introduction

"Many surveys of Bartók's music omit discussion of the Viola Concerto on the grounds that, in the form that it has become known, as completed by Tibor Serly, it cannot be considered a work by Bartók."[1] The authenticity of Béla Bartók's last composition, the Concerto for Viola and Orchestra, Sz. 120 (BB 128), has consumed violists and scholars almost since the moment when William Primrose played the final note at the premiere in 1949. Although the work was known to have been left incomplete at Bartók's death, the exact state of the manuscript (and the extent of Serly's contributions) remained shrouded in mystery for many years. Dissatisfaction with Serly's version intensified over the years, and by the early 1990s multiple attempts to produce a new version were underway.[2] A facsimile edition of Bartók's sketches, which was published in 1995, has helped clarify matters, and continued scholarship on the composer's compositional methods has shed further light on the state in which he left the work:

> It is now almost universally accepted among Bartók scholars that, when viewed beside his other late works, the draft of the Viola Concerto represents only the first layers of the compositional process of mature Bartók. Thus it is important to note that even with the most faithful transcription of the material in the manuscript, it is still only the realization of a first draft, which would have developed significantly had Bartók lived to take it to its final form.[3]

This is not to say that the viola concerto, as completed by anyone in the past or future, is not a work by Bartók. Many compositions have been left in varying states of completeness at the time of a composer's death, including W. A. Mozart's Requiem, K. 626 and Mass in C Minor, K. 427; Giacomo Puccini's *Turandot*; Aleksandr Borodin's *Prince Igor*; and Gustav Mahler's Tenth Symphony. Each unfinished composition offers its own unique problems, and each attempt to complete an unfinished work will be met with its detractors. The backlash against Serly's completion is due, in large part, to the meteoric popularity that it has enjoyed: Bartók's concerto vaulted to a prominent place in the viola repertoire shortly after its publication. Many violists remain quite happy with Serly's version; but for those who are not, there are alternatives. Given the concerto's status in the repertoire and the inherent problems with any incomplete composition, each violist must develop his or her own relationship with the work, guided by personal preferences (which may evolve over time) to determine which version is the most appropriate choice.

Biographical Sketch

Béla Bartók (1881–1945) was born in the Hungarian town of Nagyszentmiklós (now Sînnicolau Mare, Romania), to Béla and Paula Bartók. His father was headmaster of an agricultural school, and his mother a teacher and pianist. At the age of three, young Béla was tapping out rhythms on a drum. By the age of four, "he could pick out forty folksongs with one finger at the piano," and at the age of five, he began "more formal lessons with his mother."[4] In 1888, Bartók's father died, leaving Paula to care for Béla and his younger sister, Erzsébet (Elza). Over the next few years, the family moved frequently as Paula sought out opportunities to better provide for her family.

Bartók produced his earliest compositions in 1890, and on May 1, 1892, he made his first public appearance as both pianist and composer in the town of Nagyszőllős.[5] He progressed rapidly in his musical endeavors, and by 1894 he had composed more than thirty works for piano. In the summer of 1899, Bartók graduated from the Catholic Gymnasium in the town of Pozsony (now Bratislava, Slovakia). Though he had been offered a scholarship to attend the Vienna Conservatory, he chose instead to attend the Academy of Music in Budapest, enrolling in September 1899, where he studied piano with István Thomán and composition with Hans Koessler. After graduating in 1903, "Bartók pursued an itinerant life, following performing or compositional opportunities as they presented themselves."[6] He earned early acclaim as a composer with the symphonic poem *Kossuth* (1903), which was premiered by the Budapest Philharmonic Orchestra in January 1904 and performed by the Hallé Orchestra in Manchester, England, the following month. Later in 1904, during an extended stay in the Hungarian village of Gerlice puszta, Bartók heard a Transylvanian-born maid, Lidi Dósa, singing a folk song, which he notated down. This incident was a defining moment in Bartók's musical career; he soon began collecting folk songs with unbridled enthusiasm, and he would go on to earn great renown as an ethnomusicologist.[7]

In 1907, Bartók replaced his former teacher István Thomán as professor of piano at the Budapest Academy of Music. After a failed relationship with the violinist Stefi Geyer (for whom he composed his First Violin Concerto), Bartók became involved with one of his young piano students, Márta Ziegler. The couple married in 1909 and would have one son together, Béla Bartók Jr. At the outset of World War I, Bartók, who had suffered from ill health during his youth, was declared unfit for service; instead, he was "entrusted with the collection of folksongs from soldiers."[8] After the war, he reinvigorated his career as a pianist, which had taken a back seat to his efforts as a composer and ethnomusicologist. He performed on many international concert tours over the following years, often programming his own compositions. In 1923, Bartók divorced his wife and married another one of his students, Ditta Pásztory; the couple would have one son together, Peter.

Bartók left the Academy of Music in 1934 and joined the folk-music section of the Hungarian Academy of Sciences, where he remained until 1940. During this period, Bartók reached the pinnacle of his career as a composer, producing "masterpieces in each of his major genres: chamber, orchestral, vocal and piano music."[9] At the end of 1940, Bartók and his wife moved to the United States, settling in New York City. While in the United States, Bartók continued with his usual musical activities: conducting ethnomusicological research (transcribing Yugoslav materials at Columbia University), performing, composing, and lecturing. He also accepted a few private pupils for piano and composition.[10] In April 1942, Bartók was diagnosed with leukemia; after suffering from numerous illnesses over the next three and a half years, he died on September 26, 1945, at West Side Hospital in New York City.[11]

Bartók's Concerto for Viola and Orchestra, Sz. 120 (BB 128)

Béla Bartók is widely considered one of the most important and influential composers of the twentieth century. While his early compositions started off in the German Romantic tradition, he soon developed his own style:

> His chromatic system has its roots in Eastern folk music and in pentatony; his acoustic system he owed to Western harmonic thinking. He himself admitted his indebtedness to folk music and the French impressionists as the two most decisive influences on his art.[12]

Any violist who is interested in an in-depth look at Bartók's sole contribution to the viola repertoire, the Concerto for Viola and Orchestra, Sz. 120 (BB 128), would benefit from consulting the facsimile of the autograph sketches, with commentary by László Somfai,[13] and Donald Maurice's book *Bartók's Viola Concerto: The Remarkable Story of His Swansong*,[14] which extensively covers the work from many angles. Given that Maurice's book thoroughly discusses the genesis, reconstruction, and further revisions of the concerto, only minimal details are provided here.

Bartók's viola concerto was commissioned by the great Scottish-American violist William Primrose. The exact date of the commission remains unclear, but

Bartók had presumably agreed to it in early 1945 based on a letter from Primrose dated January 22:

> Dear Mr. Bartok,
> Need I tell you how gratified and thrilled I am to learn from Mr. Heinsheimer that you have so kindly consented to write for me a Viola Concerto. I really am very excited & will contact you immediately I return East in March.[15]

Bartók provided an update on the concerto's progress in a letter to Primrose dated August 5 that was apparently never sent:

> Dear Mr. Primrose:
> about mid July I was just planning to write you a rather desponding letter, explaining you the various difficulties I am in. But, then, there stirred some viola-concerto ideas which gradually crystallized themselves, so that I am able now to tell you that I hope to write the work, and maybe finish at least its draft in 4–5 weeks, if nothing happens in the meantime which would prevent my work. The prospects are these: perhaps I will be able to be ready with the draft by beginning of Sept., and with the score by end of the same month.[16]

True to his prediction, Bartók had the draft completed within five weeks, and he wrote to Primrose on September 8:

> Dear Mr Primrose
> I am very glad to be able to tell you that your viola concerto is ready in draft so that only the score has to be written which means a purely mechanical work, so to speak. If nothing happens I can be through in 5 or 6 weeks, i.e. I can send you a copy of the orchestra score in the second half of Oct., and a few weeks afterwards a copy (or if you wish more copies) of the piano score.[17]

With Bartók's death less than three weeks later, the viola concerto was left incomplete. The family turned to Bartók's friend Tibor Serly to complete both the final seventeen measures of the Third Piano Concerto and the viola concerto. On December 19, 1947, Serly wrote to Victor Bator, trustee of Bartók's estate:

> Dear Mr. Bator:
> I have completed my own sketch form of the entire Viola Concerto with all the doubtful places cleared up, corrections and additional joins made, including some technical revisions such as Bartok himself would have had to make. So far as I am concerned, the Concerto is as good as done.[18]

Serly still had to orchestrate the work, and there was a bit of a dust-up over an alternate cello version that he had prepared.[19] The work was finally premiered by William Primrose on December 2, 1949, with Antal Doráti conducting the Minneapolis Symphony Orchestra. It was well received by the audience and critics:

> A capacity crowd of 4,500 applauded so enthusiastically that both Primrose and Dorati were brought back for six bows at the conclusion of the three-move-ment, twenty-minute concerto. "Without doubt a great work," wrote John Harvey of The St. Paul Pioneer Press. "A major success," said Norman Houk of The Minneapolis Tribune.[20]

But concerns over Serly's edition soon started to surface. In his 1953 biography of Bartók, Halsey Stevens remarked:

> Primrose considers the Viola Concerto "a sensitive and inspired work and a real contribution to the literature of the viola." It would be pleasant to record that it is Bartók's crowning achievement; it is, unfortunately, nothing of the kind. This is written with full realization of the divided responsibility which brought it about; how close Serly came to the composer's intention is a question which can never be answered. Without access to the original sketches it is impossible to draw even tentative conclusions.[21]

As the work skyrocketed in popularity over subsequent years, more people began to take issue with Serly's edition. Serly attempted to address some of the concerns in his 1975 article "A Belated Account of the Reconstruction of a 20th Century Masterpiece," in which he outlined his process of reconstructing the work, including some (but not all) of the changes that he made.[22] The fac-simile publication of the original sketches in 1995 has since enabled scholars and violists to more accurately assess how much Serly deviated from Bartók's sketches. Regardless of concerns over the liberties that Serly took with the orig-inal material, he deserves a multitude of thanks from violists for his Herculean efforts in completing the viola concerto. It is difficult to imagine how differ-ently the viola's evolution may have been had Serly not completed the work when he did. (The concerto has produced a positive effect in many areas, in-cluding the expansion of violists' technique and audiences' perceptions of the viola as a solo instrument.)

As of 2019, there are two other commercially published editions of Bartók's viola concerto. The first is the revised version by Nelson Dellamaggiore and Peter Bartók, published in 1995 (see Select Later Editions at the head of this chapter). This version came about as part of a larger project by Peter Bartók to review and correct errors in his father's compositions. According to Peter, the viola concerto was, unsurprisingly, the most complex of the projects:

> Our plan was to leave this work to be one of the last tackled, since the only Béla Bartók manuscript that can be referred to is a rough sketch. Its deciphering and the orchestration were executed by my father's friend Tibor Serly (d. 1978), who can no longer be consulted. . . .
>
> Tibor Serly's task, orchestration of the Viola Concerto on the basis of the sketches, was a very difficult one, with an excellent end result. Although the project of correction resulted in a somewhat different version of his score, it is not intended to replace Mr. Serly's work but to be offered as an alternate.[23]

As with Serly, the efforts that Dellamaggiore and Peter Bartók put into their edition was immense: "Let me tell you the amount of work that Nelson and Peter did on this project," said Paul Neubauer, who worked with them on their edition, "you would not believe the hours, the painstaking hours. Not only did they prepare the revised version as closely as possible to what Bartók wrote, but they also brought out the facsimile edition of the manuscript, which contains a copy of the actual manuscript, as well as a written-out copy that is easier to read."[24]

The other version that is currently available is Csaba Erdélyi's, which has benefited from an extended period of development and from Erdélyi's consultation with Bartók scholars, including László Somfai and Elliott Antokoletz. Erdélyi's earliest revisions—from 1992 and 1996—were privately issued. In 2001, he premiered an orchestrated version, which was recorded and released on compact disc.[25] This version, with further modifications, was published by Promethean in 2004 (see Select Later Editions at the head of this chapter). In preparing the orchestration, Erdélyi "studied all of Bartók's works involving orchestra, examining the first drafts of many of these."[26] Erdélyi has continued to refine his edition; the most recent version appeared in 2016 but, as of 2019, has yet to be published.

There is no universally right or wrong edition among these three; each has its merits and shortcomings. Over time, further attempts at a completion will undoubtedly be made; it will be particularly interesting to see what conclusions artificial intelligence music composers arrive at.[27]

Despite any reservations over Serly's edition, it remains the standard version and is an excellent starting point for any violist who is learning the work (the following analysis refers to Serly's edition). Given the incomplete nature of the work, it is difficult to satisfactorily analyze it in such limited space according to measures used for Bartók's other works (such as proportion, pitch organization, and chromatic vs. diatonic systems). Readers interested in more detailed analyses are referred to chapters 5 and 8 of Donald Maurice's book *Bartók's Viola*

Concerto: The Remarkable Story of His Swansong as well as Ames Asbell's treatise, "Béla Bartók's *Viola Concerto*: A Detailed Analysis and Discussion of Published Versions."[28]

The first movement is in sonata form (Chart 2.1), opening with a virtuosic, thirteen-measure introduction. This introduction is "based initially on an octatonic scale on A (A–B–C–D–E♭–F–G♭–A♭), before it turns at bar 10 to a pentatonic scale on C (C–E♭–F–A♭–B♭) and then to a black-note pentatonic collection (D♭–E♭–G♭–A♭–B♭)."[29] In m. 14, the exposition begins with a melody that is drawn from the introduction. Unit 1.2 (mm. 41–51) "contains whole-tone trichords that interlock at the half-step, forming a six-note chromatic segment, or chromatic hexachord."[30] The first theme group ends with a "folk-like melody" in the viola (mm. 52–54),[31] which gives way to an imitative orchestral tutti. The brief second theme group (mm. 61–80) features chromatic scalar figures (often with multiple concurrent orchestral lines moving in contrary and parallel motion with the solo viola's line) and syncopated rhythms.

The development (mm. 81–146) features "a constant and free expansion and compression of intervals."[32] Bartók employs inversion in the viola's lyrical Unit 1.1 section, moving to more virtuosic writing in the following sections. The development is capped off by the viola's cadenza, which gives way to the orchestra's restatement of the exposition's Unit 1.1 material at m. 147 to start the recapitulation. After reappearances of Unit 1.2 and Unit 1.3 material from the exposition, a slightly extended orchestral tutti leads to the second theme group (mm. 184–206), which now features dotted rhythms in the viola. The exposition's principal theme (Unit 1.1) returns in the coda (mm. 207–30), which is centered on C major.

A Lento parlando section, which does not include any measure numberings in the score or piano reduction, connects the first movement with the second. In his August 5, 1945, letter to Primrose, Bartók originally indicated that the concerto would be in four movements, and that "at least 3 of them will [be] preceded by a (short) recurring introduction (mostly solo of the viola), a kind of ritornello."[33] The first six pitches of the Lento parlando are related to the notes in mm. 3–4 of the first movement (enharmonically they are a major fifth lower), and this section could qualify as one of the recurring ritornellos.[34]

Centered on E, the second movement is in an ABA form (Chart 2.2). The initial A section consists of three "strophes," each of which is largely built from the opening three-measure motive. In the third strophe (mm. 23–29), Bartók makes effective use of inversion and augmentation. The viola's dramatic, ascending passage in m. 29 leads into the B section, where the thematic material is dominated by the interval of a minor third (principally C and E♭). In the final A section (mm. 40–49), Bartók juxtaposes ideas from the two previous sections, condensing the opening motive and then appending the B section's minor-third idea. In m. 50,

Zone	Thematic Areas/Snippet	Measures
Introduction ("Ritornello")		1–13
Exposition		14–80
	Theme Group 1	14–61
	Unit 1.1	14–41
	Unit 1.2	41–51
	Unit 1.3	52–61
	Theme Group 2	61–80
Development		81–146
	Unit 1.1	81–102
	Unit 1.2	102–11
	Unit 1.3	112–26
	Unit 1.4: Cadenza	127–46

Chart 2.1 Bartók, Concerto for Viola and Orchestra, Sz. 120 (BB 128): Structural analysis, first movement, Moderato — Lento parlando.

Zone	Thematic Areas/Snippet	Measures
Recapitulation		147–206
	Theme Group 1	147–84
	Unit 1.1	147–62
	Unit 1.2	162–72
	Unit 1.3	173–84
	Theme Group 2	184–206
Coda		207–30
Lento parlando ("Ritornello")		[231–48]

Chart 2.1 (continued) Bartók, Concerto for Viola and Orchestra, Sz. 120 (BB 128): Structural analysis, first movement, Moderato — Lento parlando.

material from the first movement's introduction returns ("a sort of ritornello"), gradually accelerating into the Allegretto section, which serves as an introduction to the third movement.

Centered on A major, the third movement is cast in a rondo form (Chart 2.3).[35] Much of the movement's material "draws strongly on Romanian dance rhythms."[36] The opening A section is dominated by the viola's frenetic sixteenth notes and trill figures. To start the B section at m. 51, the orchestra presents a new thematic idea, though the viola persists with sixteenth-note figures when it re-enters in m. 65. In the following A section (mm. 84–114), the writing for the viola is even more frenetic, with double stops now added into the mix (mm. 97–103).

Zone	Thematic Areas/Snippet	Measures
A		1–29
	Unit 1.1	1–11
	Unit 1.2	12–22
	Unit 1.3	23–29
B		30–39
A		40–49
("Ritornello")		50–57
Allegretto (3rd Movement Introduction)		58–85

Chart 2.2 Bartók, Concerto for Viola and Orchestra, Sz. 120 (BB 128): Structural analysis, second movement, Adagio religioso — Allegretto.

The C section offers a major change in character, starting with a folk-like tune set over a drone. This section is largely given over to the orchestra (the viola plays in only seventeen of the sixty-three measures). The orchestra once again presents the thematic material in the return of the B section at m. 177, though the viola insists on partaking in mm. 191–95. But it is not long before the viola returns to its virtuosic sixteenth-note shenanigans, including a dramatic double-stop passage (mm. 198–212) and a long, chromatic ascent (mm. 213–20) that leads into the final A section and coda.

In 1997, a panel session at the Twenty-Fifth International Viola Congress brought together several key players who had been involved in researching or revising Bartók's viola concerto. At the session, Donald Maurice remarked:

Zone	Thematic Areas/Snippet	Measures
A		1–50
B	Vln. 1	51–83
A		84–114
C	Ob. 1	114–76
B	Tpt. 1	177–220
A		221–34
Coda		235–67

Chart 2.3 Bartók, Concerto for Viola and Orchestra, Sz. 120 (BB 128): Structural analysis, third movement, Allegro vivace.

> My final comment is that I hope these discussions haven't scared anyone from playing this piece. Rather than being put off, we should be inspired by the challenge of the choices at hand.[37]

In the ensuing years, the rhetoric surrounding Bartók's viola concerto (particularly the many negative comments about Serly's edition) has, indeed, put some violists off the work. And the prospect of sifting through the sources and weighing the considerations just to select an edition to play from can seem daunting for any violist. This is unfortunate, since all of the individuals who have devoted countless hours to producing a version have done so because of their passion for the work—and the music of Bartók, in general. However, none of the debates about Bartók's viola concerto (nor the challenges in selecting an edition) should prevent violists from tackling the work. Instead, you should seek out the opinions of your teachers, colleagues, and friends; pick an edition to start off with (you can always try the others later); and then devote your energies to conquering the many technical challenges that the concerto has to offer.

Exploring Bartók's Concerto for Viola and Orchestra, Sz. 120 (BB 128)

Bartók's Concerto for Viola and Orchestra, Sz. 120 (BB 128) has been extensively covered in the scholarly literature. These are just a few of the many sources that are worthwhile for violists to consult:

Asbell, Stephanie Ames. "Béla Bartók's *Viola Concerto*: A Detailed Analysis and Discussion of Published Versions." DMA treatise, University of Texas at Austin, 2001.

Bartók, Béla. *Viola Concerto: Facsimile Edition of the Autograph Draft.* Homosassa, FL: Bartók Records, 1995.

Maurice, Donald. *Bartók's Viola Concerto: The Remarkable Story of His Swansong.* Oxford: Oxford University Press, 2004.

"Panel Discussion: The Bartók Viola Concerto; From the 1997 International Viola Congress in Austin, Texas." *Journal of the American Viola Society* 14, no. 1 (1998): 15–49.

3

Hector Berlioz: *Harold in Italy*, op. 16

I.   Harold aux montagnes. Scènes de mélancolie, de bonheur et de joie
     [Harold in the Mountains. Scenes of Melancholy, Happiness and Joy]
II. Marche de pèlerins chantant la prière du soir
     [March of Pilgrims Singing the Evening Hymn]
III. Sérénade d'un montagnard des Abbruzes[1] à sa maîtresse
     [Serenade of an Abruzzi-Mountaineer to His Sweetheart]
IV. Orgie de brigands. Souvenirs des scènes précédentes
     [Orgy of Brigands. Reminiscences of the Preceding Scenes]

Date of Composition: January–June 1834; manuscript dated June 22, 1834

First Edition: Hector Berlioz, *Harold en Italie: Symphonie en 4 Parties avec un Alto principal*, Op: 16, Paris: Brandus et Cie, [1848], Plate No. B. et Cie. 4782bis (Score); Hector Berlioz, *Harold en Italie: Symphonie en quatre parties avec un Alto principal*, Op: 16, Partition de Piano (avec la Partie d'Alto) par F. Liszt, Paris: Brandus et Cie, [1880], Plate No. B. et Cie. 12,533 (Viola and Piano Reduction)

Select Later Edition: Hector Berlioz, *New Edition of the Complete Works*, vol. 17, *Harold en Italie*, ed. Paul Banks and Hugh Macdonald, Kassel: Bärenreiter, 2001, Bärenreiter 5457 (Score)

Dedication: dédiée à Monsieur Humbert Ferrand

Date/Place of First Public Performance: November 23, 1834, Chrétien Urhan (viola), Narcisse Girard (conductor), Salle du Conservatoire, Paris

Orchestral Instrumentation: Solo viola, 2 flutes (2nd also piccolo), 2 oboes (1st also English horn), 2 clarinets, 4 bassoons, 4 horns, 2 trumpets in C, 2 cornets, 3 trombones, ophicleide (or tuba), timpani, triangle, cymbals, 2 tambourines, harp, strings

Introduction

" 'Tone poems' by Franz Liszt and Richard Strauss are closely related to the poems they illustrate, whereas in Berlioz the subjective expression of a sentiment caused by, or seen in relation to, an event or a work of art reaches its climax. *Harold en Italie* is thus not a translation of Byron's poem into another artistic medium, but Berlioz's reaction to it, merged with a response to his own Italian experiences and expressed in musical terms."[2] No small amount of ink has been spilled attempting to reconcile Berlioz's second symphony, *Harold in Italy*, with its literary inspiration: Lord Byron's narrative poem *Childe Harold's Pilgrimage*. For his first symphony, *Symphonie fantastique*, Berlioz supplied a detailed program, indicating that it "should be distributed to the audience at concerts where this symphony is included, as it is indispensable for a complete understanding of the dramatic plan of the work."[3] Yet no such program was provided to assist with *Harold's* sketchy dramatic plan. Rather than depicting specific scenes from *Childe Harold's Pilgrimage*, the symphony instead expresses Harold's *character*—through the medium of the solo viola—using scenes from Berlioz's own travels in Italy as a backdrop.

Adding to the difficulty of relating Berlioz's version of *Harold* to Byron's is the composer's original design for the composition: a two-movement work for solo viola, chorus, and orchestra with Mary, Queen of Scots as the subject, titled *Les derniers instants de Marie Stuart* (*The Last Moments of Mary Stuart*). In its finished state, *Harold* contains vestiges of this earlier concept, leaving the impression that Harold has stumbled upon the fabled Scottish village of Brigadoon while tramping around the mountains of Italy. There is also disagreement as to what sort of composition *Harold in Italy* is: A symphony? A concerto? A tone poem? It is precisely the enigmatic features of *Harold* (along with Berlioz's exceptional music) that has captivated performers, audiences, and critics since the work debuted in 1834.

Biographical Sketch

Hector Berlioz (1803–1869) was the eldest of six children born to Louis-Joseph Berlioz, a respected doctor in the small French town of La Côte-Saint-André, and his wife, Marie-Antoinette-Joséphine. Louis was largely responsible for his son's early education, including basic training on the flageolet and flute. Around the age of thirteen or fourteen, Hector started experimenting with composition, learning the rudiments of music theory from treatises. In 1817, he began lessons with the town's newly hired music instructor, Monsieur Imbert, progressing rapidly on the flute.[4] Further music lessons came from Imbert's replacement, Monsieur Dorant, who taught Berlioz and his sister guitar. Berlioz's father, however, would not allow the budding musician to learn the piano.[5] While Louis considered music to be an acceptable pastime, he planned for Hector to pursue a career in medicine.[6]

In March 1821, Berlioz received a bachelor's degree after successfully passing an oral exam in the nearby city of Grenoble.[7] The following November, he enrolled at the Faculté de Médecine in Paris, intending to follow the path chosen by his father. Yet he was increasingly drawn to music, immersing himself in scores at the Paris Conservatoire's library and studying privately with Jean-François Le Sueur, a composition teacher at the conservatory. In January 1824, Berlioz managed to obtain the requisite medical degree, but he had already resolved to pursue his love of music. He entered the Paris Conservatoire in 1826, continuing his composition studies with Le Sueur and also studying counterpoint and fugue with Antoine Reicha. The following year he attended a performance of William Shakespeare's *Hamlet* with the actress Harriet Smithson in the role of Ophelia. Berlioz became infatuated with Smithson, conducting "an impassioned, largely imaginary relationship with her," which would inspire the program for *Symphonie fantastique*.[8]

For composition students at the conservatory, there was no greater glory than winning the Prix de Rome. Winners of this prize received a financial subsidy and were required to spend two years at the Villa Medici in Rome and at least one year in Germany and Austria.[9] After multiple attempts, Berlioz finally won the Prix de Rome in 1830, ultimately spending only fourteen months in Italy between 1831 and 1832; he disliked Rome and "seized every opportunity to leave it and escape to the mountains."[10] Berlioz returned to France in the spring of 1832, and in December he secured an introduction to Harriet Smithson. Wasting no time, Berlioz moved "heaven and earth" to win her, overcoming "every kind of opposition," including the disapproval of his family.[11] The two married in October 1833 and had one child together the following year, Louis.

By the time Berlioz's second symphony, *Harold in Italy*, premiered in 1834, he had achieved a reasonable measure of success. But his technically complex compositions had proved challenging for performers and conductors, resulting in many unsatisfactory or aborted performances. The composer's dissatisfaction reached a tipping point with a performance of *Harold in Italy* on November 22, 1835, conducted by Narcisse Girard:

> He made so serious a mistake at the end of the serenade (where, if one part of the orchestra does not double its speed, the other part cannot go on, because the whole bar of the former corresponds to the half bar of the latter) that, seeing at last that there was no hope of working up the end of the *allegro* properly, I resolved in future to conduct myself, and not allow anyone else to communicate my ideas to the performers.[12]

Berlioz's career as a conductor soon began in earnest, and within a few short years he had become "a leading exponent of modern conducting."[13] Touring widely, he earned admiration not only for the interpretations of his own works, but also for the care that he gave to works by other composers.

Composing and conducting were just two facets of Berlioz's career. He had published his first music criticism in 1823, and writing would serve as his principal source of income. In 1835, he became chief music critic for *Journal des débats*, retiring in 1863. His orchestral treatise, *Grand traité d'instrumentation et d'orchestration modernes*, was a financial success when it was published in 1843/44, and several other literary works followed. Another much-needed source of income came from his appointments at the Paris Conservatoire's library: first as associate curator in 1839 and then as Conservatoire librarian in 1850, a position he retained until his death.[14]

By the early 1840s, Berlioz's marriage was deteriorating, and he began an affair with the singer Marie Recio. He was already spending long periods abroad and was soon living apart from his wife. Nonetheless, he continued to support and care for Harriet until her death in March 1854. Later that year, Berlioz married Marie, who remained his constant companion until her sudden death of a heart attack in 1862.[15] Berlioz's final years were spent in the company of Marie's mother, who cared for him until his death on March 8, 1869.

Berlioz's *Harold in Italy*, op. 16

Berlioz was greatly influenced by C. W. Gluck and Gaspare Spontini, carrying on their French operatic traditions. Widely regarded as one of the Romantic era's greatest orchestrators, Berlioz is also admired for "the clarity and boldness of his rhythmic articulation" and his imaginative use of spatial effects.[16] With *Symphonie fantastique* (1830), he introduced the musical concept of an *idée fixe*, a "recurrent, obsessive theme," which he employed again in *Harold in Italy*.[17] Apart from a handful of juvenilia (now lost), he composed no chamber music, nor did he compose any music for solo piano; orchestral and vocal works were his specialty.[18] Violists are fortunate to have one work by Hector Berlioz: *Harold in Italy*, a symphony with solo viola. An immediate success upon its premiere, *Harold in Italy* remains one of the most well-known and frequently performed works for the instrument. It is dedicated to Humbert Ferrand, a writer and close friend of Berlioz's.

Attempting to reconstruct *Harold*'s path—from genesis to the work we know today—is challenging (Chart 3.1), and there are conflicting accounts among the surviving sources. The work originated as a commission from the virtuoso violinist Nicolò Paganini, who attended a performance of Berlioz's music on December 22, 1833:

> Some weeks after the triumphant concert which I have just described, Paganini came to see me.

December 22, 1833	Paganini attends a concert of Berlioz's works at the Paris Conservatoire.
Mid-January 1834	Paganini visits Berlioz, seeking to commission a new work to perform on his Stradivarius viola.
January 21, 1834	The commission is announced in *Le Rénovateur*: "The work will be titled: *The Last Moments of Mary Stuart*, dramatic fantasy for orchestra, chorus and solo viola."
January 24, 1834	Berlioz writes to Joseph d'Ortigue about the commission.
March 19, 1834	Berlioz writes to Humbert Ferrand: "I am finishing up the Symphony, with solo viola, that Paganini asked of me. I had planned on writing it in two movements, but then a third occurred to me, and then a fourth."
March 20, 1834	Berlioz writes to his sister Adèle: "I am at the point of finishing a large instrumental composition for Paganini, he is to perform it in London this year."
April 29, 1834	Berlioz writes to Adèle that his new symphony will be played in November in Paris.
May 15 or 16, 1834	Berlioz writes to Humbert Ferrand that three movements of his new symphony with solo viola are now complete.
June 22, 1834	Date of completion written on manuscript.
July 31, 1834	Berlioz mentions the symphony's title in a letter to Édouard Rocher: "I have composed much . . . there is, among other things, a new symphony titled *Harold*."
August 31, 1834	Berlioz writes to Humbert Ferrand: "Paganini, I believe, will find that the viola is not treated enough in concerto fashion."
September 1834?	Berlioz shows manuscript to Paganini?
November 23, 1834	Premiere of *Harold* symphony.
1834–1840 (or beyond)	Berlioz revises the work.
December 1837	Liszt sends his recently completed arrangement of *Harold* for viola and piano to Berlioz.
December 16, 1838	Paganini hears *Harold* for the first time and sends a check for 20,000 francs to Berlioz two days later.
1848	The score for *Harold in Italy* is published.
1880	Liszt's arrangement of *Harold in Italy* for viola and piano is published.

Chart 3.1 A *Harold* Chronology.

"I have a wonderful viola," said he, "an admirable Stradivarius, and should greatly like to play it in public. But I have no music for it. Would you write me a solo? I have no confidence in anyone but you for such a work."

"Certainly," I answered; "I am more flattered than I can say; but in order to fulfil your expectation, and make a composition sufficiently brilliant to suit such a virtuoso as yourself, I ought to be able to play the viola, and this I cannot do. It seems to me that you alone can solve the problem."

"No," replied Paganini; "you will succeed. As for me, I am too unwell at present to compose. I could not think of such a thing."[19]

Within days of Paganini's visit, the commission was announced in the January 21, 1834, issue of *Le Rénovateur*, also appearing in the January 26 issue of *Gazette musicale de Paris*:

Paganini, whose health is improving daily, has just requested of Mr. Berlioz a brand new composition in the genre of the *Symphonie fantastique*, which the celebrated virtuoso hopes to perform on his return to England.

The work will be titled: *The Last Moments of Mary Stuart*, dramatic fantasy for orchestra, chorus and solo viola. Paganini himself, for the first time in public, will perform the viola part.[20]

Berlioz mentioned the commission in a letter to his friend Joseph d'Ortigue on January 24:

As you know, I am working on a piece for Paganini—for chorus, orchestra, and solo viola. He came by, himself, just a few days ago, to ask it of me.[21]

Paganini, who had previously played viola only in private, had been planning his public debut on the instrument for some months: "I must return to London in April to play the large viola," he wrote in a letter to Luigi Germi in October 1833.[22] Paganini composed his *Sonata per la grand viola* for this "large viola" (a different instrument from his Stradivarius), appearing publicly as a violist for the first time on April 28, 1834, at the Hanover Square Rooms in London.[23]

How far Berlioz progressed on the work under the Mary Stuart (Mary, Queen of Scots) theme is unknown, though aspects of *Harold* are suggestive of such a theme. The ominous fugue that opens the work is more suited to Queen Mary's sorrowful fate (she was executed for treason) rather than to Harold's wanderings in the mountains. In the first movement, Berlioz reused material from his overture *Rob Roy*, including the *idée fixe* (the "Harold" theme) and the theme at m. 166. Composed in 1831 and discarded after its first performance in 1833, the overture was inspired by one of Walter Scott's Waverley Novels, *Rob Roy*, which is based on the life of Scottish outlaw turned folk hero Rob Roy MacGregor. In reusing these themes, Berlioz thus transferred material from one composition that depicted a historical Scottish figure (*Rob Roy*) to a new composition intended to depict another historical Scottish figure (*The Last Moments of Mary Stuart*). Berlioz had previously written another overture inspired by one of Scott's novels, the *Waverley* overture, op. 1. An avid fan of Scott's novels, Berlioz had contemplated two opera projects based on the author's works, and while in Italy he attended a costume ball dressed in Scottish attire as a character from Scott's *A Legend of Montrose*.[24]

In considering sources that Berlioz may have used for *The Last Moments of Mary Stuart*, it is then worthwhile to turn to another of Scott's Waverley Novels, *The Abbot*. This historical novel is centered on Mary Stuart's imprisonment in Loch Leven Castle from 1567 to 1568, twenty years before her execution. The melancholy mood of *Harold*'s opening is reminiscent of many passages in this book:

> Within the narrow circuit of [the garden's] formal and limited walks, Mary Stuart was now learning to perform the weary part of a prisoner, which, with little interval, she was doomed to sustain during the remainder of her life. She was followed in her slow and melancholy exercise by two female attendants.[25]

Harold's second movement, which depicts a procession of pilgrims singing their evening hymn, is also evocative of many passages in *The Abbot*:

> In the course of their journey the travellers spoke little to each other. Magdalen Græme chaunted, from time to time, in a low voice, a part of some one of those beautiful old Latin hymns which belong to the Catholic service, muttered an Ave or a Credo, and so passed on, lost in devotional contemplation.[26]

We cannot determine with any certainty the source of inspiration for the Mary Stuart theme, and it remains unclear at which point Berlioz altered his dramatic concept for the work. But even the later movements of *Harold in Italy* bear the stamp of this earlier concept, including the depiction of a bagpipe in the third movement (an instrument traditionally associated with Scotland that Berlioz also encountered while in Italy) and the accompanying rhythms of the final movement at measure 99 (Ex. 3.1), which "are those Berlioz would typically use for death and mortal danger; they suggest a connection to *Les derniers instants de Marie Stuart*."[27]

Returning to Berlioz's memoirs, he writes that the work's change of direction occurred shortly after completion of the first movement:

> In order to please the illustrious virtuoso, I then endeavoured to write a solo for the viola, but so combined with the orchestra as not to diminish the importance

Example 3.1 Berlioz, *Harold in Italy*, op. 16, movt. IV, mm. 99–103, orchestral reduction.

of the latter, feeling sure that Paganini's incomparable execution would enable him to give the solo instrument all its due prominence. The proposition was a new one. A happy idea soon occurred to me, and I became intensely eager to carry it out.

No sooner was the first movement written than Paganini wished to see it. At sight of the pauses, however, which the viola has to make in the *allegro*, "That is not at all what I want," cried he. "I have to wait a great deal too long. I must be playing the whole time."

"That is exactly what I said," I answered. "What you really want is a *concerto* for the [viola], and you are the only man who can write it."

To this he made no reply, but seemed disappointed, and left me without any further remarks. A few days afterwards, being already a sufferer from that throat affection which was ultimately to prove fatal to him, he went to Nice, and did not return till three years later.

Finding that my plan of composition did not suit him, I applied myself to carrying it out in another way, and without troubling myself any further as to how the solo part should be brought into brilliant relief, I conceived the idea of writing a series of scenes for the orchestra, in which the viola should find itself mixed up, like a person more or less in action, always preserving his own individuality. The background I formed from my recollections of my wanderings in the Abruzzi, introducing the viola as a sort of melancholy dreamer, in the style of Byron's *Childe Harold*. Hence the title of the symphony, *Harold in Italy*.[28]

However, Berlioz's letters from 1834 conflict with this account, suggesting that all of the work was completed before he showed it to Paganini. In a letter from March 19 to his friend Humbert Ferrand, Berlioz wrote:

The day before yesterday once again, I wrote for thirteen hours without stopping. I am finishing up the Symphony, with solo viola, that Paganini asked of me. I had planned on writing it in two movements, but then a third occurred to me, and then a fourth; I do hope that I will stop there. I still have a good month of continuous work ahead.[29]

He wrote similarly to his sister Adèle the following day:

I have been so absorbed by work for two and a half months, so pressed by several urgent compositions, that it has happened I hold the pen twelve or thirteen hours in a row. I am at the point of finishing a large instrumental composition for Paganini, he is to perform it in London this year, and I devote all the time to it that my daily [newspaper] scribbles allow me.[30]

These letters suggest that Berlioz was aiming to complete the work in time for Paganini to perform it during the virtuoso's upcoming London engagements. But on April 29, Berlioz wrote to Adèle indicating that the work was now planned for a series of concerts in Paris:

I am going to finish a new symphony, on a plan completely different from the other [*Symphonie fantastique*]. It will be for my concerts in November.[31]

A couple of weeks later, Berlioz wrote to Humbert Ferrand that the first three movements were finished, while humorously expressing his plans to dedicate the symphony to Ferrand:

I have finished the *first three movements* of my new symphony with solo viola; I'm going to set myself to finishing the fourth. I believe that it will be good and above all of a very curious quaintness. I intend to dedicate it to one of my friends whom you know well, Mr. Humbert Ferrand, if he will permit me. There is a *March of Pilgrims Singing the Evening Hymn,* which, I hope, will have fame in December. I do not know when this enormous work will be engraved; in any case, make sure to obtain the permission from Mr. Ferrand.[32]

On May 31, he wrote to d'Ortigue, indicating that the work was nearly finished:

At home I do not put down the pen, between these rascally newspapers and the finishing of my symphony, which will be born and baptized before long.[33]

Berlioz completed the symphony on June 22 in Montmartre, and the earliest mention of the work's title dates from July 31 in a letter written to his friend Édouard Rocher:

I have composed much for these next musical gatherings; there is, among other things, a new symphony titled *Harold* that the musicians and critics will have to contend with. It is about the same size as the *Symphonie fantastique.*[34]

Berlioz here gives the title simply as *Harold*; other early references to the work, including letters, newspaper announcements, and reviews, also give the title simply as either *Harold* or *Harold Symphonie.*[35] With the work now complete, Berlioz expressed his concerns about Paganini's likely reaction to the solo viola part in a letter to Ferrand on August 31:

Two months ago, and I believe I wrote it to you, my symphony with solo viola, titled *Harold*, was finished. Paganini, I believe, will find that the viola is not treated enough in concerto fashion; it is a symphony on a new level and not a composition written in order to highlight a brilliant talent like his. I owe him always for having me undertake it; it is being copied right now; it will be performed next November at the first concert that I will give at the Conservatoire. I intend to give three in a row.[36]

Paganini was back in Paris by early September, and "although there is no record of any meeting then, this is the time when Paganini had an opportunity to examine the score and to tell Berlioz that he would not be playing it."[37] Berlioz arranged for Chrétien Urhan, a prominent soloist on violin, viola, and viola d'amore who had formerly served as solo viola for the Paris Opera, to play the premiere on November 23, 1834; the work was repeated at concerts on December 14 and 28. Among those in the audience for the premiere were Fryderyk Chopin, Franz Liszt, and Victor Hugo.[38] The second movement, *Marche des pèlerins*, was encored at all three concerts, becoming a sensation:

But a piece was applauded with fury and requested again with acclaim. This piece, performed yesterday, is celebrated today. In the salons, in the homes, wherever we gather, we hear about the *March of Pilgrims*; everywhere we rhapsodize on the effect of the mysterious rhythm, of this prayer to which the arpeggios of the solo viola lend a color so religious, and of this bell which we hear first in the distance, the sound of which becomes always louder and more distinct as the monks advance to the monastery, and which, when they have entered the chapel, ends by resounding alone, leaving, however, the whisper of a grave chanting with interruptions and pauses.[39]

Berlioz regularly programmed *Harold in Italy*, both in Paris and abroad. On December 16, 1838, Paganini finally heard a performance of the symphony (Fig. 3.1):

The concert was just over; I was in a profuse [sweat], and trembling with exhaustion, when Paganini, followed by his son Achilles, came up to me at the orchestra door, gesticulating violently. Owing to the throat affection of which he ultimately died, he had already completely lost his voice, and unless everything was perfectly quiet, no one but his son could hear or even guess what he was saying. He made a sign to the child, who got up on a chair, put his ear close to his father's mouth, and listened attentively.

Achilles then got down, and turning to me, said, "My father desires me to assure you, sir, that he has never in his life been so powerfully impressed at a concert; that your music has quite [overwhelmed] him, and that if he did not restrain himself he should go down on his knees to thank you for it." I made a movement of incredulous embarrassment at these strange words, but Paganini, seizing my arm, and rattling out, "Yes, yes!" with the little voice he had left, dragged me up on the stage, where there were still a good many of the performers, knelt down, and kissed my hand.[40]

Two days later, Paganini sent 20,000 francs to the composer along with a note of appreciation. The money enabled Berlioz to begin work on his third symphony, *Roméo et Juliette*, which would be dedicated to Paganini.

A variety of performers took up *Harold*'s solo part during the nineteenth century, including many prominent violists: Chrétien Urhan in France, Henry Hill in England, Hieronymus Weickmann in Russia, and Charles Baetens in the United States. Urhan had a long association with the work; his interpretation elicited praise from the composer after a performance in 1844:

Mr. Berlioz owes a great recognition to his solo viola, to Mr. Urhan, who, always faithful, always attentive and careful, also always gives to this very difficult part so much melancholy poetry, a color so soft, a reverie so religious.[41]

Figure 3.1 Engraving by Auguste-Louis Lepère after the original painting by Adolphe Yvon, *Hommage de Paganini à Berlioz lors du concert du 16 décembre 1838 où Berlioz dirige la "Symphonie fantastique" et "Harold en Italie,"* published in the March 22, 1884, issue of *Le Monde illustré*, page 181.

At an 1843 concert in Mannheim, Berlioz indicated that "one of the violas in the orchestra, though a player with no pretensions to virtuosity, gave a capable account of the solo part."[42] The work also attracted prominent violin soloists, including Heinrich Wilhelm Ernst and Joseph Joachim as well as orchestral concertmasters, who felt entitled to play any violin or viola solo that came their way (this was particularly true of Franz Kneisel, concertmaster of the Boston Symphony Orchestra, who played the work on no fewer than five occasions between 1886 and 1899).[43] Moving into the twentieth century, Lionel Tertis and William Primrose both had strong associations with the work. Primrose made the first studio recording of *Harold* in 1944 with Serge Koussevitzky and the Boston Symphony Orchestra; his later recording with Thomas Beecham and the Royal Philharmonic Orchestra spent nineteen weeks in the top five of Billboard's classical chart from 1952 to 1953.[44] The success of that album contributed to Primrose earning his star on the Hollywood Walk of Fame. *Harold*'s solo part is now frequently taken by orchestral principal violists and occasionally by viola soloists who often pair it with a viola concerto.

Many violists are likely to play the work in a viola and piano transcription. Franz Liszt completed the first version for viola and piano by December 1837, sending the manuscript to Berlioz:

> You will soon receive from here the piano arrangement of your second symphony. If your intention was to deliver it to the public . . . Hoffmeister in Leipzig, pays me 6 francs per page for everything that I send him. This would therefore be about 600 francs.[45]

Berlioz replied favorably, and Hoffmeister announced the work's forthcoming publication in the March 6, 1838, issue of *Neue Zeitschrift für Musik*.[46] The planned publication did not materialize, and Berlioz keep the manuscript until 1852, when Liszt requested that it be returned. By this time, the full score had been published, which incorporated changes since Liszt had made his arrangement in 1837. While revisiting the arrangement at this point, Berlioz raised several concerns in a letter to Liszt, including the appropriateness of music that Liszt had transferred from the orchestra to the viola part:

> Don't you think that the part you have given to the viola, bigger than it has in the [orchestral] score, alters the character of the work? . . . the viola should not feature more prominently in the piano score than in the other. Here the piano represents the orchestra; the viola should remain separate, immersed in its sentimental musings; everything else is alien to it; it is present, but takes no part at all in the action.[47]

Liszt subsequently made alterations based on Berlioz's feedback, though the version that was published in 1880 still contained extra music for the viola in the second movement (mm. 162–68, where the solo viola incorporates the orchestral viola part) and third movement (mm. 1–31 and mm. 136–66, where the solo viola plays drones originally in the wind parts).[48] While Liszt's arrangement is remarkable for its skillful consolidation of the orchestral forces into a single piano part, it places formidable demands on the pianist. In 2001, Bärenreiter released a new version for viola and piano that aimed to reduce the demands on the pianist while giving the viola a larger share of orchestral material:

> The present arrangement is intended to make the work readily available to violists by providing a more playable piano reduction of the orchestral part and by giving the viola an element of the orchestral music when the soloist is otherwise silent. It may thus serve for rehearsals of the orchestral version and as a challenging study for violists.[49]

Given Berlioz's comments to Liszt regarding the necessary separation of the solo viola's music from that of the orchestra, this edition is less suited for performance, which Hugh Macdonald alludes to in the previous statement. Violists continue to frequently use Liszt's edition when performing the work.

Despite its concerto aspects, *Harold in Italy* is perhaps the most conventional of Berlioz's four symphonies:

> *Harold en Italie*, which consciously tries to follow Beethovenian practices, is on the whole the most conservative of his symphonies. It is the only one to have but four movements, and they are, on the surface at least, cast in traditional molds: a sonata, a slow march, a scherzo-like movement, and a finale that begins with reminiscences of the earlier movements patterned obviously after Beethoven's Ninth.[50]

Uncharacteristically, Berlioz also regularly employs four- and eight-bar phrases throughout the symphony, most notably in the *idée fixe* (the "Harold" theme, Ex. 3.2).[51] In the first movement, "there is more than a residue of sonata form; yet it flies in the face of convention by refusing to establish the complementary key in the exposition."[52] This movement does correspond to sonata form better than examples from Berlioz's other symphonies, and it is worthwhile to review the analyses by Julian Rushton and Hermann Danuser in this respect.[53] Yet, in considering Berlioz's unorthodox sonata expositions in general, Donald Tovey questioned: "Then why call them sonata expositions? They are very clear, entertaining, and all the better for the repeats

Example 3.2 Berlioz, *Harold in Italy*, op. 16, movt. I, mm. 38–45, solo viola's first statement of the recurrent "Harold" theme (*idée fixe*) that will represent Harold throughout the symphony.

which Berlioz prescribes."[54] Given the episodic nature of the complete symphony and the title of the first movement, "Harold in the Mountains. Scenes of Melancholy, Happiness and Joy," I have chosen to divide the movement into three scenes while also providing a comparison to sonata form (Chart 3.2). (The measure numbers correspond to Bärenreiter's edition from the *New Edition of the Complete Works*, which numbers the start of both the first and second endings as m. 192. Other editions and analyses may number these measures differently.)

The first scene ("Melancholy"; Adagio) opens with a double fugue: the cellos and basses play the first subject (mm. 1–3), and Bassoon I enters with the second fugal subject in m. 3. At m. 14, the winds play a minor-tinged version of the "Harold" theme. The solo viola, which Berlioz instructs is to be placed near the audience and isolated from the orchestra, enters at m. 38 with the "Harold" theme in its true form (see Ex. 3.2). Not only is the "Harold" theme recycled from *Rob Roy*, so is most of the material in mm. 38–92 (see mm. 260–63 and mm. 275–320 of *Rob Roy*). Berlioz originally wrote more complicated figurations for the viola in mm. 73–94, which he presumably discarded once Paganini was no longer involved with the work. David Aaron Carpenter incorporated this material into the solo part for his recording with Vladimir Ashkenazy and the Helsinki Philharmonic Orchestra, released in 2011.[55]

The second scene ("Happiness"; Allegro) opens with an introduction (mm. 94–130), which previews the Theme Group 1 material that will fully begin in m. 131. Berlioz also borrowed the second theme group material (mm. 166–92) from *Rob Roy* (Ex. 3.3). This material, which begins in F major, touches on several key areas but never settles on a secondary key, as one would expect from a sonata form. At mm. 180–81, Berlioz interjects an E♭ major tonality—the ♭VI—which will reappear later in the movement. After repeating the "exposition," Berlioz develops and fragments Theme Group 1 and Theme Group 2 material. At m. 249, Berlioz returns to material from this scene's introduction (see mm. 106–14), followed by more Theme Group 2 material, with the viola playing ornamented figures (mm. 259–67). Berlioz shifts to E♭ major at m. 275 and then dramatically suspends the momentum with a full measure of rest at m. 284. When the solo viola enters with the pickup to m. 290, it is now playing a variation of Theme Group 1 material.

For the third and final scene ("Joy"; animez un peu), Berlioz compresses melodic ideas from the first and second scenes. In the fugal introduction (mm. 323–52), strings pass around the "Harold" theme as winds interject Theme Group 2 figures, paralleling the opening double fugue. In mm. 349–51, the viola plays one quick interjection of the Theme Group 2 figure before taking up the "Harold" theme at m. 352, which is superimposed over Theme Group 1 material in the strings. The music crescendos to a $\boldsymbol{f\!f}$ tutti section at m. 372, where Berlioz makes his way through a sequence of fifths (mm. 378–87) before quieting down for a written-out repeat of the previous measures. At m. 438, the mood lightens

Zone	Sonata Form Zone	Thematic Areas/Snippet	Measures	Principal Tonal Areas/Function
Scene I: Melancholy			1–94	
	Introduction	Unit 1.1: Tutti introduction; includes "Harold" theme	1–37	G minor
		Unit 1.2: Solo "Harold" theme	38–94	G major
Scene II: Happiness, Part I			94–192	
	Introduction	Introduction	94–130	Dominant function
	Repeated Exposition	Theme Group 1	131–65	G major
		Theme Group 2	166–92 (1st ending)	Starts F major; principally centered on G major

Chart 3.2 Berlioz, *Harold in Italy*, op. 16: Structural analysis, first movement, "Harold aux montagnes. Scènes de mélancolie, de bonheur et de joie."

Zone	Sonata Form Zone	Thematic Areas/Snippet	Measures	Principal Tonal Areas/Function
Scene II: Happiness, Part II			192 (2nd ending) –323	
	Development	Unit 1.1	192 (2nd ending) –258	Modulatory
		Unit 1.2: Solo variation	259–89	G major; E-flat major
	Recap A in Rushton; Start of Reprise in Danuser	Unit 1.3: Solo variation	290–323	G major
Scene III: Joy			323–493	
	Recap/Coda Functions	Unit 1.1: Tutti introduction; "Harold" theme with Theme Group 2 interjections	323–52	G major
		Unit 1.2: "Harold" theme with Theme Group 2 material	352–438	G major; modulatory
		Unit 1.3: Theme Group 2 material	438–70	G major
	Closing	Closing	471–93	G major

Chart 3.2 (continued) Berlioz, *Harold in Italy*, op. 16: Structural analysis, first movement, "Harold aux montagnes. Scènes de mélancolie, de bonheur et de joie."

Example 3.3 Berlioz, *Harold in Italy*, op. 16, movt. I, mm. 166–69, cello.

for a final statement of Theme Group 2 material. As the viola concludes its statement in mm. 463–65, Berlioz begins to ramp up the volume and tempo, leading to the glorious closing tutti at m. 471.

The second movement, "March of Pilgrims Singing the Evening Hymn" (Chart 3.3), would prove to be one of Berlioz's most popular works; it was frequently encored at performances of the complete symphony and sometimes programmed separately. Berlioz describes the movement's evolution in his memoirs:

> The Pilgrims' March itself—which I sketched in a couple of hours one evening, musing by the fire—underwent many changes of detail during the next six years or more which I think greatly improved it.[56]

In this evocative movement, Harold is witness to a procession of pilgrims singing a hymn while monastery bells chime in the background. Berlioz recollected a similar scene from his journey to Italy:

> How clearly and vividly I recall that wild Abruzzi country where I wandered far and wide. . . . the rows of shrines to the Madonna along the tops of the high hills where at evening, returning late from the plain, the reapers pass, chanting their litanies, while from somewhere comes the sad jangle of a monastery bell.[57]

The entire movement is structured as a lengthy crescendo and diminuendo as the pilgrims pass by Harold. After a fifteen-measure introduction, the series of Canto I hymn stanzas begins:

> Eight-bar phrases of the pilgrims' canto are punctuated at every cadence with a bell-like chime of horns and harp playing the dissonant note C. This pitch is always resolved to B (fitting the E-Major harmony) at the beginning of the following phrase.[58]

Interrupting one of the stanzas, the viola enters in m. 60, playing four introductory measures before settling on the "Harold" theme in m. 64 (Unit 1.2). Berlioz suspends the bell-like chimes in this section with the "Harold" theme superimposed over five iterations of the canto stanzas (mm. 64–103). The bells resume in the next section, after the viola has dropped out in m. 106. While each of the ten-measure stanzas in this section (Unit 1.3) begins on the tonic, Berlioz works through an ascending series of cadences (D♯ minor in m. 111, E major in m. 121, etc.; see Chart 3.3).[59] The viola returns in the midst of these stanzas at m. 144 for the first of two fluttering statements.

Zone	Thematic Areas/Snippet	Measures	Principal Tonal Areas/Function
Introduction		1–15	Dominant function
Canto I		16–168	
	Unit 1.1: Tutti Canto statements	16–63	E major
	Unit 1.2: Solo "Harold" theme over tutti Canto	64–103	B major
	Unit 1.3: Tutti Canto	104–43	Ascending series of cadences: D-sharp minor; E major; F-sharp minor; G-sharp minor
	Unit 1.4: Viola variation over tutti Canto	144–68	Ascending series of cadences (continued): A major; B major; ends on G major
Canto II (Canto religioso)		169–248	C major
Coda		248–334	
	Unit 1.1: Canto I material	248–78	Begins C major; E major
	Unit 1.2: Bells/Canto I outlines	279–325	E minor/ C major
	Unit 1.3: Canto II arpeggios	326–34	E major

Chart 3.3 Berlioz, *Harold in Italy*, op. 16: Structural analysis, second movement, "Marche de pèlerins chantant la prière du soir."

Berlioz shifts to C major (the ♭VI of E major) at m. 169 for the Canto religioso (Canto II) section. With the pilgrims fading into the distance, the viola plays *sul ponticello* arpeggios over the Canto religioso hymn, which alternates between the winds and strings. After the viola concludes its arpeggios, the Canto I stanzas return at m. 248 for the start of the coda, with the viola periodically interjecting arpeggios until m. 275. By this point, the pilgrims have receded so far that their cantos are inaudible—all that remains are outlines of their hymn in the pizzicatos of the lower strings (mm. 283–318) as the harp and winds continue with their bells. The solo viola closes out the movement with a final group of arpeggios from mm. 326–31, ending with its own bell-like harmonic in the final measure.

The third movement, "Serenade of an Abruzzi-Mountaineer to His Sweetheart," is in an ABA form with coda (Chart 3.4). It begins with a dance-like section (mm. 1–31), inspired by the music of the *pifferari* (shepherds from the mountain regions of Italy):

Zone	Thematic Areas/Snippet	Measures	Principal Tonal Areas/Function
A	Ob. 1	1–31	C major
B		32–135	
	Unit 1.1: Tutti Eng. Hn.	32–64	C major
	Unit 1.2: Solo "Harold" theme over Serenade theme	65–98	C major
	Unit 1.3	99–135	Tonicizes D minor; ends on C major
A		136–65	C major
Coda	A and B material combined with "Harold" theme	166–208	C major

Chart 3.4 Berlioz, *Harold in Italy*, op. 16: Structural analysis, third movement, "Sérénade d'un montagnard des Abbruzes à sa maîtresse."

I only noticed one popular kind of music while I was at Rome, which may be regarded as a remnant of antiquity: that of the *pifferari*. These are wandering musicians who towards Christmas come down from the mountains four or five at a time, with bagpipes and *pifferi* (a sort of [oboe]). . . . The bagpipe, accompanied by a large bass *piffero*, gives out the harmony on two or three notes, on which a shorter *piffero* plays the tune; above this there are two very small *pifferi*, much shorter than the others, and played by children of from twelve to fifteen years of age, which make shakes and trills, and surround the rustic melody with a shower of quaint ornamentation.[60]

At m. 32, the Abruzzi mountaineer's serenade begins, once again inspired by Berlioz's recollections of Italy:

One night I was awakened by the most [singular] Serenade I had yet heard. A robust *ragazzo* [boy] was roaring out a love-song beneath the window of his *ragazza* [girl], to the accompaniment of a huge mandoline, a bagpipe, and a little iron instrument of the nature of a triangle, called here a *stimbalo*. His song, or rather shriek, consisted of a progression of four or five descending notes, ending with a long sustained wail from the leading note to the tonic. . . .
  This phrase recurs all over the Abruzzo mountains.[61]

After the English horn plays its serenade, the viola enters at m. 65 (Unit 1.2) with the "Harold" theme. Harold is once again playing the role of bystander, enjoying the sights and sounds of Italy, while the orchestra continues with statements of the serenade. Giving up the "Harold" theme at m. 95, the viola moves into a new section with *leggiero* sixteenth notes at m. 99 (Unit 1.3). The viola's sixteenth notes give way to a cantilena passage in m. 111, as if Harold were sighing in delight at his beautiful surroundings. After a tutti restatement of the opening A section (mm. 136–65), "the movement culminates in a triple thematic and metric superimposition, masterfully combining Harold's motto, the rhythm of the dance, and the theme of the serenade."[62] In this final coda, the viola plays the serenade, while the flute and harp take over the "Harold" theme.

For the final movement, Berlioz drew inspiration from Beethoven's Ninth Symphony:

Berlioz borrows from that work the idea of reviewing in the fourth movement themes from the previous three. Between repeated statements of a rhythmically disjunct theme (associated with the brigands), Berlioz introduces portions of all the earlier main themes including the motto ["Harold" theme].[63]

This movement depicts an orgy (a debauched party) of brigands (gangs of robbers who ambush travelers). Berlioz expressed fascination with the brigands while in Italy:

> It was almost dark when I left my kind hosts, and started off limping on my way home. I had lamed my right foot in coming down from Nisida; and so, when a fine carriage rolled past me on the Naples road, and I saw that the footboard behind was empty, I leapt up into it, hoping to be carried into the town in this unfashionable manner without fatigue. I had, however, counted without my hostess, a pretty little Parisian woman, lying back luxuriously in a cloud of muslin, who cried out sharply to her coachman, "Louis, there is someone behind!" whereupon I [received] a sharp cut from the whip across my face....
>
> So, meditating on the charms of a brigand's life (which, in spite of its drawbacks, would really be the only satisfactory career for an honest man, if there were not so many stupid, stinking wretches even in the smallest bands), I limped home.[64]

These remarks may shed light on why Harold (an "honest man") would observe an orgy of brigands even for the short time that he appears in the movement. Berlioz's treatment of the solo part here is intriguing: each time the dreamy wanderer is confronted with the savage orgy, he divorces himself from reality, losing himself in recollections of earlier scenes (Chart 3.5). For the first two recollections, he is completely lost in his memories, playing material that he previously only observed. He gradually becomes more self-aware in the following recollections, but as the orgy continues to intrude, he progressively moves further away from the earlier scenes' original melodic content. Coming fully unhinged at

Measures	Reference
14–18	Movement I: First scene, second fugal subject (Bassoon I, mm. 3–7)
34–41	Movement II: Canto I, fourth stanza (Bassoon III and orchestral violas, mm. 46–53)
45–54	Movement III: Serenade melody (English horn, mm. 34–40)
60–70	Movement I: Second scene, Theme Group 1 (Solo viola, mm. 126–37)
81–109	Movement I: First scene, "Harold" theme (Solo viola, mm. 38–41); highly fragmented
483–505	Movement II: Solo viola plays fragmented material over Canto stanzas

Chart 3.5 Berlioz, *Harold in Italy*, op. 16: Solo viola references, fourth movement, "Orgie de brigands. Souvenirs des scènes précédentes."

m. 81, he is capable of uttering only a few fragments of his trusty "Harold" theme. Unable to bear the "wretches" and their orgy any longer, he turns his back and flees "in terror,"[65] as the proceedings continue without his intervention. At m. 473, a pause in the raucous proceedings allows the audience to discern two offstage violins and one offstage cello playing the theme from the Pilgrims' March, with the viola joining in, *ppp*, in m. 483. This spatial effect gives the impression that Harold has wandered far away from the orgy, to a happier time and place, leaving the audience as the sole spectators to the orgy's frenzied conclusion.

While *Harold in Italy* has earned admiration as a masterful symphonic work, it has not enjoyed the same admiration as a concertante viola work—at least not among violists. Lacking a great concerto from the Romantic period, violists find *Harold* an unsuitable alternative: "Unfortunately, even today there are players who think like Paganini and steer clear of the piece, finding that it doesn't offer enough scope for their virtuosity."[66] And the work, with its ever-diminishing role for the violist, can be a challenge to execute successfully in a concert setting, in both the symphonic and piano versions. But violists have never shied away from a challenge, nor have they allowed themselves to be constrained by conventional attitudes toward music. Though *Harold in Italy* may not be a viola concerto, it is a truly brilliant work for solo viola and orchestra by one of Western classical music's greatest composers. What more could a violist want?

More about the Relationship between *Harold in Italy* and *Childe Harold*

Readers interested in learning more about the relationship between Berlioz's *Harold in Italy* and Byron's *Childe Harold's Pilgrimage* are referred to the following sources:

Banks, Paul. "Byron, Berlioz and Harold." Paper originally presented at the Royal Musical Association Annual Conference, Birmingham, UK, 1984. http://pwb101.me.uk/?page_id=460. Also published in a French translation as "Harold, de Byron à Berlioz." In *Hector Berlioz*, edited by Christian Wasselin and Pierre-René Serna, 152–61. Paris: Éditions de l'Herne, 2003.

Court, Glyn. "Berlioz and Byron and *Harold in Italy*." *Music Review* 17, no. 3 (August 1956): 229–36.

Langford, Jeffrey. "The Byronic Berlioz: *Harold en Italie* and Beyond." *Journal of Musicological Research* 16, no. 3 (1997): 199–221.

Levine, Alice. "Byron and the Romantic Composer." In *Lord Byron and His Contemporaries: Essays from the Sixth International Byron Seminar*, edited by Charles E. Robinson, 178–203. Newark: University of Delaware Press, 1982.

Rij, Inge van. "Harold en Italie." In *The Other Worlds of Hector Berlioz: Travels with the Orchestra*, 100–126. Cambridge: Cambridge University Press, 2015.

4

Ernest Bloch: *Suite hébraïque*

I. Rapsodie
II. Processional
III. Affirmation

Date of Composition: 1950–1951 (manuscripts for viola and piano version dated February 9, 16, and 17, 1951; manuscript for orchestral version dated March 10, 1951, at end of second movement)

First Edition: Ernest Bloch, *Suite Hébraïque for Viola (or Violin) and Piano*, New York: G. Schirmer, 1953, Plate No. 42892 (Viola and Piano Version); Ernest Bloch, *Suite Hébraique for Viola (or Violin) and Orchestra*, New York: G. Schirmer, 1957 (© 1953), Plate No. 43637 (Orchestral Version Study Score)

Dedication: To the Covenant Club of Illinois

Date/Place of First Public Performance: March 3, 1952, Milton Preves (viola), Helene Brahm (piano), Covenant Club of Illinois, Chicago (Viola and Piano Version, as part of *Five Jewish Pieces*); January 1, 1953, Milton Preves (viola), Chicago Symphony Orchestra, Rafael Kubelik (conductor), Chicago (Orchestral Version)

Orchestral Instrumentation: Solo viola, 2 flutes, 2 oboes, 2 clarinets, 2 bassoons, 4 horns in F, 3 trumpets in C, timpani, percussion (side drum, cymbals, tam-tam), harp, strings

Introduction

"I, for instance, am a Jew, and I aspire to write Jewish music, not for the sake of self-advertisement, but because I am sure that this is the only way in which I can produce music of vitality and significance—if I can do such a thing at all!"[1] Though his music encompasses many styles and techniques, Ernest Bloch's identity as a composer of Jewish music has remained a significant aspect of his critical reception. The composer, himself, proclaimed his Jewish heritage early on in a series of epic works known as the "Jewish Cycle."[2] He did not stop there; by the end of his career, roughly one quarter of his published compositions would "bear

Jewish titles, reveal a Jewish ethos on closer examination, or include traditional Jewish musical elements."[3] Counted among these works is the *Suite hébraïque*, a late composition in which Bloch incorporated traditional Jewish themes that he had copied from an encyclopedia years earlier.

Biographical Sketch

Born in Geneva, Switzerland, Ernest Bloch (1880–1959) was the youngest of Sophie and Maurice Bloch's three children. His paternal grandfather had served as a lay cantor at the synagogue in the small municipality of Lengnau (in the canton of Aargau), and his father practiced traditional Jewish rituals at home, occasionally taking the family to the synagogue in Geneva.[4] Bloch began studying violin at the age of nine, first with Albert Gos and later with Louis-Étienne-Ernest Reyer. In 1893, he began composition studies with Émile Jaques-Dalcroze, producing several ambitious works in the following years. Among these early works is *Symphonie orientale* (1896), which incorporated traditional Jewish tunes as sung by his father.[5] At the age of sixteen, Bloch went to Brussels, where he studied violin with Eugène Ysaÿe and Franz Schörg and composition with François Rasse. After three years in Brussels, he pursued further studies in Frankfurt, Munich, and Paris, focusing on composition while absorbing a variety of influences. Returning to Geneva in 1904, he married Margarethe Schneider, whom he had met while she was a piano student in Frankfurt; the couple would have three children together. Bloch lived in Geneva until 1916, selling tourist merchandise for his father's company while continuing with musical pursuits, including conducting, composing, and lecturing at the Geneva Conservatory. From 1911 to 1916, he composed the series of works that make up his "Jewish Cycle," including one of his most enduring compositions, *Schelomo: Rhapsodie hébraïque for Violoncello and Orchestra* (1916).[6]

Bloch traveled to the United States in 1916 to conduct the orchestra for Maud Allan's touring dance company. Though the tour turned out to be a flop, Bloch was buoyed by several successful performances of his compositions while in America, including the premiere of his String Quartet No. 1 (1916) by the Flonzaley Quartet. After bringing his family to America the following year, he started teaching at the David Mannes Music School in New York City. A watershed moment in Bloch's career came in 1919, when his Suite for Viola and Piano won the Second Berkshire Festival Competition, significantly bolstering his critical reputation. In 1920, he accepted a position as founding director of the Cleveland Institute of Music, resigning in 1925 after a disagreement with the school's directors. Later that same year, he accepted a position as artistic director of the San Francisco Conservatory of Music. During his tenure, he greatly expanded the fledgling institution, establishing an orchestra and chorus and building a theory department.[7] Wishing to devote more time to composing, Bloch resigned from the conservatory in 1930, and with financial support from multiple sources (notably the Rosa and Jacob Stern Fund) he returned to Switzerland.[8]

Bloch spent eight years in Europe and arrived back in the United States early in 1939; he eventually settled in the remote community of Agate Beach, Oregon, in 1941. To fulfill an obligation from his receipt of the Stern Fund, Bloch taught summer courses at the University of California at Berkeley from 1940 until 1952.[9] He received many further honors after returning to America, including the Gold Medal in Music from the American Academy of Arts and Letters in 1942 and three awards from the Music Critics Circle of New York. Bloch battled cancer during his final years, undergoing surgery in 1958 before finally succumbing on July 15, 1959, at the Good Samaritan Hospital in Portland, Oregon.[10]

Bloch's *Suite hébraïque*

Ernest Bloch wrote an impressive amount of music for viola, including the Suite for Viola and Piano (or Orchestra) (1919); Concertino for Flute, Viola, and String Orchestra (1950); *Suite hébraïque for Viola (or Violin) and Piano (or Orchestra)* (1951); *Meditation and Processional for Viola and Piano* (1951); and the Suite for Viola Solo (1958), which was left unfinished at the time of the composer's death. The *Suite hébraïque* stemmed from a six-day music festival in Chicago that honored the composer's seventieth birthday. As part of the event, Milton Preves, principal violist of the Chicago Symphony Orchestra, performed Bloch's Suite for Viola and Orchestra on November 30 and December 1, 1950. At the end of the festival, Preves approached Bloch with an idea for some new viola compositions:

> During Kubelik's reign here, we had a Bloch festival week where I performed the Bloch Suite and got a very nice mention from him about how I did it, thank goodness. At the end of the week I asked him if he would consider writing some pieces for viola along the lines of his *Baal Shem* suite for violin.[11]

After returning to Agate Beach, Bloch began working on *Five Jewish Pieces*, for viola and piano, consisting of a *Rhapsodie hébraïque*, *Meditation*, and *Three Processionals* (Chart 4.1). These works, indeed, resemble his *Baal Shem* suite for violin (1923). Bloch completed the *Five Jewish Pieces* on February 17, 1951, and wrote to the violinist Alfred Pochon two days later:

> I have just completed five pieces—of Hebrew character—for viola and piano. I will choose three for a small Suite with orchestra—also possibly for solo violin and orchestra.[12]

Original Movement from *Five Jewish Pieces*	Final Work and Movement	Date on Manuscript
Rhapsodie hébraïque	*Suite hébraïque:* I. Rapsodie	February 9, 1951
Meditation	*Meditation and Processional:* I. Meditation	February 16, 1951
Three Processionals: I	*Meditation and Processional:* II. Processional	February 17, 1951
Three Processionals: II	*Suite hébraïque:* II. Processional	February 17, 1951
Three Processionals: III	*Suite hébraïque:* III. Affirmation	February 17, 1951

Chart 4.1 Original movements from Bloch's *Five Jewish Pieces* and their final allocation in *Suite hébraïque* and *Meditation and Processional*.

Bloch then orchestrated three of the movements: *Rhapsodie hébraïque*, Processional II, and Processional III, forming the *Suite hébraïque*.[13] The remaining movements from *Five Jewish Pieces* were combined into the *Meditation and Processional*, dedicated to Preves, and published by Schirmer in 1954. The *Suite hébraïque*, however, was dedicated to one of the sponsors of the Chicago festival, the Covenant Club of Illinois. The group's president, Joseph H. Braun, had presented to the composer a gold Swiss watch at a banquet the day after the festival closed.[14] Bloch was greatly moved by this gift and privately promised to Braun "that there would some day be a token of his own appreciation."[15] The return token turned out to be the *Suite hébraïque*, as Bloch indicated in a letter that he sent to the organization:

> When I returned from Chicago, my heart was still overflowing with the feeling of warmth and brotherhood which surrounded me during those wonderful days in Chicago. I was particularly impressed with the fine atmosphere of the Covenant Club, and by the wonderful and symbolic gift which the members presented to me . . . It was to show them my gratitude that I thought of writing these Jewish pieces, which were the first work I composed after the Chicago Festival . . . I have used, in some of them, old and traditional melodies; but I have absorbed them to such a point that it may be difficult for future musicologists to determine what is traditional and what is Bloch.
>
> So this Suite Hebraique for Viola (or violin) and Orchestra (or piano) is dedicated to the Covenant Club of Illinois. I hope that when all of you hear the music, it will speak to your hearts better than my clumsy words, and that you will feel my own heart beating fraternally with yours.[16]

Preves premiered *Five Jewish Pieces* with pianist Helene Brahm on March 3, 1952, at the Covenant Club of Illinois. The original program lists the pieces in this order:[17]

Meditation
Processional I
        Dedicated to Mr. Milton Preves

Processional II
Processional III
Rhapsodie
        "Suite Hebraique," dedicated to the Covenant Club of Illinois

The club sponsored a recording of the pieces that year (with *Suite hébraïque* on Side A and *Meditation and Processional* on Side B), in which the movements of *Suite hébraïque* appear in the same order as the premiere. By the time that Preves premiered the orchestral version of *Suite hébraïque* on January 1, 1953, Bloch had renamed its movements, but the program lists them in the same order as when they were premiered as part of *Five Jewish Pieces*:

I.   Processional
II. Affirmation
III. Rapsodie[18]

Each movement, then, had some form of alteration to its title, the most inexplicable being the third movement, which now used the alternate spelling of "Rapsodie" in place of the more common form of "Rhapsodie." These titles were retained when Schirmer published the viola and piano version later in 1953, though the order of the movements returned to that from Bloch's manuscript.[19]

In all three movements of *Suite hébraïque*, Bloch incorporated traditional Jewish material that he had found in *The Jewish Encyclopedia*, a twelve-volume work edited by Isidore Singer.[20] Readers interested in learning more about the specific melodies that Bloch used are referred to Alexander Knapp's thorough article "Ernest Bloch's *Suite Hébraïque* and *Meditation and Processional*: Historical Overview and Analysis of Traditional Musical Materials."[21] The following charts reference these melodies, including the location (volume and page numbers) in *The Jewish Encyclopedia* where the material may be found.

Written in an ABA form (Chart 4.2), the first movement, "Rapsodie," is centered on G minor (all rehearsal numbers refer to the Schirmer edition). Bloch effectively showcases the technical capabilities of the viola in this movement with virtuosic passagework, rapid shifts in register, and bold multiple stops. These

Zone	Thematic Areas/Snippet	Measures	*Jewish Encyclopedia* Source
A		1–29 (No. 4)	
B		29 (No. 4)–68	"Shemot" Vol. IX: 220
A		69 (No. 10)–96	

Chart 4.2 Bloch, *Suite hébraïque*: Structural analysis, first movement, "Rapsodie."

aspects, along with the frequent fluctuations in tempo, give the movement an improvisatory quality, which is often associated with rhapsodies.[22] The movement opens with the piano playing the melody in octaves with the viola quietly emerging in the end of the second measure. It is not until the third iteration of the melody in m. 15 that the viola finally gets to state the beginning of the melodic idea, now centered on D minor.

The opening of the B section brings a major change in character, with the viola's multiple-stop chords embellishing the "Shemot" theme (mm. 33–38). In m. 39, the viola returns to material from the A section (see mm. 8–15), with the piano revisiting the opening of the B section in the following passage (mm. 50–59). At its entrance in m. 59 (No. 9), the viola again returns to A material as it did in m. 39, here in an embellished version that blossoms into a cadenza. When the A section returns with the pickup to m. 69, the viola now introduces the melody in its lowest register. The section continues with virtuosic, improvisatory writing for the viola, briefly referencing the B section's "Shemot" theme in mm. 86–87. Bloch ends the movement on a D major chord, which sounds like an imperfect cadence in G minor, but this corresponds to "a perfect cadence in the Jewish *Ahava Rabba* mode on D, the main octave comprising the same notes as G harmonic minor."[23]

Each of the next two movements was originally designed as a processional: "A piece of music suitable for a (religious) procession."[24] Consequently, each movement has a majestic, dignified quality that demonstrates its suitability for such an event. Cast in an ABA form (Chart 4.3), the second movement, "Processional," is centered on the E Phrygian mode, opening with a repeated ostinato in the piano that conveys the march-like procession of the participants. The viola enters with its lyrical, flowing melody with the pickup to m. 3 moving to the "Kerobot" theme in mm. 9–12.[25] In the B section, the melody is derived entirely from "Ahot Ketannah" (Ex. 4.1), with Bloch modifying the rhythms and adding dramatic chordal figures in the viola in mm. 20–23. Bloch returns to the A section at m. 25 (No. 4), first in a modified version with the viola's melody raised by a minor third and then at the original pitch level in mm. 30–36. The movement winds down with the reappearance of the "Kerobot" theme in m. 37, featuring octaves in the viola.

The final movement, "Affirmation," is also in an ABA form (Chart 4.4), opening with stately dotted rhythms in the piano. The viola enters in m. 5 with the dotted-rhythm theme, which it elaborates on, incorporating thirty-second-note figures and multiple-stop chords (e.g., mm. 11–12). In the B section, Bloch includes two themes from *The Jewish Encyclopedia*; the first is "Geshem," which appears in the viola in mm. 19–25.[26] This is followed by the first four measures of the "Hazzanut" theme (Ex. 4.2), played first by the viola (mm. 25–29) and then by the piano (mm. 29–33). The viola then continues

Example 4.1 "Ahot Ketannah," as it appears in *The Jewish Encyclopedia*, which forms the basis for the B section of the "Processional" movement.

AHOT KETANNAH

Zone	Thematic Areas/Snippet	Measures	*Jewish Encyclopedia* Source
A		1–13 (No. 2)	"Kerobot," no. 3 Vol. VII: 470
B		13 (No. 2)–25 (No. 4)	"Ahot Ketannah" Vol. I: 295
A		25 (No. 4)–43	"Kerobot," no. 3 Vol. VII: 470

Chart 4.3 Bloch, *Suite hébraïque*: Structural analysis, second movement, "Processional."

Example 4.2 The first seven measures of "Hazzanut," as it appears in *The Jewish Encyclopedia*, which Bloch splits up as part of the B section of the "Affirmation" movement.

with fragments from the next three measures of the "Hazzanut" theme in mm. 33–35,[27] concluding the section with a cadenza-like passage (mm. 36–39). In the return of the A section, the piano offers two introductory measures before the viola boldly announces the theme in m. 42. The viola continues with its jubilant statement of the theme, ending the movement with ceremonial splendor.

In reviewing the sheet music for *Suite hébraïque* in 1954, Abram Loft commented:

> Ernest Bloch likes the viola. Anyone who has played his *Suite for Viola and Piano* (or orchestra) will appreciate the truth of this statement. Bloch's feeling for the instrument has not weakened in the years since 1919, when that suite was written. In the *Suite Hébraique* the composer lavishes on the viola the same passionate lyricism of old.[28]

Zone	Thematic Areas/Snippet	Measures	*Jewish Encyclopedia* Source
A		1–18	
B		19 (No. 3)–40 (No. 6)	"Geshem" (version C) Vol. V: 645; "Hazzanut" Vol. VI: 291–92
A		40 (No. 6)–59	

Chart 4.4 Bloch, *Suite hébraïque*: Structural analysis, third movement, "Affirmation."

With its blend of "passionate lyricism" and virtuoso writing, the *Suite hébraïque* is an exceptional showpiece for the viola, one that has deservedly become entrenched in the repertoire.

Learn More about the Traditional Jewish Elements in Bloch's *Suite hébraïque*

Readers interested in learning more about the traditional Jewish elements in Bloch's *Suite hébraïque* are referred to the following source:

Knapp, Alexander. "Ernest Bloch's *Suite Hébraïque* and *Meditation and Processional*: Historical Overview and Analysis of Traditional Musical Materials." *Journal of the American Viola Society* 33, no. 2 (Fall 2017): 19–33.

5

York Bowen: Sonata No. 1 in C Minor for Viola and Piano, op. 18

I.   Allegro moderato
II. Poco lento e cantabile
III. Finale: Presto

Date of Composition: 1905

First Edition: York Bowen, *Sonata No. 1 in C-Minor for Viola & Piano*, Mainz: B. Schott's Söhne, [1906–1907], Plate No. 28028

Dedication: To Lionel Tertis

Date/Place of First Public Performance: May 19, 1905, Lionel Tertis (viola), York Bowen (piano), Aeolian Hall, London

Introduction

"Throughout my career I have endeavoured to appreciate the beauty of other people's music all the more because I am a composer myself, and I have no use for the arguments of people who try to excuse ugly music on the grounds that it expresses the ugly age in which we are living at the present time. If modern life is ugly, then there is all the more reason why music should bring beauty into it."[1] York Bowen resolutely upheld his noble, artistic ideals of beauty over the course of his lengthy career. As a young teacher at the Royal Academy of Music (RAM), he was inspired by modern attitudes, defending and teaching the music of Richard Strauss, Claude Debussy, and Maurice Ravel to the consternation of his colleagues.[2] But as musical trends changed, he became increasingly disconnected from current fashions, maintaining his own, singular style. His compositions, which had never found much of an audience outside of England, began to fade from concert programs. Fortunately, Bowen has earned a critical reappraisal in recent years, with performers and audiences rediscovering the beauty that his music has brought into the world.

Biographical Sketch

Edwin York Bowen (1884–1961) was the youngest of three sons born to Edward Bowen, a wine merchant, and his wife, Ellen Mary. Early lessons in piano and harmony came from his mother, and Bowen showed remarkable skill on the piano at a young age; he publicly performed one of Jan Ladislav Dussek's concertos at the age of eight. A scholarship permitted studies at the Royal Academy of Music starting at the age of fourteen, where he won multiple prizes for piano and composition.[3] In 1905, Bowen left the RAM, returning as a professor four short years later. He remained there for the next fifty years, teaching piano to generations of students. Bowen's consummate skills as both a pianist and composer drew comparisons to Serge Rachmaninoff and Nicolas Medtner.[4]

In 1912, Bowen married Sylvia Dalton, an actress and singer; their son, Philip, was born a year later. During the First World War, York played horn and viola in the Scots Guards while Sylvia drove an ambulance.[5] The couple later became interested in spiritualism, and their son was purported to have developed gifts as a medium. For a period of time during the 1930s, the family ran a healing clinic out of their home.[6] Bowen's later years were marred by financial difficulties, as he struggled to support a family that was living beyond their means. Teaching at the RAM remained a stable source of income, but Bowen was forced to sacrifice his pension to pay debts incurred by his son.[7] After retiring from teaching in 1959, Bowen continued with musical activities—composing, performing, recording, and writing a book—until his death in 1961.[8]

Bowen's Sonata No. 1 in C Minor for Viola and Piano, op. 18

Works for solo piano make up a substantial part of Bowen's output, though he composed in many genres. He wrote an impressive amount of original music for viola, in large part owing to his relationship with the eminent violist Lionel Tertis: *Fantasia for Viola and Organ* (1903);[9] Sonata No. 1 in C Minor for Viola and Piano, op. 18 (1905); Sonata No. 2 in F Major for Viola and Piano, op. 22 (1906); Concerto in C Minor for Viola and Orchestra, op. 25 (1907); *Melody for the C String of the Viola with Pianoforte Accompaniment*, op. 51, no. 2 (1918); *Phantasy for Viola and Piano*, op. 54 (1918); *Rhapsody for Viola and Piano* (1955); and *Piece in E♭ for Viola and Piano* (1960). Additionally, he wrote a viola obbligato for the first movement of Ludwig van Beethoven's "Moonlight" Sonata and arranged other of his compositions for viola. Several chamber works also prominently feature the viola, notably the *Fantasie for Four Violas* (1907), which was written for Tertis to play with his advanced students.[10]

Bowen became acquainted with Tertis while a student at the RAM. The spirited violist was appointed a professor in 1900 and started exerting "constant pressure for works for the viola" to any composer friends who would listen.[11] Succumbing to these requests, Bowen produced several compositions and became a frequent recital partner of Tertis's; the two musicians maintained a close association over the years. Tertis admired Bowen's works and programmed them often but, rather surprisingly, never recorded any of them. Bowen benefited from Tertis's guidance in developing an understanding of the viola, as recounted in a 1912 interview:

> I am extremely fond of the instrument. With a few hints from Mr. Lionel Tertis I gained a practical knowledge of the viola, and I am a great believer in ability to play an instrument when writing for it. Besides enjoyment in the playing, there is the added joy of knowing what kind of passages best suit the instrument.[12]

This philosophy is evident in the Sonata No. 1 in C Minor for Viola and Piano, op. 18 with writing that amply demonstrates the viola's technical and expressive capabilities. Extraordinary piano writing complements the viola, with the two instruments expertly balanced. The interval of a third plays a significant function throughout the work, both in the key relationships within and among the movements and in the melodic content. Sequential patterns are heavily used (Ex. 5.1) as a means of developing thematic ideas. Colorful harmonic touches and subtly altered accompanimental figures keep the music sounding fresh. With its fine craftsmanship and imaginative elements, Bowen's sonata is an exhilarating and musically gratifying experience for both performers.

The first movement is in sonata form with a repeated exposition (Chart 5.1). After a two-measure introduction, the viola enters with the stately theme in C minor. Two short rhythmic figures that appear throughout the movement are introduced in m. 3: a dotted-eighth–sixteenth-note figure and a dotted-quarter–eighth-note one. The second theme group begins in the relative major at m. 33 (Letter C; Unit 2.1; all rehearsal letters refer to the Schott edition) with a chordal accompaniment. At m. 49 (Letter D), the viola drops out as the piano offers new thematic material (Unit 2.2), descending sequentially through G and F minor, with the viola returning in m. 56. The section concludes at m. 70 on a B♭⁷ harmony with a fermata over the bar line delaying the resolution to E♭ major. At m. 71, the closing material starts in a lighthearted, jocular fashion, but the viola

Example 5.1 Bowen, Sonata No. 1 in C Minor for Viola and Piano, op. 18, movt. I, mm. 13–16, viola.

Zone	Thematic Areas/Snippet	Measures	Principal Tonal Areas/Function
Introduction		1–2	C minor
Repeated Exposition		3–83	
	Theme Group 1	3–32	C minor
	Theme Group 2	33 (Let. C)–70	
	Unit 2.1	33 (Let. C)–48	E-flat major
	Unit 2.2	49 (Let. D)–70	Starts G minor; descends sequentially
	Closing	71 (Let. F)–83	E-flat major
Development		84 (Let. G)–149	Begins G-flat major; modulates
Recapitulation		150 (Let. L)–213	
	Theme Group 1	150 (Let. L)–78	C minor
	Theme Group 2	179 (Let. N)–213	
	Unit 2.1	179 (Let. N)–94	E major
	Transitory	195 (Let. O)–213	Modulatory
Coda		214–22	C minor

Chart 5.1 Bowen, Sonata No. 1 in C Minor for Viola and Piano, op. 18: Structural analysis, first movement, Allegro moderato.

insists on regaining seriousness, offering snippets of the stately dotted-eighth–sixteenth-note figure in preparation for the exposition's repeat.

The development begins in G♭ major, building through a series of sequential patterns toward the viola's *ff* octaves in mm. 100–103. A sudden change of mood occurs at m. 104 with the dynamic pulling back to *p*, as the viola plays sweetly (*dolce*) in its upper register. Starting at m. 112, the piano and viola enjoy an interplay of material from the second theme group. The section culminates in an extraordinary burst of polyphony from mm. 138–41, with the viola and piano alternating loud, robust chords before quieting down in preparation for the recapitulation at m. 150.

For the recapitulation, the second theme group at m. 179 (Letter N) is not presented in the parallel major but in an even more remote key than in the exposition: E major. At m. 195 (Letter O), Bowen continues with Unit 2.1 material in an *animato* transitory passage that gives way to a short (and quiet) nine-measure coda.

Set in the remote key of A major, the second movement is in an ABA form with coda (Chart 5.2). A simple, folk-like theme in the viola opens the movement, supported by a chordal accompaniment. The theme rises sequentially by a second, tonicizing C♯ minor before making its way back to A major at m. 29, where the viola plays the opening theme an octave higher. At m. 59 (Letter C), a change of key (F major), meter (⁶⁄₈), and texture (flowing sixteenth notes in the piano) signals the start of the B section. While the opening melody suggested a folk song or church hymn, the music here suggests a German lied, with the viola's long cantilena lines soaring above the graceful murmurings of the piano. The A section returns at m. 117 with a more ornate accompanimental figure than

Zone	Thematic Areas/Snippet	Measures	Principal Tonal Areas/Function
A		1–58	A major
B		59 (Let. C)–116	F major; modulates
A		117–94	A major
Coda		194–215	A major

Chart 5.2 Bowen, Sonata No. 1 in C Minor for Viola and Piano, op. 18: Structural analysis, second movement, Poco lento e cantabile.

Example 5.2 Bowen, Sonata No. 1 in C Minor for Viola and Piano, op. 18, movt. II, mm. 206–10.

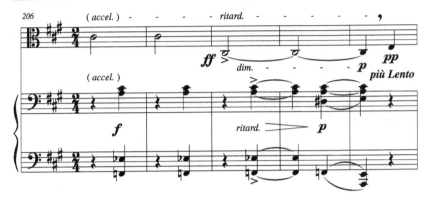

the opening. At m. 151, the music accelerates, with the viola beginning a long, descending G♯ minor arpeggio. As the music migrates to E major and then E minor, Bowen dramatically inserts a **sfp** c♯ in the viola at m. 161, turning the E minor harmony into a C♯°⁷ harmony that then deceptively resolves to F minor in m. 163. He repeats this harmonic surprise at m. 165, this time with an E°⁷ harmony that finally gets us back to G♯ minor at m. 167 for what sounds like closing material. But Bowen elongates the movement at m. 177 with the inclusion of material that originally appeared at m. 43; it is not until m. 194 that he firmly resolves to A major for the start of the coda. He continues to delay the ending with extended harmonic fluctuations, prolonging an F+⁷ chord in mm. 204–9, which he then respells to form an augmented sixth chord that resolves directly to A major (Ex. 5.2).

The final movement does not conveniently fit into a standard form, but it can be divided into sections that seem to meld ABA and sonata form (Chart 5.3). Many interrelated motivic ideas are scattered throughout the movement. In the startling introduction, the piano's opening motive is interrupted by the viola's scalar *furioso* eighth notes. Biding its time on a D°⁷ harmony, the piano resumes its thought in m. 5 after the viola reaches its apex. Pausing for a fermata in m. 10, the piano plays two notes in the following measure, as if goading the viola to interrupt again. Another fermata permits both musicians to collect themselves, and they begin the movement proper in m. 13 at a slightly relaxed tempo (Meno Presto). The music traverses several key areas with Bowen introducing a new theme at m. 45 (Unit 1.2) that bears similarities to earlier material. A flashy run by the piano in m. 55 prompts the viola to nip at its heels with a restatement of the introductory scalar passage (mm. 55–59). Another pause in the proceedings at m. 61 is followed by a rowdy double-stop version of the Unit 1.1 theme, with the

Zone	Thematic Areas/Snippet	Measures	Principal Tonal Areas/Function
Introduction		1–12	Dominant/D half-diminished seventh
A		13–77	
	Unit 1.1	13–45	C minor
	Unit 1.2	45–61	Starts F minor; ends on dominant
	Closing (Unit 1.1 material)	62 (Let. C)–77	C minor
B		78 (Let. D)–153	A major; modulates
Development		154–221	
	Unit 1.1	154–209	Modulatory
	Unit 1.2 (transitory)	210–21	C minor
A		222 (Let. K)–305 (Let. P)	
	Unit 1.1	222 (Let. K)–44	C minor; modulates
	Unit 1.2	244–305 (Let. P)	Starts F minor; modulates
Interlude / Recitative	Pno.	305 (Let. P)–46	D half-diminished seventh moving to dominant
Coda		347–95	C minor

Chart 5.3 Bowen, Sonata No. 1 in C Minor for Viola and Piano, op. 18: Structural analysis, third movement, Finale: Presto.

music finally quieting down in mm. 74–77. The B section starts at m. 78 (Letter D) in an altered mood with chordal accompaniment and highly chromatic writing. Largely centered on A major, this section exhibits Bowen's extraordinarily sophisticated harmonic writing. The subsequent section (Allegro molto; mm. 154–221) develops material from the A section in a fragmented and modulatory fashion ending with a transitory passage (Unit 1.2; mm. 210–21) that reestablishes the key of C minor, preparing for a return of the A section at m. 222 (Letter K).

Bowen continues fragmenting and developing material in the A section's return, making greater use of the second theme, climaxing with an extended *furioso* passage in the viola's upper register (mm. 297–305). The following section (mm. 305–46) serves as an interlude, starting on a $D^{\varnothing 7}$ harmony, recalling the introduction, and incorporating a *quasi recitative* passage for the viola. Bowen ramps the tempo back up to Presto at m. 347 for the coda, a dizzying ride with fluctuating dynamics and raucous double stops. The tempo pushes forward through the viola's three-octave scale (mm. 391–93), finally pulling back for the two instrumentalists' final emphatic chords.

Bowen premiered his Sonata No. 1 in C Minor for Viola and Piano, op. 18 with Lionel Tertis on a May 19, 1905, recital, which included new viola works by several composers. It received generally favorable notices, with the reviewer for the *Musical Times* writing:

> This work is another testimony to the great talent of Mr. Bowen. It is in three movements which are based upon significant and well-contrasted themes developed in a rational and musicianly manner. The first movement is the strongest in point of construction, but the central number is graceful and expressive, while the *Finale* is delightfully gay and spirited.[13]

The critic for the *Musical Standard*, however, was less enamored:

> The other new compositions by W. H. Bell, York Bowen (Sonata in C minor) and Harry Farjeon did not show a sympathetic enough regard for the viola's character. Before you can write well for the instrument, you must understand it. York Bowen, too, must avoid music-spinning in the future. It is not at all impressive.[14]

Given Bowen's belief in playing an instrument in order to write well for it, this reviewer's comments must have come as a shock. And for modern violists who appreciate the sonata's idiomatic and effective passages, these opinions seem off the mark. But in 1905, the viola was a rarity as a solo instrument, and many musicians and critics clung to outdated views regarding the instrument's proper role. For those who were oblivious to the viola's full capabilities, Bowen's audacious writing would have seemed inappropriate.

Other musicians did recognize the sonata's virtues; Thomas Dunhill considered Bowen's two viola sonatas among "the most striking works ever composed for that instrument."[15] The work enjoyed popularity at the beginning of the twentieth century but faded into obscurity along with Bowen's other compositions in the following decades. It started making a comeback in the 1980s, in large part owing to John White's determined promotion of Bowen's viola music. As violists have become acquainted with it through recordings and performances, it has reclaimed its rightful place as one of the truly masterful sonatas composed for the instrument.

6

Johannes Brahms: Sonata for Clarinet (or Viola) and Piano in E♭ Major, op. 120, no. 2

I.   Allegro amabile
II. Allegro appassionato
III. Andante con moto

Date of Composition: 1894

First Edition: Johannes Brahms, *Zwei Sonaten für Clarinette (oder Bratsche) und Pianoforte, Op. 120. No. 2. Es dur.*, Berlin: N. Simrock, 1895, Plate No. 10409

Select Later Editions: Johannes Brahms, *Sonaten Opus 120 für Klarinette und Klavier, Fassung für Viola*, ed. Egon Voss and Johannes Behr, Munich: Henle, 2013, HN 988; Brahms, *Sonaten in f und Es für Viola und Klavier, op. 120*, ed. Clive Brown and Neal Peres Da Costa, Kassel: Bärenreiter, 2016, BA 10907

Date/Place of Early Public Performance: November 17, 1896, Joseph Joachim (viola), Julius Spengel (piano), Hamburg

Introduction

"In composing the work for viola as well, Brahms took the opportunity to express his love for this instrument."[1] Brahms's final chamber works, the Two Sonatas for Clarinet (or Viola) and Piano, op. 120, were inspired by the artistry of Richard Mühlfeld, a clarinetist in the Meiningen Court Orchestra. Yet plans for a viola version of these sonatas were underway by October 1894, shortly after Brahms completed the original clarinet version. While readying the work for publication the following February, he wrote to his publisher:

> I am planning to include "for clarinet or viola" in the title. But I must still quickly prepare [the part for] the latter in Vienna.[2]

Brahms had previously sanctioned the publication of alternate viola parts in place of the clarinet parts for his Clarinet Trio, op. 114 (1891) and Clarinet

Quintet, op. 115 (1891). For these two works, no alterations were made when preparing the viola parts. But for the two opus 120 sonatas, Brahms, himself, made changes while producing the viola versions: transposing passages down an octave, making changes to notes (including adding double and triple stops), and altering articulation and expression marks. He subsequently made an arrangement for violin and piano, which necessitated changes to the piano part. While commenting on both string adaptations during the early twentieth century, Donald Tovey expressed his admiration for the viola version:

> These are on quite a different plane from the use of a viola as substitute for the clarinet in the quintet and trio, though Brahms authorized the issue of parts so transcribed. But in the trio and quintet the relation of the clarinet to the string parts makes it impossible to alter the position of anything, and transcription accordingly reveals all the points where the viola fails to represent a clarinet. But with these sonatas Brahms could use a free hand. . . . The viola version is better [than the violin version], besides being a welcome opportunity for viola players. In it the piano part is unaltered, but the viola part is a fine demonstration of the different characters of the instruments. The viola is querulous and strained just where the cantabile of the clarinet is warmest. The lowest octave of the clarinet is of a dramatic blue-grotto hollowness and coldness, where the fourth string of the viola is of a rich and pungent warmth. A comparison of Brahms's viola part with his original clarinet part makes every difference of this kind vividly real, and these viola versions deserve frequent performance in public.[3]

The two sonatas have, indeed, received many performances in public, becoming two of the most beloved works in the viola repertoire.

Biographical Sketch

Johannes Brahms (1833–1897) was born in Hamburg, the second of Johanna Henrika Christiane and Johann Jakob Brahms's three children. His father, who played several musical instruments, earned a living for many years by performing in dance halls and taverns. Around the age of four, Johannes started learning violin and cello from his father, and at the age of seven he began piano lessons with Otto Friedrich Willibald Cossel. In 1843, he began studying piano with Eduard Marxsen, a leading teacher in Hamburg, who would also instruct him in harmony, theory, and counterpoint. Beyond his musical interests, the young Brahms was an avid reader who enjoyed works by German Romantics, especially E. T. A. Hoffmann and Jean Paul. Brahms even adopted the alter ego "Johannes Kreisler Junior" after a musician that appeared in Hoffmann's stories.

By the age of twelve, Brahms was contributing to the family's finances by giving piano lessons; he also earned money in following years by playing in drinking establishments.[4]

On September 21, 1848, Brahms gave his first public recital. The following spring, he gave another recital, which included one of his own compositions, *Fantasia on a Favourite Waltz*. In 1853, Brahms embarked on a tour with the Hungarian violinist Ede Reményi, which would greatly affect the course of his musical career. Reményi's performances of music from his homeland left a deep impression on Brahms, who would develop a "lifelong fascination with the irregular rhythms, triplet figures and use of rubato" that is associated with the *style hongrois*.[5] It was Reményi who introduced Brahms to Joseph Joachim, who would become a lifelong friend and frequent musical partner. In June, toward the end of their tour, Brahms also met Franz Liszt in Weimar. After visiting with Joachim in Göttingen for a couple of months during the summer, Brahms made his way to Düsseldorf in late September, where he met Robert and Clara Schumann. The couple was greatly impressed with Brahms's playing:

> This month introduced us to a wonderful person, Brahms, a composer from Hamburg—20 years old. Here again is one of those who comes as if sent straight from God.... He has a great future before him, for he will first find the true field for his genius when he begins to write for the orchestra.[6]

The Schumanns quickly became influential champions of the budding musician. After Robert's mental breakdown in 1854, Brahms would prove a great comfort to Clara Schumann, and the two would continue an exceptionally close relationship until her death in 1896.

In 1857, Brahms accepted a three-month position in Detmold, where his duties included performing, teaching piano, and conducting the choral society. Brahms returned to this position the following two years, dividing the rest of his time among several cities, composing and performing.[7] During a visit to Göttingen in 1858, he began a romantic involvement with Agathe von Siebold. The couple exchanged rings as a token of their love, but in January 1859 they separated, ostensibly because Brahms was unwilling to commit himself to marriage.[8] Brahms would have many later romantic involvements, but he never married.

Over the next few years, Brahms continued working with choral groups: he conducted the Hamburg Frauenchor from 1859 to 1862, and in 1863 he accepted a position as director of the Vienna Singakademie, remaining there for only one season. Shortly after his mother's death in 1865, he devoted efforts to composing *A German Requiem*, which occupied him for several years. The work, as premiered in its final form on February 18, 1869, at the Leipzig Gewandhaus, brought him much critical success.[9] During the late 1860s and early 1870s, Brahms continued touring as a pianist, and in 1872, he accepted a position as artistic director of the Gesellschaft der Musikfreunde in Vienna, remaining there for three seasons. As Brahms's international reputation soared, he was honored with many accolades: King Ludwig II awarded him the Bavarian Maximilian Order for Science and Art in 1873, and the Royal Philharmonic Society in London awarded him their Gold Medal in 1877.[10] He also amassed a considerable fortune in later years, providing generous financial assistance to his family and aspiring musicians.[11] In 1890, Brahms declared his intention to give up composing, but the following year he was inspired by Richard Mühlfeld to write the Clarinet Trio, op. 114 and Clarinet Quintet, op. 115. Still, Brahms remained largely retired from composing; he produced only a few more works before the summer of 1896, when he began exhibiting symptoms of cancer of the liver. He died on April 3, 1897, at the age of sixty-three.

Brahms's Sonata for Clarinet (or Viola) and Piano in E♭ Major, op. 120, no. 2

Brahms demonstrated a fondness for the viola, composing substantial parts for the instrument in his chamber and orchestral works. Chamber works that prominently showcase the viola as a solo instrument include the Two Songs for Alto, Viola, and Piano, op. 91 (published 1884) and the Two Sonatas for Clarinet (or Viola) and Piano, op. 120 (1894). Written while Brahms was staying at his summer residence in Bad Ischl, the two opus 120 sonatas were completed by the end of August. Brahms and Richard Mühlfeld gave a private performance of the sonatas on September 22, 1894.[12] The earliest reference to a viola version comes from an October 14, 1894, letter in which Brahms invited Joachim to Frankfurt:

> If you come to Frankfurt, especially in the first half of winter, let me know. I would come too, and would invite Mühlfeld or bring along a viola part—to two Clarinet Sonatas, which I would like Frau Schumann to hear. These undemanding pieces would not disturb our comfort—but it would be nice.[13]

After Joachim responded favorably, Brahms wrote again on October 17:

> I hope Mühlfeld will be able to come—because I'm afraid, as viola sonatas, the two pieces are very awkward and unpleasant.[14]

Many violists have taken the content of this letter to suggest that Brahms was unhappy with the final arrangement of the viola versions.[15] However, this comment, written early in the development of the viola version, is more light-hearted in tone rather than critical. Brahms continued working on the viola version in the following months; readers interested in a more thorough discussion of its development are advised to read Clive Brown's preface to the Bärenreiter edition, published in 2016.[16] Violists may also wish to consult series II, volume 9 of Brahms's *Neue Ausgabe sämtlicher Werke*. This edition discusses in great detail the sources for the two sonatas, including the Stichvorlage viola part prepared by Brahms's copyist William Kupfer, which includes a number of revisions in Brahms's hand.[17] The Stichvorlage was undoubtedly derived from an earlier source that had been supplied by Brahms, since it "contains passages that could surely have come only from the composer," including the double-stop passage in the second movement of the opus 120, no. 2 sonata (mm. 126–35).[18]

Brahms was a meticulous composer who was intently involved in the editing and publication of his compositions, and editions of "his works are thus relatively error-free."[19] Violists have periodically suggested that the arrangement of the opus 120 sonatas was undertaken by someone other than Brahms or that he was pressured into making the arrangement by his publisher:

> We can be certain that this so-called arrangement was not by Brahms; we know that Brahms was an excellent arranger, who signed all his arrangements, which are never simple transcriptions but always idiomatically reworked for the instrument....
>
> The composer probably agreed to the publication of this simplified version for commercial reasons, perhaps because in his day hardly any violists could be expected to play in high positions, certainly not lyrically or with dolcezza, and gut strings made it considerably harder to control the sound. But this is no longer the case. Modern violists should have no such technical problems, so there is no longer any reason to mutilate the piece in such a way.[20]

Throughout the nineteenth century, publishers produced arrangements of all types of music for an eager market. Many solo and chamber works involving the clarinet were issued with alternate violin or viola parts during this period. The viola, in particular, worked well as a substitute for the clarinet given their similarity in register. An exhaustive comparison of published arrangements is beyond the scope of this chapter, but there is little evidence to suggest that technical demands were a major factor for composers, arrangers, or publishers when preparing alternate viola parts—even though these works were typically published with amateurs in mind. When he produced an alternate viola part for W. A. Mozart's Clarinet Quintet, K. 581, published by Schuberth in the mid-1850s, Henry Vieuxtemps made only minor changes with no concessions for the higher passages.[21] Similarly, René de Boisdeffre's *Trois pièces*, for clarinet, op. 40, was

published by Hamelle in 1888 with an alternate viola part that contains no significant changes in register (with the viola going as high as a d^{iii}), though each piece
is altered slightly, with the addition of multiple stops and even pizzicato notes in
the third piece.[22] As previously mentioned, the alternate viola parts for Brahms's
Clarinet Trio and Clarinet Quintet, both published in 1892 by Simrock, contain
no substantive differences from the clarinet parts, and both make extensive use
of the viola's upper register, each going as high as an e^{iii}. In 1897, Simrock included an alternate viola part in Walter Rabl's Quartet for Piano, Violin, Clarinet,
and Violoncello, op. 1, which was dedicated to Brahms. Once again, the viola's
upper register is frequently employed (with only a few octave transpositions),
but the viola part deviates extensively from the clarinet part, notably in passages
that are designed to integrate it more fully within the string texture (see, especially the first movement's Vivo section and the second movement's Lento gran-
dioso section).[23]

In each of these examples, the extent of changes varies based on the arranger's
preferences, but none of them suggests that technical demands played a major
role. Brahms's modifications in the viola versions of the opus 120 sonatas, including the addition of double stops and greater use of the viola's lower and
middle registers, were likely intended to bring out the best characteristics of
the instrument. Modern scholarship has found no evidence to indicate that the
viola versions of the opus 120 sonatas were undertaken by someone other than
Brahms or that he was pressured into producing an arrangement that he was unhappy with. Clive Brown notes that

> doubts about Brahms' authorship of the viola parts may therefore be set aside,
> and there is no more justification for players to take it upon themselves to
> change the notes (as William Primrose and a few later violists have done) than
> there would be to alter the texts of the clarinet or violin parts of op. 120, or any-
> thing else in Brahms' chamber music.[24]

Nevertheless, there will be violists who remain unhappy with the changes that
Brahms made and prefer to alter certain passages to more closely align with the
original clarinet version.

The first movement, in sonata form (Chart 6.1), opens with a sinuous
melody, filled with "fluent rises and dips" that are well-suited to the clarinet[25]
(though less so to the viola). The F^7 harmony in m. 17 prepares the listener for
a move to B♭ major, but Brahms deceptively cadences on E♭ minor in m. 18.
The following transitional section, from mm. 18–21, is one of the most con-
tentious among violists, since Brahms transposed most of the clarinet part
down an octave, ending with an upward leap from the d♭ to b♭ in mm. 20–21
(Exs. 6.1 and 6.2).[26]

Zone	Thematic Areas/Snippet	Measures	Principal Tonal Areas/Function
Exposition		1–55	
	Theme Group 1	1–21	E-flat major
	Theme Group 2	22–39	B-flat major
	Closing	40–55	B-flat major
Development		56–102	Starts E-flat major; modulates
Recapitulation		103–53	
	Theme Group 1	103–19	E-flat major
	Theme Group 2	120–37	C-flat major; E-flat major
	Closing	138–53	E-flat major
Coda		154–73	Starts E major; E-flat major

Chart 6.1 Brahms, Sonata for Clarinet (or Viola) and Piano in E♭ Major, op. 120, no. 2: Structural analysis, first movement, Allegro amabile.

Example 6.1 Brahms, Sonata for Clarinet (or Viola) and Piano in E♭ Major, op. 120, no. 2, movt. 1, mm. 18–21, clarinet in B♭ (transposed).

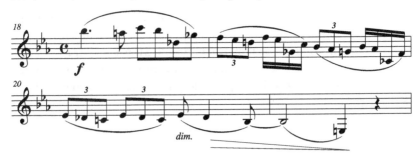

Example 6.2 Brahms, Sonata for Clarinet (or Viola) and Piano in E♭ Major, op. 120, no. 2, movt. I, mm. 18–21, viola.

Theme Group 2 begins in B♭ major at m. 22 with a strict canon at the twelfth between the viola and the piano's bass (separated by a quarter note), which is maintained until m. 27, after which the viola continues with a variation of this material. The closing section (mm. 40–55) begins with a figure in the viola consisting of three quarter notes, which recalls earlier figures in the piano (e.g., mm. 5–6 and mm. 26–27),[27] while the octave leaps starting at m. 48 recall the opening of Theme Group 2.

The development begins at m. 56 with the appearance of Theme Group 1 material in the tonic. After working through Theme Group 1 material, Brahms turns to Theme Group 2 material at m. 65, in the piano. The viola takes up this material in m. 69 with Brahms retaining the earlier imitative writing between the two instruments. At m. 78, the instruments begin an extended exchange that heavily involves triplet arpeggios.

In the recapitulation, Brahms follows a similar path as in the exposition, with Theme Group 2 starting in m. 120 in the remote key of C♭ major before moving to E♭ major in m. 126. The coda begins in the distant key of E major at m. 154. When comparing this harmonic area to that of the development (which began in E♭ major), the relationship is a half-step, which parallels the half-step difference between the key areas at the start of the Theme Group 2 statements in the exposition (B♭ major) and recapitulation (C♭ major). The music finally moves to E♭ major in m. 162 at the start of the Tranquillo, where Brahms revisits the arpeggios from the development section.

The second movement is a turbulent scherzo (Chart 6.2) in the parallel minor (E♭ minor). It opens with an eight-measure theme in the viola, which the piano then repeats (mm. 9–16), starting out an octave higher. After a strong, ** ff ** cadence on E♭ minor in m. 27, the viola's subsequent upward leap of a sixth suggests that a repeat of the opening theme will follow. But Brahms instead rhythmically prolongs the theme so "that the original six-note motive becomes a full four-measure phrase."[28] The opening motive finally returns in its original form in m. 37 to close out Unit 1.1. In mm. 48–49, Brahms takes a fragment of the opening motive (the four descending eighth notes) and fashions a new theme (Unit 1.2), played *p*. In the following passage, Brahms indulges in a bit of imitative writing between the two instruments. After arriving on a diminished seventh harmony in mm. 63–64, Brahms suspends the momentum with a full measure of rest in m. 65. Another upward leap of a sixth (this time a major sixth) follows, with Brahms further pulling the momentum back by augmenting the eighth-note figure from mm. 48–49 into quarter notes as the viola gradually descends to close out the A section.

Zone	Thematic Areas/Snippet	Measures	Principal Tonal Areas/Function
A		1–80	
	Unit 1.1	1–48	E-flat minor
	Unit 1.2	49–80	E-flat minor
B		81–138	
	Unit 1.1	81–108	B major
	Unit 1.2	109–38	Starts G-sharp major; B major
A		139–223	
	Unit 1.1	139–88	E-flat minor
	Unit 1.2	189–223	E-flat minor

Chart 6.2 Brahms, Sonata for Clarinet (or Viola) and Piano in E♭ Major, op. 120, no. 2: Structural analysis, second movement, Allegro appassionato.

Brahms moves to B major for the Sostenuto B section (mm. 81–138), marked *ma dolce e ben cantando.* After the piano plays the opening fourteen-measure statement (divided into an eight-measure and a six-measure phrase), the viola joins in for another fourteen-measure statement. A twelve-measure phrase at m. 109 opens with a D♯ major harmony. In this section, both "the bass motion and the harmonies suggest that D-sharp now serves as a 'dominant' for the unusual key of G-sharp major."[29] The key of B major is restored at m. 121 with a return of the B section's opening material. In the following passage, the viola part deviates extensively from the original clarinet version with Brahms taking advantage of the viola's polyphonic capabilities to add dramatic triple and double stops (Exs. 6.3 and 6.4).

For the return of the A section at m. 139, Brahms revisits the piano's material from mm. 34–36 before beginning the theme proper with the viola's pickup to m. 141. The remainder of the movement is largely an exact repeat of the opening A section until m. 217, when Brahms augments the rhythms from mm. 77–80 to produce a seven-measure ending.

Example 6.3 Brahms, Sonata for Clarinet (or Viola) and Piano in E♭ Major, op. 120, no. 2, movt. II, mm. 126–35, clarinet in B♭ (transposed).

Example 6.4 Brahms, Sonata for Clarinet (or Viola) and Piano in E♭ Major, op. 120, no. 2, movt. II, mm. 126–35, viola.

The final movement is a Classically modeled set of variations on a fourteen-measure theme in $\frac{6}{8}$ (Chart 6.3). Brahms maintains a consistent structure throughout the theme and first four variations, consisting of a four-measure phrase ending on B♭ major, another four-measure phrase ending on B♭ major, a two-measure phrase ending on G minor, and a four-measure phrase ending on E♭ major.[30] The first variation is a stripped-down version of the theme with syncopated counterpoint in the piano. Dotted rhythms and triplet figures characterize the second variation, while the third uses *grazioso* thirty-second notes. A fermata at m. 56 strikingly sets apart the subdued fourth variation, which employs syncopated rhythms.

For the fifth variation at m. 71, the tempo changes to Allegro, the key shifts to E♭ minor, and the meter changes from $\frac{6}{8}$ to $\frac{2}{4}$. This variation follows a similar structure as the previous ones, though the phrase lengths are now doubled, and G♭ major serves as the stopping point in m. 90 instead of G minor. The final cadence on E♭ major at m. 98 coincides with the start of the Più tranquillo coda, in which Brahms develops the cadential figure from m. 4, climaxing "in a brief display of gleeful virtuosity for both instruments."[31]

Zone	Thematic Areas/Snippet	Measures	Principal Tonal Areas/Function
Theme		1–14	E-flat major
Variation I		15–28	E-flat major
Variation II		29–42	E-flat major
Variation III		43–56	E-flat major
Variation IV		57–70	E-flat major
Variation V		71–98	E-flat minor
Coda		98–153	E-flat major

Chart 6.3 Brahms, Sonata for Clarinet (or Viola) and Piano in E♭ Major, op. 120, no. 2: Structural analysis, third movement, Andante con moto.

In reviewing an early performance of the opus 120, no. 2 sonata played on clarinet, Eduard Hanslick wrote: "The first movement of the E-flat major Sonata is delightful. Its theme—which seems to have descended from heaven, or more properly, to exhale the sweet fragrance of beautiful youth—abounds in sweet rapture and the urgent bliss of love!"[32] Both sonatas earned critical acclaim and were quickly embraced by clarinetists. They also attracted the attention of violists; known performances of the E♭-major sonata during the nineteenth century include one by Joseph Joachim with Julius Spengel in Hamburg on November 17, 1896,[33] and one by Lionel Tertis with Margaret Glyde in London on November 29, 1899 (one of Tertis's earliest viola recitals).[34] Though originally for clarinet, the two works have since become equally well-known as viola sonatas, with some critics favoring the viola versions: "My personal preference is for the versions with viola, whose darker, huskier tone seems to suit their elusive moods even better than the veiled and silken clarinet."[35]

Analyzing Brahms's Sonata for Clarinet (or Viola) and Piano in E♭ Major, op. 120, no. 2

Readers interested in more detailed analyses of Brahms's Sonata for Clarinet (or Viola) and Piano in E♭ Major, op. 120, no. 2 are referred to the following sources:

Evans, Edwin. *Handbook to the Chamber & Orchestral Music of Johannes Brahms*. Vol. 2, Second Series Op. 68 to the End, 320–35. London: William Reeves, 1935.

Hansen, Kelly Dean. "Clarinet (or Viola) Sonata No. 2 in E-Flat Major, Op. 120, No. 2." *Listening Guides to the Works of Johannes Brahms*. http://www.kellydeanhansen.com/opus120-2.html.

Mason, Daniel Gregory. "The Clarinet Sonata in E Flat, Opus 120, No. 2." Chap. 24 in *The Chamber Music of Brahms*. Reprint ed. Ann Arbor, MI: Edwards Brothers, 1950.

7

Benjamin Britten: *Lachrymae,* op. 48

Date of Composition: 1950 (manuscript dated May 16, 1950; published score dated April 1950)

First Edition: Benjamin Britten, *Lachrymae: Reflections on a song of Dowland*, for Viola and Piano, viola part ed. William Primrose, London: Boosey & Hawkes, 1951, Plate No. B. & H. 17817; Benjamin Britten, *Lachrymae: Reflections on a Song of Dowland,* for Solo Viola and String Orchestra, Op. 48a, London: Boosey & Hawkes, 1977, Plate No. B. & H. 20364 (Orchestral Version Pocket Score)

Dedication: For William Primrose

Date/Place of First Public Performance (Piano Version): June 20, 1950, William Primrose (viola), Benjamin Britten (piano), Third Aldeburgh Festival, Aldeburgh Parish Church, Aldeburgh, Suffolk

Date/Place of First Public Performance (Orchestral Version): May 3, 1977, Rainer Moog (viola), Westphalian Symphony Orchestra, Karl Anton Rickenbacher (conductor), Recklinghausen

Date/Place of Other Early Public Performance (Orchestral Version): June 21, 1977, Cecil Aronowitz (viola), Northern Sinfonia Orchestra, Steuart Bedford (conductor), Thirtieth Aldeburgh Festival, Snape Maltings Concert Hall, Snape, Suffolk

Orchestral Instrumentation: Solo viola, second violins (divided), violas (divided), cellos (divided), double basses (divided)

Introduction

"Music for me is clarification; I try to clarify, to refine, to sensitize. Stravinsky once said that one must work perpetually at one's technique. But what is technique? Schoenberg's technique is often a tremendous elaboration. My technique is to tear all the waste away; to achieve perfect clarity of expression, that is my aim."[1] Benjamin Britten's technical mastery did not happen by chance. Rather, it was the product of careful deliberation and hard work;[2] each composition was well thought out and refined to strip away any excess. Given the perfection he sought in himself as a composer, he expected no less perfection from his interpreters, often "giving very precise instructions about how he wanted his score played."[3] Despite Britten's goal of "clarification," his music can be challenging to grasp, as William Primrose noted:

> That work of genius, Britten's *Lachrymae*, is usually garbled in a manner that shocks me, because Britten was quite unable, for all his skill, to set down exactly what his wishes were—and which he conveyed to me so clearly during our rehearsals for the first performance. I would suggest, however, that a comprehensive study and knowledge of his style of composition, along with a lively imagination, might lead the performers to decorous conclusions. I say "performers" designedly, as the subtleties of performance reside equally with the pianist and the violist.[4]

It is worthwhile for performers who are approaching *Lachrymae* to take a cue from Britten's compositional method, stripping away any excess from their interpretation while aiming for "perfect clarity of expression."

Biographical Sketch

Born in Lowestoft, Suffolk, England, Edward Benjamin Britten (1913–1976) was the youngest of Robert and Edith Britten's four children. Robert was a dentist and Edith an amateur soprano and pianist who regularly hosted musical soirées in her home.[5] Britten's mother was responsible for her son's earliest musical instruction. At age seven, he began piano lessons with Ethel Astle, who ran a local day-school, and at age ten he began viola lessons with Audrey Alston, a friend of his mother's. It was through Alston that Britten met Frank Bridge in 1927, with whom he would soon start studies in composition. By this point, Britten had been composing for many years and already had "100 opus numbers to his credit."[6] Bridge would exert the greatest influence on Britten's musical development, instilling discipline and emphasizing the importance of good technique.[7]

In 1930, Britten won a composition scholarship to the Royal College of Music, where he studied piano with Arthur Benjamin and composition with John Ireland. While a student, he won several prizes, including the Cobbett Chamber Music Prize in 1932 for his *Phantasy in F Minor*, for string quintet. After completing his studies in 1933, Britten spent time traveling on the continent before landing a job with the General Post Office Film Unit in 1935. The job, writing music for documentary films, was a learning experience for Britten: "I had to work quickly, to force myself to work when I didn't want to, and to get used to working in all kinds of circumstances."[8]

Britten lost both of his parents in the mid-1930s: his father in 1934 and mother—with whom he was especially close—in 1937. Only five weeks after his mother's death, Britten met Peter Pears, who would become his lover, musical partner, and lifelong companion.[9] Britten's profile as both a composer and pianist was greatly raised with a bravura performance of his Piano Concerto at a Promenade Concert in August 1938. The following spring, Britten and Pears embarked on a trip to America, making their way first to Canada and then on to the United States.[10] Both men were pacifists, and with Britain's entry into World War II later that summer, the couple decided to extend their stay. In America, Britten made his first attempt at an opera with *Paul Bunyan*, which was a critical failure. He also continued to play piano publicly and viola privately: "When we were in America," recalled Pears, "we used to call at the local library for works for viola and piano. I used to play the piano part."[11]

Upon returning to England in April 1942, Britten and Pears each applied for status as a conscientious objector. While Pears was granted exemption at his first hearing, the tribunal decided that Britten "was to be called up for non-combatant duties."[12] A few months later, Britten was also exempted upon appeal. In 1945, Britten earned a triumphant success with the premiere of his opera *Peter Grimes*. He would go on to write fourteen more operas, reviving an art form that had languished in England since the Baroque era. During a trip to the Lucerne Festival in 1947, Britten and Pears—along with Eric Crozier—hit upon the idea of establishing their own music festival.[13] The resulting Aldeburgh Festival of Music and the Arts was held June 5–13, 1948, and has continued as an annual event. Britten solidified his status as a major composer over the following years, while still finding time to perform and manage the Aldeburgh Festival. His contributions to England were recognized in June 1976 when he was awarded a life peerage. Baron Britten, of Aldeburgh, in the County of Suffolk enjoyed his new title for only a short period; after years of declining health, he died on December 4, 1976, in the arms of Peter Pears.[14]

Britten's *Lachrymae*, op. 48

During his youth, Britten composed a substantial number of works for viola, several of which have been published since his death. As of 2018, his published works include: *Reflection*, for viola and piano (1930); *Elegy*, for solo viola (1930); *Two Portraits*: No. 2 ("E.B.B."), for solo viola and string orchestra (1930); Double Concerto for Violin, Viola, and Orchestra (1932); and *Lachrymae: Reflections on a Song of Dowland*, for viola and piano (1950), which Britten later orchestrated. More than a dozen original compositions for viola, in varying states of completion, remain in manuscript.[15]

Lachrymae owes its existence to the Aldeburgh Festival. During a concert tour of the United States in 1949, Britten met the great Scottish-American violist William Primrose and offered to compose a new work if Primrose would participate in the third festival the following year. Primrose wrote an effusive letter shortly after their meeting:

> I hasten to thank you most warmly for two very gracious experiences. First of all for your concert of a few hours ago which I found a very rewarding experience. It was all so beautifully accomplished, and so simply: this latter is a rare virtue in concerts here. Secondly, for your heartwarming compliment the other evening at the Hawkes' when you said I was "needed" at Aldeburgh. Believe me I would regard it as a privilege, without a viola piece from you, but with it my cup would indeed overflow! Please let me know when you would wish me to come.[16]

A few days later, Britten wrote to Elizabeth Sweeting, general manager of the festival:

> Everyone here knows about the Festival—I think we might advertise a bit here for next year. I think I landed William Primrose (the viola-player—a great one) for a recital—but more of that later.[17]

With Primrose's participation assured, Britten set to work on *Lachrymae* in the spring of 1950; the published version indicates that the work was written in April 1950 at Aldeburgh, while Britten's manuscript is dated May 16, 1950. The work's full details—including its title—were not settled prior to publication of the souvenir Festival Programme Book, which described it as: "A New Work for Viola and Pianoforte," by Benjamin Britten, which was "to be given its first performance by William Primrose, for whom it was specially written."[18]

Primrose reappeared at the Aldeburgh Festival in 1951 and then again in 1952, when he performed *Lachrymae* with the Australian pianist Noel Mewton-Wood. Britten's program note for that performance succinctly describes the work's design:

> Written for William Primrose, this piece was first performed at the Aldeburgh Festival of 1950. It is a series of variations on the first phrase of Dowland's song "If my complaints could passions move," one of his most characteristically passionate melodies. After a *lento* introduction in which the song is quoted in the bass of the piano-part, the Reflections continue with the following indications: Allegretto molto commodo, Animato, Tranquillo, Allegro con moto, Largamente (big chords for both instruments), Appasionato (in

which another song of Dowland's is quoted "Flow my tears"), Alla valse mode-rato (Waltz tempo), Allegro marcia (syncopated march rhythms for the viola), Lento (very high on the piano, harmonics on the viola) and L'istesso tempo which after a slow crescendo imperceptibly returns to Dowland's original tune and harmony, completing it for the first time. John Dowland put at the top of one of his pieces Semper Dowland, semper dolens, and this piece darkly reflects that introspective melancholy that was so much a part of the Elizabethan temperament.[19]

Even for a composer who sought to minimize excess, Britten was exceptionally spare in his use of musical material in *Lachrymae,* with the first strain (mm. 1–8) of Dowland's "If My Complaints Could Passions Move" (Ex. 7.1) serving as the principal material for the work until the final variation:

> In the sequence of variations that comprises *Lachrymae,* virtually each phrase, each motivic cell, each harmonic progression, can be traced back to Dowland's song "If my complaints could passions move," on which Britten's piece is based and which emerges in its original tranquil clarity only at the work's conclusion.[20]

Lachrymae opens with fragments of this strain: in mm. 1–2, the viola plays the first three notes from Dowland's tune (motive *x*), while the piano plays the three notes from m. 5 of the tune (motive *y*). In m. 3 of *Lachrymae,* Britten extends the viola part to include the fourth note from Dowland's tune (establishing motive *x'*) while simultaneously starting motive *x* a fifth higher (Ex. 7.2).[21] Elsewhere, Britten also extends motive *y* by a note to establish motive *y'* (Ex. 7.3). After five iterations of motive *x* in the viola (mm. 1–8), the complete first strain of Dowland's tune is heard in the bass line of *Lachrymae* starting at m. 9.

After the introduction, Britten works through a series of variations on "If My Complaints," deftly manipulating all four versions of the motives, both horizon-tally and vertically (Ex. 7.4). He also explores textures and string techniques, in-cluding pizzicato, double stops, *quasi ponticello,* and harmonics (Chart 7.1; all rehearsal numbers refer to the Boosey & Hawkes edition). In the sixth variation, Britten introduces the second song by Dowland, "Flow My Tears." Published in 1600, "Flow My Tears" borrows its tune from Dowland's earlier instrumental pavan, titled *Lachrimae.* Britten quotes only from the second strain (Ex. 7.5), and he encloses the viola's first phrase within quotation marks.

"Flow My Tears" is just a brief interlude, and Britten returns to "If My Complaints" in Variation 7. It is in the final variation that Britten reveals Dowland's complete tune, beginning in mm. 295–302, when the entire first strain (slightly altered) appears in the viola. Britten then fragments this strain from mm. 303–12 with the second and third strains closing out the work (mm. 313–28).

Example 7.1 Dowland, "If My Complaints Could Passions Move" (melody only), from *The First Booke of Songes or Ayres* (1597), with motives *x*, *x′*, *y*, and *y′* indicated.

Example 7.2 Britten, *Lachrymae*, op. 48, mm. 1–5, with motives *x*, *x′*, and *y* indicated.

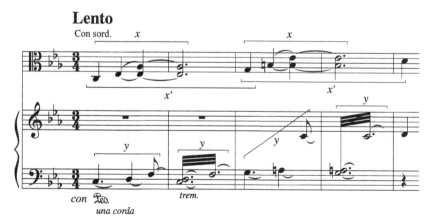

Example 7.3 Britten, *Lachrymae*, op. 48, mm. 46–50, viola, showing motive *y′*.

On June 22, 1970, Cecil Aronowitz performed *Lachrymae* at the Aldeburgh Festival with Britten at the piano. "During rehearsals Britten realised he was dissatisfied with the ninth variation [at Number 9]."[22] He quickly composed an alternative part, which the pair performed in place of the original. This alternative part was added to the piano score in later printings.[23]

In February 1976, Britten orchestrated the work for Aronowitz, intending for him to premiere it. The violist expressed his appreciation in a reply to Britten:

> I would like you to know how deeply honoured and moved I felt for your generous gesture in asking me to give the "premiere" of your *Lachrymae* for Viola and String Orchestra. I will try to give as fine a performance as possible.[24]

Unfortunately, a mix-up with Boosey & Hawkes permitted Rainer Moog to perform this version in May 1977, prior to Aronowitz's performance the following month at the Aldeburgh Festival.[25]

Both versions of *Lachrymae* have proved popular with performers and critics. Reviewing the premiere in 1950, the critic for the *Times* wrote:

> "Lachrymae," or Reflections on a Song of Dowland, for viola and piano, is not an easy piece to assimilate at first hearing without a score, partly because the listener has to wait till the last few bars for an overt reference to Dowland's "If my complaints could passions move," which constitutes the main theme, easily missed on its first furtive appearance in the piano bass beneath atmospheric muted tremolo references to it from the viola. An extract from the same composer's "Flow, O my tears" is heard during the 10 continuous variations, but the fertility of Britten's invention again enables him to make a very little thematic material go a very long way, while the introspective, undemonstrative character of the music will no doubt make a deeper impression at each successive performance.[26]

The work has made a deeper impression upon successive performances, of which there have been many. Britten was happy enough with the "reverse variation" structure to use it again in two later works: *Nocturnal after John*

Variation	Rehearsal No./ Measures	Tempo	Idea/Technique
Introduction	1–28	Lento	Tremolo
1	No. 1; 29–63	Allegretto molto comodo	Eighth notes (staccato and slurred)
2	No. 2; 64–78	Animato	Pizzicato sixteenth notes (rubato)
3	No. 3; 79–102	Tranquillo	Syncopated double stops in viola (canonically following the piano), followed by *ad libitum* triplet flourishes
4	No. 4; 103–56	Allegro con moto	Elongated, sustained motive in viola with moving notes in piano
5	No. 5; 157–74	Largamente	Chords followed by triplet eighth notes
6	No. 6; 175–215	Appassionato	"Flow My Tears"
7	No. 7; 216–47	Alla valse moderato	Waltz, with string crossings
8	No. 8; 248–71	Allegro marcia	March (dotted-eighth–sixteenth-note rhythms with pizzicatos at end); *quasi ponticello, a punta*
9	No. 9; 272–79	Lento	Harmonic double stops with a triplet rhythm (alternative viola part eliminates double stops, retains concept of harmonics, and expands on the triplet rhythm; played *flautando*)
10	No. 10; 280–328	L'istesso tempo	Repeated thirty-second notes; closing section includes the complete tune of "If My Complaints Could Passions Move"

Chart 7.1 Overall design of Britten's *Lachrymae*, op. 48

Example 7.4 Britten, *Lachrymae*, op. 48, mm. 79–82, with motives *x'* and *y* indicated.

Example 7.5 Dowland, "Flow My Tears" (melody only), from *The Second Booke of Songs or Ayres* (1600), second strain (mm. 8–15).

Dowland: Reflections on "Come Heavy Sleep," op. 70, for guitar (1963) and the Cello Suite No. 3, op. 87 (1971), based on four Russian themes.[27]

More about *Lachrymae*

Readers interested in an in-depth analysis of Britten's *Lachrymae* are referred to the following source:

Sills, David. "Benjamin Britten's *Lachrymae*: An Analysis for Performers." *Journal of the American Viola Society* 13, no. 3 (1997): 17–34.

8

Max Bruch: *Romanze for Viola and Orchestra*, op. 85

Date of Composition: 1911

First Edition: Max Bruch, *Op. 85, Romanze für Bratsche mit Orchester*, Mainz: B. Schott's Söhne, 1911, Plate No. 29361 (Score); Plate No. 29362 (Piano Reduction)

Select Later Edition: Max Bruch, *Romanze für Viola und Orchester, F-dur, Opus 85*, ed. Norbert Gertsch, Munich: Henle, 2004, HN 785 (Piano Reduction)

Dedication: Herrn Maurice Vieux, Solobratschisten der Großen Oper und der Conservatoire-Concerte in Paris zugeeignet

Date/Place of First Private Performance: April 25, 1911, Willy Hess (viola), Orchestergesellschaft, Leo Schrattenholz (conductor), Berlin

Date/Place of Early Public Performances: November 2, 1911, Herman Meerloo (viola), Royal Concertgebouw Orchestra, Cornelis Dopper (conductor), Amsterdam; February 18 and 25, 1912, Maurice Vieux (viola), Orchestre de la Société des Concerts du Conservatoire, Philippe Gaubert (conductor), Salle des Concerts, Paris Conservatoire, Paris

Orchestral Instrumentation: Solo viola, flute, oboe, 2 clarinets in B♭, 2 bassoons, 3 horns in F, 2 trumpets in C, timpani, strings

Introduction

"The violin can sing a melody better than the piano can, and melody is the soul of music."[1] Bruch's comment, made in response to the question as to why he, a pianist, had taken such an interest in the violin, aptly characterizes the music for which he is known: beautifully melodic string compositions. While the bulk of Bruch's compositional output is vocal music, including three operas and numerous songs and choral works that equally demonstrate his gift for melody, the immediate success of his Violin Concerto No. 1 in G Minor, op. 26 established his reputation as a string composer in the minds of audiences and performers. His sensitive string writing appealed to virtuoso violinists of the day, including Joseph Joachim, Pablo de Sarasate, and Ferdinand David, who eagerly promoted his music. Bruch's lengthy career extended well into the twentieth century, though his style remained firmly rooted in the German Romantic tradition of Felix Mendelssohn and Robert Schumann.

Biographical Sketch

Born in Cologne, Max Bruch (1838–1920) received his early musical training from his mother, a singer. At the age of nine, Bruch surprised her with a song written for her birthday—his first composition. Encouraged by his parents, Bruch began privately studying theory with Heinrich Breidenstein, eventually adding composition studies with Ferdinand Hiller. In 1852, he earned the Frankfurt Mozart-Stiftung Prize, which allowed him to study composition with Hiller and piano with Carl Reinecke and Ferdinand Breunung until 1857.[2]

After those studies ended, Bruch began a period of travel, obtaining performances of his compositions and interesting publishers in his music, notably Breitkopf & Härtel. In the summer of 1864, Bruch began work on the piece that would prove to be a pivotal success: his Violin Concerto No. 1 in G Minor, op. 26. The concerto was premiered two years later, but Bruch was not completely satisfied and sent the manuscript to Joseph Joachim for advice. Joachim replied with suggestions in a lengthy letter dated August 17, 1866. Bruch incorporated some of Joachim's suggestions and also showed the work to Ferdinand David and others. Joachim premiered the revised version of the concerto on January 7, 1868, in Bremen.[3]

From 1865 to 1870, Bruch held positions as music director in Koblenz and Sondershausen, and it was during this time when he began his first serious romantic involvement, with Emma Landau. The relationship ended badly, leaving Bruch "battered and bruised."[4] He suffered another ill-fated romantic entanglement in 1873, becoming secretly engaged to the nineteen-year-old Amalie Heydweiller. Bruch was, by this time, working as a freelance composer, and Amalie's mother was none too happy with the prospect of her daughter marrying a penniless composer. Bruch endeavored to secure a permanent position with steady income but was discontented with his options, and the engagement was broken off.[5] His romantic fortunes finally improved in 1880, when he became engaged to the sixteen-year-old Clara Tuczek on August 22. The two wed shortly after the New Year and remained happily married until her death in 1919.[6]

Only days after his engagement in 1880, Bruch departed for England to assume a new post as director of the Liverpool Philharmonic Society. It was in Liverpool that he completed work on *Kol Nidrei*, for cello and orchestra; Bruch subsequently arranged *Kol Nidrei* and a later cello work, *Canzone*, for viola.[7] His tenure in Liverpool was marked by turmoil, involving disagreements with the orchestra's governing committee and complaints from Bruch about the quality of the chorus. After Bruch left Liverpool, he held a conducting post at Breslau from 1883 until 1890. He then taught composition at the Hochschule für Musik in Berlin from 1890 until his retirement in 1911, where Ottorino Respighi and Ralph Vaughan Williams were among his students.[8] During his final years, Bruch suffered from a number of ailments; he died peacefully in the early morning hours of October 2, 1920.[9]

Bruch's *Romanze for Viola and Orchestra,* op. 85

Bruch's works that prominently feature the viola include *Eight Pieces for Clarinet, Viola, and Piano*, op. 83 (c. 1908; published 1910); *Romanze for Viola and Orchestra*, op. 85 (1911); and the *Double Concerto for Clarinet, Viola, and Orchestra*, op. 88 (1911). *Romanze* was written for Bruch's friend Maurice Vieux, who served as principal viola solo with the Orchestre de la Société des Concerts du Conservatoire and the Paris Opera Orchestra. A letter from Bruch to Vieux, dated February 23, 1911, suggests that the work came about as a request from the violist for a concerto:

> I thank you for your good letter on the 13th of this month. It goes without saying that it would be a true pleasure for me to write for you; but it seems to me that it would be a bit audacious at my age to compose a great <u>Concerto</u> for viola and orchestra. It would be better to finish my writing career now! However—if by chance I have ideas for an <u>Adagio</u> etc., you will be the first one who will have the manuscript.
>
> I am delighted to hear from your friend [Joseph] Débroux that you will play my op. 83 in March with your excellent colleague Mr. Mimart. But it might be a little too much, to play all 8 pieces; it would be better to choose 4 to 6.
>
> Accept, dear sir, the assurance of my distinguished consideration.[10]

Ideas must have quickly struck Bruch, since the *Romanze* was completed within the next two months. Bruch preferred to organize private hearings of his works before having them published,[11] and he arranged for his friend Willy Hess to play through the work in Berlin on April 25. Bruch prepared the work for publication shortly afterward, and Vieux performed the work in Paris the following winter.

As a musical form, the German vocal Romanze is indebted to French models, imitating their "strophic form, simple melodies, phrase structure and harmonies" while incorporating "elements of folksong."[12] The instrumental Romanze retains the lyrical aspects of the vocal version, but the term was typically "applied to slow movements with a rondo, ABA or variation structure" or to "small character-pieces with no common formal pattern."[13]

The lyrical, vocal aspect suggested by Bruch's choice of title is evident in his *Romanze for Viola and Orchestra*, op. 85, but the single-movement work is uncharacteristically in sonata form (Chart 8.1). After a brief, two-measure introduction, the viola's lyrical four-measure theme (Unit 1.1) is first presented in F major and then repeated a third higher in A minor. A return to F major is established with an orchestral statement of the theme in m. 18 (Letter B; all rehearsal letters refer to both the Schott and Henle editions), with the viola briefly re-entering with thematic material in D♭ major before the appearance of new material (Unit 1.2) in m. 24 in A♭ major. These "modulating sidesteps . . . are typical fingerprints of Bruch's style."[14] Theme Group 2 at m. 32 (Letter C) is in the customary dominant (C major). The solo viola presents the theme in double stops, which are used sparingly (this theme's return at m. 93 is the only other instance of double stops, while triple stops are used only in mm. 58–59). Bruch's limited use of polyphonic writing in the viola part further reflects the vocal nature of the solo line.

The development begins in m. 50 in A♭ major before moving to an extended section in G minor at m. 58. Here, the solo viola exhibits elements of recitative, particularly in mm. 61–63 and mm. 69–72.[15] This highly dramatic and operatic section bears a strong resemblance to the *Romanze* from Carl Maria von Weber's *Der Freischütz*, with its tremolo string accompaniment and shared key of G minor. The bravura opening arpeggios of Weber's *Romanze* (Ex. 8.1) are echoed in m. 60 of Bruch's *Romanze* (Ex. 8.2). In modeling this section after such a famous viola solo in the operatic literature, Bruch seems to be alluding to Vieux's position at the Paris Opera.

Bruch prepares for the recapitulation with a brief stop in E♭ major in m. 69 before turning to F major for the full recap at m. 73 (Letter G). *Romanze* finishes with a typical Bruchian ending, with the viola slowly making its way to a final glorious note suspended in the stratosphere.

Attractively written for the viola, Bruch's *Romanze for Viola and Orchestra*, op. 85 is a favorite of violists, who routinely program the viola and piano version on recitals. It is surprising, then, that the work was slow to come into the standard repertoire and that even today its performance history in orchestral concert halls is wanting. World War I broke out in 1914 shortly after the work's premiere, and Bruch remained loyal to Germany while anti-German sentiment ran high. He renounced an honorary doctorate that he had received from Cambridge University and was ejected from the Paris Académie, losing friends (and potential champions of his music) in the process.[16] And compared to the newer, more challenging viola works that were being composed during

Zone	Thematic Areas/Snippet	Measures	Principal Tonal Areas/Function
Introduction		1–2	Dominant
Exposition		3 (Let. A)–49	
	Theme Group 1	3 (Let. A)–32 (Let. C)	
	Unit 1.1	3 (Let. A)–24	F major
	Unit 1.2	24–32 (Let. C)	A-flat major
	Theme Group 2	32 (Let. C)–44 (Let. D)	C major
	Closing	44 (Let. D)–49	C major
Development		50–72	
	Unit 1.1	50–57	Begins A-flat major; modulates
	Unit 1.2	58–72	G minor
Recapitulation		73 (Let. G)–104 (Let. I)	
	Theme Group 1	73 (Let. G)–92 (Let. H)	
	Unit 1.1	73 (Let. G)–84	F major
	Unit 1.2	84–92 (Let. H)	G-flat major
	Theme Group 2	92 (Let. H)–104 (Let. I)	F major
Coda		104 (Let. I)–18	F major

Chart 8.1 Bruch, *Romanze for Viola and Orchestra*, op. 85: Structural analysis.

Example 8.1 Weber, *Der Freischütz*, Act III, "Romanze und Arie," mm. 2–3, viola obbligato.

Example 8.2 Bruch, *Romanze for Viola and Orchestra*, op. 85, m. 60, solo viola.

the early twentieth century, Bruch's *Romanze* can be seen as old-fashioned and lacking sufficiently interesting material to have attracted performances by viola soloists of the day. It was not until 1973 that *Romanze* received its first commercial recording, and it remains infrequently performed by major orchestras in America.[17]

9

Henri Casadesus: Concerto in B Minor for Viola and Orchestra (attributed to G. F. Handel)

I. Allegro moderato
II. Andante ma non troppo
III. Allegro molto

Date of Composition: Completed c. 1918

First Edition: G. F. Händel, *Concerto en si mineur pour Alto avec accompagnement d'orchestre; Réalisation de la basse et orchestration par Henri Casadesus*, Paris: Éditions Max Eschig, 1924, Plate No. M. E. 1311 (Piano Reduction); Georg-Friedrich Haendel, *Concerto en si mineur pour alto avec accompagnement d'orchestre; réalisation de la basse et orchestration par Henri Casadesus*, Paris: Éditions Max Eschig, 1925, Plate No. M. E. 1643 (Score)

Date/Place of Early Public Performances: January 8, 1912, Henri Casadesus (viola), Société des Nouveaux Concerts, Lodewijk Mortelmans (director), Antwerp; December 10 and 11, 1926, Samuel Lifschey (viola), The Philadelphia Orchestra, Leopold Stokowski (conductor), Philadelphia

Orchestral Instrumentation: Solo viola, 2 flutes, 2 bassoons, strings

Introduction

"The work as it stands will neither gain nor lose in intrinsic value, if, in the future, we should be supplied with more exact information as to how much of a hand Casadesus or Saint-Saëns or any other person had in its creation."[1] The assessment by Abraham Veinus of the so-called viola concerto by G. F. Handel raises an interesting question: Do we judge a work of art solely by its intrinsic value—considering only the work itself—or do other factors come into play? There is ample evidence that our valuation is affected by wide-ranging factors, including geography (where a work was made), provenance (who owned the work), and most important, authorship (who created the work). A painting, possibly by Jackson Pollock and contested for more than sixty years, would be worth millions of dollars if authenticated, while the same work would be estimated at no more than $50,000 if merely attributed to him.[2] The painting itself has not changed; the difference rests in the value that we place on the name Jackson Pollock.

Likewise, there are a number of works previously attributed to J. S. Bach and entered into Schmieder's Bach-Werke-Verzeichnis (BWV) catalogue that "enjoyed great popularity until the attribution was called into question or authoritatively disproved. Now they tend to be neglected, perhaps with a touch of embarrassment that we should have fallen for the misattribution in the first place."[3] Did these works suddenly cease being worthy of attention merely because they were not composed by Bach?

The case with the "Handel" viola concerto is a bit different than these examples in that Henri Casadesus was deliberately deceitful about the authorship of the work. While he consistently maintained the concerto was an original work by Handel, the lack of any sources attributable to Handel and the sizable number of spurious works that Casadesus—and other members of his family—have been associated with have led scholars to deem this concerto a musical hoax composed entirely by him. Should we disregard the concerto because of Casadesus's deception, or should we value it even more as a clever forgery? Or, should we solely consider its intrinsic value in our judgment?

Biographical Sketch

Henri Casadesus (1879–1947) was the fourth of nine children born to Luis and Mathilde Casadesus. His father was a self-taught musician who conducted café orchestras and imparted a love of music to his children, eight of whom went on to professional careers.[4] Henri entered the Paris Conservatoire at a young age and became one of the earliest viola students of the great French pedagogue Théophile Laforge, earning a premier prix in 1899. Credited as the first French violist to give recitals entirely devoted to viola music,[5] Henri quickly made a name for himself on the instrument: he played viola for a period in quartets led by Lucien Capet and George Enescu, and Arthur Honegger dedicated his Sonata for Viola and Piano (1920) to Casadesus. In addition to performing, he also composed, producing a number of works under his own name, including operettas and film scores.

As a performer, Casadesus is best remembered for his involvement with the Société des Instruments Anciens, an early-music ensemble that he founded in 1901 with Camille Saint-Saëns as honorary president (Fig. 9.1). The ensemble would remain his life's work and was a family affair, involving his wife, Lucette,

Figure 9.1 Early members of the Société des Instruments Anciens de Paris; from left to right: Albert Périlhou, Marcel Casadesus, Maurice Devilliers, Camille Saint-Saëns, Henri Casadesus, and Jacques Malkin.

his brother Marius, and his sister Régina playing on period instruments, including the quinton, harpsichord, viola d'amore, and viola da gamba. The ensemble toured the world for the next thirty-plus years, earning widespread acclaim in Russia, the United States, Japan, Egypt, and Europe.

Casadesus ostensibly searched through libraries to locate music for the ensemble to play, but questions about their repertoire arose early: "Almost all of the music played was either apocryphal or had at least been cleverly 'retouched' by that talented and sympathetic rascal of a [Henri] Casadesus."[6] Casadesus did not discriminate; he falsely attributed works to little-known composers (Joseph Antoine Lorenziti and Chevalier de Saint-Georges) and well-known composers (C. P. E. Bach and Handel). The audacity of Henri was matched (if not beaten) by his brother Marius, who composed the Adélaïde Concerto ascribed to W. A. Mozart. Marius came clean about his authorship of that concerto shortly before his death and also admitted to the violist and conductor Pierre Monteux that the brothers had composed much of the Société's repertoire themselves.[7] Henri's wife also confirmed suspicions that Henri composed the "Handel" viola concerto in a personal letter written to Walter Lebermann in 1963.[8]

The Casadesus brothers may have begun their fraudulent activities out of necessity, as a source of music for their concerts. They may then have expanded them as a practical joke, or even a contest, to see whether audiences and critics would fall for their deceptions. The brothers may also have felt that compositions written under their own name would not be appropriately appreciated, a motive credited to many master forgers.[9]

Henri's deception has sadly overshadowed his other musical contributions; he performed with some of the greatest artists of the day and was highly admired for his playing on both the viola and viola d'amore. He made several recordings with the Société des Instruments Anciens, and the quality of his forgeries attest to his consummate compositional skills. In his personal life, he was described as a kind-hearted and charismatic gentleman who lived for art and beauty.[10]

Casadesus's Concerto in B Minor for Viola and Orchestra (attributed to G. F. Handel)

There are two known works by Casadesus for solo viola and orchestra: Concerto in B Minor for Viola and Orchestra (Handel) (completed c. 1918; published 1924) and Concerto in C Minor for Viola and Orchestra (J. C. Bach) (published 1947). Casadesus also composed the Concerto in D Major for Violin or Viola with Piano or Orchestral Accompaniment (C. P. E. Bach) (published 1931).

Given the peculiar circumstances surrounding Casadesus's compositions for viola, the genesis of his "Handel" concerto remains murky. Samuel Lifschey provided a bit of insight in 1926 when he was preparing the American premiere of the work:

> A few years ago, when Henri Casadesus was in America with the "Société des Instruments Anciens," he showed me a manuscript copy of a viola concerto, the original of which he believed was an unpublished work of Handel in the British Museum.[11]

As part of his research into the concerto, Lifschey sent letters to multiple sources, including the British Museum and Library of Congress as well as to Casadesus, who replied to his query:

> The information you requested in regard to the Handel concerto is quite simple. It was written for the viola. I was the one who realized the bass and did the orchestration.... The most important information I can give you is to say that the Concerto is an entirely original composition for the viola.[12]

So immediate was the success of the concerto, and the doubts about its authenticity, that Henri Casadesus provided greater detail in a letter from the early 1930s:

September 1, 193[_]

Your letter of this past August 22, reached me at the Ile de Re, where I spend my vacations. I have been eager to respond to your request. As far as the Handel Concerto is concerned, it is an original for viola. The manuscript, or, rather, the edition of that period was passed along to me by Camille Saint-Saëns. I have never held in my hands anything other than the viola part, with the bass, which was not even figured. As indicated by the Eschig edition in which it appeared, I realized the concerto, which is to say that I provided complete harmonization and orchestration. That was 30 years ago. I toyed with this concerto in manuscript form during all those years, during stays in Paris, Berlin, London, Petrograd, Moscow, etc., etc., and it was only in 1918 that I added it to the edition. This work is, without doubt, original, and is a concerto which should be added to the Handel collection—In my orchestration and harmonization I have been as deferent as possible, and I believe that this work is one of the most successful for the viola. The adagio is utter beauty, and the first movement is of a most admirable style.

The Eschig Edition has made several transcriptions of the Concerto for violin, cello, oboe, and trumpet.[13]

Saint-Saëns was deceased by the time of this letter and could not defend himself against the charge of providing the manuscript. Casadesus's mention that the harmonization and orchestration were completed some thirty years prior suggests that the concerto may have been largely written around the turn of the twentieth century but not fully completed until around 1918. Casadesus is known to have performed the concerto in 1912 and possibly on other occasions while continuing to fully develop the composition.[14]

The false attribution to Handel also presents challenges in analyzing the work and approaching it from a performance perspective. With its decidedly non-Baroque characteristics, including nineteenth-century harmonizations and extensive use of the viola's upper register, the concerto cannot be considered a Baroque work stylistically. It is also unclear to what extent Casadesus was familiar with Handel's concertos or how rigorously he explored their characteristics in an attempt to imitate Handel's style. Handel's original concertos display diversity in their orchestration, form, and texture and do not fall into consistent patterns,[15] but he favored the four-movement format of slow–fast–slow–fast rather than the three-movement format that Casadesus selected. Casadesus was most likely concerned with attempting to mimic Handel's motivic style, and it is here that he is most successful, with many critics commenting on the appropriate Handelian mood of the concerto.[16]

All three movements of the concerto are in B minor. The first movement is in a ritornello form, with the soloist and orchestra alternating sections. But

Casadesus seems to be toying with a general sonata-form scheme, with the "exposition" ending in m. 52 (No. 6; all rehearsal numbers refer to the Eschig edition). The orchestra then repeats its opening statement in F♯ minor followed by the longest, and most developmental, solo section for the viola (mm. 58–75). The "recapitulation" starts at m. 76 (No. 8), repeating the opening material (minus the opening tutti) until m. 104 (No. 11), when Casadesus cuts short the violist's earlier material (see mm. 35–39) and moves directly to the orchestra's ritornello (see m. 40; No. 4). The ensuing viola section at m. 109 (No. 12) is now set in B minor, as opposed to its earlier appearance at m. 45 (No. 5) in F♯ minor.

The second movement, largely built around the opening theme, "features the wide melodic arches, the impersonal yet deeply absorbing grandeur, which one finds often in Handel."[17] This movement demonstrates Casadesus's skill at orchestration: the texture is lightened by the omission of bassoons, and the solo viola engages in lovely exchanges with the principal flute and solo cello.

The third movement appears to have been influenced by Handel's propensity for including dance forms in his concertos, since it resembles a gigue, though in a three-part form rather than the customary binary. Like the first movement, this movement can be viewed as a quasi-sonata form, with the "exposition" ending in m. 79 on a V/V harmony. The thematic material is then extensively developed, with the pickups to m. 147 signaling the start of the "recapitulation."

Casadesus's viola concerto gained widespread adoption by violists immediately after publication and has remained a standard of the repertoire. While its early success can be attributed to the attachment of the name Handel (and some people still believe it to be a work by him), it has remained popular among violists who recognize it for what it is: a beautifully wrought composition that is enjoyable to play. The test of time has proved Abraham Veinus right: the concerto remains an intrinsically outstanding work, regardless of who composed it. And Casadesus gets the last laugh.

10

Rebecca Clarke: Sonata for Viola and Piano

I. Impetuoso
II. Vivace
III. Adagio

Date of Composition: 1918–1919 (manuscript dated July 1919)

First Edition: Rebecca Clarke, *Sonata: For Viola (or Violoncello) and Piano*, London: J. & W. Chester, 1921, Plate No. J.W.C. 805

Date/Place of First Public Performance: September 25, 1919, Louis Bailly (viola), Harold Bauer (piano), Second Berkshire Festival of Chamber Music, Pittsfield, MA

Introduction

"This is easily the best work we have had from a woman composer for a long time—though music has no genders and such a consideration is really irrelevant to its quality."[1] Rebecca Clarke shocked the musical world when her viola sonata tied with Ernest Bloch's suite at the 1919 Berkshire Festival Competition. After the festival's patron, Elizabeth Sprague Coolidge, cast the winning vote for Bloch's suite, the jury demanded to know the identity of the other composer. "And," Coolidge later told Clarke, "you should have seen their faces when they saw it was by a woman!"[2] Soon, Clarke's identity as a composer was intertwined with her gender, much to her chagrin:

> "Art," she declared, "has nothing to do with the sex of the artist. I would sooner be regarded as a sixteenth-rate composer than be judged as if there were one kind of musical art for men and another for women."[3]

Even today, a significant amount of scholarship has focused on Clarke's gender. Given the biases that women have faced in classical music—particularly as composers—the promotion of Rebecca Clarke as a "woman composer" seems warranted. Yet, by viewing her viola sonata on its own merits, irrespective of the composer's identity (just as the judges at the 1919 competition had to do), one readily sees a great work of art that transcends notions of gender.

Biographical Sketch

Born in Harrow, England, Rebecca Clarke (1886–1979) was the eldest of Agnes and Joseph Thacher Clarke's four children. Her American father served as the European Patent Expert for the Eastman Kodak Company. He loved music, playing the cello and singing duets with his German wife, who was also "quite a serviceable pianist."[4] At the age of eight, Rebecca began learning the violin alongside her younger brother Hans; the pair studied with Mr. Cave, a nearby teacher. The family was soon playing string quartets together (with Agnes on viola), and chamber music would remain an important part of Rebecca's musical development over the following years. At the age of sixteen, she entered the Royal Academy of Music (RAM), where she studied violin with Hans Wessely and harmony with Percy Hilder Miles, a friend of the family's.[5] While at the academy, she received an unexpected marriage proposal from Miles, prompting her father to remove her from the school in 1905.[6]

Afterward, Clarke devoted more efforts to composing while at home. Her father sent a few songs to the eminent composition teacher Charles Villiers Stanford, who responded favorably:

> I think there may be some talent in your daughter, tho' the songs are very slight to judge by, & they are (as can be expected) quite inexperienced in workmanship. There is a possibility of poetical feeling lurking in them, & a certain independence of idea. Whether she has melodic invention & can arrive at expressing it musically is a matter which only time & work can show. But I would be pleased to try my hand at what training her will do, tho' I don't conceal from you that it means (like every art) a lot of drudgery for her, & not a little disappointment at intervals, & apparent stand stills occasionally.[7]

Following Stanford's suggestion, Rebecca enrolled as a composition student of his at the Royal College of Music (RCM) in 1908. It was Stanford who persuaded Clarke to take up the viola in the school's orchestra, "Because then you are right in the middle of the sound, and can tell how it's all done."[8] Meanwhile, Clarke's situation at home was getting worse; she had a complicated relationship with her volatile father—they were both strong-willed and frequently butted heads. Things reached a breaking point in 1910 when she pulled a prank involving letters from one of her father's paramours: "It was meant to show Papa that I was aware of the situation between them. It was playing with fire, I knew—half mischievous deviltry, half malicious criticism."[9] In the end, Rebecca got burned: she was thrown out of the house by her furious father and forced to earn a living as a violist. She played in various chamber groups and orchestras, joining Henry J. Wood's orchestra in 1913 once he began admitting women.[10]

Clarke traveled to America in 1916, staying with family members while touring as a solo and chamber artist. A major recital with the cellist May Mukle at Aeolian Hall in New York on February 13, 1918, included three recent compositions: *Lullaby* and *Grotesque*, for viola and cello, programmed under Clarke's own name, and *Morpheus*, for viola and piano, programmed under the pseudonym Anthony Trent. Though the reviewer for *Musical America* felt that Trent's work was "lacking originality," he liked Clarke's viola and cello duos, commenting that "as a composer the young woman likewise shone."[11] Clarke's major breakthrough as a composer came the following year at the 1919 Berkshire Festival Competition. Out of seventy-two anonymous entries, the six judges were divided between Clarke's viola sonata and Bloch's suite. The competition's patron, Elizabeth Sprague Coolidge—who was personal friends with both composers—ultimately cast the winning vote for Bloch's suite. Still, Clarke's sonata was performed at the festival, and she received a tremendous amount of publicity. Coolidge's friendship would prove beneficial over the following years: after Clarke's Piano Trio received an honorable mention in the 1921 Berkshire Festival Competition, Coolidge commissioned the *Rhapsody for Cello and Piano* for the 1923 festival.

Clarke enjoyed success as both a composer and performer in the following years, continuing to travel widely while principally residing in England. But a trip to visit family in America during the summer of 1939 turned into a life-altering event when displaced musicians were denied return visas after Britain's entry into World War II.[12] A burst of creative activity followed, including a number of new compositions "in a leaner, more neo-classical idiom."[13] In 1944, she reconnected with a former classmate from the RCM, James Friskin, and the couple married on September 23 of that year, residing in New York City. Owing to health issues, Clarke largely retired from playing but continued with a variety of music-related activities, including teaching, lecturing, and hosting a weekly radio program.[14] Though Clarke's visibility as a composer faded over the following decades, she was never totally forgotten. In 1976, Robert Sherman devoted a WQXR radio program in honor of her ninetieth birthday—which included a performance of the viola sonata by Toby Appel and Emanuel Ax—that helped bring new attention to her.[15] Toby Appel's performance of the sonata at Alice Tully Hall the following year further stoked interest in Clarke's music, which has only grown in strength. After enjoying a long and varied career, Clarke died on October 13, 1979, at the age of ninety-three.

Clarke's Sonata for Viola and Piano

Clarke's output consists of vocal works (primarily songs) and chamber music. As might be expected, she composed a number of works for viola: *Lullaby*, for viola and piano (c. 1909); *Lullaby: An Arrangement of an Ancient Irish Tune*, for viola and piano (c. 1913); Untitled Movement, for viola and piano (1917–1918); *Morpheus*, for viola and piano (1917–1918); Sonata for Viola or Violoncello and Piano (1918–1919); *Passacaglia on an Old English Tune*, for viola or violoncello and piano (1941); and *I'll Bid My Heart Be Still* (Old Scottish Border Melody), arranged for viola and piano (1944). She also arranged one of her violin and piano works, *Chinese Puzzle (Adapted from a Chinese Tune)* (1921), for viola and piano (arr. 1922) and prominently included the viola in several chamber works.

In a program note from 1977, Clarke detailed the genesis of the viola sonata:

> The first sketches were made during the winter of 1918–1919 while I was in Honolulu, playing in a series of chamber concerts. The viola was my instrument; composition with Sir Charles Stanford had been my chief study at the Royal College of Music in London; and when I heard that a thousand-dollar prize for a viola sonata was being offered by Mrs. Elizabeth Sprague Coolidge I thought I would try my hand at one.
>
> The work was completed in Detroit during the spring and summer of 1919, while I was on a visit to a brother of mine.[16]

While staying with her brother Eric (affectionately dubbed "Monkey") and his wife, Beryl, in Detroit, Clarke charted the sonata's progress in a series of diary entries,[17] many of which are included below:

> April 3, 1919: Spent the rest of the day working at my Viola Sonata, which I am beginning to get quite excited about.

> April 22, 1919: Worked hard again at the Sonata all day. It is beginning to come out extremely well.

> April 26, 1919: Put finishing touches to first movement of Sonata, & played it with Beryl.

> May 5, 1919: Began working at my slow movement in the morning.

> May 20, 1919: After dinner we [Beryl and I] played Monkey [Eric] my slow movement for criticism.

> June 11, 1919: Had breakfast with Louise on her nice porch. Then walked to the Detroit Institute of Music, about a mile away, & got a room with a piano, to work in all the morning. Starting my Scherzo now.

June 29, 1919: In the afternoon the others went to a base-ball game, but I begged off, as I wanted to work at my Sonata—In the evening Louise & the others came to hear the Scherzo. Everybody liked it.

July 3, 1919: My last day of working at the Institute. Shall be sorry to stop. The Sonata is finished now, & I have only a few small corrections to do, & the marking & copying before sending it off. Feel very proud to have actually got it done.

These entries indicate that after finishing the first movement, Clarke progressed to the third movement ("slow movement") and then the second movement ("Scherzo"). She started copying the sonata on July 5 and played through the complete work on July 8, noting in her diary: "Had a performance of the whole thing in the evening. Expected to hate it after all that work, but really am rather pleased with it."[18] Clarke then traveled to Buffalo to stay with her brother Hans, mailing the fully copied manuscript on July 11 to the secretary for the competition, Hugo Kortschak. In early August, Clarke traveled to Pittsfield, Massachusetts (the site of the Berkshire Festival), to visit with friends, joyfully writing news of the competition in her diary on August 24:

A red-letter day for me. Mrs Coolidge & [Hugo] Kortschak walked in while we were having supper to tell us the result of the Sonata Competition. Apparently the jury made a tie between two, & as Mrs Coolidge would not divide the prize she gave the casting-vote, which turned out to be for Bloch. The other was mine, which was given special mention. Very excited indeed.[19]

According to a diary entry written two days later, there were originally no plans for Clarke's sonata to be performed at the festival:

Went for a drive with Mrs Coolidge.... Drove all the morning & until a quarter to two, & talked our heads off. She had decided long ago that the second Sonata should not be performed at the Festival, but late in the afternoon she came to see me & said it should be after all, by [Louis] Bailly & Harold Bauer.[20]

The work was premiered at the Second Berkshire Festival on September 25, 1919, by Bailly and Bauer, receiving favorable reviews. While neither the manuscript nor published version bears a dedication, the premiere program does: Dedicated to Mrs. E. S. Coolidge.[21] The program also includes two lines from Alfred de Musset's 1835 poem "La nuit de Mai" ("The Night of May"):

Poète, prends ton luth; le vin de la jeunesse
Fermente cette nuit dans les veines de Dieu.

(Poet, take up thy lute; the wine of youth
Ferments this night in the veins of God.)[22]

Clarke had inscribed these lines on her submitted manuscript, and they also appear in the published edition. The general tone of Clarke's sonata reflects the atmosphere of Musset's poem, as many commenters have noted: "She has all but vocalized the free spirit of the verses," remarked a reviewer for the *New York Times* in 1920.[23]

With its complex formal and harmonic aspects, there are many possible approaches to analyzing Clarke's sonata. The work is characterized by fragmented motives, intricate rhythms, and abrupt harmonic and melodic shifts. Like her other compositions, it displays a wide range of influences, including English folk song, French Impressionism, and Orientalism.[24] Ralph Vaughan Williams, Claude Debussy, Maurice Ravel, and Ernest Bloch were all major influences on Clarke's music, and one can detect traces of their styles in the viola sonata.

The first movement opens with a bold, declamatory statement from the viola in the E Dorian mode, set over a sustained chord (A–B–E) in the piano. After twelve measures of this cadenza-like introduction, the viola's move from a repeated e[ii] to an e♭[ii] in m. 13 (No. 1; all rehearsal numbers refer to the Chester edition) creates a dramatic shift in tonality to start the exposition (Chart 10.1). The sense of instability is enhanced in the following measures with harmonic fluctuations and dynamic swells. Though the exposition opens with new thematic material (Theme Group 1), it soon incorporates motives from the introduction (Exs. 10.1 and 10.2), which will serve as substantial thematic material throughout this movement as well as in the third. For the second theme group at m. 39 (No. 4), Clarke relaxes the tempo and thins out the texture with the piano playing alone for the first time. At m. 50, the serene atmosphere continues with the viola's *dolce espressivo* entrance. In earlier sections, Clarke made extensive use of the viola's A string, but here she restricts the viola to its lower three strings (specifically marking Sul D in mm. 51–54).

At m. 75 (No. 7), the development begins with material from the introduction, starting with the piano's *misterioso* statement of the opening fifth motive (m. 75), which is followed by the viola's cadenza-like flutterings in mm. 75–78. The music here is bitonal, with the piano's chords set harmonically apart by a third: the right

Example 10.1 Clarke, Sonata for Viola and Piano, movt. I, mm. 1–2, viola.

Example 10.2 Clarke, Sonata for Viola and Piano, movt. I, mm. 20–22, viola.

Zone	Thematic Areas/Snippet	Measures	Principal Tonal Areas/Function
Introduction		1–12	E Dorian
Exposition		13 (No. 1)–74	
	Theme Group 1	13 (No. 1)–38	Begins Fm⁷ chord; many seventh chords, along with emphasis on tri-tone relationship
	Theme Group 2	39 (No. 4)–74	Begins G major; ends C Mixolydian
Development		75 (No. 7)–109	Starts C Aeolian/ A-flat Lydian
Recapitulation		110 (No. 9)–67	
	Theme Group 1	110 (No. 9)–34	Begins Fm⁷ chord; many seventh chords, along with emphasis on tri-tone relationship
	Theme Group 2	135 (No. 12)–67	E major
Coda		167–85	E major

Chart 10.1 Clarke, Sonata for Viola and Piano: Structural analysis, first movement, Impetuoso.

hand outlines C Aeolian (along with the viola), while the left outlines A♭ Lydian. After working through earlier material, Clarke concludes the tautly constructed development with a restatement of the opening four measures in mm. 106–9, played *ppp* in octaves by the piano, now set over an It+^{6} chord in the piano's lower system. The recapitulation starts with a quick *impetuoso* measure in m. 110 (No. 9), which abruptly gives way to a repeat of Theme Group 1 (mm. 111–34). Forgoing the earlier transitional measures (see mm. 37–38), the music imme- diately shifts to the second theme group in m. 135 (No. 12). Starkly contrasting with the relaxed atmosphere in the exposition, the viola here loudly plays the theme in E major over *appassionato* arpeggios in the piano. The music finally calms down in m. 159 (No. 14) with *ppp* arpeggios in the viola as the piano takes over the melody, leading to the final coda in m. 167.

Using a small amount of thematic material, Clarke fills the marvelously witty second movement (Chart 10.2) with many colorful harmonic and melodic touches, including octatonic and pentatonic scales, as well as interesting string techniques, including harmonics, pizzicato, glissandos, and con sordino (the viola is muted throughout the entire movement). The movement begins with a single- voiced melody in the piano, accompanied by pizzicato chords in the viola. After the piano's pentatonic glissando in m. 12, the viola takes over the melody—intending to build on the piano's material from m. 7—but does not progress far before the piano interrupts with a return of the opening melody in m. 15. Finally getting its say in m. 27 (No. 17), the viola expands on its earlier thought from m. 13. Clarke concludes the section with a pentatonic passage centered on E♭ (mm. 43–58).

The B section (mm. 59–102) is bitonal, demonstrating the influence of both Ravel and Vaughan Williams, with the right and left hands of the piano outlining chords set a tritone apart (starting with A major and E♭ major in mm. 59–61, echoing the A section's two tonal centers). A new mood is established by the slower tempo and the arpeggios in the piano, but flashes of earlier material soon intrude in the viola (Exs. 10.3 and 10.4). The resemblance to earlier material becomes more pronounced with the viola's staccato eighth notes at m. 79 (No. 20; *Più mosso*) in an extended octatonic passage (mm. 79–102).

The A section returns at m. 103 (No. 21) with the piano's melody an octave lower and the viola's accompanimental chords now transferred to the pianist's left hand. After a few sequential passages, mm. 131–46 brings a return of the viola's earlier material from mm. 27–42, now set against a more elaborate piano part. At m. 147, the viola is prepared to continue to the pentatonic passage, but the piano has other ideas and jumps ahead to the bitonal sixteenth notes that transitioned us to the B section (see mm. 57–58). After hesitating, the viola repeats its mate- rial (mm. 149–50), only to have the piano persist. The viola finally agrees to the piano's demands and returns to the B section in m. 151 (No. 23), but the piano

Zone	Thematic Areas/Snippet	Measures	Principal Tonal Areas/Function
A	*(Pno. music notation)*	1–58	Centered on A; E-flat
B		59 (No. 19)–102	
	Unit 1.1 *(music notation)*	59 (No. 19)–78	Bitonal (tritone apart)
	Unit 1.2 *(music notation)*	79 (No. 20)–102	Bitonal (tritone apart)
A	*(Pno. music notation)*	103 (No. 21)–50	Centered on A
Coda		151 (No. 23)–81	
	Unit 1.1: B material *(music notation)*	151 (No. 23)–62	Begins centered on E-flat
	Unit 1.2: A material *(Pno. music notation)*	163 (No. 24)–81	Centered on A; ends on C

Chart 10.2 Clarke, Sonata for Viola and Piano: Structural analysis, second movement, Vivace.

Example 10.3 Clarke, Sonata for Viola and Piano, movt. II, mm. 63–66, viola.

Example 10.4 Clarke, Sonata for Viola and Piano, movt. II, mm. 51–54, viola.

now demurs, offering only a few chords in response. Having had enough, the viola vamps with the theme from the first measure (mm. 159–62), encouraging the piano to return to the A section. By mutual consent, the pair revisit their respective roles from the opening in m. 163 (No. 24), closing the movement out with more of their playful banter.

The final movement is the most fragmented, with quick shifts between motives, including a significant return of material from the first movement. Clarke's interest in songwriting is demonstrated in this movement with simple, lyrical melodies and entirely monophonic writing for the viola until m. 106 (as the material from the first movement is returning). This movement is the most indebted to Vaughan Williams, opening with a simple, modal melody in the piano.[25] At its entrance in m. 8, the viola plays an altered version of this melody, set over an increasingly elaborate piano part. After the viola's prayer-like statement of the melody in mm. 24–31, a new motive (Ex. 10.5) begins the next section (mm. 32–73), which features highly chromatic writing and complex rhythms. To close this section, Clarke revisits the opening melody at m. 64 (No. 29) in a climactic passage featuring the viola's upper register.

At m. 75, the viola returns with the prayer-like statement of the opening melody (see mm. 24–31), which is followed, as before, with the piano's statement of the motive in Ex. 10.5 at m. 84 (No. 30). But here it is just a fleeting memory, and the viola begins a transitional passage in m. 86 with the piano returning to the movement's opening melody in m. 94, set over the viola's *ponticello*, tremolo c pedal. In m. 98, the piano revisits material from the first movement's introduction, culminating in a return of that movement's Theme Group 1 material at m. 114 (No. 32). Clarke continues with fragmented motives from the first movement, incorporating material from the development in m. 137 (No. 34) (see movt. I, mm. 80–81). These reminiscences are interrupted in m. 161 (No. 35) with a brief *Comodo quasi pastorale* section in the E♭ Dorian mode followed by a *Quasi fantasia* section at m. 173 (No. 36) that blends movement I material with the third movement's opening theme in a frenzied manner.

Example 10.5 Clarke, Sonata for Viola and Piano, movt. III, mm. 32–33, piano.

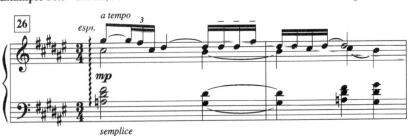

Example 10.6 Clarke, *Pomposo*. Copyright © 2004, Christopher Johnson. Reproduced by permission.

The music is interrupted at m. 206 with a quiet, *Poco meno mosso* statement of the third movement's opening theme, but material from movement I once again reasserts itself in m. 212 (No. 39), with Clarke closing the sonata out in sweeping fashion.

Upon its premiere, Clarke's sonata was greeted with generally favorable reviews, and it became a favorite work of hers to perform:

> When a work wears well after several hearings one may regard it as having attained definite status. "It will wash," Beethoven used to say—very high praise, if the laundries of his day were as destructive as ours! It was this quality of persisting excellence which most distinguished the concert of her own compositions given by Miss Rebecca Clarke at Wigmore Hall on Oct. 21. Her Sonata for viola and pianoforte, her Duets for viola and violoncello, and her Trio for pianoforte, violin and violoncello, have all been heard before. They emerge from the test of rehearing extremely well.[26]

Louis Bailly, who premiered the work, continued to perform and teach it while at the Curtis Institute of Music, and other notable violists, including Lionel Tertis, also programmed it. But, over time, the sonata largely disappeared from the repertoire until Toby Appel performed it in Alice Tully Hall in 1977. Since then, it has exploded in popularity among violists, who have re-established it as a cornerstone of the repertoire and made it almost an anthem for their beloved instrument.

In addition to reviving the sonata, Appel inspired Clarke's final "composition" for viola, a short tune demonstrating that her charm and wit were still as strong as ever, well into her nineties (Ex. 10.6). After coaching Appel in advance of the WQXR broadcast, and then again before his Tully Hall recital, Clarke was so taken with his engaging personality and mischievous sense of humor that she started trying to capture both in music. According to family members whom she spoke to about it at the time, it was unclear whether she thought of it as a free-standing trifle or as the kernel of some larger work.[27] Either way, it stands as a fascinating pendant to a work that many violists regard as one of the finest sonatas in the repertoire.

11

George Enescu: *Concertstück for Viola and Piano*

Date of Composition: 1906

First Edition: Georges Enesco, *Concertstück pour Alto avec accompagnement de Piano*, Paris: Enoch & Cie, [1908], Plate No. E. & C. 6786

Dedication: A Monsieur Th. Laforge

Date/Place of First Public Performance: July 4, 1908, six students of Théophile Laforge: Claude-Ludovic-Henri Barrier, Fernande-Louise-Madeleine Desnoyers, Thérèse-Marie-Vulfranie Dumont, Charles-Emile-Paul Mayeux, Lucien-Marcel Rousseau, and Georges-Jules Taine (viola); George Enescu (piano); Paris Conservatoire; Paris

Introduction

"A sense of constant, organic development of melody is something that runs through Enescu's entire oeuvre. And yet the ways he learned, or invented, of developing melodic forms—superimposing them, taking small elements out of a melody, recombining them in different forms—are things that could only have been possible for someone who had absorbed not only a folk legacy, but also all the richest and most developed parts of the national musical traditions of all of the great cultures of Europe."[1] George Enescu was a true eclectic, drawing inspiration from a wide range of sources. Though best remembered for compositions inspired by his homeland, including the two *Romanian Rhapsodies* for orchestra and the third sonata for violin and piano, his music displays markedly diverse stylistic traits. Extensive chromaticism, complex musical textures, and arresting orchestrations are qualities frequently found in his compositions. But the most distinctive characteristic of Enescu's musical style is his organic—and inventive—method of developing melodic ideas.

Biographical Sketch

Born in Liveni Vîrnav, Romania, to Costache Enescu, an estate manager and amateur violinist, and his wife, Maria, George Enescu (1881–1955) started playing the violin at age four and composing at age five, as soon as he acquired a piano.[2] The precocious musician went to Vienna at age seven, where he attended the Konservatorium der Gesellschaft der Musikfreunde, studying violin with Sigismund Bachrich and Joseph Hellmesberger Jr. and harmony with Robert Fuchs. Enescu graduated from the conservatory in 1893, and, on the recommendation of Hellmesberger, went to France, entering the Paris Conservatoire in 1895. Desiring most to be a composer, he studied with Jules Massenet and Gabriel Fauré, achieving an early triumph when his *Poème Roumain*, op. 1, was performed in 1898. But the violin would not be denied, and Enescu pursued studies with Martin Pierre Marsick, earning a premier prix on the instrument in 1899.

Following graduation, Enescu began a pattern that lasted throughout his career, dividing "his energies between performance and composition."[3] The two *Romanian Rhapsodies*, each of which was premiered in Bucharest in 1903, garnered immediate attention—and enduring fame for Enescu. But he would never match the success of these two works, which incorporated folk tunes, and grew to resent the way that they "dominated and narrowed his reputation as a composer."[4]

While trying to establish himself as a composer, Enescu was also performing throughout Europe as a violinist and pianist. Audiences and critics adored his brilliant violin playing, which combined virtuosity, unorthodox technique, and "an intensely personal style, improvisational yet disciplined."[5] He came to be viewed, first and foremost, as a violinist, much to his annoyance:

> Mad about composing, I grudged every minute I had to give to my violin, and although I had no delusions about what I was writing, I very much preferred my own humble attempts to the persistent study of an instrument that gave me so little satisfaction in return for all my efforts. I have so often looked at my fiddle in its case and said to myself: You are too small, my friend, much too small.[6]

Enescu was primarily based in Paris until the outbreak of the First World War, when he returned to Romania. There, he started an affair with Princess Maria "Maruca" Cantacuzino, the wife of an aristocrat. They remained devoted to one another, and the "turbulent course of their romance" was followed by all of Romania.[7] After the war, he resumed a heavy performance schedule, including frequent tours to the United States, where the young American violinist Yehudi Menuhin heard him in 1925. Though Enescu had been "reluctant to become a violin teacher," he accepted Menuhin as a pupil the following year.[8] Returning to his homeland for the duration of the Second World War, Enescu finally married Maruca in 1939 (her husband having died more than a decade earlier). With the Communist party's rise to power in Romania after the war, Enescu relocated again to Paris. During this late stage of his career, he devoted more time to teaching, recording, and conducting, while trying to satisfy the demands of an erratic and financially irresponsible wife. His final years were "clouded by poverty as well as ill health"; a stroke in July 1954 left him partially paralyzed, and he died ten months later.[9]

Though largely remembered as a composer and violinist, Enescu was a truly multifaceted artist who also excelled as a conductor and pianist. His feats of musical recall are legendary: he knew every note of Richard Wagner's *The Ring* cycle, all of Ludwig van Beethoven's symphonies and string quartets, and at least 150 of J. S. Bach's cantatas, any of which he could play from memory on the piano.[10] Menuhin recalled an occasion when Enescu sight-read Maurice Ravel's recently completed Violin Sonata No. 2 with the composer, then set the music aside and played the entire piece again from memory.[11]

Enescu's *Concertstück for Viola and Piano*

Enescu's perfectionist nature limited his productivity as a composer, though he left a sizable number of manuscripts "in varying degrees of rough draft or near-completion."[12] The *Concertstück for Viola and Piano*, Enescu's only known composition for the instrument, was written in 1906 as a commissioned *morceau de concours* for the Paris Conservatoire. With the establishment of a viola class at the conservatory in 1894, violists could participate in the examination contest (*concours*) to demonstrate their advancement while at the school. The contest required performance of a compulsory piece, which was typically commissioned expressly for the examination. Enescu composed three other *morceaux de concours* for the conservatory: one for flute (*Cantabile et presto*, 1904), chromatic harp (*Allegro de concert*, 1904), and trumpet (*Légende*, 1906). The *Concertstück*, which is dedicated to the conservatory's first viola teacher, Théophile Laforge, was performed by six students at the 1908 *concours* with the composer at the piano.[13] Enescu played the piano part on many later occasions, including for a radio broadcast in 1943 with the Romanian violist Alexandru Rădulescu, which has been commercially released.[14] In 1945, Enescu declined a request from the noted violist Ernst Wallfisch to orchestrate the work,[15] but the composer and violist Amable Massis produced an orchestration in 1963.

The following comments by Enescu regarding his compositional approach are particularly pertinent to the *Concertstück*:

> I am essentially a polyphonist, and not at all a man of pretty chords in sequence. I hate what is stagnant. For me, music is not a state, but an action, that is to say a collection of phrases that express ideas, and movements that carry these ideas in such-and-such directions. The sequence of harmonies comes about, it seems to me, from simple improvisation. However brief it may be, a work deserves the name *composition* only if one can discern a line, a melody, or better still, an overlay of melodies.[16]

The highly rhapsodic work shifts rapidly between thematic ideas and moods, featuring four primary themes (Chart 11.1) that are juxtaposed and combined in compelling ways. When preparing the *Concertstück*, it is helpful to consider how these themes align and intertwine (Chart 11.2). Within this framework, Enescu incorporates appropriate technical challenges worthy of a competition piece. Primarily in F major, the work tends to "depart from the functional principle of harmonic thinking" in its manner of development.[17] The single-movement composition is in an unusual sonata form with a jumbled recapitulation. A similarly unorthodox recapitulation can be found in the first movement of *Dixtuor*, op. 14, for wind instruments—also written in 1906—where the themes from the exposition are "mixed up on an area of approximately thirty bars, in a sort of fortuitous reallocation, the way fragments scattered away by an explosion might fall back again."[18]

Chart 11.1 Four primary themes in Enescu's *Concertstück for Viola and Piano*.

The *Concertstück* starts with octave Ds in the piano, producing immediate harmonic uncertainty before moving to F major in m. 3. Enescu's gift for melody and "a line" is demonstrated by theme 1, which serves as the principal thematic material. An abrupt shift in mood and texture occurs at the pickup to m. 7 with the appearance of the graceful (*gracieux*) theme 2. Following a strong F major cadence at m. 31, theme 3 is boldly announced in the piano, like a brass fanfare, giving way to a return of theme 1 three measures later. At m. 44, theme 1 underpins a transitory passage with French-inspired harmonies, leading to a key change (E major) at m. 55 and the introduction of theme 4. After another brief appearance of theme 3 at m. 74, the viola presents theme 1 material at m. 77 in a variation designed to further showcase the instrumentalist's technical agility. The section closes out quietly in E major with harmonics and a final pizzicato note in the viola (m. 96).

Zone	Measures	Primary Theme	Notes
Exposition	1–97		
(Theme Group 1)	1–6	Theme 1	
	7–14	Theme 2	
	14–20	Theme 1	
	21–31	Theme 2	Extended by technical devices (double stops, runs, arpeggios)
	31–34	Theme 3	
	34–37	Theme 1	
	37–40	Theme 3	
	40–43	Theme 1	
	44–54	Theme 1	Transitory, with theme 1 periodically in bass
(Theme Group 2)	55–66	Theme 4	Theme 1 appears in piano, mm. 64–65
	66–71	Theme 1	Transitory
	72–73	Theme 4	
	74–77	Theme 3	
	77–87	Theme 1	Technical variation for viola (mm. 81–83 revisits material from the viola line in an earlier transitory section; see mm. 44–54)
	87–90	Theme 3	
	90–97	Theme 1	

Chart 11.2 Enescu, *Concertstück for Viola and Piano*: Structural analysis.

Zone	Measures	Primary Theme	Notes
Development	98–148		
	98–106	Theme 3	
	106–10	Theme 2	
	110–17	Theme 3	
	117–23	Theme 2	
	123–27	Theme 3 (viola)	With theme 2 in piano
	127–33	Theme 4 (viola)	With theme 2 in piano
	133–48	Theme 1 (viola)	With theme 2 in piano (theme 3 at m. 135, m. 140, and end of m. 142); theme 1 in piano starting m. 146
Recapitulation	149–94		
(Theme Group 1)	149–56	Theme 2	
	156–60	Theme 1	
	161–71	Theme 1	Transitory, with theme 1 periodically in bass
(Theme Group 2)	172–83	Theme 4	Theme 1 appears in piano, mm. 181–82
	183–87	Theme 1	Transitory
	188–89	Theme 4	
	190–94	Theme 1	Transitory
Coda	194–216		
	194–207	Theme 3	mm. 200–202 revisits material from the viola line in an earlier transitory section; see mm. 161–71
	208–16	Theme 1	

Chart 11.2 (continued) Enescu, *Concertstück for Viola and Piano*: Structural analysis.

The development starts with a *ff* presentation of theme 3 material, which was used sparingly in the exposition but is substantially developed here. Enescu's structuring of thematic material is ingenious, not only through the linear arrangement but also in the way they are superimposed. Most intricate is the area from mm. 117–48, during which all four themes appear in progressively complex arrangements, notably from mm. 133–42, where flashes of theme 3 punctuate the piano's theme 2 utterances, all layered underneath theme 1 material in the viola (Ex. 11.1). The recapitulation starts with a return of the *gracieux* theme 2 at m. 149 and continues with an unusually ordered presentation of thematic material. In a nod to traditional sonata form,

Enescu retains the key of F major at m. 172 for the reappearance of theme 4, which serves a general function as Theme Group 2 material. A strong F major cadence at m. 194 starts the coda, with the viola closing the work out in bravura style.

Example 11.1 Enescu, *Concertstück for Viola and Piano*, mm. 133–38.

Initial reaction to Enescu's *Concertstück for Viola and Piano* was mixed, with the reviewer for *Le Radical* calling it "an exquisite piece, capricious, unpredictable, a charming fantasy."[19] But the reviewer for *Le Ménestrel* wrote that he "tried in vain to understand the plan, perhaps because there was none," and that it had "a certain number of harmonies, but not the hint of a melody."[20] Given the work's formal and thematic complexities, these comments seem understandable. Quickly gaining favor among violists, *Concertstück* was reused for the Paris Conservatoire's *concours* three more times (in 1913, 1920, and 1927). It has remained one of the most popular French-inspired showpieces for the instrument.

12

Cecil Forsyth: Concerto in G Minor
for Viola and Orchestra

I.   Moderato — Con moto, Agitato — Allegro con spirito
II. Andante un poco sostenuto
III. Allegro con fuoco

Date of Composition: 1903

First Edition: Cecil Forsyth, *Concerto sol mineur ~ g-Moll pour Viola et Orchestre ou Piano*, Mainz: B. Schott's Söhne, 1904, Plate No. 27459, Edition Schott No. 1077 (Piano Reduction); Cecil Forsyth, *Concerto*, Mainz: B. Schott's Söhne, [1910], Plate No. 47067 (Score)

Dedication: à son ami Férir [Émile Férir]

Date/Place of First Public Performance: September 12, 1903, Émile Férir (viola), Queen's Hall Orchestra, Henry J. Wood (conductor), Queen's Hall, London

Orchestral Instrumentation: Solo viola, 2 flutes, oboe, English horn, 2 clarinets, 2 bassoons, 4 horns in F, 2 trumpets in F, 3 trombones, tuba, timpani, cymbals, strings

Introduction

"He was regarded as a unique authority on music by all of his contemporaries, and even his elders, many of whom frequently sought his advice on technical matters. Amongst those who from time to time sat at his feet were Vaughan Williams, John Ireland and Frank Bridge."[1] Cecil Forsyth is primarily known for two things—his viola concerto and his *Orchestration* treatise. He was considered an expert on the subject of orchestration, with Ralph Vaughan Williams commenting that "Cecil Forsyth before he went to America 'vetted' many of my scores, giving out from his incomparable store of knowledge obtained 'straight from the horse's nosebag.'"[2] But Forsyth was mainly a composer of vocal music and a lover of opera who expended much energy—before the days of Benjamin Britten—toward building interest in native English operas. His failure in this undertaking, coupled with a disastrous marriage, led Forsyth to immigrate to America during World War I. Settling in New York, he began a new phase of his musical life working for the publisher H. W. Gray while continuing to write songs and books.

Biographical Sketch

Cecil Forsyth (1870–1941) was born in Greenwich, England, to Katherine and Alexander Forsyth; his father was a prominent physician originally from Edinburgh, Scotland. Little is known about his early musical training, though he played violin in his youth. From 1888 to 1891, he studied at the University of Edinburgh; class records do not document any musical studies while he was a student there, though Forsyth indicated that he first studied harmony with Herbert Stanley Oakeley, who was a longtime professor of music at the university. After publishing several songs in 1894, Forsyth entered the Royal College of Music (RCM) in 1896, initially studying theory and violin, but switching to composition and viola before he left in 1898. While at the RCM he studied composition with Hubert Parry and history with Charles Villiers Stanford, the legendary educators who influenced a new generation of English composers.[3]

After his studies at the RCM, Forsyth played viola in the Queen's Hall Orchestra, and it was here that he enjoyed his first great triumph as a composer in 1903 with the Concerto in G Minor for Viola and Orchestra, composed for Émile Férir, principal violist of the orchestra:

> The work is described by its composer as "an attempt to write a concerto in which the beauties and possibilities of the viola are used without any imitation of the technique of the violin or violoncello." He complains that the viola is so little used as a solo instrument that listeners, hearing it, usually make a sort of mental comparison of it with the violin and 'cello; and this, of course, is not only unfair, but leads to an overlooking of the individual merits of the viola. . . . The work is exceedingly refined, its scoring is delicate and reticent.[4]

During the nineteenth century, many composers had ignored the viola's potential as a solo instrument, and Forsyth's success with his concerto did wonders for both his reputation and the viola's. The concerto was revived on at least three other occasions in England by 1907 and was widely performed by violists over the next twenty years.

Following on the heels of his viola concerto, Forsyth produced additional orchestral works and turned toward operatic writing. These efforts met with less success, and he vented his frustration in his first book from 1911: *Music and*

Nationalism: A Study of English Opera, in which "he discusses the historical, political, and sociological causes concerning the lack of support for English National Opera."[5] While this book was well received, it was his next one—*Orchestration*, published in 1914—that would become a classic. Forsyth had become an expert on the history and development of instruments, in part thanks to the collection of instruments assembled at the RCM. His knowledge of instruments and keen understanding of orchestration in general make *Orchestration* a valuable contribution on this topic. But it is his caustic wit, which permeates the book, that makes the work a joy to read:

> If we turn now to the Scores that represent this period—that is to say the Haydn-, Mozart-, and even early Beethoven-Scores—we feel that the Viola is often merely a source of anxiety to the composer.... The instrument was there and had to be written for. Interesting but subordinate contrapuntal middle-parts were, however, still a thing of the future. The Viola, therefore, either did nothing or something which by the ingenuity of the composer was made to appear as much like nothing as possible.[6]

In 1914, Forsyth immigrated to America, working as an executive for the music publisher H. W. Gray. He continued to publish songs and choral works that gained a measure of popularity during his lifetime, the most successful being *The Bell-Man*, which was frequently sung by Richard Crooks,[7] "the most popular singer of the day," with whom William Primrose would later tour in joint recitals.[8] He also continued to publish books on various musical topics and kept in touch with friends from England on their visits to the United States. But he mostly stayed under the radar, leading a quietly respectable life in the musical world. Forsyth died on December 7, 1941, following a street accident that had befallen him weeks earlier.[9]

Forsyth's Concerto in G Minor for Viola and Orchestra

Forsyth's output consists principally of vocal and orchestral music; only a few short solo instrumental and chamber works by him are known. His compositions for viola include the Concerto in G Minor for Viola and Orchestra (1903); *Chanson Celtique*, for viola and orchestra (1905); *The Dark Road*, for viola and string orchestra (1922); and *Tiger, Tiger, Burning Bright: Song without Words for Viola and Piano (or Chamber Orchestra)* (1927). His early works, in particular, exhibit the influence of German music (which was revered by his teacher Hubert Parry), but they also display the influence of British and French sources. Like other composers of the English Musical Renaissance, Forsyth was involved in the research and preservation of British folk music. His *Chanson Celtique*, for viola and orchestra, incorporates an Irish tune from a collection that he helped organize.[10]

Written in 1903, Forsyth's Concerto in G Minor for Viola and Orchestra is dedicated to the principal violist of the Queen's Hall Orchestra, Émile Férir, who would go on to hold principal viola positions with orchestras in Boston, Philadelphia, and Los Angeles. Férir trained in Brussels under Eugène Ysaÿe and Léon Firket, and his technique undoubtedly inspired the virtuosity of the solo part. Written in a late-Romantic style in the standard three-movement format (fast–slow–fast), the work displays Forsyth's flair for melody and orchestral color while also demonstrating his love of song and opera. The first movement, in sonata form (Chart 12.1), begins in a dramatic, operatic fashion. Dispensing with a lengthy opening orchestral tutti, Forsyth has the viola enter immediately after a *ff* orchestral G, playing an extended, recitative-like solo passage. Measure 2 follows the same pattern—this time starting with a C#°7 chord—before moving to the Moderato section. Forsyth continues the dramatic buildup as the viola persists with recitative-like statements over tremolo strings, while the cellos and basses hint at thematic material that will appear in the exposition. The intensity increases at m. 26 as the orchestra, now Con moto, Agitato, continues its foreshadowing of the exposition with fragments of thematic material ending on a *ff* C°7 chord. The exposition proper begins at m. 47 (Allegro con spirito) with a sweeping viola melody (Unit 1.1) over triplet wind chords. After a tutti statement at m. 64 (Letter F; all rehearsal letters refer to the Schott edition), the solo viola enters with new thematic material in m. 71 (Unit 1.2). Forsyth combines these two thematic ideas at m. 79 (Letter G) with the orchestra playing Unit 1.2 material while the viola revisits the opening Unit 1.1 motive.

The second theme group starts in the relative major of B♭, though from the shape and pitches of the solo line, it appears that the viola wants to remain in G minor (Ex. 12.1). The tonal ambiguity of this theme is compounded by its initial fragmented appearance in the introduction at m. 30, where a C7 chord resolved to F minor (Ex. 12.2). A relatively brief development section follows, which is extended by a written-out cadenza. The timpani joins in for the final seven measures of the cadenza, with the recapitulation starting at m. 199 (Allegro). Theme Group 2 now appears in the parallel major at m. 235 followed by an animated coda with the solo part concluding in a flourish of arpeggios spanning all four strings.

Forsyth makes extensive use of chromaticism in the second movement, which is cast in an ABA form (Chart 12.2). After an introductory wind chorale that opens in D minor, the solo viola begins section A with pickups to m. 17 (Letter C), establishing the movement's primary tonal center of D major. The solo viola leads the muted orchestral strings in a lovely chorale, filled with suspensions and seventh chords. The thematic material moves to E minor at m. 49 (Letter D) before the viola gives way to the English horn at m. 63 (Letter E), now tonicizing E major. The B section (mm. 76–120) brings a change in tempo, *con moto*, and mood, with the viola playing ferociously (*feroce*) over tremolo orchestral strings. The tension builds, briefly pulling back at m. 100 with a change of orchestral texture, and then moving forward with a *sempre stringendo* at m. 110 as the viola

Zone	Thematic Areas/Snippet	Measures	Principal Tonal Areas/Function
Introduction		1–46	
	Unit 1.1: Solo	1–25	Begins G minor; Moderato begins B-flat minor; modulates
	Unit 1.2: Tutti	26–46	Dominant (diminished chords)
Exposition		47–137	
	Theme Group 1	47–104 (Let. I)	
	Unit 1.1	47–71	G minor
	Unit 1.2 (with Unit 1.1 material)	71–104 (Let. I)	G minor; D minor; D major
	Theme Group 2	104 (Let. I)–37	B-flat major; G major; F major
Development		138 (Let. K)–70	
	Solo development	138 (Let. K)– 58 (Let. M)	Starts with an upward sequential progression (by major seconds)
	Tutti transition	158 (Let. M)–70	Sequential
Cadenza		171–98	Dominant

Chart 12.1 Forsyth, Concerto in G Minor for Viola and Orchestra: Structural analysis, first movement, Moderato — Con moto, Agitato — Allegro con spirito.

Zone	Thematic Areas/Snippet	Measures	Principal Tonal Areas/Function
Recapitulation		199–249	
	Theme Group 1	199–234	
	Unit 1.1a: Solo	199–217 (Let. P)	G minor; modulates sequentially
	Unit 1.1b: Tutti	217 (Let. P)–34	Sequential; moves to a dominant function
	Theme Group 2	235–49	G major; E minor
Coda		250–78	Begins A minor; modulates to G major

Chart 12.1 (continued) Forsyth, Concerto in G Minor for Viola and Orchestra: Structural analysis, first movement, Moderato — Con moto, Agitato — Allegro con spirito.

Example 12.1 Forsyth, Concerto in G Minor for Viola and Orchestra, movt. I, mm. 104–7, solo viola.

Example 12.2 Forsyth, Concerto in G Minor for Viola and Orchestra, movt. I, mm. 30–32, orchestral reduction.

Zone	Thematic Areas/Snippet	Measures	Principal Tonal Areas/Function
Introduction		1–16	Begins D minor; modulates
A		17 (Let. C)–75	D major; E minor; E major; highly chromatic
B		76 (Let. F)– 120 (Let. H)	Begins A minor; modulates
A		120 (Let. H)–71	
	Unit 1.1: Tutti	120 (Let. H)–40	D major; lots of stepwise chromaticism
	Unit 1.2: Solo	140–71	Predominant to dominant; moves to D major

Chart 12.2 Forsyth, Concerto in G Minor for Viola and Orchestra: Structural analysis, second movement, Andante un poco sostenuto.

makes its way to a climactic high point in mm. 119–20. The orchestra takes over at m. 120 (Letter H) with a forceful recasting of the A section, but calm returns when the viola re-enters in m. 140 to serenely close out the movement.

The third movement is in an expansive ABAB form (Chart 12.3), a common form for strophic songs that borders here on sonata form. This movement, like the first, opens dramatically: a run of eighth notes in the violins hurriedly propels the movement forward; the dust from the introductory tutti settles with a timpani roll in measures 17 through 20. The dotted rhythms in section A pay homage to Forsyth's Scottish heritage, while the extensive use of multiple stopping showcases the stout tonal qualities of the viola, another way that Forsyth shows off "the beauties and possibilities" of the instrument. In contrast, section B features a sweeping, lyrical melody in E♭ major, which Forsyth interrupts with more multiple stops at m. 211 as a bridge to a return of the A section at m. 239. The lyrical B section returns at m. 276, this time in G major, with Forsyth bookending the movement with a compact coda, where a frenzy of eighth notes in the winds and solo viola give way to an abrupt orchestral conclusion in G major.

An immediate success, Forsyth's Concerto in G Minor for Viola and Orchestra was critically well-received at its premiere: "A very refined gift of melody and the power of inventing characteristic themes both belong to Mr. Forsyth, while his ability for emotional expression was impressively shown in the beautiful slow

Zone	Thematic Areas/Snippet	Measures	Principal Tonal Areas/Function
Introduction		1–22	G minor
A		23–146	
	Unit 1.1	23–67 (Let. D)	G minor
	Unit 1.2	67 (Let. D)–117 (Let. G)	D minor
	Unit 1.3: Tutti	117 (Let. G)–46	G minor
B		147 (Let. H)–211	E-flat major; modulates
Bridge		211–38	Dominant
A		239–75	G minor
B		276–328	G major
Coda		328–55	G major

Chart 12.3 Forsyth, Concerto in G Minor for Viola and Orchestra: Structural analysis, third movement, Allegro con fuoco.

movement."[11] It was also well-received by violists, who were in need of original works, particularly ones that were written so advantageously for the viola. After enjoying widespread popularity for twenty years, the work fell out of favor during the middle of the twentieth century, but it has been resurrected in recent years. "Forsyth was another Romantic who's been neglected," said Lawrence Power, whose outstanding recording of the work released in 2005 jump-started its revival. "His concerto is a really touching piece of music. . . . with a real melting pot of influences."[12]

13

Lillian Fuchs: *Sonata Pastorale* for *Unaccompanied Viola*

I.   Fantasia
II. Pastorale
[III. Allegro]

Date of Composition: c. 1953

First Edition: Lillian Fuchs, *Sonata Pastorale for Unaccompanied Viola*, New York: Associated Music Publishers, 1956, Plate No. AMP - 95519 - 7

Dedication: To Rosalie J. Leventritt

Date/Place of First Public Performance: March 9, 1953, Lillian Fuchs (viola), Town Hall, New York

Introduction

"For the personality of the writing, as a showpiece for the violist and *for the viola*, and as the crown of Miss Fuchs's devotion to her chosen instrument, the *Sonata Pastorale* deserves great esteem."[1] Lillian Fuchs's devotion to her chosen instrument, the viola, was boundless, and her solid technique and superb musicality enabled a brilliant career as teacher, soloist, chamber musician, and recording artist. Her championship of J. S. Bach's cello suites on viola, through her teaching and recordings, was integral to their adoption as standards of the viola repertoire. She was also a champion of contemporary music who inspired numerous composers, including Bohuslav Martinů and Quincy Porter, to compose works for her. A composer herself, Fuchs made several notable contributions to the viola literature. Appreciation of these compositions has grown over time, bringing further recognition to Fuchs and her remarkable lifetime devoted to the viola.

Biographical Sketch

Lillian Fuchs (1902–1995) was born in New York City to Philip and Kate Fuchs; her father was an amateur violinist who offered free lessons to neighboring children.[2] Both of her brothers played string instruments: her younger brother, Harry, played cello, while her older brother, Joseph, played the violin. After early studies on the piano, Lillian was inspired by Joseph's playing to take up the violin, initially studying with Louis Svečenski, violist of the Kneisel Quartet. She would continue "following in her brother's footsteps" by enrolling at the Institute of Musical Art (which would later become the Juilliard School), studying violin with Franz Kneisel and composition with Percy Goetschius.[3] Upon graduation in 1924, she won honors for both her violin playing and her work in composition.

Like many violists before and since, Lillian's conversion to viola came about through a desire to play chamber music. In 1926, she fulfilled a request by Franz Kneisel to play viola in his daughter Marianne's quartet; the following year she accepted a position as violist of the Perolé String Quartet. She also had occasion to perform chamber music with Jascha Heifetz, Mischa Elman, and the Budapest String Quartet, identifying a concert played with the latter ensemble in the mid-1930s as a "turning point in her career because it immediately increased her stature as a chamber music artist."[4]

Another turning point occurred in 1945, when she appeared as soloist with her brother Joseph in W. A. Mozart's Sinfonia concertante, K. 364 at Carnegie Hall. The reviews were glowing, especially for Lillian: "The viola playing of Miss Fuchs was particularly delightful, and, if one must choose, it may be said that she communicated rather more of the essence of Mozart than did her virtuoso brother."[5] The praise for Lillian was meaningful, as she had long felt overshadowed by her brother: "I just developed quietly because nobody ever paid any attention to me even in my family. They were always fussing over Joseph."[6] In addition to furthering the solo careers of each, the concert spurred them to continue their collaboration. When Joseph became a co-founder of the Musicians' Guild in 1947, the pair began to regularly program duos together, earning them fame as one of the great violin-viola partnerships. Even still, there remained a bit of sibling rivalry between them, apparent during a recording session for Mozart's Sinfonia concertante in 1961: "The soloists vied constantly with one another for control of subtle changes of tempo; it was a classic example of two strong wills in conflict. Lillian would have her way no matter what, stamping her foot if things were not right."[7]

Music and family would remain intertwined throughout Fuchs's life. While playing chamber music with friends in the 1920s, she met her future husband,

Ludwig Stein—a businessman and amateur violinist and violist. Fuchs credited the financial and emotional support that he provided as enabling her to pursue a professional musical career while also raising a family.[8] Their twin daughters, cellist Barbara Stein Mallow and violinist Carol Stein Amado, were born in 1935. In addition to performing with their mother privately at home, they also performed publicly with her in the early 1980s as the Lillian Fuchs String Trio.

Teaching formed a substantial part of Fuchs's career, though for many years she chose not to be associated with a major conservatory, offering private lessons for free. She eventually joined the faculty of the Manhattan School of Music in 1962, teaching chamber music, and later joined the faculty of Juilliard in 1971. Fuchs was associated with other schools and summer training programs, notably the Aspen Music Festival and School. In 1979, the American String Teachers Association honored her with the ASTA Artist-Teacher Award (her brother Joseph had previously won in 1971). Always upholding the highest artistic ideals, she earned a reputation as a demanding—but caring—teacher, who "was truly concerned about each student's progress."[9] Fuchs also believed that teaching the viola required "entirely individual treatment for each student,"[10] mostly due to the non-standard size of the instrument. Through her nurturing and careful attention, she inspired students to be the best musicians that they could be. She continued teaching at conservatories past the age of ninety and died on October 5, 1995, at the Actors Fund Nursing Home in Englewood, New Jersey.[11]

Fuchs's *Sonata Pastorale for Unaccompanied Viola*

With so many competing musical endeavors, Fuchs found little time for composing; among her small published output are four works for solo viola: *Twelve Caprices for Viola* (c. 1948; published 1950), *Sonata Pastorale for Unaccompanied Viola* (c. 1953), *Sixteen Fantasy Etudes* (1959), and *Fifteen Characteristic Studies for Viola* (1965). The *Sonata Pastorale* is her only concert work for viola and is dedicated to Rosalie J. Leventritt, a friend and patron who shared Lillian's birthday.[12]

The published edition of the sonata lists only two movements, "Fantasia" and "Pastorale," and those are the movements that have been used for identification and numbering purposes here (Chart 13.1; the published music contains neither measure numbers nor rehearsal letters or numbers). However, several other sources list a third movement separate from the "Pastorale," starting at either the Allegro (m. 73) or the energico (m. 84).[13] Elements of the sonata resemble her earlier *Twelve Caprices*, and Fuchs indicated that "the Sonata is a direct result of these caprices."[14] Most recognizable is the use of drones from Caprice No. 3 and No. 6, with similar melodic material in the first movement of the sonata (Exs. 13.1 and 13.2).

Movement	Tempo Marking	Measures
I. Fantasia		1–121
	Maestoso	1–12
	Risoluto	13–20
	Allegro	21–121
II. Pastorale Andante semplice portion		1–72
	Andante semplice	1–62
	Tempo I	63–72
II. Pastorale Allegro portion		73–201
	Allegro	73–83
	energico	84–120
	L'istesso tempo	121–44
	Maestoso	145–56
	Risoluto	157–64
	Allegro	165–75
	energico	176–85
	più vivo	186–201

Chart 13.1 Fuchs, *Sonata Pastorale for Unaccompanied Viola*, table of published movements with tempo markings and measure numbers.

Example 13.1 Fuchs, *Twelve Caprices for Viola*, No. III, mm. 37–38.

Example 13.2 Fuchs, *Sonata Pastorale for Unaccompanied Viola*, movt. I, mm. 85–88.

The first movement alternates thematic statements with contrasting rhythmic linking passages (Chart 13.2). After three introductory measures, the quietly tender primary theme begins in m. 4. A series of accelerating sixteenth notes in m. 12 segues to the Risoluto, characterized by a dotted-eighth–sixteenth-note figure that extends into the following Allegro. At the pickup to m. 28, the primary theme appears again, this time set against an open-string drone. The drone recurs at m. 36 with the undulating melodic material descending through a fully chromatic scale. Another linking passage begins at m. 59 with the primary theme returning at the pickup to m. 77. While the drone and melodic material were set far apart in the second thematic statement, Fuchs sets them close together here. After the final linking passage (mm. 101–12), the movement closes with material drawn from mm. 40–46.

The second movement is built around the pitch center C, with the Andante semplice portion (mm. 1–72) starting in the C Dorian mode and the Allegro portion

Zone	Thematic Areas/Snippet	Measures
Thematic Statement 1		1–12
Linking Passage 1		13–27
Thematic Statement 2		28–59
Linking Passage 2		59–76
Thematic Statement 3		77–101
Linking Passage 3		101–12
Closing		113–21

Chart 13.2 Fuchs, *Sonata Pastorale for Unaccompanied Viola*: Structural analysis, first movement, "Fantasia."

(mm. 73–201) built around C minor. With its largely monophonic writing, quiet dynamics, and slow pulse (in the first forty-six measures, the shortest duration is a quarter note), the Andante semplice portion evokes the simple life implied by the term "pastorale." Fuchs would frequently escape New York City for the peace and quiet of her family's farm in rural Pennsylvania, and this portion offers a similarly idyllic respite from the sonata's more animated areas.

Fuchs uses the Allegro at m. 73 to deftly transition from the prior pastoral mood to the vigorous energico one at m. 84. The Allegro portion (mm. 73–201) of movement II incorporates earlier material, either obliquely or quoted in full. Rhythmically and melodically, the energico section resembles the "linking passages" of the first movement; for example, mm. 106–9 outlines an exact enharmonic statement from the Risoluto section of movement I (Exs. 13.3 and 13.4). Fuchs returns to the Andante semplice portion's melodic material in m. 121 (L'istesso tempo), giving way to a full return of the sonata's opening in m. 145 (Maestoso). Twenty measures later, the Allegro and energico material returns, and the sonata culminates with the frenzied *più vivo* at m. 186, propelling the work to its "whirlwind ending."[15]

The *Sonata Pastorale for Unaccompanied Viola* was positively received at its premiere by the reviewer for the *New York Times*: "The sonata is attractively written. The slow movement reveals that Miss Fuchs has a pleasant gift of melodic inventiveness."[16] Fuchs performed the sonata herself on many later occasions, and the work gained a following shortly after publication, thanks in part to its promotion by her students. It has remained popular among violists, who admire its effective display of the tonal and technical capabilities of the viola.

Example 13.3 Fuchs, *Sonata Pastorale for Unaccompanied Viola*, movt. I, mm. 13–14.

Example 13.4 Fuchs, *Sonata Pastorale for Unaccompanied Viola*, movt. II, mm. 106–9 (lower notes only are displayed) with enharmonic notes corresponding to Ex. 13.3 indicated by †.

14

Aleksandr Glazunov: *Élégie for Viola and Piano*, op. 44

Date of Composition: Completed October 12, 1893

First Edition: Alexandre Glazounow, *Elégie pour Alto avec accompagnement de Piano, Op. 44*, Leipzig: M. P. Belaieff, 1894, Plate No. 858

Select Later Editions: Alexander Glasunow, *Elegie g-Moll für Viola und Klavier, Opus 44*, ed. Rüdiger Bornhöft, Frankfurt: C. F. Peters, 2011, Plate No. 33165, EP 11327; Alexander Glasunow, *Élégie Opus 44 für Viola und Klavier*, ed. Dominik Rahmer, Munich: Henle, 2014, HN 1241

Dedication: A son ami Monsieur Franz Hildebrand

Date/Place of Early Public Performance: April 15, 1894, Pierre Monteux (viola), Société nationale de musique concert, Paris

Introduction

"Glazunov began changing the moment he became director of the Petersburg Conservatory and eventually he turned into another person altogether."[1] The story of Glazunov reads like that of two separate individuals, divided by the turn of a century and two vastly different worlds. The Glazunov of the nineteenth century, affectionately called "Sasha," enjoyed seemingly effortless success as a composer, earning admiration from his elder Russian peers, including Pyotr Tchaikovsky and members of The Five (Mighty Handful). By the beginning of the twentieth century, Glazunov was, himself, an elder musical statesman. Thrust into administrative duties, he found himself desperately trying to reconcile a society torn apart by war and revolution. Like many, he fell victim to the perilous times that would follow, with his living conditions greatly reduced.[2] But he still held a position of respect and influence, which he wielded for the benefit of students at the St. Petersburg Conservatory, willingly sacrificing "his time, his serenity, and finally, his creativity."[3]

Biographical Sketch

Aleksandr Glazunov (1865–1936) was born into a wealthy family in St. Petersburg, Russia. His father, Konstantin Ilyich, was a book publisher and amateur violinist, and his mother, Elena Pavlovna, a pianist. In his youth, Glazunov studied the piano and was "encouraged to play the viola and cello," to partake in chamber music with the family.[4] After piano and harmony studies with N. Elenkovsky, Glazunov next studied with Nikolay Rimsky-Korsakov, on the recommendation of Mily Balakirev:

> Casually, Balakireff once brought me the composition of a 14 or 15 year old high school student, Sasha Glazunoff. It was an orchestral score written in childish fashion. The boy's talent was indubitably clear. Shortly afterwards (in the season of 1879–80) Balakireff introduced him that he might take up studies under me. While giving lessons in elementary theory to his mother Yelyena Pavlovna Glazunova, I began also to teach the youthful Sasha.[5]

Glazunov progressed rapidly as a composer and fortuitously came to the attention of Mitrofan Belyayev, a timber merchant and amateur violinist and violist. Belyayev became Glazunov's patron, guiding his career and arranging performances of his music. In 1885, Belyayev founded the M. P. Belaieff publishing house, principally to issue Glazunov's music.[6] During the following years, Glazunov produced an impressive number of critically acclaimed compositions. He earned admiration for his technique as an orchestrator and for his astounding musical memory (there are numerous accounts of Glazunov playing back or writing down music that he had heard only once).[7]

In 1899, Glazunov's career began to turn with his appointment as professor of orchestration and composition at the St. Petersburg Conservatory. The 1905 Russian Revolution brought upheaval to the school and prompted Glazunov's resignation, but he returned at the end of the year and was elected director of the conservatory shortly afterward. In this position, Glazunov became a fierce advocate for the students' welfare. Glazunov's advocacy took many forms at the conservatory: he renounced his salary, established an opera studio and a philharmonic orchestra, and assisted Jewish students who endured anti-Semitic laws.[8] As Russia suffered through World War I and the rise of the communist state, Glazunov fought to obtain necessities for his students, including food and firewood. He knew the names of all his students and reportedly knew what pieces they played and "exactly where a given student had made mistakes during an examination."[9]

In 1928, Glazunov traveled to Vienna for celebrations marking the centennial of Franz Schubert's death. He elected to remain abroad, though he would retain his position as director of the conservatory for two more years. Settling near Paris, he married Olga Gavrilova in 1929, adopting her daughter, Elena.[10] During his final years, Glazunov spent time traveling, conducting, and composing, though deteriorating health limited his activities. Glazunov died in 1936 and was buried in Neuilly-sur-Seine, France. His body was returned to Russia in 1972, where he was reburied at the Tikhvinskoe Cemetery at the Aleksandr Nevskii Monastery in St. Petersburg, reuniting him with former colleagues, including Tchaikovsky and Rimsky-Korsakov.

Glazunov's *Élégie for Viola and Piano*, op. 44

Though Glazunov composed in a variety of formats, orchestral works make up roughly half of his output. Among his chamber works are a number of short "salon pieces of the sort that wiled away many a dull evening in a St Petersburg winter."[11] Glazunov's single contribution to the viola literature, the *Élégie for Viola and Piano*, op. 44, is such a work. *Élégie* is dedicated to Franz Hildebrand, a leading chamber musician and viola player during the late nineteenth century who premiered works by major Russian composers, including Glazunov.[12] Originally from Copenhagen, Hildebrand was engaged in the Imperial Chapel in St. Petersburg in 1868. He also taught at the St. Petersburg Music School and was offered a position as viola professor at the Imperial Conservatory, which he declined.[13] A documented performance of the *Élégie* by Hildebrand has remained elusive, though he presumably performed it on some occasion. While the autograph manuscript indicates that the work was completed on October 12, 1893, it likely originated as a work for Belyayev during the summer of 1886.[14] Belyayev frequently played viola in chamber gatherings, and the fairly limited technical demands of the viola part seem more appropriate for the amateur Belyayev rather than the professional Hildebrand.

The *Élégie* is in an ABA form with coda (Chart 14.1). With its lilting accompaniment and flowing melodic line, the work is essentially a barcarolle in a nontraditional meter of $\frac{9}{8}$.[15] A placid sense of calm prevails, owing to the work's fairly static harmonic scheme and rhythmic consistency: there is no duration shorter than an eighth note, and there are only a few measures without an eighth note at the end of each beat (specifically m. 48, mm. 71–72, m. 111, m. 113, and mm. 115–17).

After a two-measure introduction, the viola enters with its gliding melody. The piano remains in the background, coming to the fore in m. 31 and briefly taking over the melody at m. 35. As the viola resumes the melody in m. 39, the

Zone	Thematic Areas/Snippet	Measures	Principal Tonal Areas/Function
A		1–48	G minor
B		49–74	E-flat major
A		75–101	G minor
Coda		102–17	G minor

Chart 14.1 Glazunov, *Élégie for Viola and Piano*, op. 44: Structural analysis.

music becomes agitated and crescendos to the first f of the piece in m. 43. The intensity quickly subsides as the section winds down with a slight ritard in m. 48 leading into the B section.

Like the opening of the A section, the B section's theme is marked *dolce*. Contrast is achieved through the major mode and greater use of the viola's upper register. In m. 67, the music once again becomes agitated with the viola climbing to a high d[iii] before quickly pulling back with the *calando* at m. 71. Glazunov's omission of a final eighth note on the first beat of m. 71 is striking, since it dramatically suspends the momentum, setting the stage for the transition back to the A section at m. 75. After a shortened restatement of the A section, the coda at m. 102 provides a sense of poignant reflection, with the viola repeating an upwardly questioning figure before resignedly descending into despair.

In 1918, the influential critic and musicologist Boris Asaf'yev wrote that "the redeeming beauty of Glazunov's music lies in the noble 'portly' balance of his lyricism, which is sincere and of crystalline transparency."[16] The *Élégie for Viola and Piano*, op. 44 embodies these qualities with its soaring lyricism and perfectly balanced instrumentation. The entirely monophonic writing for the viola and frequent quiet dynamics creates an ethereal atmosphere, with the viola floating over the piano. The *Élégie* became popular immediately after publication, particularly in France, where it was programmed multiple times before the end of the nineteenth century. It remains one of the most popular salon pieces written for viola and piano.

15

Paul Hindemith: Sonata for Viola and Piano, op. 11, no. 4

I.   Fantasie
II. Thema mit Variationen
III. Finale (mit Variationen)

Date of Composition: February 27–March 9, 1919

First Edition: Paul Hindemith, *Sonate, Bratsche und Klavier, Opus 11 Nr. 4*, Mainz: B. Schott's Söhne, 1922, Plate No. 30597

Date/Place of First Public Performance: June 2, 1919, Paul Hindemith (viola), Emma Lübbecke-Job (piano), Kleiner Saal des Saalbaues, Frankfurt am Main

Introduction

"I cannot give analyses of my works because I don't know how to explain a piece of music in a few words (I would rather write a new one in the time). Besides I think that for people with ears my things are perfectly easy to understand, so an analysis is superfluous. For people without ears such cribs can't help."[1] Written in 1922, this statement expresses the wry humor that is often associated with Paul Hindemith. It also underscores a key aspect of his musical philosophy: that music should be playable by performers and understandable by audiences. Hindemith expressed this concept more forcefully in 1927:

> It is to be regretted that in general so little relationship exists today between the producers and the consumers of music. A composer should write today only if he knows for what purpose he is writing. The days of composing for the sake of composing are perhaps gone forever. On the other hand, the demand for music is so great that composer and consumer ought most emphatically to come at last to an understanding.[2]

From the "performers as consumers" perspective, no group of instrumentalists appreciates Paul Hindemith's music more than violists. Audiences' attitudes toward Hindemith, however, have fluctuated over the years. But one work that has remained a favorite of performers and audiences is his Sonata for Viola and Piano, op. 11, no. 4, the composer's first foray into the viola repertoire.

Biographical Sketch, 1895–1932

Born in Hanau, Paul Hindemith (1895–1963) was the eldest of Maria Sophie and Robert Rudolf Hindemith's three children. His father, who worked as a house painter, struggled to support the family, and Paul lived with his paternal grandparents in Naumburg am Queis, Lower Silesia, from 1899 to 1902. Passionate about music, Robert Rudolf subjected his children "to unrelenting musical training from early childhood."[3] Paul's instrument was the violin; his early studies were with Eugen Reinhardt in Mühlheim. In 1907, he began studies with Anna Hegner in Frankfurt. After Hegner moved to Switzerland in 1908, Hindemith transferred to Hegner's own teacher, Adolf Rebner. In the winter of 1908, Hindemith entered the Hoch Conservatory as a student of Rebner's. While Hindemith's focus was on the violin during his first years at the conservatory, he also dabbled with composing. In 1912, he added composition studies: first with Arnold Mendelssohn and then with Bernhard Sekles.[4] Hindemith soon found himself in demand as a violinist: starting in 1913, he accepted a string of professional violin engagements. In 1915, he joined Rebner's string quartet as second violinist and also joined the Frankfurter Opern- und Museumsorchester, where he eventually rose to the rank of first concertmaster.

World War I greatly affected the Hindemith family: Robert Rudolf was killed in combat in September 1915, and Paul, himself, was conscripted in August 1917. He officially served as a drummer in the regimental band but—thanks to his commanding officers' enjoyment of music—spent much of his time playing string quartets:

> Recently, when our dear Count [the regimental commanding officer] died so suddenly, we were all in a mood of deep depression. No one knew what would happen next; we were left hanging by a thread with our quartet. But now all our worries are over. The count has a worthy successor, a colonel who in civil life is court intendent in Gera and knows a lot about music. Everything remains as it was. He has quartets played to him, and, since he is familiar with the entire

chamber music repertoire, he arranges his own programmes. He is a very attentive listener, so playing for him is a pleasure. — Now to tell you something
amusing. I have been made a corporal. Not on account of bravery or any other
of my military virtues, but just because the last time we played quartets for him
our colonel amused himself by "giving me a stripe." If the war goes on long
enough, I'll maybe finish up a captain![5]

After the war, Hindemith returned to his concertmaster position in Frankfurt
but switched to playing viola in the Rebner Quartet.[6] On June 2, 1919, he
presented a recital of his own compositions in the Kleiner Saal (small hall) at the
Frankfurt Saalbau. Shortly after this recital, the publisher B. Schott's Söhne accepted Hindemith's String Quartet, op. 10 for publication, beginning a long and
profitable relationship for both parties.[7] The young composer earned a measure
of notoriety with the premiere of his one-act operas *Mörder, Hoffnung der Frauen*
and *Das Nusch-Nuschi* on June 4, 1921; the audience was scandalized by the
sexual themes in both operas as well as Hindemith's overt parodying of German
Romantic composers (notably Richard Wagner) in *Das Nusch-Nuschi*. Later that
year, a performance of his String Quartet, op. 16 at the Donaueschingen Festival
led to the formation of the Amar Quartet; Hindemith played viola with the ensemble from its inception until 1929.

In 1924, Hindemith married Gertrud Rottenberg, who would go on to handle
many aspects of his professional business affairs. By this time, he was being
"hailed as the leading representative of the new generation of composers in
Germany."[8] Hindemith accepted an appointment to teach composition at the
Hochschule für Musik in Berlin in 1927. Even with his activities as a composer
and teacher, Hindemith furthered his status as a leading viola soloist during the
late 1920s and early 1930s. In addition to performing his own compositions, he
premiered viola concertos by William Walton and Darius Milhaud in 1929.[9]
During this period, he also turned his attention to new musical interests, including mechanical music, ancient instruments, works for amateurs, and
the Jugendmusikbewegung (youth music movement).[10] In 1930, Hindemith
stressed the importance of his work in these areas while responding to a request
from Elizabeth Sprague Coolidge:

> I could set about writing a piece for you at the end of June after the conclusion
> of the music festival here in Berlin. All the same, there are still certain consid-
> erations on my side. In the last few years, I have turned my back almost com-
> pletely on concert music and have been writing almost exclusively for amateurs,
> for children, for radio, for mechanical instruments etc. I consider composing
> in this manner to be more important than writing for concert purposes, since

the latter is little more than a technical exercise for a musician and contributes hardly anything to the development of music.[11]

Hindemith's comments here reflect an emerging philosophical distinction between *eigenständige Musik* (autonomous music) and *Gebrauchsmusik* (utility music). *Eigenständige Musik*, in which aesthetic considerations were often considered paramount, was associated with concert music, while *Gebrauchsmusik*, in which aesthetic considerations were considered "secondary or even irrelevant," was the music of everyday life, intended to serve a useful purpose.[12] While the concept of *Gebrauchsmusik* reflects many of Hindemith's musical attitudes of the time, he later expressed displeasure with the term's association with him:

> When . . . I first came to [the United States], I felt like the sorcerer's apprentice who had become the victim of his own conjurations: the slogan *Gebrauchsmusik* hit me wherever I went, it had grown to be as abundant, useless, and disturbing as thousands of dandelions in a lawn. Apparently it met perfectly the common desire for a verbal label which classifies objects, persons, and problems, thus exempting anyone from opinions based on knowledge.[13]

Hindemith's Sonata for Viola and Piano, op. 11, no. 4

Overall, Hindemith's compositions are marked by "a distaste for self-indulgent expression and an emphasis on clarity of line, texture, and form."[14] His earliest compositions display a variety of influences, including Romanticism, Impressionism, and Expressionism. In the 1920s, he became a leading representative of the Neue Sachlichkeit (New Objectivity) movement in Germany, in which artists moved away from "Impressionistically vague" and "Expressionistically abstract" tendencies toward a more "positive, tangible reality."[15] Given Hindemith's emphasis on "clarity of line," as well as his interest in earlier models of music, the terms "neo-Baroque" and "neo-classical" have frequently been applied to his music.

Hindemith composed seven sonatas for viola: Sonata for Viola and Piano, op. 11, no. 4 (1919); Sonata for Solo Viola, op. 11, no. 5 (1919); Sonata for Solo Viola, op. 25, no. 1 (1922); Sonata for Viola and Piano, op. 25, no. 4 (1922); Sonata for Solo Viola, op. 31, no. 4 (1923); Sonata for Solo Viola (1937); and Sonata for Viola and Piano (1939). The two sonatas from 1919 are part of his opus 11 set, "the first batch in the large output of instrumental sonatas which form so important a part of his life's work."[16] While working on two sonatinas for violin in 1918 (which would ultimately become the opus 11, no. 1 and opus 11, no. 2 sonatas), he wrote to his friend Emmy Ronnefeldt:

> I want to write a whole series of these sonatinas, which in fact = small sonatas, since they are too lengthy for sonatinas. Each one is to be totally different in character from the one before, in form too. I want to see whether in a series of pieces I can extend the expressive possibilities—which are not very great in this kind of music and with this combination of instruments—and bring them closer to the horizon. Many years will pass before I finish this work—if I live to see it, or keep my health. I believe it will be an interesting task.[17]

The Sonata for Viola and Piano, op. 11, no. 4 is distinct in character and form from the rest of the opus 11 set (and from Hindemith's later sonatas for viola). It was composed between February 27 and March 9, 1919, but includes material from Hindemith's earlier sketchbooks.[18] Exhibiting German, Russian, and French influences, the sonata is clearly indebted to Claude Debussy. While sections of the work have clear tonal centers, traditional harmonic aspects, including dominant-tonic cadences and diminished-seventh chords, are used sparingly.[19] The piano score is preceded by this text:

> Note: The Sonata is to be played without pauses between the movements. The second and third movements, especially, must be so closely connected that the listener does not have the impression of hearing a Finale, but grasps the last movement only as a continuation of the Variations.[20]

Effectively serving as a prologue to the remaining movements, the opening "Fantasie" has a free-flowing, improvisatory quality. The thematic material for the short, forty-measure movement is derived from the first three measures; only two measures (m. 4 and m. 31) contain material that cannot be traced back to this opening motive.[21] Centered on F major, the movement opens calmly (*Ruhig*) and quietly with a singing melody in the viola. The music soon becomes restless: the piano's glittering thirty-second notes in mm. 10–13 give way to the viola's *veloce* passage in m. 14, which then broadens out (*Sehr breit*), culminating with the viola's cadenza in m. 16 on a dominant (C major) harmony. Quiet returns at the *Im Zeitmaß* (*a tempo*) section at m. 17 with fluttering utterances in the viola. Hindemith once again propels the music forward with an *un poco accelerando* in m. 27, reining in the momentum with a *ritard* four measures later in preparation for a return of the full opening motive in mm. 32–35. The movement ends with three iterations of the viola's D-major figure from m. 3 in different registers (mm. 34–38) followed by a final iteration, raised by a major third (mm. 39–40), which connects the first movement with the second.

The second movement (Chart 15.1) is cast as a theme with four variations. Fluctuating between $\frac{2}{4}$ and $\frac{3}{4}$, the Theme section (mm. 1–33) is centered on E♭ minor. The opening ten-measure period presents two iterations of the five-measure folk-like melody, the first (mm. 2–6) ending on the dominant and the second (mm. 7–11) on an E♭ major chord. At m. 13 (No. 4; all rehearsal numbers refer to the Schott edition), the viola presents a new idea in a passage that intermingles whole-tone scales with descending chromatic embellishments. Starting at m. 20, the piano interjects two elided statements of the opening melody (mm. 20–28), while the viola contributes a descending chromatic line in mm. 24–28. The section ends with the viola's statement of the five-measure melody ending on E♭ minor (mm. 29–33).

The graceful Variation I, in $\frac{6}{8}$, persists with aspects from the opening Theme, including the principal key area of E♭ minor, descending chromatic lines, and whole-tone passages. Whole tones also figure prominently in Variation II, marked "a little capricious" (*ein wenig kapriziös*). In this lengthy variation, the impish viola and sprightly piano romp together in an enchanting manner. The lyrical, flowing Variation III follows, with Hindemith highlighting material from mm. 12–20 of the Theme section in mm. 120–28. Variation IV, marked "even more lively" (*noch lebhafter*), gushes forth directly from the previous one. This short, nine-measure variation "is nothing but an elaboration of the whole-tone ostinato G♯–F♯–E–D."[22] Above this ostinato, the viola surges ahead with a syncopated version of the principal melody, which collides directly into the following movement.

Zone	Thematic Areas/Snippet	Measures	Principal Tonal Areas/Function
Theme		1–33	E-flat minor
Variation I		34–65	E-flat minor
Variation II		66–112	Whole-tone (centered on E-flat)
Variation III		113–38	E-flat major
Variation IV		139–47	Whole-tone

Chart 15.1 Hindemith, Sonata for Viola and Piano, op. 11, no. 4: Structural analysis, second movement, "Thema mit Variationen."

Overall, the final movement is in sonata form (Chart 15.2), but Hindemith's comment that the listener should grasp "the last movement only as a continuation of the Variations" is important in considering its structure. Indeed, movements II and III sound like a lengthy Theme and Variations in which

Zone	Thematic Areas/Snippet	Measures	Principal Tonal Areas/Function
Exposition		1–135	
	Theme Group 1	1–80	
	Unit 1.1	1–53	C-sharp minor
	Unit 1.2	54 (No. 17)–80	F-sharp minor; B minor; E-flat major
	Theme Group 2: Variation V	81–128 (No. 21)	Starts A-flat major; moves to B major at end
	Closing (Unit 1.1 material)	128 (No. 21)–35	E major; D major; ends G-sharp^7
Development: Variation VI		136–200	Whole-tone
Recapitulation		200–301	
	Theme Group 1	200–247	
	Unit 1.1	200–224	E-flat minor
	Unit 1.2	225 (No. 26)–47	A-flat minor; D-flat minor; F-sharp major
	Theme Group 2	248 (No. 27)–95 (No. 30)	Begins B major; moves to D major at end
	Closing (Unit 1.1 material)	295 (No. 30)–301	B-flat major; whole-tone
Coda: Variation VII		302–92	E-flat minor

Chart 15.2 Hindemith, Sonata for Viola and Piano, op. 11, no. 4: Structural analysis, third movement, "Finale (mit Variationen)."

Example 15.1 Hindemith, Sonata for Viola and Piano, op. 11, no. 4, movt. III, mm. 30–33, viola.

Example 15.2 Hindemith, Sonata for Viola and Piano, op. 11, no. 4, movt. II, mm. 14–17, viola.

Hindemith inserts a few deviations. Hindemith enhances the continuity between the two movements with the opening motive (Unit 1.1), which, in rhythm and melodic contour, complements the second movement's melody (particularly the version as it appears in Variation IV). From the listener's perspective, the opening of the third movement could easily be mistaken for another variation. Likewise, the dreamy material in mm. 26–40, marked "a little expansive" (*ein wenig ausladend*), bears similarities with material from mm. 13–19 of the second movement (Exs. 15.1 and 15.2). A broad, sweeping theme is introduced at m. 54 (No. 17; Unit 1.2), marked "Light and Flowing" (*Leicht fließend*). For the second theme group (mm. 81–128), Hindemith returns to the second movement's thematic material, labeled Variation V, but he closes the section by revisiting Unit 1.1 material (mm. 128–35).

Variation VI (mm. 136–200), which forms the development section, is a fugato marked "to be played with bizarre ungainliness" (*mit bizarrer Plumpheit vorzutragen*).[23] The bizarre ungainliness can be heard "in the music's heavily lumbering ostinato, its aimless melodic looping, and later, in its *fortissimo* octave doublings [mm. 182–98]."[24]

The recapitulation follows a similar pattern as the exposition, though Hindemith forgoes an official variation label for the return of Variation V material in mm. 248–95. In the final closing section (mm. 295–301), Hindemith returns to a descending ostinato whole-tone pattern spanning an augmented fourth (which he had used in Variation IV) as a lead-in to Variation VII, which serves as the coda for the movement.

Hindemith frequently performed the Sonata for Viola and Piano, op. 11, no. 4. It appeared on the program for his second (1938) and third (1939) concert tours of the United States (Fig. 15.1), receiving favorable reviews:

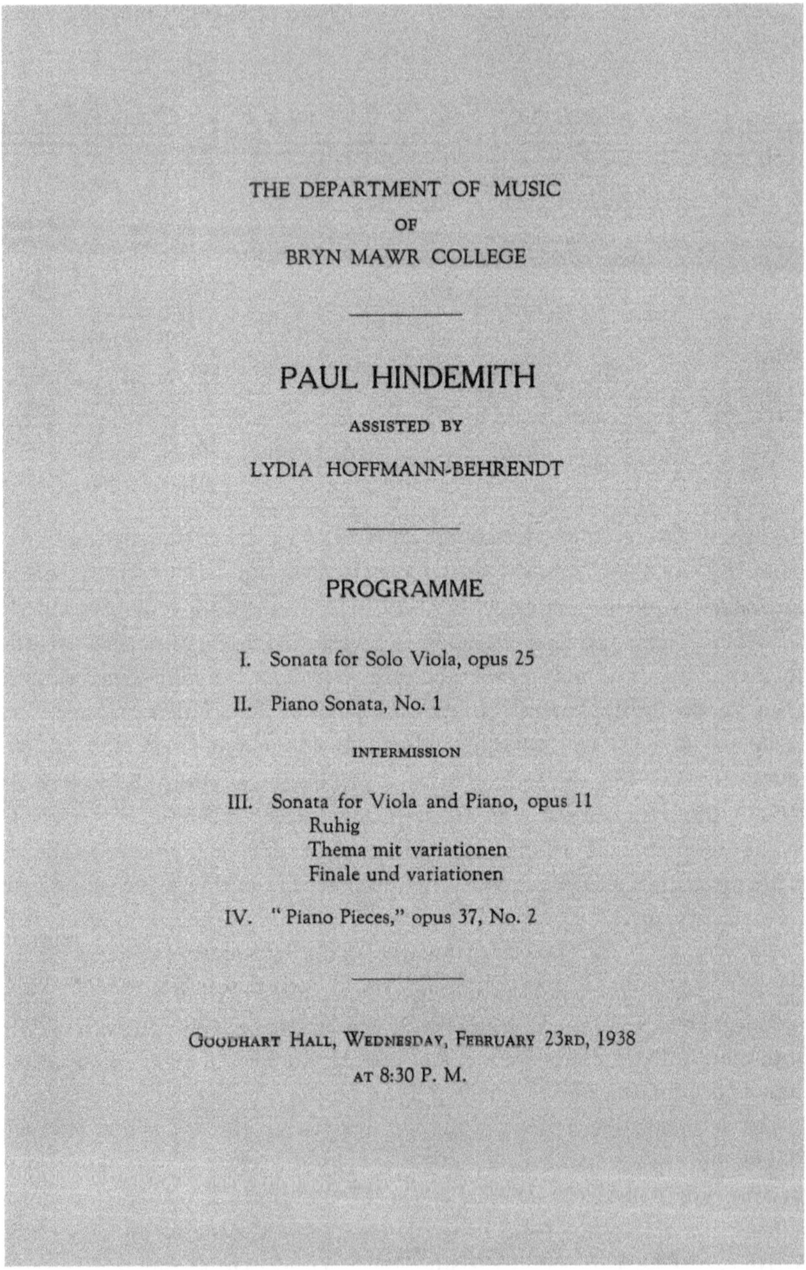

THE DEPARTMENT OF MUSIC

OF

BRYN MAWR COLLEGE

PAUL HINDEMITH

ASSISTED BY

LYDIA HOFFMANN-BEHRENDT

PROGRAMME

I. Sonata for Solo Viola, opus 25

II. Piano Sonata, No. 1

INTERMISSION

III. Sonata for Viola and Piano, opus 11
     Ruhig
     Thema mit variationen
     Finale und variationen

IV. "Piano Pieces," opus 37, No. 2

GOODHART HALL, WEDNESDAY, FEBRUARY 23RD, 1938

AT 8:30 P. M.

Figure 15.1 During Hindemith's second concert tour of the United States in 1938, he programmed his "old viola sonata with piano," opus 11, no. 4. The tour, which included seven chamber-music concerts and four orchestral appearances, began with a February 23 recital at Bryn Mawr College, a women's liberal arts college in Bryn Mawr, Pennsylvania.

I would venture that every one present last night found much that was pleasing in the final sonata for viola and piano, with its broad majestic opening fantasia, followed by several extremely interesting and brilliant variations upon a folk tune theme. Perhaps this being an early work it could be more easily understood, but to the writer it held many moments of great beauty.[25]

With its beautiful music and effective writing for both instruments, it is not surprising that it has become the most frequently performed of Hindemith's sonatas for viola.[26]

Analyzing Hindemith's Sonata for Viola and Piano, op. 11, no. 4

Readers interested in a more in-depth analysis of Hindemith's Sonata for Viola and Piano, op. 11, no. 4 are referred to the following source:

Hilse, Walter Bruno. "Hindemith and Debussy." *Hindemith-Jahrbuch* 2 (1972): 48–90.

16

Paul Hindemith: *Der Schwanendreher: Concerto after Old Folksongs for Viola and Small Orchestra*

I. "Zwischen Berg und tiefem Tal"
II. "Nun laube, Lindlein, laube" — Fugato: "Der Gutzgauch auf dem Zaune saß"
III. Variationen "Seid ihr nicht der Schwanendreher"

Date of Composition: September–early October 1935 (completed October 13, 1935); revised 1936

First Edition: Paul Hindemith, *Der Schwanendreher: Konzert nach alten Volksliedern für Bratsche und kleines Orchester (1935)*, Mainz: B. Schott's Söhne, © 1936, Plate No. B·S·S 34532, Edition Schott 3308 (Score); © 1937, Plate No. B·S·S 34534, Edition Schott 2517 (Piano Reduction)

Date/Place of First Public Performance: November 14, 1935, Paul Hindemith (viola), Concertgebouw Orchestra, Willem Mengelberg (conductor), Amsterdam

Orchestral Instrumentation: Solo viola, 2 flutes (2nd also piccolo), oboe, 2 clarinets in B♭, 2 bassoons, 3 horns in F, trumpet in C, trombone, harp, timpani, 4 cellos, 3 double basses

Introduction

A minstrel, joining a merry company, displays what he has brought back from foreign lands: songs serious and gay, and finally a dance-piece. Like a true musician, he expands and embellishes the melodies, preluding and improvising according to his fancy and ability.

This mediaeval scene was the inspiration of the composition.[1]

Biographical Sketch, 1933–1963

By 1932, Paul Hindemith (1895–1963) had achieved fame at home and abroad as a composer and viola soloist. But his fortunes changed in 1933, the year in which Adolf Hitler was appointed chancellor of Germany and the National Socialist German Workers' Party (Nazi Party) took control of the government. Hindemith had been a target of critical attacks by the Nazis since the late 1920s, which increased once the party was in power. On April 5, 1933, his publisher, Willy Strecker, informed him that a number of his works were being banned: "You yourself are to fifty per cent condemned as a cultural bolshevist on account of your earlier works."[2] A year later, Hindemith's music was subject to a total radio broadcast ban while the government investigated critical remarks that the composer had made about Hitler. Rising to Hindemith's defense, the conductor Wilhelm Furtwängler wrote an article titled "Der Fall Hindemith" ("The Hindemith Case"), which appeared on the front page of the Berlin newspaper *Deutsche Allgemeine Zeitung* on November 25, 1934. The article backfired, providing more ammunition to the Nazis. Without explicitly mentioning Hindemith's name, Reich Minister for National Enlightenment and Propaganda Joseph Goebbels attacked the composer during a speech on December 6:

> Purely German his blood may be, but this only provides drastic confirmation of how deeply the Jewish intellectual infection has eaten into the body of our own people. . . . Certainly we cannot afford, in view of the deplorable lack of truly productive artists throughout the world, to turn our backs on a truly German artist. But he must be a real artist, not just a producer of atonal noises.[3]

As a result of the controversy, Hindemith took an extended leave from his teaching position at the Hochschule für Musik in Berlin and retreated to Lenzkirch to work on orchestrating his opera *Mathis der Maler.*

In April 1935, Hindemith made the first of several trips to Turkey as an adviser on musical life in that country. His standing within Germany remained precarious over the following months, though he resumed teaching at the Hochschule für Musik and accepted an official commission by representatives of the German Luftwaffe in June 1936.[4] But German officials grew alarmed over a performance of Hindemith's Sonata in E for Violin and Piano by Georg Kulenkampff and Walter Gieseking in the fall of 1936, which was met with such " 'demonstrative' applause," that they "considered it expedient for the time being to ban further performances of all Hindemith's works."[5] Hindemith eventually came to realize that any hope for an improvement in his situation was fruitless; on March 25,

1937, he resigned his position at the Hochschule für Musik before embarking on his first tour of the United States.[6] During the tour, he was approached by many admirers who wanted him to settle in the United States:

> I had to take the place of honour beside [Elizabeth Sprague Coolidge], and I had a long conversation with her. Like all the others, she tried to persuade me to move here permanently, saying that any arrangement that would suit me could be made. What she would like best, she said, would be for me to teach at one of the universities or large music colleges, even if not on a permanent basis.[7]

Though these recruiting efforts were not immediately successful, Hindemith did return to the United States for concert tours in each of the following two years. He did, however, move to Bluche, Switzerland, in September 1938 with his wife, Gertrud. With the outbreak of World War II a year later, his American friends increased their efforts to induce him to their country. He arrived for his fourth visit to the United States in February 1940, taking up teaching and lecturing posts during the winter and spring at the University of Buffalo, Cornell University, Wells College, and Yale University and during the summer at the Berkshire Music Center (Tanglewood).[8] In April, Hindemith was offered a position as visiting professor of the theory of music at Yale University to begin in September 1940. He gladly accepted, and plans were made for his wife to join him. After enduring a delay of several months, she arrived in New York in the middle of September.[9] Hindemith enjoyed great success in America: his position at Yale turned into a permanent post; he became a citizen in 1946; and he received many commissions and honors, including honorary doctorates from the Philadelphia Musical Academy and Columbia University and full membership in the National Institute of Arts and Letters.

After the war, Hindemith returned to Europe for a concert tour that started in April 1947. As part of his second European tour the following year, American military authorities requested that he contribute to their reorientation program by conducting and lecturing in German cities.[10] In 1951, Hindemith began teaching at the University of Zürich while retaining his position at Yale. He initially alternated between the two posts, but in 1953 he resigned his professorship at Yale and returned permanently to Europe, settling in the Swiss village of Blonay. In 1957, Hindemith retired from his teaching position in Zürich but continued with numerous musical activities, including composing, conducting, lecturing, and performing, until his death in Frankfurt on December 28, 1963.

Hindemith's *Der Schwanendreher: Concerto after Old Folksongs for Viola and Small Orchestra*

Hindemith composed four concertante works for viola: *Kammermusik No. 5, op. 36, no. 4* (1927); *Konzertmusik for Solo Viola and Large Chamber Orchestra, op. 48* (1930); *Der Schwanendreher: Concerto after Old Folksongs for Viola and Small Orchestra* (1935); and *Trauermusik for String Orchestra with Solo Viola* (1936). *Der Schwanendreher*, the most famous of his viola concertos, has been extensively covered in the scholarly literature (see the list of sources at the end of the chapter); consequently, the discussion and analysis here only touch on the basics. Readers interested in learning more about the concerto are particularly encouraged to read Louise Lansdown's article "Paul Hindemith's *Der Schwanendreher*: A Biographical Landmark," which includes reproductions of many archival sources.[11]

As with his two earlier viola concertos, Hindemith composed *Der Schwanendreher* for himself to perform. He had considered writing a new concerto in the spring of 1935 for a possible tour of the United States.[12] While the tour did not materialize, the idea of a new concerto had taken hold, and on June 15, he mentioned the concerto in a letter to Willy Strecker:

> The score [for the opera *Mathis der Maler*] is going well, it will be finished in a few weeks. Then comes the new viola concerto.[13]

He began sketching the concerto while on holiday in Brenden (in the Black Forest) in early September and completed the fair copy of the score in Berlin on October 13.[14] A month later, on November 14, Hindemith premiered the work with the Concertgebouw Orchestra in Amsterdam, conducted by Willem Mengelberg. In the summer of 1936, Hindemith reworked the ending of the concerto, replacing Variation XII, which originally closed the third movement (and covered mm. 280–309), with a "definitive, more virtuosic closing section which proceeds from bar 269ff."[15]

Aspects of *Der Schwanendreher* reflect the socio-political turmoil that Hindemith faced while composing the work. It does not take much imagination to connect Hindemith's preface (see this chapter's Introduction) with his personal circumstances at the time:

> Let us remember: Hindemith writes the *Schwanendreher* during a time when the basis for his artistic work in Germany, be it as a composer or as a violist, is largely deprived of him; he is thus threatened in his existence. He originally writes the piece for his own use for an American tour. The equating of

the minstrel of the preface, who spreads songs of his homeland abroad, with Hindemith, who introduces German folk songs abroad, is certainly not far-fetched. The minstrel as a symbol of the homeless and the cultural-political outlaw Hindemith are identical.[16]

Der Schwanendreher also bears the influence of his theoretical work from the period. In 1933, he began drafting a book, "Komposition und Kompositionslehre" ("Composition and Composition Theory"), which offered his "reflections on his experience in teaching composition in Berlin" and also included "the out-line of a new pedagogical method."[17] Given the political climate (and the con-troversy surrounding Hindemith at the time), the publisher did not release the book, and Hindemith instead turned to writing the first part of The Craft of Musical Composition in 1935.[18] The first German edition of The Craft of Musical Composition, published in 1937, contained an appendix with a list of compositions (including Der Schwanendreher) that was preceded by this text: "The realisation of the views presented in this book on the technique of composition can best be observed in the following works by the author."[19] In this book, and later theoret-ical writings, Hindemith took issue with so-called atonal music. He also bristled at the application of the term atonal to his music during an interview in 1937:

My music is not atonal. I don't care what others say about it; and I ought to know. It's not even polytonal. But both impressions might be given because it exploits more of the possibilities of a single tonality than most other music. If you listen carefully to even the most complicated of my compositions you will hear that all the tunes and chords revolve around a single tonal center, and that makes the music just as tonal as any product of the romantic period.[20]

Hindemith's music from this period—whether in response to the political cli-mate in Germany or owing to an evolution in his compositional and theoretical philosophies—did, indeed, turn more conspicuously tonal:

In these works the triad is the harmonic point of reference, and harmonic phrases controlled by major or minor triads are often simply juxtaposed with phrases controlled by sonorities developed from augmented or diminished triads.... Hindemith in this period came closest to working in terms of a linear harmonic logic analogous to the older diatonic tonal system.[21]

In Der Schwanendreher, Hindemith used four selections from Franz Magnus Böhme's Altdeutsches Liederbuch, a source that he had previously turned to for compositions as well as student exercises.[22] Böhme's book, originally published in 1877, gathered German folk songs from the twelfth through seventeenth centuries. In each movement of Der Schwanendreher, Hindemith included the first line of the text as the identifier for the song that he used. In three of the four instances, this line differs from the title of the song in Böhme's collection (Chart 16.1).[23] For convenience, further references to the songs in this chapter use Hindemith's titles.

The first movement is generally described as having a sonata form at its core, which is bookended by an introduction and coda (Chart 16.2).[24] In the introduction, the viola-minstrel demonstrates his ability at "preluding and improvising," selecting Theme Group 2 material for his opening, declamatory prologue. In m. 11 (Letter A; all rehearsal letters and measure numbers refer to the Schott edition, with the repeated section in movt. III, mm. 27–32, counted only once in the numbering), the orchestra enters with the Dorian-mode melody from the first of the folk tunes, "Zwischen Berg und tiefem Tal" (Ex. 16.1), in the French

Movement	Böhme No.	Böhme Title	Hindemith Title
I	163	"Guter Rath für Liebesleute"	"Zwischen Berg und tiefem Tal"
II: A section	175	"Nun laube, Lindlein, laube!"	"Nun laube, Lindlein, laube"
II: B section (Fugato)	167	"Kuckuk"	"Der Gutzgauch auf dem Zaune saß"
III	315	"Der Schwanendreher (Tanzlied)"	"Seid ihr nicht der Schwanendreher"

Chart 16.1 Folk songs used by Hindemith in *Der Schwanendreher: Concerto after Old Folksongs for Viola and Small Orchestra*, comparing the titles as they appear in Franz Magnus Böhme's *Altdeutsches Liederbuch* with the titles as they appear in *Der Schwanendreher*.

Example 16.1 "Zwischen Berg und tiefem Tal," from Franz Magnus Böhme's *Altdeutsches Liederbuch*.

horns and trombone, punctuated by the solo viola's improvisatory comments. Hindemith sketched this introductory *Langsam* material after he had sketched the movement's main section,[25] which begins in m. 34 with a vigorous melody in the solo viola. The more lyrical Theme Group 2—which was previewed in the

Zone	Thematic Areas/Snippet	Measures	Principal Tonal Areas/Function
Introduction		1–33	
	Unit 1.1: Cadenza	1–11 (Let. A)	C
	Unit 1.2: "Zwischen Berg und tiefem Tal"	11 (Let. A)–33	C
Exposition		34–87	
	Theme Group 1	34–61 (Let. F)	C
	Theme Group 2	61 (Let. F)–87	G
Episode/ Development		87–130 (Let. N)	
	Unit 1.1: Transitory	87–96	E
	Unit 1.2: "Zwischen Berg und tiefem Tal"	96–124	A; E; B
	Unit 1.3: Theme Group 1 material/false reprise	124–30 (Let. N)	E-flat

Chart 16.2   Hindemith, *Der Schwanendreher: Concerto after Old Folksongs for Viola and Small Orchestra:* Structural analysis, first movement, "Zwischen Berg und tiefem Tal."

Zone	Thematic Areas/Snippet	Measures	Principal Tonal Areas/Function
Recapitulation		130 (Let. N)–63 (Let. Q)	
	Theme Group 1	130 (Let. N)–51 (Let. P)	C
	Theme Group 2	151 (Let. P)–63 (Let. Q)	F
Episode		163 (Let. Q)–83	
	Unit 1.1: Theme Group 1 (with fragments of Theme Group 2)	163 (Let. Q)–74 (Let. R)	D-flat
	Unit 1.2: Theme Group 1 material	174 (Let. R)–83	C
Coda		184–214	
	Unit 1.1: Cadenza	184–92	C
	Unit 1.2: "Zwischen Berg und tiefem Tal"	193–214	C

Chart 16.2 (continued) Hindemith, *Der Schwanendreher: Concerto after Old Folksongs for Viola and Small Orchestra:* Structural analysis, first movement, "Zwischen Berg und tiefem Tal."

introduction—begins in m. 61 (Letter F), centered on G. An episodic/developmental section begins at m. 87 with a forceful transitory passage for the soloist. At m. 96, the "Zwischen Berg und tiefem Tal" theme returns, which "inaugurates a tonal sequence of rising fifths, A major, E major and B major, reaching its climax in a dramatic false reprise in E flat [mm. 124–30]."[26]

The recapitulation starts at m. 130 (Letter N) with the return of Theme Group 1, centered on C, which is followed by a brief statement of Theme

Group 2 (mm. 151–63), centered on F. Another episode begins at m. 163 (Letter Q) with the viola's triplet figures recalling the earlier transitory passage (see mm. 87–96). Meanwhile, the orchestra offers fragments of Theme Group 1 and Theme Group 2 material. The section culminates in a passage in which the orchestra and soloist struggle for supremacy (mm. 174–83). Just as it seems that the orchestra will emerge the winner, the violist interrupts with a triumphant return of its opening cadenza in m. 184. The movement closes with a reappearance of "Zwischen Berg und tiefem Tal" in the oboe and first clarinet (mm. 193–205), after which the violist is finally entrusted with the folk tune, playing two iterations of its final line (see Ex. 16.1, mm. 11–14) in the movement's closing measures (mm. 205–14).

The second movement, in an ABA form (Chart 16.3), opens with a lovely, melancholy theme in the viola. Here, the forlorn viola-minstrel has only his harp to keep him company. At m. 35, woodwinds enter with the Mixolydian-mode folk tune "Nun laube, Lindlein, laube" (Ex. 16.2) in a glorious chorale setting that is punctuated by the viola's plaintive comments.

Hindemith moves from a "serious" song to a "gay" song in the Fugato B section (mm. 73–218), which uses the folk tune "Der Gutzgauch auf dem Zaune saß" (Ex. 16.3). The opening subject is given over to the orchestra, with Hindemith shortening "the fugue subject by quasi-stretto entries,"[27] providing variety while adding to the gaiety. At m. 114, the viola enters for the start of the first episode. As the fugue continues in all its contrapuntal glory, Hindemith slips in the "Nun laube, Lindlein, laube" tune starting in m. 180 (Letter N), which fully takes over at m. 195 (Letter O) in a statement that is split between the trumpet and viola. For the return of the A section at m. 218, the viola plays its opening melody an octave higher, still accompanied by the harp but now combined with the "Nun laube, Lindlein, laube" tune in a pair of French horns.

The final movement is a set of variations (Chart 16.4) on the folk tune "Seid ihr nicht der Schwanendreher" (Ex. 16.4).[28] This folk tune, which Hindemith described as "a sort of round-dance," provides the name for the entire concerto.[29] Hindemith combines variation techniques in this movement, mixing "strict variations," in which "the original form of the theme is closely preserved,"[30] with "free variations" or "fantasy variations," which "allude to or develop elements of the theme."[31]

After the orchestra states the first strain of the tune, the solo viola immediately repeats the strain at its entrance in m. 7; the remainder of the tune is then divided between the soloist and orchestra. At m. 27 (Letter B), the viola-minstrel proceeds to expand and embellish the melody, "according to his fancy and ability"—here he seems intent on showing off technical facility, since the first three variations have him rapidly traversing around the fingerboard. At m. 103,

Example 16.2 "Nun laube, Lindlein, laube," from Franz Magnus Böhme's *Altdeutsches Liederbuch*.

Zone	Thematic Areas/Snippet	Measures	Principal Tonal Areas/Function
A		1–72	
	Unit 1.1	1–35	A major
	Unit 1.2: "Nun laube, Lindlein, laube" Fl. 1	35–72	A major
B		73–218	
	Unit 1.1: "Der Gutzgauch auf dem Zaune saß" Bsn. 1	73–195 (Let. O)	F major; modulates
	Unit 1.2: "Nun laube, Lindlein, laube" Tpt. 1	195 (Let. O)–218	Starts D major
A	"Nun laube, Lindlein, laube"	218–60	A major

Chart 16.3 Hindemith, *Der Schwanendreher: Concerto after Old Folksongs for Viola and Small Orchestra*: Structural analysis, second movement, "Nun laube, Lindlein, laube" — Fugato: "Der Gutzgauch auf dem Zaune saß."

Variation IV introduces a new theme, derived from the final notes of the folk tune (the viola's first five pitches in mm. 103–4 are a retrograde version of the final five notes of the original tune; see Ex. 6.4, mm. 19–20).[32] A pair of "closely related" free variations follow:[33] first a slow variation centered on F major (mm.

Example 16.3 "Der Gutzgauch auf dem Zaune saß," from Franz Magnus Böhme's *Altdeutsches Liederbuch*.

127–56) and then a fast, virtuosic variation centered on F minor (mm. 157–89), which leads to a cadenza that forms Variation VII (mm. 190–209), centered on B♭. The next variation retains the tonal center of B♭, with the folk tune in the first French horn, which is followed by the ninth variation, in which the tune is treated canonically. After the dense texture of the previous variation, the opening of the tenth variation at m. 249 (Letter T), which features only solo viola and the first French horn, comes as a dramatic change. Hindemith maintains the drama by alternating sparsely accompanied solo passages with orchestral outbursts in the following measures. For the final variation (mm. 269–79), Hindemith returns to material from Variation IV, which quickly leads to the coda, in which "Hindemith dismantles his material . . . in dense and breathless combinations, then puts it together again until he blows it all away."[34]

Der Schwanendreher formed a centerpiece of Hindemith's first concert tour of the United States in 1937; he performed the work in Washington, DC; Boston; New York City; Chicago; and Buffalo. Many notables turned out for each of these concerts, lauding Hindemith and his new concerto:

> After the concert, Nadia Boulanger gave a reception that was as distinguished as it was boring. . . . Stravinsky, who is in New York for rehearsals of his ballet and who sat in the front row at the concert, very decoratively detached, was also there, followed by his satellite [Samuel] Dushkin. He was telling everybody that Der Schwanendreher is an immensely important piece, and I heard in the following days that he was still dropping this sage discovery into various thirsting ears.[35]

Of the conductors that he worked with during the tour, Hindemith was happiest with Arthur Fiedler in Boston. During his third American tour,

Zone	Thematic Areas/Snippet	Measures	Principal Tonal Areas/Function
Theme	*[musical notation]*	1–26	G to C
Variation I	*[musical notation]*	27 (Let. B)–46	C
Variation II	*[musical notation]*	47–77	G
Variation III	*[musical notation]*	78–102	A
Variation IV	*[musical notation]*	103–26	D to E
Variation V	*[musical notation]*	127–56	F to D
Variation VI	*[musical notation]*	157 (Let. M)–89	F to D
Variation VII	*[musical notation]*	190–209	B-flat
Variation VIII	*[musical notation]*	210–28	B-flat
Variation IX	*[musical notation]*	229–48	G to C
Variation X	*[musical notation]*	249 (Let. T)–68	G
Variation XI	*[musical notation]*	269–79 (Let. V)	C
Coda	*[musical notation]*	280–336	D to C

Chart 16.4 Hindemith, *Der Schwanendreher: Concerto after Old Folksongs for Viola and Small Orchestra:* Structural analysis, third movement, Variationen "Seid ihr nicht der Schwanendreher."

Example 16.4 "Seid ihr nicht der Schwanendreher," from Franz Magnus Böhme's *Altdeutsches Liederbuch.*

Hindemith recorded *Der Schwanendreher* with Fiedler and his Sinfonietta on April 12, 1939.

Learn More about *Der Schwanendreher: Concerto after Old Folksongs for Viola and Small Orchestra*

Readers interested in learning more about Hindemith's *Der Schwanendreher* are referred to the following sources:

Kemp, Ian. "Some Thoughts on Hindemith's Viola Concertos." *Hindemith-Jahrbuch* 35 (2006): 68–117.

Kohlhase, Hans. "Paul Hindemiths Bratschenkonzert 'Der Schwanendreher.'" In *2. Viola-Symposium 1990: Dokumentation*, edited by Rolf Fritsch, 47–84. Trossingen, Germany: Bundesakademie für musikalische Jugendbildung, 1991.

Lansdown, Louise. "Paul Hindemith's *Der Schwanendreher*: A Biographical Landmark." *Journal of the American Viola Society* 28, no. 2 (Fall 2012): 33–51.

Neumeyer, David. "*Der Schwanendreher* (1935)." In *The Music of Paul Hindemith*, 188–95. New Haven, CT: Yale University Press, 1986.

Schubert, Giselher. Preface to *Der Schwanendreher: Concerto after Old Folksongs for Viola and Small Orchestra*, by Paul Hindemith, iii–ix. Translated by Penelope Souster. London: Ernst Eulenburg, 1985. Miniature score.

17

Franz Anton Hoffmeister: Concerto for Viola and Orchestra in D Major

I.   Allegro
II. Adagio
III. Rondo

Date of Composition: by 1799

First Edition: F. A. Hoffmeister, *Concert in D-Dur für Viola und Orchester*, Leipzig: Paul Günther, 1941 (Piano Reduction); Franz Anton Hoffmeister, *Konzert für Viola und Orchester D dur*, ed. Ulrich Drüner, Adliswil, Switzerland: Edition Kunzelmann, 1982, No. 10 185 (Score)

Select Later Editions: Franz Anton Hoffmeister, *Violakonzert D-dur*, ed. Norbert Gertsch and Julia Ronge, Munich: Henle, 2003, HN 739 (Piano Reduction); Franz Anton Hoffmeister, *Concerto in D-dur für Viola und Orchester*, ed. Yvonne Morgan, Winterthur: Amadeus, 2011, BP 1050 (Score); BP 342 (Piano Reduction)

Date/Place of Early Public Performance: [September 26, 1805, Peter Albrecht von Hagen Jr., Concert Hall, Boston?]

Orchestral Instrumentation: Solo viola, 2 oboes, 2 horns in D, strings

Introduction

"No good and much harm comes from the statement on the title-page: this concerto, 'an enchanting work, could almost have been written by Mozart.' That little word, 'almost,' calls attention to the large, important gap between talent and genius, away from the genuine Hoffmeister virtues. He was no Mozart but a man content with the clichés of his time."[1] Louise Rood easily homes in on a great misfortune that has plagued Hoffmeister's Concerto for Viola and Orchestra in D Major: Lacking an original concerto by W. A. Mozart, violists have sought alternatives. Turning to a work that is "almost Mozart," many discover that Hoffmeister's concerto does not live up to their expectations. On the surface, a comparison to Mozart is understandable, since the work "is probably the finest viola concerto from the period of the Viennese Classics and comes closest to the models of Haydn and Mozart."[2] But it is *not* by Mozart, nor does it pretend to be.

Active during the height of the Viennese Classical period, Hoffmeister earned "a well-deserved and wide-spread reputation through the original content of his works."[3] He enjoyed the company—and respect—of contemporary composers, and his music was popular among performers and audiences in Vienna and abroad. Given the circles in which Hoffmeister moved, comparisons to Mozart, Joseph Haydn, and even Ludwig van Beethoven have been inevitable—comparisons in which Hoffmeister has always come up short. But how many composers can measure up to the genius of those three masters? Instead, Hoffmeister deserves the courtesy of evaluating his works on their own merits. And if you approach his music on these terms, you will find an abundance of grace, clarity, charming melodies, and even the occasional flashes of genius.

Biographical Sketch

Born into a respected family in Rottenburg am Neckar, Franz Anton Hoffmeister (1754–1812) went to Vienna in 1768 to study law. After completing those studies, he became increasingly involved in music; starting in 1778, he served as Kapellmeister to the Hungarian Count Franz von Szecsenyi for three years.[4] Hoffmeister had several works published in Lyon before announcing plans in 1784 to issue his compositions "at his own expense" through a new publishing enterprise located in Rudolf Gräffer's Viennese bookshop.[5] By the following year, he had established an independent business and was advertising new publications by leading composers of the day, including W. A. Mozart, Joseph Haydn, and Ignaz Pleyel.

For the next twenty years, Hoffmeister divided his activities between composing and publishing. As a publisher, he secured rights from fashionable composers, advertised broadly, and expanded his business. But as Hoffmeister devoted more time to composition, his attention to the business waned, and he auctioned off a branch of the firm and sold off assets indiscriminately.[6] In 1790, Hoffmeister married Theresia Haas; the couple would not have any children.[7]

Hoffmeister traveled to Prague in 1799 as part of a concert tour that was expected to continue on to London. His plans changed when he met Ambrosius Kühnel in Leipzig, and the two decided to establish the Bureau de Musique publishing firm, which would become the basis of the legendary music publisher C. F. Peters.[8] Even with this new business venture, Hoffmeister maintained his Viennese firm, which was apparently entrusted to his wife.[9] Hoffmeister finally gave up his publishing activities in 1806 and died six years later.

Hoffmeister's Concerto for Viola and Orchestra in D Major

A prolific composer, Hoffmeister produced hundreds of chamber works and more than sixty symphonies and fifty concertos. Much of his music was written with the tastes and capabilities of amateurs in mind, a reflection of the musical environment in Vienna where connoisseurs and amateurs performed alongside one another.[10] Among his compositions are three works for viola: the Concerto for Viola and Orchestra in D Major (by 1799), Concerto for Viola and Orchestra in B♭ Major (by 1799), and the 12 Études for Viola (published 1803), as well as a number of duos prominently involving the viola.

Little is known about the origins of the viola works; stylistically, both concertos likely date from the 1780s or early 1790s. An autograph manuscript of the Concerto for Viola and Orchestra in D Major has yet to surface, and modern editions are based on a single contemporaneous source, a set of handwritten parts that once belonged to the violist Joseph Schubert bearing the title *Concerto ex D♯ [sic] a Viola Principale, Due Violini, Due Oboi, Due Corni in D, Viola, et Basso, del Signor Hoffmeister.*[11] It was not until the twentieth century when the concerto was published, though a 1799 catalogue from music dealer and copyist Johann Traeg lists the work as available for sale in a handwritten edition.[12] The work was undoubtedly performed during Hoffmeister's lifetime; in 1805, the American violist Peter Albrecht von Hagen Jr. performed a viola concerto by Hoffmeister in Boston, though it is uncertain which one.[13]

The concerto adheres to Viennese Classical ideals regarding harmonic design, clarity, balance, and "the equal importance of formal and expressive features."[14] A sense of elegance and refinement dominates, with pleasing melodies and tastefully ornamented figures. Thematic elements are generally broken into two-measure units, though phrase lengths often extend beyond a four- or eight-measure statement. While the technical demands are impressive, the writing is less overtly virtuosic and more graceful, highlighting the viola's lyrical and sweet tone, making extensive use of the middle and upper registers. Like many composers of the period, Hoffmeister confines the winds to the tutti passages of the outer movements.[15]

Cast in a Classical concerto (sonata) form (Chart 17.1), the first movement opens with a ritornello consisting of two theme groups, the second of which appears only in the first two ritornellos. At its solo entrance in m. 36, the viola states the first theme from the opening ritornello, which Hoffmeister extends beyond the original eight-measure period with an outburst of arpeggios in m. 43. The second theme group, in A major, begins on beat three of m. 60. Following a short tutti statement (mm. 68–72), the violist's technique is on display, with the only extended passage of double stops in the concerto (mm. 73–79) followed by a passage with rapid string crossings and arpeggios (mm. 82–91). After the second tutti ritornello, the viola begins the development section with a delicate restatement of

Zone	Thematic Areas/Snippet	Measures	Principal Tonal Areas/Function
Opening Ritornello		1–35	
	Theme Group 1	1–15	D major to A major
	Theme Group 2	16–35	Dominant; D major
Solo Exposition		36–91	
	Theme Group 1	36–60	D major to A major
	Theme Group 2	60–91	A major
Second Ritornello		91–116	
	Theme Group 1	91–103	A major to E major
	Theme Group 2	104–16	V/V; A major
Development		117–61	
	Solo development	117–51	A major; B minor
	Tutti retransition	151–61	B minor to dominant
Recapitulation		162–207	
	Theme Group 1	162–79	D major
	Theme Group 2	179–207	D major
Closing Ritornello and Cadenza		207–17	D major

Chart 17.1 Hoffmeister, Concerto for Viola and Orchestra in D Major: Structural analysis, first movement, Allegro.

the principal theme. The music soon moves from A major to B minor, becoming stormy at m. 139 with the orchestra taking over at m. 151 to transition us back to D major for the start of the recapitulation in m. 162. Hoffmeister quickly moves to the second theme group at m. 179, now in the tonic. As he did in the exposition,

Hoffmeister provides an opportunity for technical display, this time with a passage of bariolage in mm. 189–92. An orchestral ritornello, interrupted by the viola's cadenza, closes out the movement in typical fashion.

While the second movement may be considered in ABA or even sonata form, it closely follows the form described as Aria or Ariette by the German music theorist Heinrich Koch (Chart 17.2).[16] After an opening ritornello, the viola enters

Zone	Thematic Areas/Snippet	Measures	Principal Tonal Areas/Function
Opening Ritornello		1–6	D minor
First Main Period		7–31	
	Unit 1.1	7–12	D minor
	Unit 1.2	13–17	D minor; moves to F major
	Unit 1.3	18–24	F major
	Unit 1.4	24–31	F major
Second Ritornello		31–37	F major
Second Main Period		38–69	
	Fragmentation/development	38–53	F major; moves to dominant function
	Unit 1.1 (return of Unit 1.1 material from First Period)	53–60	D minor
	Unit 1.2	60–69	D minor
Closing Ritornello and Cadenza		69–80	D minor

Chart 17.2 Hoffmeister, Concerto for Viola and Orchestra in D Major: Structural analysis, second movement, Adagio.

with its initial theme (Unit 1.1) at m. 7. The second thematic unit begins in D minor but quickly tonicizes F major with the third thematic unit at m. 18 fully establishing a move to the relative major. After another orchestral ritornello (mm. 31–37), the second main period begins with fragmentation/development of themes from the first period. At m. 47, the orchestra drops out after the first beat, leaving the viola conspicuously alone in a dramatic change of texture. Hoffmeister then uses a chromatic bass line in mm. 48–51 to transition us from F major back to D minor and a return of the viola's initial theme at m. 53. The theme breaks off at m. 56 with the viola recycling the chromatic bass pattern from a few measures earlier. At m. 67, the orchestra once again drops out after the downbeat, providing another dramatic textural change in preparation for the final ritornello and cadenza.

The third movement is in rondo form with three episodes (Chart 17.3) starting with a refrain consisting of an eight-measure solo period (mm. 1–8), which is then restated by the orchestra (mm. 9–16). A brief episode follows (mm. 17–36), flowing directly from the rondo refrain as if an extension of the theme. The second episode (mm. 53–96) begins with a lyrical theme in the relative minor with a short orchestral figure in mm. 61–62 transitioning us back to D major. At m. 63, the viola launches into a series of runs and arpeggios, making extensive use of the lower register. While this middle section (Unit 1.2) is twenty-four measures long, Hoffmeister varies the phrase lengths so that the return of the lyrical B-minor theme at m. 87 seems to interrupt the orchestral transition that started in m. 84. The third episode (mm. 113–48) is constructed similarly to the second, this time in the parallel minor. But the middle section is shorter, offering just one quick round of runs and bariolage before returning to the lyrical D-minor theme at m. 137.

The concertos by Hoffmeister and Carl Stamitz (see chapter 28) are the two Classical-era works that most violists learn, routinely appearing on audition and competition lists. Hoffmeister's Concerto for Viola and Orchestra in D Major was quickly embraced upon publication in the 1940s and has retained its stature despite the subsequent availability of numerous other viola concertos from the period. Given the popularity of the work, it is no surprise that at least a dozen different editions have been produced. The editing process has been complicated by the lack of an autograph manuscript as well as questionable spots in the existing source. Adding to the complexities, several editions suffer from misprints and varying degrees of editorial liberties.

Reviewing the concerto in 1951, Louise Rood described it as "a true period-piece, of use to student and recitalist alike," and compared it to Stamitz's D-major concerto, which she considered "a less sophisticated predecessor."[17] Hoffmeister's concerto demonstrates a high degree of sophistication with its coherent formal and tonal plan and attractive treatment of material. While Stamitz's concerto

Zone	Thematic Areas/Snippet	Measures	Principal Tonal Areas/Function
A		1–16	
	Solo	1–8	D major
	Tutti	9–16	D major
B		17–36	D major; A major
A		37–52	D major
C		53–96	
	Unit 1.1	53–63	B minor
	Unit 1.2	63–87	D major to B minor
	Unit 1.3 (with Unit 1.1 material)	87–96	B minor
A		97–112	D major
D		113–48	
	Unit 1.1	113–28	D minor
	Unit 1.2	128–37	D major
	Unit 1.3 (with Unit 1.1 material)	137–48	D minor; moves to dominant
A		149–64	D major

Chart 17.3 Hoffmeister, Concerto for Viola and Orchestra in D Major: Structural analysis, third movement, Rondo.

offers more technical challenges, Hoffmeister's requires more finesse. The work may not bear Mozart's stamp of genius, but it does bear Hoffmeister's stamp of expertise, resulting in a superb concerto by any standard.

18

Johann Nepomuk Hummel: Sonata for Piano and Viola, op. 5, no. 3

I.   Allegro moderato
II. Adagio cantabile
III. Rondo con moto

Date of Composition: by 1798

First Edition: Jean Nep. Hummel, *Trois Sonates pour le Piano-Forte. Les deux premieres avec Accompagnement d'un Violon, la troisieme avec Alta Viola obligé, Oeuvre 5ᵉ*, Vienna: self-pub., n.d. (c. 1798)

Select Later Edition: Johann Nepomuk Hummel, *Sonate für Klavier und Viola Es-dur Opus 5 Nr. 3*, ed. Ernst Herttrich, Munich: Henle, 2012, HN 1029

Dedication: Composées et dediées (avec Permission) A Son Altesse Madame la Princesse Royal de Dännemarc

Introduction

"Johann Nepomuk Hummel is a classic example of an artist enormously successful and revered in his lifetime but consigned by posterity to its more thorough history books."[1] What determines the ongoing success of an artist? Is it talent? Or fate? Or luck? Many factors contribute to an artist's reception by contemporary audiences and critics. And many factors contribute to that same artist's ensuing reputation: tastes change, advocates come and go, research casts the artist in a new light. An artist's reputation is not permanently fixed but instead moves freely, sometimes swinging between extremes like a pendulum. Perhaps no composer has suffered more significantly from the swing of the pendulum than Hummel. Flourishing during "one of the most dynamic periods in music history," Hummel enjoyed immense success as a composer, with "every new composition being heralded as a major event by critics, the public, and fellow musicians."[2] Yet he primarily remained a Classicist while Romanticism was coming into vogue, and his music quickly came to be viewed as old-fashioned, resulting in a "rapid descent in public esteem."[3] For more than a century after his death, performers and historians largely ignored his music, grouping him among the Classical period's also-rans. But new champions have emerged in recent decades who have revealed the splendors of his music, allowing the pendulum to once again swing in Hummel's favor.

Biographical Sketch

Johann Nepomuk Hummel (1778–1837) was born in Pressburg (now Bratislava, Slovakia) to Johannes Hummel, a violinist and conductor, and his wife, Margarethe. Johannes was responsible for his son's early musical education, including lessons on the violin and piano.[4] Hummel made remarkable progress on the piano, and shortly after the family moved to Vienna in 1786 W. A. Mozart accepted the young prodigy as a student. As part of the arrangement, Hummel moved in with Mozart's family, becoming a member of the household and receiving lessons for free.[5] In 1788, Hummel and his father embarked on an extensive concert tour, covering numerous cities over the next five years. Returning to Vienna in 1793, he devoted the next decade to "study, composition and teaching."[6]

Thanks to a recommendation from Joseph Haydn, Hummel became Konzertmeister to Prince Nikolaus Esterházy in 1804, effectively serving as Kapellmeister, though Haydn retained that title.[7] Hummel's years at the Esterházy court were riddled with jealousies and controversies; he was dismissed in 1808 for dereliction of duties but persuaded the prince to re-engage him. Failing to learn his lesson, Hummel continued to ignore his obligations at the court and was dismissed for good in 1811. Hummel returned to Vienna, where he married the singer Elisabeth Röckel in 1813; the couple would have two sons together.

Throughout these early years, Hummel received considerable acclaim as a composer and performer. His skill as a pianist rivaled that of Ludwig van Beethoven. While Beethoven's style of playing was considered "far ahead of his time," Hummel's "purling, brilliant style" was described as being "much more comprehensible and pleasing to the public."[8] The two men had a complicated relationship that "fluctuated between warm friendship and outright hostility."[9] Nevertheless, Hummel would serve as a pallbearer at Beethoven's funeral in 1827.

Hummel accepted another permanent post in 1816, as Kapellmeister to the Württemberg court in Stuttgart. The position proved to be a disappointment, leaving little time for composing or concert tours. Animosity with a colleague, Baron Karl von Wächter, added to Hummel's unhappiness.[10] In 1819, Hummel found a more hospitable post as Kapellmeister at the Weimar court, which he retained until his death. This position allowed regular leaves, permitting Hummel to devote efforts to other musical activities, including teaching, composing, conducting, and touring. In the 1820s, Hummel's fame reached its pinnacle, but by the 1830s his star had begun to fade. After several years of declining health, Hummel died in 1837.

Hummel's Sonata for Piano and Viola, op. 5, no. 3

Hummel's compositions cover the major genres, with the notable exception of the symphony. Among his compositions are two works for viola, the Sonata for Piano and Viola, op. 5, no. 3 (by 1798) and the *Potpourri for Viola and Orchestra*, op. 94 (1820). In 1898, the violist Clemens Meyer published a substantially truncated version of the *Potpourri*, retitled *Fantasie*, which has become a popular work among violists. Little is known about the origins of the Sonata for Piano and Viola, which likely dates from the period 1793–1797 after Hummel had resettled in Vienna. It was originally published in a mixed set of three sonatas, of which the first two are for piano with violin. Since music was often published in sets of three or six works during this period, it is not uncommon to find groupings with mixed instrumentations.[11] Hummel announced the availability of the sonatas in the January 3, 1798, issue of *Wiener Zeitung*:

> Announcement for Friends and Lovers of Music
> The applause and encouragement with which I was honored everywhere on my travels throughout Germany, England, Scotland, Holland, and Denmark, etc., inspires me so much that I continue to work devotedly on musical works. Therefore, at the present time, I have the honor of announcing to lovers of music 3 sonatas for the *Piano-Forte*, which you will certainly welcome, and of which two are accompanied by violin and the third by *Alta Viola*.
>
> This work is dedicated with the most gracious permission to Her Royal Highness the Crown Princess of Denmark. Since I had it engraved here in Vienna at my own expense, I did not fail to arrange for a pure, correct, and beautiful edition.[12]

The work underwent multiple editions during Hummel's lifetime; the full set of three sonatas was subsequently released by Johann André in 1798 and by Artaria in 1815. Separate editions of the viola sonata—bearing the opus number 19 and including an alternate part for violin—started appearing around 1818 by publishers in Leipzig (Peters), Paris (Richault, Pleyel, and Sieber), Copenhagen (Lose), and London (T. Boosey & Co.). The numerous editions are not only a testament to Hummel's popularity as a composer but also suggest that the sonata was popular with amateur violists. Nonetheless, the author has not been able to identify any performances prior to the twentieth century.[13]

Stylistically, the Sonata for Piano and Viola, op. 5, no. 3 displays characteristics that would appear in Hummel's later compositions, including "basically homophonic textures, florid ornate Italianate melodies, and virtuoso embroidery supported by modernized Alberti accompaniments."[14] Though the work is a piano sonata with viola accompaniment, the viola is a full-fledged partner with a suitable share of melodic material. And while the piano exhibits more virtuosic writing overall, the viola has many technically brilliant passages.

The first movement is in sonata form with a repeated exposition (Chart 18.1). After two bold E♭ major chords played jointly by both instruments, the piano softly plays four b♭[ii]s, each preceded by a grace note an octave lower. An ornamented string of sixteenth notes concludes the brief introduction, flowing directly into the first theme (Unit 1.1) at m. 4, played by the piano and then by the viola at m. 12 (all measure numbers refer to the Henle edition; other editions may number the first movement's repeated exposition—with a first and second ending—differently). In m. 24, the end of the first theme nicely dovetails with a new thematic idea (Unit 1.2), prefaced by octaves in the piano, echoing the movement's introductory material. The piano plays more octave grace-note figures in mm. 38–39, signaling another transition. Here, the arpeggiated F[7] harmony prepares a shift to B♭ major at m. 41 for the second theme group. Once again, the piano initially states the theme, with the viola taking it up at m. 49. This section offers an opportunity for technical display with the instruments alternating sixteenth-note passages starting in m. 60, briefly teaming up at mm. 72–73 as a lead-in to the closing section, where the viola finally gets first crack at the theme.

Incorporating motivic ideas from the exposition, the development begins with a melody related to Theme Group 1, Unit 1.2 material. After the viola's soaring legato version (mm. 92–99), the piano plays an ornamented, *dolce* version at m. 100. The music turns turbulent in m. 112, following a strong cadence on C minor, with sixteenth notes in the piano and staccato markings in both instruments. Hummel closes the section with a nice harmonic touch in mm. 126–28 (Ex. 18.1): a chromatic line between the piano's highest and lowest voices moves in contrary motion, enabling a progression from B♭[7] to D minor back to a B♭[7] chord. Hummel then uses the same string of sixteenth notes that appeared in m. 3 to lead us into the recapitulation at m. 130, where the piano presents a more ornamented version of the first theme. At m. 164, the second theme group appears in the tonic, and the instruments once again alternate sixteenth-note passages later in this section. Meeting up at m. 193, the two instruments play an extended passage in thirds, emphasizing neighboring tones while prolonging the dominant. The tension finally resolves at the start of the coda (m. 204) with the

Zone	Thematic Areas/Snippet	Measures	Principal Tonal Areas/Function
Introduction		1–3	E-flat major
Repeated Exposition		4–91	
	Theme Group 1	4–41	
	Unit 1.1	4–24	E-flat major
	Unit 1.2	24–41	E-flat major
	Theme Group 2	41–76	B-flat major
	Closing	76–91	B-flat major
Development		92–130	Begins B-flat major; modulates
Recapitulation		130–204	
	Theme Group 1	130–64	
	Unit 1.1	130–50	E-flat major
	Unit 1.2	150–64	E-flat major
	Theme Group 2	164–204	E-flat major; moves to dominant at end
Coda		204–21	E-flat major

Chart 18.1 Hummel, Sonata for Piano and Viola, op. 5, no. 3: Structural analysis, first movement, Allegro moderato.

Example 18.1 Hummel, Sonata for Piano and Viola, op. 5, no. 3, movt. I, mm. 126–29, piano.

Zone	Thematic Areas/Snippet	Measures	Principal Tonal Areas/Function
A		1–13	B-flat major
B		13–25	B-flat major; F major
A		25–42	B-flat major

Chart 18.2 Hummel, Sonata for Piano and Viola, op. 5, no. 3: Structural analysis, second movement, Adagio cantabile.

movement ending in the same manner in which it began, with two bold E♭ major chords played jointly by both instruments.

While the second movement can be viewed as an ABA form (Chart 18.2), it has an improvisatory, fantasia-like quality, drawing on Hummel's interest in variation.[15] An eight-measure period starts with the principal idea in the piano: a short, two-measure statement, followed by a complementary two-measure statement ending on the dominant. The viola then echoes the opening in mm. 4–8, ending on the tonic. Two measures of ornamented figures transition to another statement of the principal idea at m. 10, now on the downbeat of the measure. At the end of m. 13, the B section starts with the viola playing ornamented figures over the piano's accompaniment. The two instruments begin a dialogue of this material in m. 16 with increasingly elaborate figurations propelling the music to an F^7 harmony in mm. 23–25, culminating in the piano's cadenza-like passage at the Presto. For the return of the opening material at m. 25, Hummel varies the

Zone	Thematic Areas/Snippet	Measures	Principal Tonal Areas/Function
A		1–35	
	Unit 1.1	1–23	E-flat major
	Unit 1.2	23–35	F major
B		35–91	B-flat major
A		91–107	E-flat major
C	Development	107–43	C minor
B		143–92	E-flat major
A		192–213	E-flat major

Chart 18.3 Hummel, Sonata for Piano and Viola, op. 5, no. 3: Structural analysis, third movement, Rondo con moto.

ornaments in both the piano and viola, closing out the movement with more florid writing.

The final movement is a sonata-rondo form (Chart 18.3) in the ABACBA variety favored by Mozart.[16] Combining elements of sonata and rondo forms, the movement opens with an eight-measure statement of the rondo refrain by the piano, ending on the dominant. A varied statement by the viola follows (mm. 9–17), ending on the tonic. A short closing section (Unit 1.2; mm. 23–35), tonicizing F major, leads to the first episode (B; mm. 35–91), which opens with the viola playing a *dolce* theme in B♭ major. At m. 52, the piano starts an extended section of triplets, which is followed by a dialogue between the two instruments of dotted-eighth–sixteenth-note figures at m. 66. The piano's triplets resume at m. 74 in a series of arpeggiated figures set over a long pedal B♭ starting at m. 76. After statements of the refrain by each of the instruments (mm. 91–107), the

Example 18.2 Hummel, Sonata for Piano and Viola, op. 5, no. 3, movt. III, mm. 9–13, viola.

Example 18.3 Mozart, *Così fan tutte*, "Ah lo veggio," No. 24, Act II, Scene II, mm. 1–4, tenor (melody only).

second episode (C) begins at m. 107 in C minor, serving a developmental function. At m. 143, the B episode returns, now in E♭ major. While triplets dominated the earlier appearance of this episode, Hummel uses sixteenth-note figures at m. 162 before returning to triplets at m. 175, now initiated by the viola. The movement closes out with a varied version of the refrain at m. 192.

Hummel often incorporated existing tunes into his works, particularly in variations and potpourris.[17] In addition to such explicit instances of musical borrowing, scholars have detected other musical references in Hummel's compositions, notably in the trumpet concerto.[18] Jacek Dumanowski has identified several motives in Hummel's Sonata for Piano and Viola, op. 5, no. 3 that appear to be borrowed from other sources, including Beethoven's "Pathétique" Sonata and Mozart's *Così fan tutte* (Exs. 18.2 and 18.3).[19] Not surprisingly, Hummel frequently drew inspiration from Mozart's music. But Hummel "was something more than a mere talented imitator" of his teacher,[20] and his compositions—including the Sonata for Piano and Viola—display many original harmonic and formal traits.

When the three opus 5 sonatas were reviewed as a group in 1798 in *Allgemeine musikalische Zeitung*, the critic was unimpressed, writing that "one cannot say that they are distinguished by anything."[21] Twenty years later, the same publication offered a more enthusiastic review of the viola sonata:

> Despite the almost incalculable flood of new piano music, we certainly do not possess too much of it. And of all the many skillful composers for the piano, certainly few could write in such an interesting way as Herr Kapellmeister Hummel. The sonata is most favorable with the accompaniment of the viola, especially because this instrument's best and most effective tonal region is used so well, but it does not lose much, either, with the accompaniment of the violin.[22]

Since its rediscovery in the twentieth century, the sonata has been embraced by violists. The piano writing demonstrates Hummel's mastery of the instrument, and the viola writing is quite accomplished. Throughout the work, the two instruments engage in charming interplay to great effect (particularly striking are the passages from mm. 42–45 and mm. 173–76 in the first movement, where the viola's percussive pizzicato notes double the right hand of the piano). One extraordinary aspect of the sonata is the number of different editions published during Hummel's lifetime—quite a feat for any viola composition. Modern editions have varied depending on which sources the editor selected as well as individual editorial practices. The work was a favorite of Paul Doktor and Louise Rood, both of whom published editions during the middle of the twentieth century that contributed to the work's resurrection. It has gone on to become the most popular of the eighteenth-century viola sonatas written in the Classical style.

19

Bohuslav Martinů: *Rhapsody-Concerto for Viola and Orchestra*, H. 337

I. Moderato
II. Molto adagio — Allegro

Date of Composition: March 15–April 18, 1952

First Edition: Bohuslav Martinů, *Rhapsody-Concerto für Viola und Orchester*, Kassel: Bärenreiter, 1972, BA 4316a (Piano Reduction); 1980 (©1978), BA 4316 (Score)

Date/Place of First Public Performance: February 19, 1953, Jascha Veissi (viola), The Cleveland Orchestra, George Szell (conductor), Severance Hall, Cleveland

Orchestral Instrumentation: Solo viola, 2 flutes, 2 oboes, 2 clarinets in B♭, 2 bassoons, 4 horns in F, 2 trumpets in C, timpani, snare drum, strings

Introduction

"He was born in a tower, completely isolated from the outside world."[1] Bohuslav Martinů spent his formative years in a bell tower, looking down on the small Bohemian town of Polička. As he made his way out of the tower and into the world, he found himself ill prepared to deal with the stresses of the larger cities to which he gravitated: Prague, Paris, and New York. Naturally shy and taciturn, even in his native Czech language, he struggled to communicate in French and English. There are many stories of Martinů's unwillingness—or inability—to engage in the most basic forms of polite conversation: "Even when socializing with fellow musicians, he could be terse. When meeting new people, his reticence could cause conversation to cease awkwardly."[2] Rather than engaging in small talk, Martinů often appeared absorbed in his own thoughts. Fond of solitary, nighttime walks in which he could work out compositions in his mind, he found himself, on more than one occasion, completely lost and in need of assistance.[3]

Martinů's experience growing up in a bell tower undoubtedly affected his personal interactions later in life. But what effect did it have on his compositional style?

> Many a time I have wondered what kind of an influence my living in the tower had on my musical composition. From the time of my first coming to Paris I have always had in my room a picture postcard with a miniature view of the Polička market square as seen from the tower. But this view and many others are firmly imprinted in my memory. . . . Everything in miniature, with little houses and little people, and above it all a great, boundless space. I think that this space is among the strongest impressions of my childhood and one that I am most conscious of and which probably plays a great part in my whole attitude to composition. Not the small interests of people, their cares, joys and griefs, was what I saw from a great distance, or rather, from a great height. It was this space that I had constantly before me and which, it seems to me, I am for ever seeking in my compositions. Space and Nature, not people.[4]

These early impressions greatly affected Martinů's approach to space, expression, and form in his compositions.[5] Embodying the unique view from the tower, Martinů's music offers perceptive insights into space, nature—and the human spirit.

Biographical Sketch

Bohuslav Martinů (1890–1959) was born in Polička, the youngest child of Ferdinand Martinů and his wife, Karolina. A cobbler by profession, Ferdinand also maintained the bell tower in the Church of St. James and kept watch for fires, a post that allowed the family to live rent-free in a single room within the tower.[6] In 1897, Bohuslav started group violin lessons with Josef Černovský, a tailor who taught local children. The violin proved a welcome diversion, and he advanced quickly. Martinů also tried his hand at composing, producing a string quartet by the age of ten.

In 1906, Martinů was admitted to the Prague Conservatory as a violin student. The school's regimented method of instruction, vastly different from his small-town upbringing, came as a culture shock. He missed classes and neglected the violin. Rather than practicing, Martinů preferred to soak up the cultural activities that Prague had to offer; he read voraciously and attended the theater almost daily.[7] Falling behind in his violin studies, he eventually transferred to the Prague Organ School in 1909, where he could also study composition. He continued to miss classes and was expelled the following year "for incorrigible negligence."[8] But his musical path was now clear, and he threw himself into composition.

Martinů avoided conscription during World War I through a series of faked (and occasionally real) illnesses.[9] After the war, his first major success came with a performance of the *Czech Rhapsody*, H. 118, a large-scale cantata that differed markedly from his earlier works.[10] Over the next few years, he experimented with Impressionism and discovered English madrigals, a form that would leave a lasting mark on his compositional style.[11] In 1920, he joined the Czech Philharmonic as a full member, having played violin with them intermittently since 1913. He briefly re-entered the Prague Conservatory in 1922 to study with Josef Suk but felt increasingly drawn to the musical scene in Paris. A three-month travel scholarship permitted him to leave for Paris in October 1923; he would call the city home for the next seventeen years.[12]

Shortly after his arrival in Paris, Martinů began private studies with Albert Roussel. Like many others, Martinů was swept up by the musical currents swirling throughout the city: Stravinsky, neoclassicism, Les Six, and jazz. Within a few years, his music was attracting international attention. In 1926, he met Charlotte Quennehen, a seamstress whom he would marry in 1931. Charlotte remained married to Martinů until his death, even while he carried on two major affairs (first with Vítězslava Kaprálová in Paris and later with Roe Barstow in America). In June 1940, the couple fled Paris during the German invasion, spending several months in Aix-en-Provence until they secured visas for America.

The Martinůs arrived in America on March 31, 1941, eventually settling in New York City. Several friends offered support, including Serge Koussevitzky, who commissioned Martinů's Symphony No. 1, H. 289 and invited him to teach during the summers at the Berkshire Music Center (Tanglewood). Charlotte was particularly unhappy in America, and the couple planned a return to Europe in the spring of 1946. But Martinů accepted another appointment at Tanglewood for that summer, leaving Charlotte to return alone. While at Tanglewood, he suffered a serious accident, falling ten feet from an unenclosed balcony:

> In the evening he went out in the dark on to the balcony which was not railed off at one end (a neglected precaution for which he later sued the school). Somebody had closed the door of his apartments and Martinů, not wishing to disturb anyone and under the impression that steps led down from the balcony, wished to return by way of the ground-floor entrance. The first step brought him on to the roof of a lean-to pantry and the second step into emptiness.[13]

Martinů landed on the side of his head, fracturing his skull and crushing his spinal cord. Though he was fortunate to have escaped paralysis, recovery was slow and painful, and the accident left him with hearing loss and heightened sensitivity. With Charlotte in Europe, he was nursed by Roe Barstow, a divorcée with whom he had recently begun an affair. Martinů remained in America until 1953, ultimately reconciling with his wife. After a couple of years spent in France, he returned to New York in 1955, taking up a teaching position at the Curtis Institute of Music in Philadelphia. The following year he accepted a one-year residency at the American Academy in Rome and afterward moved to Schönenberg, Switzerland. He died of stomach cancer in the nearby town of Liestal on August 28, 1959.

Martinů's *Rhapsody-Concerto for Viola and Orchestra*, H. 337

Martinů's works for viola include the *Divertimento (Serenade No. 4) for Solo Violin, Solo Viola, and Chamber Orchestra*, H. 215 (1932); the *Rhapsody-Concerto for Viola and Orchestra*, H. 337 (1952); and the Sonata for Viola and Piano, H. 355 (1955). Among his chamber works involving the viola are two important duos for violin and viola: *Three Madrigals*, H. 313 (1947) and Duo No. 2, H. 331 (1950). In a program note from 1953, Martinů explained the origin of the *Rhapsody-Concerto*:

> I composed this piece on commission for Jascha Veissi, who is an old friend. I had known him years ago in Paris, and I saw him again in New York last year and was very much impressed by his playing. He has a rare instrument made by Gasparo da Sallo in 1540 [*sic*] which sounds like a human voice. This is inspiring in itself and provides the reason for calling the piece a rhapsody, which actually means a song.[14]

Born in Odessa, Russia, Veissi came to America in 1920, playing in the first violin section of the Cleveland Orchestra from 1921 through 1929.[15] He subsequently served as principal viola of the San Francisco Symphony and then played viola with the Los Angeles Philharmonic. Veissi sustained a significant injury to his left hand in 1941 while a member of the Kolisch Quartet, narrowly averting amputation of the index finger.[16] He recovered and went on to enjoy a modest solo career.

In the *Rhapsody-Concerto*, Martinů exploits the viola's inherent vocal qualities, writing many long, cantilena passages that make extensive use of the instrument's middle register. He intersperses these areas with more rhythmic, virtuosic writing that one expects from a concerto. This juxtaposition of contrasting elements is characteristic of the composer: "Martinů's key sound is the presence of lyrical moments syncopated in a rather special way, usually surrounded by passages meant to suggest an opposing state."[17]

Example 19.1 Martinů, *Rhapsody-Concerto for Viola and Orchestra*, H. 337, movt. I, mm. 48–49, solo viola.

Example 19.2 Martinů, *Rhapsody-Concerto for Viola and Orchestra*, H. 337, movt. I, m. 112, solo viola.

Throughout the work, Martinů uses "cellules" (or "cells"), his term for short motivic germs from which he builds larger musical ideas.[18] A favorite cellule of Martinů's is a "falling and rising minor third," which the viola plays at its first entrance (Ex. 19.1).[19] Cellules can be rhythmic, as is the case with the repeated sixteenth-note and two thirty-second-notes pattern that occurs in both movements (Ex. 19.2). An exhaustive survey of the cellules used in the *Rhapsody-Concerto* is beyond the scope of this chapter; the following analysis is intended to provide a broad overview of the work's form along with brief references to this cellule technique.

The first movement follows a general concerto (sonata) form (Chart 19.1), opening with an orchestral tutti in B♭ major. This section, built around the orchestra's principal thematic idea, is dominated by syncopated rhythms, homophonic textures, and plagal cadences. At m. 48 (all measure numbers and rehearsal numbers refer to the Bärenreiter edition), the solo viola enters with a new, *cantabile* melody (Theme Group 1). This song breaks off in m. 73 as the tempo slows slightly (Poco meno) and a new rhythmic figure is introduced (Theme Group 2). Starting in A♭ major, this section soon returns to B♭ major in m. 82. The viola is afforded a greater opportunity here for technical display with double stops, runs, and complex rhythmic figures. At m. 117, the viola climaxes on a b♭,ii as the orchestra briefly states its opening theme (mm. 117–20), followed by a return of the viola's Theme Group 1 material at m. 120.

The tutti development begins at m. 146 with a brief passage featuring syncopated rhythms in the winds (Unit 1.1). At m. 155, muted strings enter with material derived from Theme Group 2 (Exs. 19.3 and 19.4), which the viola takes

Zone	Thematic Areas/Snippet	Measures	Principal Tonal Areas/Function
Opening Tutti	Opening theme	1–48	B-flat major
Exposition		48–146	
	Theme Group 1	48–73	B-flat major
	Theme Group 2	73–117	Starts A-flat major; B-flat major
	Tutti (opening theme)	117–20	B-flat major
	Closing (Theme Group 1 material)	120–46	B-flat major; ends on D-flat major
Development		146–248	
	Unit 1.1: Tutti	146–55	Starts D-flat major
	Unit 1.2: Tutti	155–89	Starts F major; modulates
	Unit 1.3: Solo	189–231 (No. 23)	Starts B-flat minor; modulates
	Tutti/Solo retransition	231 (No. 23) –48	E-flat major
Recapitulation		248–86	
	Theme Group 1	248–86	
	Unit 1.1	248–73	B-flat major
	Unit 1.2 (with snippets of exposition's Theme Group 2 material)	274–86	A-flat major
Closing	Opening theme	287–95	B-flat major

Chart 19.1 Martinů, *Rhapsody-Concerto for Viola and Orchestra*, H. 337: Structural analysis, first movement, Moderato.

Example 19.3 Martinů, *Rhapsody-Concerto for Viola and Orchestra*, H. 337, movt. I, mm. 75–76, violin I.

Example 19.4 Martinů, *Rhapsody-Concerto for Viola and Orchestra*, H. 337, movt. I, mm. 155–58, violin I & II.

up in m. 189. After working through several key areas in this section, Martinů makes his way to E♭ major for the retransition at m. 231 (No. 23). Here, the roles are reversed with the orchestra playing the viola's Theme Group 1 material in mm. 231–36, while the viola takes up material from the orchestra's opening tutti (see mm. 7–10) when it enters in m. 237. The retransition merges seamlessly with the recapitulation at m. 248, where the viola repeats its lyrical song (Theme Group 1; Unit 1.1). Martinů teases us with snippets of the exposition's Theme Group 2 rhythmic patterns in the oboe and clarinets from mm. 274–76, but the viola persists with its flowing melody (Unit 1.2). The movement closes with a return of the opening theme at m. 287, now led by the solo viola.

The second movement is substantially more free-form than the first, effectively fulfilling the functions of a concerto's slow movement (Molto adagio) and finale (Allegro). It makes greater use of orchestral colors, opening with a pair of flutes in their lower register, mixing E♭ major and minor through a rising third cellule. The viola's lyrical opening passage (mm. 27–46) also prominently features the interval of a third (both rising and falling). At m. 46, the mood changes with the introduction of a new rhythmic cellule: three pickup sixteenth notes followed by a sixteenth note on the downbeat (Ex. 19.5). Variations of this cellule will appear throughout the remainder of the movement. The sixteenth-note and two thirty-second-notes cellule (see Ex. 19.2) also makes an appearance in this section (mm. 77–88). Martinů lightens the atmosphere at m. 100 with the introduction of a *Molto tranquillo* song, which is followed by an orchestral tutti (mm. 108–23) that begins by revisiting the rising third cellule. A quasi cadenza in m. 124 segues into a Poco allegro section (mm. 125–34), which prepares us for the energetic Allegro.

Example 19.5 Martinů, *Rhapsody-Concerto for Viola and Orchestra*, H. 337, movt. II, mm. 46–48, solo viola.

The Allegro portion (mm. 135–262) is dominated by sixteenth-note figurations starting with a return of the sixteenth-note "pickup" cellule (see Ex. 19.5). After a section featuring bouncing staccato double stops (mm. 144–57), the sixteenth-note "pickup" cellule reappears at m. 161. More fancy passage-work follows, with the violist leaping around the fingerboard. A series of fierce multiple stops (mm. 202–8) finally exhausts the soloist, who gives way to the orchestra for a vigorous tutti (mm. 208–38). By the time the viola re-enters in m. 239, the orchestra has exhausted themselves as well, save for a single snare drum, which bravely accompanies the soloist until m. 246 (No. 25). The viola continues its lyrical passage alone until the orchestral strings intrude at m. 260. A tempo change at m. 263 (Andante) ushers in a return of the song from m. 100, providing a serene conclusion to the movement.

At its premiere, critics found the *Rhapsody-Concerto for Viola and Orchestra*, H. 337 to be a pleasant, if not particularly exciting, work:

> The character of the Martinu piece, except for a short and spicy allegro episode, is generally serene, idyllic and pleasant. There is certainly nothing in its harmonies that could be the least bit offensive to the tenderest and most unsophisticated ears.
>
> The viola speaks out eloquently in melodies that have a tinge of folk song, as well as a faint suggestion of medieval monody. The writing is competent and smooth, and the composer seems content not to introduce any very disturbing elements into the seriously reflective picture.
>
> In so doing he perhaps robs it of a certain emotional impact it might have, were there only at least some undercurrent of opposition. It is a little like a story without a villain. But it is wholly agreeable music.[20]

Upon publication of the piano reduction, Michael Tilmouth was more scathing in his assessment:

> Martinů's Rhapsody-Concerto is an uneven work by an uneven composer. There are some beautiful moments: the closing Andante strikes a vein of tender

simplicity which is not less captivating for sounding like a page of Dvořák. But so much of the work seems to bear those hall-marks of the rhapsodic style—a kind of aimless meandering coupled with mere note-spinning—which seem unlikely to give it any very secure place even in the slender repertory of the viola.[21]

David Cope was equally unimpressed when he reviewed the full score in 1980:

> This is certainly not Martinů's most imaginative score. It is riddled with clichés and hackneyed approaches to folk tunes and so repetitive at times that any real drama or musical drive is thoroughly negated.[22]

Contrary to these critical remarks, violists have embraced the *Rhapsody-Concerto*, and it has become one of Martinů's more frequently performed and recorded works. The writing is highly suited to the viola, bringing out both the lyrical and more rugged aspects of the instrument. Martinů orchestrated the work in a manner that allows the viola to shine through using many subtle effects that enhance the solo part: the luscious scoring of the accompanying strings in mm. 30–35 of the second movement and the *col legno* slaps in mm. 155–56 of the same movement are just two instances that appear simplistic on the page but sound marvelous in person. Indeed, such "simplistic" elements are what make Martinů's music special:

> It is possible that my thoughts dwell upon objects or events of an almost everyday simplicity familiar to everyone and not exclusively to certain great spirits. They may be so simple as to pass almost unnoticed but may still contain a deep meaning and afford great pleasure to humanity, which, without them, would find life pale and flat.[23]

A work of great beauty and vitality, Martinů's *Rhapsody-Concerto for Viola and Orchestra*, H. 337 is a sheer delight to perform—and, thankfully, its deep meaning has not gone unnoticed by violists.

20

Felix Mendelssohn: Sonata in C Minor for Viola and Piano

I.   Adagio — Allegro
II. Menuetto — Trio
III. Andante con Variazioni

Date of Composition: November 23, 1823–February 14, 1824

First Edition: Felix Mendelssohn Bartholdy, *Sonate C-moll für Bratsche und Klavier*, Leipzig: VEB Deutscher Verlag für Musik, 1966, DVfM 8103

Select Later Edition: Felix Mendelssohn Bartholdy, *Sonate c-moll für Viola und Klavier*, ed. Ernst Herttrich, Munich: Henle, 2011, HN 1035

Introduction

"Every composer is capable of surprising inequalities in his output, but no one has achieved more baffling extremes than Mendelssohn, and in no other instance does the reputation of one group of works cast so forbidding a shadow over our assessment of the others."[1] For violists accustomed to Mendelssohn at his best—the Octet, op. 20; the Violin Concerto in E Minor, op. 64; and the symphonies—his Sonata in C Minor for Viola and Piano can prove to be something of a letdown. Completed shortly after his fifteenth birthday, the sonata dates from a pivotal phase in Mendelssohn's artistic development. His music underwent "a significant stylistic shift" during this period,[2] and the sonata exhibits a mixture of youthful and emerging influences. It was not published during Mendelssohn's lifetime, though this may have had less to do with concerns over the quality of the work and more to do with his recycling of material from the Menuetto in his Symphony No. 1, op. 11.[3] While the sonata may not rank among the composer's masterpieces, it is an accomplished work filled with "the qualities people associate with Mendelssohn's best music—brilliance, clarity, and cleverness."[4]

Biographical Sketch

Felix Mendelssohn (1809–1847) was born into a wealthy banking family in Hamburg. His parents, Abraham and Lea Mendelssohn, moved the family to Berlin in 1811, where Lea oversaw the early musical education of Felix and his older sister, Fanny. By 1819, Carl Friedrich Zelter had been hired to instruct both children.[5] Zelter's method of instruction was based on his own teacher's—Carl Friedrich Christian Fasch—progressing through four- and five-part chorales, counterpoint, canon, and three-part composition before finally coming to the fugue.[6] Reflecting "a conservative theoretical tradition extending back to J. S. Bach,"[7] this approach greatly influenced Mendelssohn's compositional style.

A sensitive, artistic child, Felix was encouraged to pursue a wide range of intellectual and creative endeavors. He became adept at playing several instruments, including the piano, violin, viola, and organ. By 1822, he was routinely performing at "lavish Sunday 'musicales' at the family home," which "attracted the cultural élite of Berlin."[8] These concerts also provided an opportunity for showcasing his budding compositional talents. In 1827, Mendelssohn entered the University of Berlin to further his general education. Two years later, he conducted Bach's *St. Matthew Passion* at the Sing-Akademie zu Berlin, a defining moment that is generally credited with invigorating the revival of Bach's music.[9] Mendelssohn then embarked on a Grand Tour of Europe, traveling for the next three years. In 1833, he accepted a three-year appointment as music director in Düsseldorf but soon became dissatisfied with this position. He requested termination of his contract in May 1835 and officially accepted a position as director of the Gewandhaus Orchestra in Leipzig the following month.[10] By this time, Mendelssohn was already enjoying "an international reputation secured by several important works," including the Symphony No. 1, the Octet, two string quartets, and *A Midsummer Night's Dream* overture.[11] On a trip to Frankfurt in 1836, he met Cécile Charlotte Sophie Jeanrenaud, whom he would marry the following year; the couple would have five children.

In 1840, Mendelssohn was approached about a position under Prussia's new king, Friedrich Wilhelm IV, who hoped to "revitalize the arts in Berlin."[12] Mendelssohn accepted the position of Kapellmeister at the king's court in 1841 but negotiated a change of duties the following year, enabling him to resume activities in Leipzig. One of his significant projects in Leipzig was the founding of a conservatory in 1843 (now the Hochschule für Musik und Theater "Felix Mendelssohn Bartholdy" Leipzig), where he taught "solo singing, instrumental playing, and composition."[13] In his final years, Mendelssohn experienced a "downward physical spiral,"[14] brought on by overwork and emotional distress. After suffering a series of strokes in the fall of 1847, Mendelssohn died on November 4 at the age of thirty-eight.

Mendelssohn's Sonata in C Minor for Viola and Piano

Mendelssohn's Sonata in C Minor for Viola and Piano (1823–1824) remained largely unknown until the middle of the twentieth century, when Ernst and Lory Wallfisch discovered the manuscript in the archives of the Preußische Staatsbibliothek (now the Berlin State Library). The couple started programming the work frequently, including at Pablo Casals's Prades Festival in 1959. First published in 1966, the sonata was recorded shortly afterward by Georgii Bezrukov and Anatolii Spivak.[15] The inspiration for the work is unknown, though Mendelssohn may have intended the viola part for himself.[16] Like other works of Mendelssohn's dating from the same period, the sonata shows the influence of Ludwig van Beethoven, particularly in the hefty final movement, a theme and variations structured "not as a loose sequence of individual numbers, but as a through-composed and purposeful 'process.'"[17] Several scholars have commented on cyclic aspects among the sonata's movements; most noticeable is the shared "suspension of the upper neighbor across the bar line" in both the second and third movements (Exs. 20.1 and 20.2).[18]

Example 20.1 Mendelssohn, Sonata in C Minor for Viola and Piano, movt. II, mm. 1–4.

Example 20.2 Mendelssohn, Sonata in C Minor for Viola and Piano, movt. III, mm. 36–39, viola.

The first movement is in sonata form with an introduction and repeated exposition (Chart 20.1). Mendelssohn's training in counterpoint is reflected in the opening Adagio, which resembles a chorale setting. At m. 20 (all measure numbers refer to both the VEB Deutscher Verlag für Musik and Henle editions), the viola begins the Allegro with a sweeping theme (Unit 1.1). The two instruments swap roles at m. 34 with the piano taking over the melody while the viola plays a condensed version of the accompaniment. Mendelssohn progresses to B♭ major at m. 46 with new melodic material in the piano (Unit 1.2), supported by a pedal B♭ in the viola. Instead of moving directly to the relative major for the second theme group, the viola provides only a hint of E♭ major at m. 56, while the piano persists with the key of B♭ (serving a dominant function) in its melodic material at m. 58. There is no strong confirmation that we have arrived in the relative major until m. 74 (Unit 2.2).[19] Here, the piano takes over the viola's eighth notes playing an ascending E♭ major scale that is answered by the viola with a

Zone	Thematic Areas/Snippet	Measures	Principal Tonal Areas/Function
Introduction		1–19	C minor; ends on dominant
Repeated Exposition		20–93	
	Theme Group 1	20–55	
	Unit 1.1	20–46	C minor
	Unit 1.2	46–55	B-flat major
	Theme Group 2	56–93	
	Unit 2.1	56–74	V/III; E-flat major
	Unit 2.2	74–93	E-flat major
Development		94–145	Begins C minor; modulates; dominant

Chart 20.1 Mendelssohn, Sonata in C Minor for Viola and Piano: Structural analysis, first movement, Adagio — Allegro.

Zone	Thematic Areas/Snippet	Measures	Principal Tonal Areas/Function
Recapitulation		146–200	
	Theme Group 1	146–67	
	Unit 1.1	146–60	C minor
	Unit 1.2	160–67	Dominant
	Theme Group 2	168–200	
	Unit 2.1	168–86	Dominant; C major
	Unit 2.2	186–200	C major
Coda		200–222	C minor

Chart 20.1 (continued) Mendelssohn, Sonata in C Minor for Viola and Piano: Structural analysis, first movement, Adagio — Allegro.

descending scalar passage. The section closes with a bit of imitative counterpoint between the viola and piano in mm. 86–92 prior to the exposition's repeat.

The development is concentrated on Theme Group 1, Unit 1.1 material. Mendelssohn thins out the texture at m. 103, with monophonic writing in each of the three instrumental lines until m. 126. A sustained dominant harmony begins at m. 130, with a G pedal in the bass. At m. 139, the final measures of the introduction (mm. 18–19) are echoed, first in the viola's figure and then in the piano's.

For the recapitulation, Mendelssohn omits material that originally appeared at m. 29 (Ex. 20.3) and moves quickly to Unit 1.2 material, now in the dominant (G major) in preparation for the second theme group's appearance in the parallel major. While the key signature change at m. 163 heralds the move to C major, the viola stubbornly sticks to a♭s at the beginning of Theme Group 2 (m. 168), allowing Mendelssohn to preserve the half-step relationship from the exposition. Meanwhile, the piano continues on a G dominant function, with a full confirmation of the modulation to C major at m. 186. A return to C minor at m. 200 signals the start of the coda, where the previously omitted material (see Ex. 20.3) makes an appearance at m. 202.

Example 20.3 Mendelssohn, Sonata in C Minor for Viola and Piano, movt. I, mm. 29–33, viola.

Movement two is a minuet and trio (Chart 20.2) with the Menuetto portion (Allegro molto) in a typical rounded binary form. The opening section (A; mm. 1–35) contains two themes; the first (Unit 1.1) emphasizes a half step, both in the theme and in the descending chromatic bass line. Over the course of two eight-measure periods, the viola and piano trade melodic material. In mm. 14–15, the music modulates to E♭ major, anticipating the start of the second theme (Unit 1.2) at m. 16. Here, the music broadens out with the viola's *dolce*, legato theme making use of wider intervals over arpeggiated figures in the piano's right hand. Serving a developmental function, the B section (mm. 36–75) explores several key areas while fragmented portions of Unit 1.1 material flit about. At m. 76, the A section returns with the opening melody now entirely in the piano. The second theme is presented in C minor at m. 91, which is followed by a coda from mm. 107–22.

The chorale-like Trio (più lento) shifts to C major and common time, never getting louder than *p*. After a four-measure introductory idea (mm. 123–26), the piano presents an eight-measure period ending on G major followed by an eight-measure period in the viola. The second portion of the Trio (Second Reprise) is an expanded version of the first with the four-measure introductory idea presented twice (mm. 143–50). Next comes a reharmonized version of the piano's earlier eight-measure period followed by a modified version of the viola's period, ending with a C major cadence in mm. 165–66. A return to ¾ and the Allegro molto tempo at m. 166 enables a smooth return to the opening minuet.

Like the previous movements, the Andante con Variazioni is in C minor. The Andante theme, which begins with an upbeat figure, is in binary form with both sections repeated; the first is eight measures in length (ending on E♭ major), while the second is ten measures. Variations 1 through 3 employ sixteenth-note figurations, and variations 2 and 3 dispense with the second section's repeat. For the fourth variation, the piano plays sextuplets underneath the viola's presentation of the theme, and Mendelssohn extends the second section by one measure. In the fifth variation, the rhythmic momentum is pulled back, with the viola playing pedal sixteenth notes, creating a wonderfully hypnotic effect underneath the piano's theme. Mendelssohn now begins to deviate "from the original melodic

Zone	Thematic Areas/Snippet	Measures	Principal Tonal Areas/Function
Menuetto		1–122	
	First Reprise (Repeated)	1–35	
	(A) Unit 1.1	1–16	C minor
	(A) Unit 1.2	16–35	E-flat major
	Second Reprise (Repeated)	36–122	
	(B) Developmental	36–75	C minor; modulates; ends on dominant
	(A) Unit 2.1	76–91	C minor
	(A) Unit 2.2	91–107	C minor
	Coda	107–22	C minor
Trio		123–82	
	First Reprise (Repeated)	123–42	C major to dominant
	Second Reprise (Repeated)	143–66	Dominant to C major
	Closing	166–82	C major; dominant
Da Capo (senza repeats)		1–122	

Chart 20.2 Mendelssohn, Sonata in C Minor for Viola and Piano: Structural analysis, second movement, Menuetto — Trio.

course" in Variation 6,[20] which features thirty-second notes in the piano. Only the first section is repeated (Variation 4 and Variation 5 dispensed entirely with repeats), while the second section is extended to eighteen measures. Following a similar plan (with a repeated first section and an extended second one), Variation 7 uses dotted-sixteenth–thirty-second-note figures. Having gotten progressively further away from the theme's original framework, Mendelssohn makes a nearly clean break in the two final sections. Variation 8 shifts to the downbeat for a "free, florid *adagio* in C major featuring the piano. A brief recitative then leads to a turbulent return to C minor in an *allegro* coda."[21]

For such a youthful work, Mendelssohn's sonata demonstrates great compositional maturity. It has been critically well-received, praised for its "impressive musical quality."[22] Despite admiration from critics, the sonata has yet to fully win the hearts of violists. It is in the model of a piano sonata with viola accompaniment, and many of the accompanimental figures (particularly the frequent repeated notes) may not satisfactorily sustain a violist's interest. The final movement, in which the pianist is increasingly taxed while the violist has extended periods of rest, often proves tiresome to violists, and they have occasionally made cuts to alleviate the perceived imbalance between the instruments.[23] More engaging for violists is the second movement. Though labeled a Menuetto, it exudes the sprightly scherzo style associated with the composer. Regardless of any reservations, the work is a significant contribution to the nineteenth-century viola sonata repertoire and is worthy of study and performance by every violist.

21
Darius Milhaud: *Quatre Visages for Viola and Piano*, op. 238

I.   La Californienne
II. The Wisconsonian
III. La Bruxelloise
IV. La Parisienne

Date of Composition: November 16–December 1, 1943

First Edition: Darius Milhaud, *Quatre Visages Pour Alto et Piano*, 4 vols., Paris: Heugel et Cie, 1946, Plate No. H.31 120

Dedication: à Germain Prévost

Date/Place of First Public Performance: January 9, 1944, Germain Prévost (viola), Gunnar Johansen (piano), Music Hall Auditorium, The University of Wisconsin, Madison

Introduction

"Before we approach the music of Milhaud, before we can absorb its expressiveness and appreciate its genius and skill, we must first imagine ourselves in Provence."[1] The prolific French composer Darius Milhaud traveled widely, finding inspiration in far-flung locales: the Botanical Gardens of Rio de Janeiro, the dance halls of London, the theaters of Harlem. But the greatest source of inspiration came from the sights and sounds of his youth in Aix-en-Provence: fields of wheat; gardens filled with magnolias, lime trees, and crape myrtles; peasants playing cards in cafés; villagers herding flocks of sheep to the Alps; and pealing bells at nearby convents.[2] For Milhaud, Provence was a paradise of earthly delights: real people, leading real lives within a landscape of utter beauty. These joyous surroundings worked their way deep into Milhaud's psyche, imbuing his musical style with a "Mediterranean lyricism" that extends throughout all of his compositions.[3]

Biographical Sketch

Darius Milhaud (1892–1974) was born into a Jewish family in Marseille but raised in nearby Aix-en-Provence. His father, Gabriel, was an almond exporter and amateur pianist who was involved in the local musical society; his mother, Sophie, was a contralto who had studied singing in Paris. By the age of three, Milhaud was picking out tunes on the piano and playing duets with his father. At age seven, he began violin lessons with Léo Bruguier, advancing rapidly on the instrument.[4] In 1909, he entered the Paris Conservatoire, remaining there until 1915. Initially concentrating on violin, he gradually turned toward composition, studying harmony with Xavier Leroux and fugue with Charles-Marie Widor. His most influential studies were in counterpoint and composition with André Gédalge, who "impressed upon him the need to make melody the essence of musical composition."[5]

Exempted from service in World War I on medical grounds, Milhaud instead joined the Foyer Franco-Belge, an organization that assisted Belgian refugees.[6] Later, he began working at the Maison de la Presse, which was responsible for France's wartime propaganda efforts. During this period, he became increasingly interested in polytonality, thoroughly investigating every combination of two and three keys.[7] He also continued playing violin and occasionally viola, most notably in the first private performance of Claude Debussy's Sonata for Flute, Viola, and Harp on December 10, 1916. In January 1917, Milhaud accompanied his friend Paul Claudel to Rio de Janeiro. Claudel had recently been appointed Minister to Brazil and offered Milhaud a position as secretary in charge of propaganda. Even with his regular duties, Milhaud found time to compose and organize concerts in aid of the Red Cross.[8]

Following his return to France in 1919, Milhaud became entrenched in the postwar avant-garde scene, earning a spot in Henri Collet's group of modern composers who were reviving French music—famously dubbed "Les Six."[9] Milhaud's ballet Le Bœuf sur le toit, which used Brazilian melodies and rhythms, premiered to great success in February 1920. Later that year, a performance of his polytonal work Suite symphonique no. 2 caused a scandal—reportedly on par with that of Igor Stravinsky's Le Sacre du printemps—in which balconies were cleared of hecklers and the conductor implored the restless audience to give the music a fair hearing.[10] Milhaud proved immune to criticism and continued composing in a manner that he found satisfying. His adoption of modern techniques, including jazz and polytonality, reflected a genuine interest in music and humanity rather than a desire to appear trendy.

In 1925, he married the actress Madeleine Milhaud, his cousin; the couple would have one son, the painter and sculptor Daniel Milhaud. Ill health plagued the composer with severe bouts of rheumatoid arthritis confining him to bed for extended periods and ultimately to a wheelchair in later life. In 1940, as France fell to Germany, the Milhauds were forced to flee from the Nazi threat. Traveling to the United States, Darius was offered a job at Mills College, a private women's college in Oakland, California. After returning to France in 1947, Milhaud spent alternate years teaching at Mills and the Paris Conservatoire. In 1951, the Milhauds added the Aspen Music Festival and School to their teaching schedule, with Madeleine teaching drama and directing opera performances. Darius Milhaud retired from teaching at Mills in 1971 and died in Geneva, Switzerland, three years later.

Milhaud's *Quatre Visages for Viola and Piano*, op. 238

With more than four hundred works to his credit, Milhaud composed in practically every genre. Among his compositions are a number of pieces for viola: Concerto for Viola and Orchestra, op. 108 (1929); *Quatre Visages for Viola and Piano*, op. 238 (1943); Sonata No. 1 [Première sonate] for Viola and Piano, op. 240 (1944); *Air de la Sonate for Viola and Orchestra*, op. 242 (1944); Sonata No. 2 [Deuxième sonate] for Viola and Piano, op. 244 (1944); *Concertino d'été for Viola and Chamber Orchestra*, op. 311 (1951); and Concerto No. 2 [Deuxième concerto] for Viola and Orchestra, op. 340 (1954–1955), as well as several duos prominently involving the viola.

Quatre Visages (*Four Faces*) was the first of three works for viola and piano commissioned by the Belgian violist Germain Prévost, a founding member of the Pro Arte Quartet and a friend of Milhaud's. Each movement is a tribute to "young womanhood,"[11] inspired by Prévost's love of "friends, youthful faces, and music."[12] According to Milhaud's wife, the movements are not based on specific women, but instead are "pure imagination."[13] Milhaud typically "endeavoured to find the style that would suit a particular work,"[14] and all of the compositions for Prévost "were written in order to please Germain and his sentimentality."[15]

Prévost commissioned *Quatre Visages* at the end of 1943 and premiered it in early January of the following year.[16] Each of the titles corresponds to an important place where Prévost worked with the Pro Arte Quartet: California (the quartet had a regular summer residency at Mills College during the 1930s), Wisconsin (the quartet had established a residency in 1940 at the University of Wisconsin in Madison, where they are still based), Brussels (where the quartet was founded), and Paris (a city integral to their early success). In 1946, each movement was individually published, and violists have frequently programmed one or two movements rather than the entire set.

Light and breezy, "La Californienne" depicts the type of student that Milhaud encountered at Mills: "self-confident and free from complexes and inhibitions."[17]

Example 21.1 Milhaud, *Quatre Visages for Viola and Piano,* op. 238, movt. I. "La Californienne," mm. 1–4, viola.

Example 21.2 Milhaud, *Quatre Visages for Viola and Piano,* op. 238, movt. I. "La Californienne," mm. 47–51, viola.

Centered on F major, the movement is built around two motivic ideas that appear in the first four measures (Ex. 21.1). After the initial eight-measure phrase, Milhaud fragments and combines these motives in different ways, presenting the motive from m. 3 in a sequence descending by a second (mm. 9–12) and then in an inverted form in another descending sequential pattern (mm. 15–17 and mm. 23–25). A transitory passage with trills (mm. 27–31) takes us to a passage with a new rhythmic pattern at m. 32 followed by another transitory passage (mm. 41–47). The movement closes with two varied statements of the opening eight-measure phrase (mm. 48–63), the first of which Milhaud ingeniously merges with material from m. 32 (Ex. 21.2).

The personality of "The Wisconsonian" is reflected in the tempo marking: Vif et gai (Lively and cheerful). This charming young woman is bubbly and chatty, if a bit repetitive and flighty, wandering all over the place. Centered on G, this movement has the character of a *perpetuum mobile,* opening with rapid sixteenth-note figurations that emphasize the intervals of a second and a third. After winding down its sixteenth notes in mm. 31–36, the viola presents a new idea at m. 37 while the piano continues with sixteenth notes. The opening material returns at m. 48 with the music winding down once again in mm. 66–67 in preparation for a return of material from m. 37. Here, the viola spends only four measures (mm. 68–71) catching its breath before one final chipper outburst of sixteenth notes at m. 72.

"La Bruxelloise" is the most serious in temperament. The movement begins with a strict canon at the octave between the viola and the right hand of the piano, set over a chromatic bass line. In mm. 13–14, the canon breaks off as the

Example 21.3 François van Campenhout, *La Brabançonne*, mm. 21–25 (melody only).

Example 21.4 Milhaud, *Quatre Visages for Viola and Piano*, op. 238, movt. III. "La Bruxelloise," mm. 51–56, viola.

music transitions to a new section at m. 18. Here, the piano's texture briefly thins out but retains its chromaticism. The canon returns at m. 29 with the viola line moving about: the first six notes are an octave below the piano's line subsequently moving to the unison and finally an octave above (mm. 39–40). Milhaud also harmonizes this section differently than the opening. At m. 45, the material from m. 18 returns, abruptly ending at m. 51 on a fermata note. The movement closes out with a tag that incorporates music from the Belgian national anthem, *La Brabançonne* (Exs. 21.3 and 21.4).[18] Milhaud frequently incorporated popular tunes in his music, usually in a slightly altered form,[19] and the inclusion of the anthem is an obvious nod to Prévost's Belgian heritage.

"La Parisienne" exudes the most sophisticated countenance: a fashionably dressed young woman with impeccable taste. Milhaud uses mixed meters to add complexity, setting this movement apart from the others. After a four-measure statement of the principal thematic idea in the piano, the viola enters at m. 5 with the notation *avec chic et apreté* (with style and bite). A more subdued quality pervades the section that starts at m. 20, with its quiet dynamics and harmonics in the viola. At m. 34, the viola and piano trade motivic ideas from the beginning of the movement, and a decisive return of the opening section occurs at m. 44. This time, the viola plays along from the outset, asserting itself with dramatic chords and string crossings. The intensity escalates in the final six measures (mm. 52–57), with a *ff* dynamic and heavily accented chords in the piano, to conclude the movement in a rousing manner.

Reviewing a performance of *Quatre Visages* by Ferenc Molnar in 1945, the critic Donald Fuller wrote:

Though Milhaud too does not often strike us with his novelty, one always finds in him fresh little touches to delight. The *Quatre Visages*, a group of sunny disposition on Ferenc Molnar's viola recital, offered such variations as a widespread, leaping lyricism and a spirited adaptation of conventional string figurations.[20]

The work's lyricism and clever portrayals of four faces makes for engaging programming in any context. Yet behind its light and airy façade is a multifaceted, skillfully crafted work. Each movement is the musical equivalent of a portrait miniature, in which Milhaud perfectly captures the sitter's likeness.

22

Wolfgang Amadeus Mozart: Sinfonia concertante for Violin, Viola, and Orchestra, K. 364 (320d)

I. Allegro maestoso
II. Andante
III. Presto

Date of Composition: 1779 (summer or fall)

First Edition: W. A. Mozart, *Sinfonie concertante pour Violon & Alto*, Oeuvre 104, Offenbach: Jean André, [c. 1801–1802], No. 1588 (Parts)

Select Later Editions: Wolfgang Amadeus Mozart, *Sinfonia concertante in Es für Violine, Viola und Orchester, KV 364 (320^d)*, ed. Christoph-Hellmut Mahling, Kassel: Bärenreiter, 1987 (© 1975), TP 176 (Study Score); W. A. Mozart, *Sinfonia concertante in Es für Violine, Viola und Orchester, KV 364 (320^d)*, Kassel: Bärenreiter, 1990, BA 4900-90 (Piano Reduction; includes two viola parts, one with and one without the scordatura tuning); Wolfgang Amadeus Mozart, *Sinfonia concertante für Violine, Viola und Orchester, Es-dur KV 364*, ed. Wolf-Dieter Seiffert, Wiesbaden/Munich: Breitkopf & Härtel/Henle, 2006, EB 10798/HN 798 (Piano Reduction; includes two viola parts, one with and one without the scordatura tuning)

Date/Place of Early Public Performance: Winter season 1808, Bartolomeo Campagnoli (violin), Johann Georg Hermann Voigt (viola), Leipzig

Orchestral Instrumentation: Solo violin, solo viola, 2 oboes, 2 horns in E♭, 2 violins, 2 violas, violoncello and basso

Introduction

"We also meet with two works in one of Mozart's most lucky keys—E flat major—in the course of 1779, and these stand out by enduring qualities, particularly the *Sinfonia concertante* for violin, viola and orchestra (K. 364), a beautiful, dark-coloured work in which a passion not at all suited to an archiepiscopal court, and perhaps disclosing active revolt against it, seems to smoulder under a perfectly decorous style and exquisite proportions."[1] By the time that Mozart composed his Sinfonia concertante, K. 364, he was quite unhappy at the prince-archbishop's court in Salzburg. Having left the archbishop's employ in 1777, he reluctantly returned in early 1779 after failing to secure an appointment elsewhere. Only a few months before returning, he wrote to Abbé Joseph Bullinger:

> You know, my dear friend, how I hate Salzburg!—not only on account of the injustices that my father and I have suffered there, which would be reason enough to forget such a place altogether, indeed wipe it from your memory! . . . I have far *more* hope to live a pleasurable and happy life anywhere else!—Perhaps you misunderstand me and think that I feel Salzburg is too small for me?—if you think that, you are quite mistaken;—I told my father some of the reasons already; let me tell you just one: Salzburg is no place for my talent!—First of all, the court musicians do not enjoy a good reputation, second, there's nothing going on musically; there is no theater, no opera![2]

Mozart's attitude toward the prince-archbishop did not improve during his remaining years of employment: he fulfilled his musical obligations at the court in a perfunctory manner and focused instead on composing instrumental works, few of which "would have been heard at court, where instrumental music was little favoured."[3] Perhaps the greatest of the instrumental works composed during Mozart's final years in Salzburg is the Sinfonia concertante, in which he took a fashionable genre of the day and turned it on its head, producing a work that is "exceptional not only in its symphonic intensity and cogency, but also in the seriousness of its tone."[4]

Biographical Sketch

Born in Salzburg, Wolfgang Amadeus Mozart (1756–1791) was the last of Maria Anna and Leopold Mozart's seven children, of whom only two—Wolfgang and his older sister, Maria Anna "Nannerl"—survived beyond infancy. Leopold, who served as a violinist in the prince-archbishop of Salzburg's orchestra, is believed to have been entirely responsible for his children's education. Wolfgang's talent manifested itself early: having learned to play keyboard pieces from his sister's music book at the age of four, he produced his earliest known compositions at the age of five and taught himself to play the violin at the age of six. Leopold, eager to showcase his children's talents, traveled to Munich in January 1762, where Wolfgang and Nannerl performed at the court of Maximilian III Joseph,

Elector of Bavaria; at the end of the year, they traveled to Vienna, where the children performed for several noble families. After Leopold was elevated to deputy Kapellmeister at the court in 1763, the family embarked on a tour that would last for over three years and cover England, France, Germany, the Low Countries, and Switzerland.[5] Leopold arranged further tours in the following years, and the young Wolfgang continued to astound audiences with his musical feats. During these travels, he was awarded many honors: Pope Clement XIV conferred the Order of the Golden Spur on him in 1770, and he was admitted to the Accademia Filarmonica in Bologna in 1770 and the Accademia Filarmonica in Verona in 1771.[6]

The election of Hieronymus Colloredo as the new prince-archbishop of Salzburg in 1772 brought changes to musical life at the court. On August 21, 1772, Colloredo officially employed Wolfgang as Konzertmeister, a post that he had held on an honorary basis since 1769. But Colloredo made other changes that were less to the Mozarts' liking, placing restrictions on performances of purely instrumental music at the court and eventually closing the university theater in 1778.[7] Under Colloredo's reign, Wolfgang grew unhappy with court life; rather than principally devoting himself to church music—as would be expected from someone in his position—he "established himself as the chief composer in Salzburg of instrumental and secular vocal music."[8] During these years, he produced many serenades and divertimentos for festive occasions and composed all five of his violin concertos.

In August 1777, Mozart petitioned to leave Colloredo's employ but got more than he bargained for; the archbishop happily released both Wolfgang *and his father* from service. Leopold managed to retain his position, while Wolfgang traveled with his mother in search of a new position, visiting Munich, Augsburg, and then Mannheim, where he became smitten with Aloysia Weber, a singer. After dallying for nearly five months in Mannheim, he proceeded to Paris, where his attempts at attaining a suitable position came to nothing. To compound matters, his mother died during their stay, on July 3, 1778. He dejectedly returned to Salzburg early in 1779, where his father had secured the position of court organist for him. Mozart remained discontented with court life and resented being treated like a servant; matters reached a breaking point in the spring of 1781 while Colloredo was on an extended visit to Vienna. After a heated interview with the archbishop on May 9, Mozart formally requested his discharge. The release was finally granted during a meeting on June 8 with one of Colloredo's court officials, Count Karl Joseph Felix Arco, who threw Mozart out of the room with "a kick in his Behind."[9]

Mozart remained in Vienna, taking on pupils and quickly earning a reputation as the finest keyboard player in the city, performing in many public and private concerts over the following years.[10] On July 16, 1782, he scored a major success with the premiere of his opera *The Abduction from the Seraglio*. Only a few weeks later, on August 4, Mozart married Constanze Weber, younger sister of his former love, Aloysia. The couple would have six children together, of whom only two sons, Carl Thomas and Franz Xaver Wolfgang, survived beyond infancy.

In December 1784, Mozart joined the freemasons; he composed a number of works for Masonic occasions over the following years and reaped many professional benefits from his association with the organization. Mozart scored another operatic success in 1786 with *The Marriage of Figaro*, the first of his three great collaborations with the librettist Lorenzo Da Ponte. In December 1787, he was appointed court *Kammermusicus* (chamber composer) by Emperor Joseph II, which provided a small, but welcome, annual salary of 800 gulden. Mozart's financial situation throughout the Vienna years had been unstable, and by his final years he was mired in debt, frequently imploring friends for assistance.[11] Mozart fell ill late in November 1791 and took to his bed; he died in the early hours of December 5 and was buried two days later "in a common grave, in accordance with contemporary Viennese custom."[12]

Mozart's Sinfonia concertante for Violin, Viola, and Orchestra, K. 364 (320d)

In addition to the violin, Mozart also enjoyed playing the viola.[13] He composed several works that prominently involve the instrument, including the Sinfonia concertante for Violin, Viola, and Orchestra, K. 364 (320d) (1779); 2 Duos for Violin and Viola, K. 423–24 (1783); the "Kegelstatt" Trio for Clarinet, Viola, and Piano, K. 498 (1786); and the Divertimento in E♭ Major for Violin, Viola, and Cello, K. 563 (1788). These works demonstrate a penchant for flat keys (J. S. Bach likewise favored flat keys when showcasing the viola), notably E♭ major, considered to be one of Mozart's "richest keys, allowing for a wide range of expression, from the queenly-regal, dignified, and commanding without being imperious, to the exuberant and the energetic."[14]

The circumstances surrounding Mozart's composition of the Sinfonia concertante are unknown, including the intended performers; many authors have speculated that Mozart composed the viola part for himself.[15] Christoph-Hellmut Mahling notes that there were many capable instrumentalists in Salzburg who could have taken the solo parts; he specifically mentions the violinists Antonio Brunetti and Joseph Hafeneder as possible soloists.[16] The original manuscript for the work is presumed to be lost; only fragmentary sketches, along with an autograph fair copy of Mozart's original cadenzas for the first two movements, are known to exist. When Ludwig Ritter von Köchel initially compiled his thematic catalogue of Mozart's works (first published in 1862), he dated the Sinfonia concertante to 1780, assigning it a catalogue number of 364 in his chronological arrangement of Mozart's compositions. Subsequent research redated the work to the summer or early fall of 1779, and it was assigned a revised Köchel number of 320d. Both Köchel numbers remain in use, but the original number, 364, is more common. The work was first published around 1801–1802 by Johann André.[17] Though there were undoubtedly performances of the work during Mozart's lifetime, the early performance history of the work is uncertain. There are several recorded performances from the nineteenth century, including one in Leipzig during the winter season of 1808 by Bartolomeo Campagnoli and Johann Georg Hermann Voigt,[18] and one in Manchester, England, on January 16, 1868, by John Carrodus and Charles Baetens with Charles Hallé's orchestra.[19]

The symphonie concertante is a musical genre for solo instruments with orchestra that swiftly rose to popularity starting around 1770. Its popularity reflected broader social and musical changes of the period, including "an increasing fascination with virtuoso display, a fondness for big sonorities, and particularly an all-pervading enthusiasm for the pleasing melodic line."[20] The genre was particularly popular in Mannheim and Paris, cities that Mozart had visited before returning to Salzburg in 1779. In form and function, symphonies concertantes are generally light and entertaining:

> The symphonie concertante resembles the lighter Classical genres, such as the serenade and divertimento, in character. Melodic variety is its hallmark. Although a symphonie concertante may include a poignant Andante, the prevailing mood is usually relaxed, gracious and happy, rarely dramatic, never sombre or intense.[21]

While Mozart's Sinfonia concertante, K. 364 exhibits many characteristic qualities of the genre, including melodic variety and virtuoso display, it "adds richness, depth of expression, and invention that raises it far above other works of this type."[22] The achingly beautiful second movement notably stretches the normal bounds of the genre, and Mozart's egalitarian treatment of the solo violin and viola, in terms of melodic distribution and technical demands, is also noteworthy.[23]

Mozart wrote the solo viola part in D major with the indication that the instrument was to be tuned up a half step (*accordata un mezzo tono più alto*). Many concertante works for viola from the Classical period employ such scordatura tuning "in an attempt to give the small violas, in general use at the time, a more brilliant and more resonant projection."[24] Historically, many violists have played the viola part using standard tuning, in part because of the scarcity of printed editions with the scordatura tuning. The scordatura part is now readily available in multiple modern editions, and it is worthwhile for any violist to investigate performing the work with the original tuning. Both solo parts are designated to

Zone	Thematic Areas/Snippet	Measures	Principal Tonal Areas/Function
Opening Ritornello		1–74	
	Theme Group 1	1–38	
	Unit 1.1	1–11	E-flat major
	Unit 1.2	11–27	E-flat major
	Unit 1.3	27–38	E-flat major
	Theme Group 2	38–74	E-flat major
	Unit 2.1	38–46	E-flat major
	Unit 2.2	46–74	E-flat major
Solo Exposition		74–158	
	Theme Group 1	74–125	
	Unit 1.1	74–94	E-flat major
	Unit 1.2	94–105	Tonicizes C minor and B-flat major
	Unit 1.3	105–25	Modulatory; moves to B-flat major
	Theme Group 2	125–58	
	Unit 2.1	125–33	B-flat major
	Unit 2.2	133–58	B-flat major
Second Ritornello		158–74	B-flat major; moves to G minor

Chart 22.1 Mozart, Sinfonia concertante for Violin, Viola, and Orchestra, K. 364 (320d): Structural analysis, first movement, Allegro maestoso.

Zone	Thematic Areas/Snippet	Measures	Principal Tonal Areas/Function
Development		174–223	
	Unit 1.1 *S. Vln.*	174–94	G minor; C minor
	Unit 1.2 *S. Vln.*	194–223	C minor; modulates
Recapitulation		223–328	
	Tutti Opening	223–33	E-flat major
	Theme Group 1	233–84	
	Unit 1.1 *S. Vla.*	233–53	E-flat major
	Unit 1.2 *S. Vla.*	253–64	Tonicizes F minor and E-flat major
	Unit 1.3 *S. Vln.*	264–84	Modulatory; moves to E-flat major
	Theme Group 2	284–328	
	Unit 2.1 *S. Vla.*	284–93	E-flat major
	Unit 2.1a: Tutti interruption	293–301	E-flat major
	Unit 2.2 *S. Vla.*	301–28	E-flat major
Closing Ritornello & Cadenza		328–57	E-flat major

Chart 22.1 (continued) Mozart, Sinfonia concertante for Violin, Viola, and Orchestra, K. 364 (320d): Structural analysis, first movement, Allegro maestoso.

play during the principal orchestral tuttis, and many performers have followed this practice. In these passages, the solo viola doubles the Viola I part, with minor deviations.

The Sinfonia concertante for Violin, Viola, and Orchestra, K. 364 (320d) is widely considered one of Mozart's masterpieces from his Salzburg years and a pivotal work in the evolution of his mature artistic style. Overall, the work is marked by an orchestral richness that shows the influence of Mannheim, including the use of a Mannheim crescendo (movt. I, mm. 46–61) and divided viola parts.[25] The work also displays the influence of opera (e.g., recitative-like passages in the first movement and the use of binary form in the second movement). Mozart's treatment of the violin and viola serves almost as an essay on the similarities and differences between the two instruments' tone, providing immediate comparisons on many levels.

The first movement, in concerto (sonata) form (Chart 22.1), is overflowing with melodies; Leonard Ratner notes that "there are at least eighteen distinctive melodic members in this movement."[26] The choice of tempo marking, Allegro maestoso, is exceptional: "Mozart used the marking 'maestoso' infrequently, and always with a purpose. Rarely did he use it with such significance as he did for the first movement of K364."[27] The majestic quality is evident from the first chords, and the entire opening ritornello is replete with orchestral splendor. In m. 72, the soloists break away from the tutti, emerging on equal footing with their joint statement in octaves. Each soloist then gets to independently introduce itself (mm. 79–84), with the two joining forces once again in mm. 84–90. From this point, Mozart prefers to showcase the soloists in an independent, but egalitarian manner with the two taking turns at the melodic material, politely passing it off to one another. The pair do not join forces again until the latter part of the second theme group at m. 143 (widely separated by the interval of a tenth).

After a robust ritornello (mm. 158–74), the development begins with recitative-like statements from each of the soloists (Unit 1.1). The soloists then alternate rapid-fire sixteenth-note figures that are finely woven within a vibrant orchestral tapestry. In m. 218, the orchestra suddenly drops out, and the soloists join forces in a closely spaced (separated by a third) ascending scalar passage. Two measures later, the soloists momentarily pause on a half note (allowing the orchestra to re-enter) before releasing a final flurry of sixteenth notes that cascade into the recapitulation.

To start the recapitulation, Mozart provides just a brief snippet of the opening ritornello's Theme Group 1, Unit 1.1 material (mm. 223–29), before jumping ahead to material from m. 70. Mozart then reverses the order of the soloists' appearance in the following section; that is, if the violin led the statement of material in the exposition, the viola leads it in the recapitulation (and vice versa). While the form generally follows the same plan as in the solo exposition, Mozart throws in one detour during the second theme group at m. 293, inserting an orchestral statement of its Theme Group 2, Unit 2.1 material from the opening ritornello. The soloists pick back up where they left off in m. 301 with their Unit 2.2 material to lead us into the closing ritornello and cadenza.

Mozart turns to the relative minor for the second movement (Chart 22.2), infusing it with a pathos more suitable to an opera than a symphonie concertante:

The aria and operatic style also have a special influence on the slow middle movement, which falls into two sections of approximately the same length (sixty-two

Zone	Thematic Areas/Snippet	Measures	Principal Tonal Areas/Function
Opening Ritornello		1–8	C minor
First Main Period		8–53	
	Theme Group 1	8–35	
	Unit 1.1	8–24	C minor; E-flat major
	Unit 1.2	24–35	Modulatory
	Theme Group 2	35–53	E-flat major
Second Ritornello		53–62	E-flat major
Second Main Period		62–116	
	Theme Group 1	62–91	
	Unit 1.1	62–79	E-flat major; modulatory
	Unit 1.2	79–91	C minor
	Theme Group 2	91–116	C minor
Closing Ritornello & Cadenza		116–29	C minor

Chart 22.2 Mozart, Sinfonia concertante for Violin, Viola, and Orchestra, K. 364 (320d): Structural analysis, second movement, Andante.

and sixty-eight bars). It follows the pattern of many binary arias, in the second half of which the text of the first is repeated while the harmonic arc which drew away from the tonic during the first half is led back to it; during this process the thematic material and the musical structure remain essentially the same.[28]

Zone	Thematic Areas/Snippet	Measures	Principal Tonal Areas/Function
A	Tutti Statement	1–79	
	Unit 1.1	1–16	E-flat major
	Unit 1.2	16–32	E-flat major
	Unit 1.3	32–48	E-flat major
	Unit 1.4	48–64	E-flat major
	Closing	64–79	E-flat major
B		80–204	
	Unit 1.1 S. Vln.	80–112	E-flat major
	Unit 1.2 S. Vln.	112–36	E-flat major to B-flat major
	Unit 1.3 S. Vln.	136–52	B-flat major
	Unit 1.4 S. Vln.	152–204	B-flat major
A		204–46	
	Unit 1.1 S. Vla.	204–19	E-flat major
	Unit 1.2 S. Vla.	219–35	E-flat major
	Unit 1.3: Tutti transition	235–46	E-flat major; ends on G major chord

Chart 22.3 Mozart, Sinfonia concertante for Violin, Viola, and Orchestra, K. 364 (320d): Structural analysis, third movement, Presto.

Zone	Thematic Areas/Snippet	Measures	Principal Tonal Areas/Function
B		247–343	
	Unit 1.1 S. Vla.	247–79	A-flat major
	Unit 1.2 S. Vla.	279–303	A-flat major to E-flat major
	Unit 1.3 S. Vln.	303–19	E-flat major, moving to E-flat minor
	Unit 1.4 S. Vln.	319–43	E-flat minor; moves to dominant function
A		343–432	
	Unit 1.1 S. Vla.	343–58	E-flat major
	Unit 1.2 S. Vla.	358–74	E-flat major
	Unit 1.3 Vln. 1	374–400	E-flat major; B-flat major
	Unit 1.3a (material from B section Unit 1.4) S. Vln.	400–416	E-flat major
	Unit 1.4: Tutti Hn. 1	416–32	E-flat major
Coda	S. Vla.	432–90	E-flat major

Chart 22.3 (continued) Mozart, Sinfonia concertante for Violin, Viola, and Orchestra, K. 364 (320d): Structural analysis, third movement, Presto.

Material from the opening ritornello (mm. 1–8) is elaborated on by the solo violin at its entrance in m. 8, still in C minor. When the viola's turn comes in m. 16, it further elaborates on the material, moving away from C minor toward a sunnier major mode. A dialogue between the soloists begins in m. 24 (Unit 1.2), concluding in m. 35, where the orchestra introduces the second theme group with a beautiful canonical passage between the orchestral violins and Viola I. The soloists embellish this theme when they re-enter in m. 40, continuing with the canonical dialogue set over a sparse orchestral texture consisting of the orchestral violins in unison. More canonical dialogue between the soloists (mm. 46–52) gives way to a sweeping orchestral ritornello at m. 53, which returns to material from the opening in m. 58.

The second main period opens at m. 62 with a fragmentation of the earlier Theme Group 1, Unit 1.1 material (now in E♭ major). In the first movement, Mozart reversed the roles of the soloists during the recapitulation, but in this movement, the violin continues to lead the way on each occasion. After the soloists join forces again in m. 74, they continue with a return of Unit 1.2 material (mm. 79–91) and then Theme Group 2 material (mm. 91–116) from the first main period, now in C minor. A final breathtaking tutti and cadenza closes the movement out with a sense of despair.

The buoyant final movement is a complete change in mood from the previous one. Cast in a rondo form (Chart 22.3), the second episode consists of the same material as the first, resulting in an ABABA form. This movement, like the first, has no shortage of melodies, and Mozart again highlights the symphonic nature of the symphonie concertante genre with an extensive opening tutti, which comprises the entire initial A section.

At m. 80, the first B section begins with independent statements by the soloists. But they soon engage in an extended period of playful dialogue (mm. 128–204), with Mozart exploring a variety of registers on the two instruments. At m. 204, the soloists return to the opening A section, which Mozart truncates, ending with the orchestra's statement of Unit 1.3 material. The section ends on a G major chord in m. 245, suggesting a transition to C minor (the relative minor was a popular choice for the "C" section of a rondo). But Mozart provided plenty of C minor in the second movement, so he instead turns to A♭ major with a return of the opening theme from the B section in m. 247. As he did in the first movement, Mozart reverses the roles of the soloists with the two swapping their material from the earlier B section until m. 303, when the violin again takes the lead for Unit 1.3. Mozart finally throws in a bit of the parallel minor for variety, starting in m. 311. The major mode returns for the final A section, during which all of the melodies from the opening section are revisited. Here, Mozart's inventiveness shines through with his delightful variation on the Unit 1.2 material (mm. 358–74) and his incorporation of material from the B section (mm. 400–416, which is drawn from mm. 152–68). In the final coda (mm. 432–90), Mozart explores the upper region of both instruments, allowing each soloist a final virtuosic passage before the final tutti.

In 2007, *Strings* magazine asked eleven violists to share their all-time favorite works; only one piece was named more than once: Mozart's Sinfonia concertante for Violin, Viola, and Orchestra, K. 364 (320d).[29] Treasured by violinists and violists alike, Mozart's masterful work is truly in a class by itself.

23

Krzysztof Penderecki: *Cadenza*
for Viola Solo

Date of Composition: 1984

First Edition: Krzysztof Penderecki, *Cadenza per viola sola*, Mainz: B. Schott's Söhne, 1986, 45 855, VAB 52

Select Later Edition: Krzysztof Penderecki, *Cadenza per viola sola*, Kraków: Polskie Wydawnictwo Muzyczne, 1988 (© 1986), Plate No. PWM-8838

Dedication: Grigorij Zyslin gewidmet

Date/Place of First Public Performance: September 10, 1984, Grigori Zhislin (viola), Third Festival of Chamber Music, summer residence of Krzysztof Penderecki, Lusławice

Introduction

"The contemporary artist, despite his longing for universality, is fragmented and alienated. For me, the conscious use of tradition became an opportunity for overcoming this dissonance between the artist and the audience."[1] Penderecki burst onto the avant-garde scene in 1959 when three of his works—submitted anonymously—won top prizes at the Young Composers Competition hosted by the Union of Polish Composers. A spate of experimental works followed, including *Anaklasis* and *Threnody to the Victims of Hiroshima*, in which he explored a sonoristic style focused on timbre and unconventional sounds. To achieve these sounds, Penderecki constructed his own system of musical notation. But, over time, he determined that this style was limiting his compositional voice.[2] By the middle of the 1970s, his music had become more lyrical, looking back toward Romanticism. Thereafter, tradition played an important role in the advancement of his personal style, not only as a means of respecting the past but as part of his continued search "for something which is new."[3]

Biographical Sketch

Krzysztof Penderecki (1933–2020), the second child of Tadeusz and Zofia Penderecki, was born in the small town of Dębica, Poland. A lawyer by profession, Tadeusz enjoyed playing violin and piano, hosting chamber music gatherings in his home until the Second World War. Following the Nazi invasion of Poland in 1939, the devoutly Roman Catholic family found themselves caught in a period of great social and political upheaval: first with the war and then with the subsequent rise of Stalinism. Krzysztof Penderecki's witness to oppression during these formative years would have a profound effect on his outlook toward life.

As a young boy, Krzysztof played piano; he later studied violin with Stanisław Darłak.[4] In 1951, he moved to Kraków, attending Jagiellonian University while privately studying violin with Stanisław Tawroszewicz and composition with Franciszek Skołyszewski. He switched to the State Higher School of Music (now the Academy of Music in Kraków) in 1954, studying composition with Artur Malawski and then with Stanisław Wiechowicz. While still a student, Penderecki married his first wife, Barbara; the couple would have one child together in 1955.[5]

After graduating from the school of music in 1958, Penderecki joined the faculty as an instructor of composition and counterpoint. Success came swiftly, beginning with his impressive showing at the 1959 Young Composers Competition and then with *Threnody to the Victims of Hiroshima*. Written in 1960 and awarded the Tribune Internationale des Compositeurs UNESCO prize the following year, *Threnody* brought widespread international attention to Penderecki. More innovative works followed, including a substantial number for films and puppet theaters. In 1965, Penderecki married his second wife, Elżbieta, with whom he would have two more children. Penderecki began to assume more teaching and administrative responsibilities, serving as a lecturer at the Folkwang Hochschule für Musik (1966–1968), as a professor at Yale University (1973–1981), and as rector of the Academy of Music in Kraków from 1972 to 1987.[6] In 1971, he made his conducting debut, adding a further dimension to his career.[7]

Penderecki's musical style started to transform in 1974 with the orchestral work *The Awakening of Jacob*, which introduced "melody and harmony as serious devices for the first time in the composer's work."[8] Subsequent compositions continued in a more lyrical vein, making use of traditional forms and standard musical notation. While this stylistic change confounded some critics, it also attracted new admirers, and Penderecki went on to earn many more honors, including the Grawemeyer Award in 1992 for his Symphony No. 4 and multiple Grammy Awards. By the time of his death in 2020, he had firmly established his reputation as one of the most respected composers of the post–World War II era.

Penderecki's *Cadenza for Viola Solo*

Large-scale orchestral and vocal works form a significant portion of Penderecki's output, though he composed in many genres. Political and religious themes appear frequently, reflecting the influence of social consciousness on his music: "I am interested in the general problems of Man, particularly the problem of intolerance."[9] Penderecki's compositions for viola include the Concerto for Viola and Orchestra (1983), *Cadenza for Viola Solo* (1984), and the Double Concerto for Violin, Viola, and Orchestra (2012). All of these works fall into the composer's post-avant-garde stylistic period. *Cadenza* was written for the Russian violinist and violist Grigori Zhislin as a token of appreciation; Zhislin had previously given captivating performances of Penderecki's violin and viola works, including the European premiere of the viola concerto with the composer conducting on April 21, 1984.[10] Modeled on the viola concerto, *Cadenza* employs "many of the same techniques and several motifs."[11] It was first performed by Zhislin on September 10, 1984, in the drawing room of Penderecki's summer home during the composer's Third Festival of Chamber Music.[12]

The score for *Cadenza* lacks time signatures or bar lines; Schott's edition is laid out on four pages divided into thirty-four staves (the numbering in the following analysis refers to individual staves in Schott's edition). An accidental (sharp or flat) applies only to the succeeding note; there are many instances when courtesy naturals are used for clarity, but there are also numerous notes without them (e.g., the 9th note of staff 18, which is an e♮i). The spot likely to cause the most confusion is the 18th note of staff 30 (Ex. 23.1), which is an unmarked e♮ii following immediately after an e♭ii.[13]

At some point after the first printing by Schott, Penderecki made corrections/ alterations to the music, which have been incorporated into later printings (Chart 23.1).[14] The following discussion factors in these changes. Additionally, the edition published by Polskie Wydawnictwo Muzyczne (PWM) in 1988 differs in numerous spots from Schott's edition. While many of these differences appear to be errors, there are several differences worth noting (see Chart 23.2, which compares multiple sources).

Example 23.1 Penderecki, *Cadenza for Viola Solo*, staff 30, notes 14–20 (not counting rests) with the 18th note marked to clarify the e♮ii.

Cast in a ternary form, *Cadenza* opens with a sighing semitone, an interval that has been "the unmistakable cornerstone of Penderecki's vocabulary throughout his career."[15] The semitone plays a significant role throughout the piece, as does the inverse of the semitone (a diminished octave or major seventh), particularly in double stops and chords (e.g., staves 4, 5, and 9). Rests are used to great effect in the opening section, giving the music a halting, tentative quality. As the viola overcomes its hesitancy, Penderecki builds tension through a variety of means: first through a *poco a poco cresc.* in staves 2 and 3; then by adding double stops in staff 3; and then by introducing shorter rhythmic durations, adding triplets in staff 5 and then runs of thirty-second notes in staff 6. The tension reaches a fever pitch in staff 8 with a series of down-bow triple stops. A rest briefly breaks the tension, but the viola presses on with fierce chords, finally relaxing in staff 9 as the chords give way to double stops and then a new figure, marked *subito* ***p***. The tension escalates once again with the viola playing a series of triplet sixteenth notes (staves 10–11) that crescendo and accelerate to the Vivace section.

Like the Lento, the Vivace section (staff 12) opens with a downward semitone, and rests are initially used to interrupt the music's flow. Stopped notes are alternated with open strings to imply polyphony, recalling the solo string

Staff Number	Note Number (Not Counting Rests)	Change in Later Printing
Staff 1	15th note	a-natural (previously marked as an a-flat)
Staff 1	21st note (penultimate note)	courtesy natural (b-natural) added
Staff 5	10th note (first triplet of this staff)	*poco più mosso* marking added above
Staff 7	18th note (first triplet of this staff)	alla corda designation added above
Staves 15–17, 19–20, 23–25	Groupings of three beamed eighth notes	No triplet markings (see also Chart 23.2)
Staff 25	1st note	*p* dynamic added below
Staff 26	25th note (9th note from the end of the staff)	*cresc.* marking added below
Staff 27	7th note	*ff* dynamic added below
Staff 29	9th note (at Tempo I marking)	*f* dynamic added below

Chart 23.1 Changes in Schott's later printing of Penderecki's *Cadenza for Viola Solo* compared to the original printing.

Staff No.	Note No. (Not Counting Rests)	Editorial Manuscript (Redaktions-vorlage)	First Schott Printing (1986)	PWM Edition (1988)	Violin Version; First Schott Printing (1989)	Later Schott Printing
Staff 3	5th to 6th notes	Slur over notes	No slur	Slur over notes	Slur over notes	No slur
Staff 4	12th note	Quarter note	Quarter note	Eighth note	Eighth note	Quarter note
Staves 15–17, 19–20, 23–24	Groupings of three beamed eighth notes	Marked as triplets	Marked as triplets	*Not* marked as triplets; two spots have an eighth note = eighth note indication prior to the groupings of two beamed eighth notes that are interspersed among the groupings of three beamed eighth notes	*Not* marked as triplets	*Not* marked as triplets
Staff 25	Groupings of three beamed eighth notes	Marked as triplets	Marked as triplets	Marked as triplets	*Not* marked as triplets	*Not* marked as triplets

Chart 23.2 Select differences among the editorial manuscript (Redaktionsvorlage), Schott's first printing, PWM's first printing, Schott's first printing of the violin version, and Schott's later printing of the viola version for Penderecki's *Cadenza for Viola Solo*.

works of J. S. Bach. The implied polyphony gives way to real polyphony at the end of staff 15 in a series of double stops played at the frog. At the end of staff 17, the opening of the Vivace section is revisited (now down a fifth) with sixteenth notes once again giving way to a series of double stops (staff 19). In staff 22, the Vivace section's opening material returns in earnest, enhanced by double stops. Penderecki prepares this return by revisiting ideas from staves 9–11 that originally preceded the Vivace. Here, the order is reversed with triplet sixteenth notes appearing first (staves 20–21), followed by down-bow double stops (staff 22). While staff 9 used widely spaced double stops that accentuated the inverted semitone relationship, the down-bow double stops in staff 22 are now tightly compacted, emphasizing the semitone. Starting in staff 22, Penderecki quickly works his way through earlier ideas while introducing new elements, including the *poco rubato grazioso* figure in staff 25, where the dynamic drops down to $\boldsymbol{p}$. The music rapidly crescendos at the end of staff 26, culminating in "a spectacular passage involving octaves on the D and G strings and open A and C strings" in staff 27.[16]

Staff 29 marks a return of the opening at the Tempo I marking. Instead of an exact repeat of the opening Lento, the material is raised a fifth with double stops and a $\boldsymbol{f}$ dynamic, linking it to the preceding Vivace section. The dynamic finally softens at staff 33 with the music returning to the pitch level of the opening. But Penderecki reminds us that the viola has matured since it began its journey, retaining double stops in the final two staves while adding a new technique: false harmonics.

In his 1989 review of *Cadenza for Viola Solo*, David L. Sills wrote:

> *Cadenza* announced its independence early: though there is little new here for those acquainted with the Concerto, there is, oddly, little exact repetition either. This work is, in effect, a commentary on its larger counterpart, which may be the sense in which its title is to be taken.[17]

Michael Newman emphasized that "in no way however is *Cadenza* a scaled-down version of the concerto," and likened the work to a nineteenth-century caprice.[18] The work does have a capricious nature in the many playful ways that Penderecki fragments and combines snippets of motives, leaving one guessing in which direction he will dart next. Yet the overall intensity of the music, particularly the extensive use of a $\boldsymbol{f}$ dynamic, suggests a more serious character. In *Cadenza*, Penderecki has managed to brilliantly craft a work that captures the monumental tone found in many of his large-scale works, as if the weight of the world were placed on the shoulders of a single, solitary viola.

24

Quincy Porter: *Suite for Viola Alone*

Lento
Allegro furioso
Larghetto espressivo
Allegro spiritoso

Date of Composition: Completed October 15, 1930

First Edition: Quincy Porter, *Suite para viola solo*, in "Suplemento Musical," supplement, *Boletín Latino-Americano de Música* 5 (October 1941): 90–94

Select Later Editions: Quincy Porter, *Suite for Viola Alone*, South Hadley, MA: Valley Music Press, 1946; Quincy Porter, *Suite for Viola Alone*, ed. David M. Bynog, [Dallas, TX]: American Viola Society Publications, 2010, AVS 008

Date/Place of First Public Performance: February 10, 1931, Quincy Porter (viola), American Library, Paris

Date/Place of Additional Early Public Performance: February 18, 1931, Quincy Porter (viola), Salle Chopin, Paris

Introduction

"Porter's music went its own way."[1] This sentiment, expressed by Quincy Porter's friend Howard Boatwright, refers to Porter's music compared to his fellow American contemporaries, yet it equally applies within the broader context of music composition during the middle of the twentieth century. This is not to suggest that Porter's musical style was without influence, noticeably in his early works—shades of jazz and Béla Bartók are apparent as is a fondness for Renaissance and Baroque music. But Porter listened "only to his 'inner ear'" and was unmoved by the latest avant-garde trends.[2] Hallmarks of Porter's style include simplicity of subjects, clarity of textures, "mildly dissonant unrest," and music that is driven naturally by its "melodic and rhythmic propulsion."[3] Though Porter's music was well-regarded during his lifetime, it went out of favor later in the century. Fortunately, it has been gaining greater attention during the twenty-first century by musicians who recognize Porter as a master craftsman who wrote beautiful, elegant music in a truly individual style.

Biographical Sketch

Quincy Porter (1897–1966) was born in New Haven, Connecticut, to Delia and Frank Chamberlin Porter. His father served as Winkley Professor of Biblical Theology at the Yale Divinity School; his maternal grandfather had also been a professor at Yale. Having studied violin with Herbert Dittler during his youth, Porter furthered his musical education at Yale, playing first violin in a string quartet that he organized while an undergraduate.[4] His composition studies there, with Horatio Parker and David Stanley Smith, were thoroughly steeped in the German Romantic tradition. Porter expanded on this training with a year of study at the Schola Cantorum in Paris in 1920, where he enrolled in courses with Vincent d'Indy, and then through private composition studies with Ernest Bloch in New York.

In 1922, he joined the De Ribaupierre Quartet in Cleveland as violist and soon began teaching theory and viola at the Cleveland Institute of Music. It was here that he met Lois Brown, a violinist who was to become his wife in 1926. The two continued a musical partnership that lasted for decades; they frequently played chamber music together and were both involved in promoting contemporary composers through performances. Porter's love of playing chamber music spilled over into his compositions with chamber music forming the bulk of his output.

A Guggenheim Fellowship enabled Porter to move to Paris in 1928, where he focused on composing. His time in Paris was fruitful as he experimented with various styles; some of his best-known compositions, including the String Quartet No. 3, Second Sonata for Violin and Piano, and *Blues Lointains for Flute and Piano*, date from this period. While in Paris, Porter elected not to study with Nadia Boulanger, a favorite teacher of and great influence on his American contemporaries, but she attended his recital at the Salle Chopin on February 18, 1931, where he officially premiered the *Suite for Viola Alone*, writing him a note the following day: "Everything was so perfect,—peacefully, beautifully, charmingly prepared and presented."[5]

Porter returned to Cleveland in 1931, staying for only a year before being offered a teaching position at Vassar. Administrative posts at the New England Conservatory of Music followed: first as dean of faculty (1938–1942) and then as director (1942–1946). In 1946, Porter's father passed away, and an opening at Yale allowed him to come full-circle back to his *alma mater* as a professor of music, where he joined his fellow violist-composer Paul Hindemith in teaching

theory and composition. Porter spent many happy years at Yale until his retirement in 1965 with summers devoted to composition at a studio on the idyllic
Squam Lake in New Hampshire (Squam Lake would later be immortalized in
the 1981 film *On Golden Pond*). Ever the Yale man, Porter suffered a seizure on
November 12, 1966, while watching the Yale–Princeton football game on televi-
sion; he died instantaneously.[6]

Porter's *Suite for Viola Alone*

Over the course of his career, Porter received numerous accolades: he was
awarded the Elizabeth Sprague Coolidge Medal in 1943, was elected to the
National Institute of Arts and Letters later that same year, and won the Pulitzer
Prize for Music in 1954. He was also a major force in the advancement of
American music. In 1940, he cofounded the American Music Center as a means
"to foster and encourage the composition of contemporary music and to pro-
mote its production, publication, distribution, and performance in every way
possible."[7] Porter is perhaps best remembered for his string compositions: his
nine string quartets form "one of the most substantial contributions to the literature by any American composer,"[8] while his *Suite for Viola Alone* was the first
American composition for solo viola to earn prominent attention.

Porter's works for viola include the *Suite for Viola Alone* (1930), Concerto for
Viola and Orchestra (1948), and *Speed Etude for Viola and Piano* (1948). He also
arranged two other of his works for viola, *Blues Lointains for Viola and Piano*
(1928; originally for flute and piano) and *Poem for Cello (or Viola) and Piano*
(1948), and he wrote several duos and trios that include the viola.[9]

The *Suite for Viola Alone* was composed in Paris, and Porter gave several private performances of the work prior to his public performances at the American
Library on February 10, 1931, and the Salle Chopin on February 18, 1931.[10] An
accomplished violist, Porter frequently played chamber and solo recitals (with
large-scale works by Ernest Bloch and Paul Hindemith as part of his repertoire)
and made a handful of recordings; he performed the suite on multiple occasions
and also recorded it.[11]

The suite consists of four unnumbered movements (the AVS edition uses continuous measure numbers throughout the entire piece, and those numbers are
referenced in the following discussion). The first movement, Lento, explores
instrumental coloring in its brief twenty-three measures. Porter creates tonal
ambiguity at the outset: the opening g^i harmonic, with its wind-like sonority,
momentarily confuses the listener as to what type of instrument is playing. And
the first three notes—with an interval of a tritone followed by a perfect fourth,
outlining a major seventh—establish the tension between consonance and

dissonance that is to follow. The first phrase, from mm. 1–5, is a monophonic exploration of the three upper strings. In sharp contrast, the following phrase is largely polyphonic and increasingly dissonant. But the discord is brought to a pleasing resolution in mm. 10–11 as Porter firmly resolves to C major. The movement finishes with more instrumental coloring, contrasting close registers of the viola, eventually settling on a tonal center of G and finishing on the same g^i harmonic that began the movement.

The second movement, Allegro furioso, starts with a pulsating and frenetic rhythm that propels the music forward. From the g^i harmonic that ends the first movement, Porter moves in m. 24 to the same $d♭^i$–$a♭$ interval from m. 2 of the first movement, which is now stacked vertically. The opening measure (m. 24), with its alternating intervals of perfect fourths and minor ninths, lays the groundwork for even greater tension between consonance and dissonance throughout this movement. The first phrase is cast in an ambiguous tonal area (seemingly centered on D♭). With a nod to his traditional training, Porter uses a Ger+^{6} chord in m. 32, resolving to G in the following measure, before returning to the movement's opening at m. 35, now a perfect fifth higher and at a faster tempo. After another Ger+^{6} chord in m. 41, Porter resolves to D in m. 42, introducing a new rhythmic motive. Porter quickly brings the tension back at full force, culminating in mm. 51–53 with harsh major and minor seconds interspersed with consonant intervals. Porter then pulls the volume and tempo level back, returning to material from the beginning of the movement in m. 66. The return allows a further quiet winding down of the movement, but Porter does not fully resolve the tension, ending the movement with an ambiguous tonality.

That tonality is resolved at the start of the third movement, Larghetto espressivo, as the final two measures of the second movement become clearer as a C♯^{o7} set-up for a resolution to the opening d^{ii} at m. 78. From this point, the writing is entirely monophonic until the suite's final two measures. The third movement, influenced by Renaissance vocal models, is a welcome change from the relentless second movement. With its emphasis on linear melody and harmony, the movement is built around the opening melodic cell spanning a minor sixth that establishes a tonal center of B♭. Porter develops this brief cell for sixteen measures before returning to a restatement of the opening melody at m. 94, played two octaves lower. The movement concludes with preparatory material that moves *attacca* into the final movement.

Marked Allegro spiritoso, the final movement is a fancy feat of fiddling for the viola. Centered on A major, harmony and polyphony are evoked through the many arpeggios, string crossings, and open strings. Porter uses sequences and repeated patterns throughout (Ex. 24.1), and the interval of a perfect fourth permeates the movement (Ex. 24.2). By the end of the piece, it is clear that consonance has triumphed in its struggle with dissonance, but Porter throws in a final

Example 24.1 Porter, *Suite for Viola Alone*, Allegro spiritoso, mm. 128–31.

Example 24.2 Porter, *Suite for Viola Alone*, Allegro spiritoso, mm. 161–64.

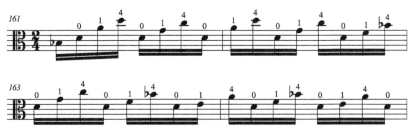

tussle in the penultimate measure with major seconds alternating with major sixths before the final perfect-fifth harmonics.

Porter's *Suite for Viola Alone* is idiomatically and effectively written for the viola, and at eight to nine minutes in length, it can fit well in a variety of performance situations. The work has been well-received across the spectrum: "From a purely musical point of view, it is a rewarding work for listener and performer alike," commented Louise Rood in 1951.[12] By the 1970s, its reputation for excellence was well-established: "Porter's *Suite* is something of a classic: it is one of the first American pieces for solo viola, one of the best, and an outstanding original composition."[13] In recent years, David Aaron Carpenter programmed the work on his 2007 Weill Hall Recital as part of his Walter W. Naumburg Viola Competition prize,[14] while Eliesha Nelson included the work on a 2009 recording devoted to Porter's viola music, which garnered a Grammy Award.[15]

25
Max Reger: Three Suites for Solo Viola, op. 131d: No. 1 in G Minor

I.   Molto sostenuto
II. Vivace — Andantino
III. Andante sostenuto
IV. Molto vivace

Date of Composition: 1915 (likely November–December)

First Edition: Max Reger, *Opus 131d, Drei Suiten für Bratsche allein: Nr. 1 G Moll*, Berlin: N. Simrock, 1916, Plate No. 13785

Select Later Edition: Max Reger, *Drei Suiten für Viola solo Opus 131d*, ed. Franz Beyer, Munich: Henle, 1991, HN 468

Dedication: Meinem lieben Freunde Prof. Dr. Walther zugeeignet [Heinrich Walther]

Date/Place of First Public Performance: October 28, 1916, Karl Doktor (viola), Wiener Konzerthaus, Vienna

Introduction

"Reger edited, arranged, or transcribed 428 individual pieces by Bach. No other composer since Bach himself was so deeply, indeed pathologically, involved with his works."[1] The esteem that Reger felt for the great composers of the German tradition—Johannes Brahms, Ludwig van Beethoven, and above all, J. S. Bach—is reflected in his compositions, which often imitate these composers to the point of near plagiarism.[2] As a performer, Reger's imitation of Bach was even more pronounced: his faithful interpretations generated an almost "metaphysical authority" among audiences, who "believed they heard Bach himself."[3] Reger's affection for music of the past was not born of conservatism or lack of original inspiration. Rather, he considered an understanding and appreciation of German musical tradition—extending back to Bach—as essential for musical progress:

> Sebastian Bach is for me the beginning and end of all music; upon him rests, and from him originates, all real progress!
>
> What does—pardon, what should—Sebastian Bach mean for our era?
>
> A really powerful, inexhaustible medicine, not only for all those composers and musicians who suffer from "misunderstood Wagner," but for all those "contemporaries," who suffer from spinal maladies of any kind. To be "Bachian" means: to be authentically German, unyielding.
>
> That Bach could be misunderstood for so long, is the greatest scandal for the "critical wisdom" of the eighteenth and nineteenth centuries.[4]

This is not to say that Reger merely recycled music of the great composers. Instead, he built on their efforts, developing a highly idiosyncratic style that pushed the boundaries of traditional harmony and tonality. To Reger's many supporters, he "seemed able to effect a union between the modern spirit and the forms employed by the masters of the seventeenth and eighteenth centuries."[5] But to Reger's many critics, his contrapuntally complex compositions, with their unusual modulations and lack of singable melodies, seemed "like mathematical problems and solutions, sheer brain-spun and unlyrical works."[6] While musicians and audiences remain divided over Reger's merits, scholars have increasingly viewed his music, with its blend of traditional and progressive attitudes, as a critical link between that of Johannes Brahms and Arnold Schoenberg.

Biographical Sketch

Max Reger (1873–1916) was born in Brand, Bavaria, to Joseph and Philomena Reger. His father, a schoolteacher who played multiple instruments, accepted a new position a year after Max's birth, moving the family to Weiden. Both of Reger's parents were involved in his early musical education, which started at the age of five with piano lessons from his mother. In 1884, he was entrusted to Adalbert Lindner for piano and organ lessons. It was a trip to the Bayreuth Festival in 1888, where Reger heard Richard Wagner's *Parsifal* and *Die Meistersinger von Nürnberg*, that inspired him to pursue a musical career. Returning to Weiden, he produced his first composition: an Overture in B Minor for small chamber ensemble. In a sign of things to come, the contrapuntally overloaded work ran to 120 pages, exhausting every variation of its thematic material.[7] Lindner was impressed enough with the work to send it to the musicologist Hugo Riemann, who responded encouragingly by supplying textbooks to aid in Reger's studies. By 1890, Reger had advanced to studying directly under Riemann, first at the Sondershausen Conservatory and then at the Wiesbaden Conservatory.

Riemann's mentorship was pivotal to Reger's musical development. It was Riemann who impressed upon Reger a reverence for Bach, Beethoven, and Brahms. Riemann also secured Reger's first publishing contracts and recommended him for a teaching post at the Wiesbaden Conservatory.[8] After teaching for several years in Wiesbaden, Reger began his mandatory military service in 1896 but was discharged the following year owing to health reasons. A series of professional failures, coupled with Reger's excessive tobacco and alcohol use, precipitated a mental and physical breakdown in 1898. He returned to live with his family in Weiden, also accompanying them when they relocated to Munich in 1901. These were productive years compositionally for Reger, who taught privately to support himself. In 1902, Reger married Elsa von Bercken (née von Bagenski), a divorced protestant. The marriage caused a rift with his devoutly Roman Catholic parents and resulted in his excommunication from the church.

A major turning point in Reger's career came in 1903 with the highly successful premiere of his Piano Quintet in C Minor, op. 64. Over the next decade, he busied himself with numerous musical activities; in addition to teaching and composing he frequently served as an accompanist and chamber musician. In 1905, Reger accepted a teaching position at the Munich Akademie der Tonkunst, resigning the following year. He was appointed director of music at the University of Leipzig and professor at the Royal Conservatory in 1907. Though he stepped down as director the following year, he continued to teach a master class in composition at the conservatory until his death.[9] Reger's last major appointment was as music director at the court of Duke Georg II of Saxe-Meiningen, in 1911. The hectic pace of Reger's life—fueled by overwork and a reliance on alcohol— eventually took its toll: he collapsed after a concert in February 1914, spending the next month at a sanatorium to recuperate. After resigning his position in Meiningen, he moved to Jena in 1915, where the relative peace and quiet revitalized his creative spirit: "Now begins the free, Jena style," he happily proclaimed to his friend Karl Straube.[10] Alas, his newfound leisurely existence was short-lived; Reger suffered a heart attack on May 11, 1916, in Leipzig, dying at the age of forty-three.

Reger's Three Suites for Solo Viola, op. 131d: No. 1 in G Minor

Reger's compositions for viola include the Sonata in B♭ Major for Clarinet (or Viola or Violin) and Piano, op. 107 (1908–1909) and the Three Suites for Solo Viola,

Opus	Title	No. of Works	Date of Composition
131a	Six Preludes and Fugues for Solo Violin	Six	April 1914
131b	Three Duos: Canons and Fugues in the Old Style for Two Violins	Three	April 1914
131c	Three Suites for Solo Violoncello	Three	December 1914/January 1915
131d	Three Suites for Solo Viola	Three	November/December 1915

Chart 25.1 Works within Max Reger's opus 131 set.

op. 131d (1915). Each of the suites was dedicated to a different individual: the first suite is dedicated to the gynecologist Heinrich Walther, an acquaintance who lived in the town of Giessen.[11] Simrock separately published each suite at the beginning of 1916, and the first suite was premiered in late 1916 by noted violist Karl Doktor, who served for many years as solo viola with the Vienna Konzertverein Orchestra.[12] Reger evidently planned a fourth suite for Doktor—even playing the violist themes from the work—but died before writing any of the music down.[13]

The viola suites round out Reger's opus 131 set, which consists of fifteen compositions for strings (Chart 25.1), all of which are in keys that correspond to the open strings of the violin: G (major or minor), D (major or minor), A (major or minor), and E minor. As with many of Reger's other compositions, the influence of Bach is readily apparent in each of these works. Bach's compositions for solo violin (BWV 1001–1006) and solo cello (BWV 1007–1012) seem obvious exemplars for opus 131a and 131c, yet there is no such parallel for the opus 131d suites for viola. Bach's cello suites, which would later become a standard part of a violist's repertoire, had scarcely been played on the viola when Reger composed his suites.[14]

More than eighteen months separate the first from the last of Reger's opus 131 solo works, yet there are many similarities in the motivic and melodic figurations among them (Exs. 25.1, 25.2, and 25.3).

In some instances, there are large-scale similarities: the second movement of the first viola suite (Ex. 25.4) is cut from the same cloth as the second movement

Example 25.1 Reger, Six Preludes and Fugues for Solo Violin, op. 131a: No. 1 in A Minor, m. 7.

Example 25.2 Reger, Three Suites for Solo Violoncello, op. 131c: No. 2 in D Minor, movt. I: Präludium, m. 3.

Example 25.3 Reger, Three Suites for Solo Viola, op. 131d: No. 1 in G Minor, movt. I, m. 5.

Example 25.4 Reger, Three Suites for Solo Viola, op. 131d: No. 1 in G Minor, movt. II, mm. 41–57.

Example 25.5 Reger, Three Suites for Solo Violoncello, op. 131c: No. 3 in A Minor, movt. II: Scherzo, mm. 77–89.

(Scherzo) of the third cello suite (Ex. 25.5). (The third movement of the second viola suite likewise resembles these two movements in structure, motivic content, and key relationships.)

Yet there are notable differences separating the viola suites from the earlier solo works: None of the movements is titled nor is there a fugue among them. Each of the viola suites, unlike the cello suites, is in four movements, resulting in a more classically inspired form overall. And the viola suites are more concise in scale than the cello suites.[15] The reduced scope reflects Reger's "free Jena style":

> Growing out of the relaxed professional circumstances Reger found in Jena
> compared to the rigors of his previous position as conductor of the Meiningen
> court orchestra, this style is marked by light texture, flowing melodic line, and a
> subtle manipulation of form, harmony, and motive.[16]

Reger's compositions often place formidable technical demands on the performer, and the first viola suite is no exception: most challenging are the numerous double stops, primarily sixths and thirds. Sequential patterns appear frequently in the suite—often consisting of two consecutive ones rising by a second (e.g., movt. I: mm. 1–2, m. 6, and m. 20). The suite also includes highly detailed dynamic and expressive markings; Reger has been criticized for an excess of such notations in other instances:

> Through an overabundance of dynamic and agogic markings he tried to explain his own view clearly. It is not only the organ works, but also the wonderful
> D-minor string quartet, the Sinfonietta and G-major Serenade, the violin

concerto and the Hiller Variations, which suffer the same burden that more or less achieved the opposite of what Reger wished to accomplish.[17]

The Suite No. 1 in G Minor opens with a plaintive, resonant G minor chord, setting the tone for the introspective first movement, which is cast in an ABA form (Chart 25.2). Reger nicely balances polyphonic and monophonic writing, creating the illusion of polyphony through various means: alternating voices on different strings (mm. 10–12), using arpeggios to outline chords (m. 13), and rapidly changing registers (mm. 22–25).

At the beginning of the B section, Reger introduces a new rhythmic figure: triplet sixteenth notes in m. 14. While this section starts in F minor, the music briefly touches on B♭ minor in mm. 16–17 before making its way to a cadence on D major in m. 23. Reger then revisits material from the beginning of the B section in mm. 23–25, inverting relationships and placing them within a different melodic and harmonic context (Exs. 25.6 and 25.7). In the return of the

Zone	Thematic Areas/Snippet	Measures	Principal Tonal Areas/Function
A		1–13	G minor; ends on F minor
B		14–26	Starts F minor; ends on dominant
A		27–34	G minor

Chart 25.2 Reger, Three Suites for Solo Viola, op. 131d: No. 1 in G Minor: Structural analysis, first movement, Molto sostenuto.

Example 25.6 Reger, Three Suites for Solo Viola, op. 131d: No. 1 in G Minor, movt. I, mm. 13–15.

Example 25.7 Reger, Three Suites for Solo Viola, op. 131d: No. 1 in G Minor, movt. I, mm. 23–24.

A section, Reger restates the first six measures in their entirety (mm. 27–32), changing course in m. 33 for a quick and efficient conclusion to the movement.

The second movement is a witty scherzo, bordering on the grotesque (Chart 25.3). Only two rhythms are used in the Vivace portion (mm. 1–53): a quarter note and an eighth note. To counteract the squareness that such a limitation can create, Reger employs various means of offsetting the music, including hemiola effects (e.g., mm. 5–7 and mm. 12–15). The A section of the Vivace consists of two themes (Unit 1.1 and Unit 1.2), which are developed in the B section (mm. 20–40). In the return of the A section (mm. 41–53), Reger condenses material from these two themes, ritarding into the Andantino (Trio) section.

The lyrical, flowing Trio is in E♭ major. Like the Vivace, this portion uses a limited rhythmic palette (half and quarter notes) with two anomalies thrown in: a dotted-quarter–eighth-note figure in m. 77 and m. 79. The A section (mm. 54–67) uses a lilting half-note and quarter-note rhythm, while the B section (mm. 68–84) features moving quarter notes. Reger closes out the Trio with a repeat of the A section before returning to the Vivace.

The third movement, like the first, is in an ABA form (Chart 25.4) with the opening A and B sections each thirteen measures in length. Tully Potter considered this movement to have "one of the most beautiful themes ever written for a solo stringed instrument."[18] Reger enhances the lovely opening theme with double stops, fully exploiting the glorious sonority of the viola's middle and lower registers. The mood turns dark at m. 14 with the change to G minor and the first *f* of the movement. Reger then builds tension in mm. 22–24 by repeating the syncopated rhythm from the opening measure before relaxing the tempo in m. 26 prior to the return of the A section in m. 27.

The *perpetuum mobile* final movement, with its arpeggiated and scalar sixteenth notes, is reminiscent of Bach's instrumental preludes.[19] However, the movement does not function here as a Baroque prelude, but rather as a virtuosic, Romantic finale. The opening is dominated by terraced dynamics with sudden changes from *f* to *p* in mm. 1–9. A stepwise pattern begins in m. 14 with the first note of each measure ascending as the music crescendos. After the *ff* apex

Zone	Thematic Areas/Snippet	Measures	Principal Tonal Areas/Function
Vivace		1–53	
	A	1–19	
	Unit 1.1	1–7	G minor
	Unit 1.2	8–19	G minor; D minor
	B: Developmental	20–40	Modulatory
	A	41–53	G minor
Andantino		54–100	
	A	54–67	E-flat major
	B	68–84	Starts F minor; ends on B-flat^7 harmony
	A	85–100	E-flat major; ends on dominant of G minor
Da Capo		1–53	

Chart 25.3 Reger, Three Suites for Solo Viola, op. 131d: No. 1 in G Minor: Structural analysis, second movement, Vivace — Andantino.

Zone	Thematic Areas/Snippet	Measures	Principal Tonal Areas/Function
A		1–13	B-flat major
B		14–26	G minor
A		27–40	B-flat major

Chart 25.4 Reger, Three Suites for Solo Viola, op. 131d: No. 1 in G Minor: Structural analysis, third movement, Andante sostenuto.

in m. 22, a new pattern appears in mm. 23–26 with the first note of each measure descending by a second while the music diminuendos. Reger briefly relaxes the momentum in mm. 38–39 as the music ritards in preparation for a return of the opening at m. 40. The music slows again in m. 61, with Reger introducing the first multiple stops of the movement to close the suite out with a decisive flourish.

Frédéric Lainé nicely summed up the brilliance of Reger's viola suites:

> Reger succeeds in finding a balance between a harmonic richness (with an ever-moving chromaticism) and an expressive fluidity that is perfectly suited to the viola. With a real technical complexity (many double stops, especially thirds and sixths), a variety in the articulations, sharp contrasts in the dynamics, he alternates sections of great vitality and more poetic moments, showing his perfect comprehension of the resources of the instrument.[20]

Written in 1915, Reger's suites are a glorious achievement for the viola. Not only do they capture the *modern* spirit, they also encapsulate Baroque, Classical, and Romantic sensibilities. Through his adept fusion of styles, Reger combines two hundred years of German musical progress into a cohesive whole, simultaneously carving out a past and a future for the viola's solo repertoire.

26

Robert Schumann: *Märchenbilder*
for Viola and Piano, op. 113

1. Nicht schnell
2. Lebhaft
3. Rasch
4. Langsam, mit melancholischem Ausdruck[1]

Date of Composition: March 1–4, 1851

First Edition: Robert Schumann, *Mährchen-Bilder: Vier Stücke für Pianoforte und Viola (Violine ad libitum), Op. 113*, 2 vols., Kassel: C. Luckhardt, [1852], Plate No. 273 and Plate No. 274

Select Later Editions: Robert Schumann, *Märchenbilder für Klavier und Viola Opus 113*, ed. Wiltrud Haug-Freienstein, Munich: Henle, 2000, HN 632; Robert Schumann, *Märchenbilder für Viola (Violine) und Klavier opus 113*, ed. Armin Koch, Mainz: Schott Music, 2018, 57 922, VAB 93

Dedication: Herrn J. von Wasielewskÿ zugeeignet [Wilhelm Joseph von Wasielewski]

Date/Place of First Read-Through: March 15, 1851, Wilhelm Joseph von Wasielewski (viola), Clara Schumann (piano), Schumann residence, Düsseldorf

Date/Place of First Private Performance: March 19, 1852, Ferdinand David (viola), Clara Schumann (piano), Preußer family residence, Leipzig

Date/Place of First Public Performance: November 12, 1853, Wilhelm Joseph von Wasielewski (viola), Clara Schumann (piano), Zum goldenen Stern (Golden Star) inn, Bonn

Introduction

"Once upon a time there was an Enchanter who collected around him a great crowd of folks, before whom he performed his wonderful tricks."[2] As if by magic, a great storyteller draws you in, spinning tales of mystery, delight, and wonder. In his later years, Robert Schumann composed a number of enchanting works that rely on the art of storytelling: "An art that reaffirms the importance of telling old tales and singing old songs."[3] An outstanding example of his skill as storyteller is the *Märchenbilder* (*Fairy-Tale Pictures*), for viola and piano, written in 1851. Though Schumann provided no descriptive titles for the movements, his vivid musical settings so expertly capture the aura of fairy tales that they have inspired countless performers and listeners to conjure their own images of far-off lands, fantastical creatures, and heroic adventures.

Biographical Sketch

Born in the small town of Zwickau, Saxony, Robert Schumann (1810–1856) was the fifth and final child of August and Johanna Christiana Schumann. His father was a respected bookseller, publisher, and lexicographer, and Robert was raised in an environment that valued literature and learning. At the age of seven, he began piano lessons with Johann Gottfried Kuntsch, a local organist and choir-master, and within a year he had written his first compositions (now lost). He also took flute and cello lessons starting around 1822 from Carl Gottlieb Meissner.[4] Music and literature would serve as dual loves during his formative years; in addition to composing music, he wrote poetry, essays, and dramatic works. At the age of fourteen, he was entrusted by his father to help gather and translate material for a book, and in 1825 he co-founded a literary society devoted to German literature at his school, the Zwickau Gymnasium.[5] Over the following years, Schumann became captivated by a number of German literary figures, including Friedrich Schiller, Jean Paul, and E. T. A. Hoffmann.

Schumann's father died in 1826, and to appease his mother and fulfill the terms of his inheritance, he entered the University of Leipzig as a law student in 1828. Disliking the study of law, he continued with his literary and music efforts, becoming a piano student of Friedrich Wieck in August of that year. Wieck's then nine-year-old daughter Clara would eventually become Schumann's partner in marriage and the most ardent promoter of his music. After a year of university studies in Heidelberg (1829–1830), Schumann wrote an impassioned letter to his mother, imploring her to let him abandon law and pursue a career as a pianist under Wieck's tutelage. She "grudgingly approved her son's proposed course of action,"[6] and Schumann returned to Leipzig in late 1830, living with Wieck and practicing for up to seven hours a day.

In the summer of 1831, Schumann started harmony and counterpoint lessons with Heinrich Dorn, an opera director, studying with him for less than a year. During this period, Schumann wrote frequently about a weakness that had been developing in his right hand, including stiffness of the middle finger. While the exact cause remains unclear, Schumann's use of a chiroplast, a device designed to strengthen a pianist's fingers, did not help the situation.[7] He eventually abandoned any hope of a career as a pianist and devoted energies toward composition and music criticism. In 1833–1834, his article *Der Davidsbündler*, published in *Der Komet*, publicly introduced an imaginary society of crusaders—the Davidsbund—who were leading the fight against the musical Philistines of the day. Two of Schumann's alter egos were the society's principal members: the "fiery and impetuous" Florestan and the "dreamy" Eusebius.[8] The Davidsbund soon found a permanent home in a new journal, *Neue Leipziger Zeitschrift für Musik*, which was reorganized as the *Neue Zeitschrift für Musik* in 1835 with Schumann as editor. Schumann held this position for the next ten years, which "would be infinitely more important in promoting his name than his compositions."[9]

In early 1835, Schumann's affections toward Clara Wieck began to change—affections that were returned by Clara—and by the end of the year they were mutually declaring their love.[10] Her father bitterly opposed the relationship and resorted to extreme measures to keep the two apart. After winning a court case against Clara's father, the couple married on September 12, 1840; they would go on to have eight children together.

Most of Schumann's early compositions were piano works, but starting in 1840 he turned, almost systematically, to other genres, exploring lieder in 1840–1841 (composing about 125 lieder within a period of twelve months), followed by orchestral music (1841), chamber music (1842), and choral music (1843).[11] After selling the *Neue Zeitschrift für Musik* in 1844, Schumann and his family moved to Dresden. In September 1850, he took up a new position as municipal music director in Düsseldorf. Schumann had suffered from severe depressive episodes since the early 1830s, and his mental state worsened after the first, exhausting year in Düsseldorf:

> Even in 1851, alarming symptoms of this terrible, slowly-developing, and anxiously-watched disease, appeared. He wrote of it, June 11, 1851, "We are all tolerably well, except that I am the victim of occasional nervous attacks, which sometimes alarm me; especially a few days ago, when I fainted after hearing [Robert] Radecke play the organ." These "nervous attacks" increased in 1852.[12]

His illness reached an acute stage in February 1854, as recorded by Clara in her diary:

> On the night of Friday the 10th and Saturday the 11th, Robert suffered from so violent an affection of the hearing that he did not close his eyes all night. He kept on hearing the same note over and over again, and at times he heard chords. . . .

The following nights were very bad—we hardly slept at all. . . . He tried to work by day, but he could do so only at the cost of the most terrible effort. He said frequently, that if this did not cease, his mind must give way.[13]

On February 27, Schumann threw himself into the Rhine river but was rescued by fishermen. At his own request, he was taken to a private asylum in Endenich on March 4, where he remained until his death, over two years later, on July 29, 1856.

Schumann's *Märchenbilder for Viola and Piano,* op. 113

Schumann composed two works that prominently involve the viola, both of which have fairy-tale themes: *Märchenbilder for Viola (or Violin) and Piano,* op. 113 (1851) and *Märchenerzählungen for Clarinet (or Violin), Viola, and Piano,* op. 132 (1853). *Märchenbilder* was composed over the course of four days between March 1 and March 4, 1851, as recorded by Schumann in his *Haushaltbücher* (daily household account books):

March 1, 1851: *Viola*geschichten (*Viola* Stories)
March 2, 1851: "Mährchengeschichten" (*Fairy-Tale Stories*)
March 3, 1851: "Mährchen" (*Fairy Tales*)
March 4, 1851: 4tes Mährchen (4th Fairy Tale)[14]

On March 15, he noted a read-through of the work with Wilhelm Joseph von Wasielewski, concertmaster of the Düsseldorf Musikverein, under the title "Mährchenlieder" (*Fairy-Tale Songs*). And on March 18, he referenced the title *Mährchenbilder* (*Fairy-Tale Pictures*) in his account book, indicating that he had engaged the copyist Otto Hermann Klausnitz to work on the piece.[15]

An extensive discussion of *Märchenbilder*'s genesis, publication, reception, performance history, and sources can be found in the New Edition of the Complete Works by Robert Schumann; readers interested in learning more are advised to read Armin Koch's extensive critical notes.[16] One of the sources that Koch reproduces only in part is a letter from the poet Louis du Rieux, dated February 19, 1851—days before Schumann began work on *Märchenbilder*. In that letter, du Rieux included a poem titled "Märchenbilder," suggesting that it might serve as "a stimulus for a musical creation":[17]

Very esteemed Sir,
A few years ago, I first became acquainted with the products of your genius and have since had them played for me repeatedly. I have followed the ever

more brilliant development of your musical activity not merely with atten-
tiveness but with awe; but I will refrain here from recounting my opinions
of your works, since you will yourself recognize in them the greatness of
your genius not only more beautifully but more purely. However, I have
long wished to put my feelings of reverence into words, and with pleasure
I grasp the opportunity [to do so] by sending you a few stanzas, which have
earned the approval of my friends. I allow myself to relay them here.

Fairy-Tale Pictures

1.
During childhood, magical fairy tales
Explain to us the actions of spirits
And we cheer or wail,
When we listen to their deeds.
Then within ourselves resound
Laments, as yet unrecognized by us;
But our early-spoiled
Ear cannot express the inner sound.

2.
Until a picture, like the red glow of dawn,
Has arisen out of the night of pain—
Beloved, calls the weary warrior,
Your gazes release the bonds
That are woven around my eyes and mind;
Resting on your breast, I recover
My strength, in your words
[I find] gentle, beautiful fairy-tale songs!
Leave the sweet words of love
Vibrating in my arms,
To find there a solid bond;
Pain must bind us together,
This our love shall tell us:
Two spirits tightly entwined,
While storms rage about them,
As fairy tales sing of it!

3.
But with a shudder, he seizes her,
[And] wrenches her into the dance of life;

Anxiously she reaches for the garland
On her head; but in vain—
Fluttering, its blossoms fall—
And as in the old fairy tales,
The wild delight of the dancers intensifies—
They themselves are a fairy tale to each other.

4.
And as life was sleeping
That evening in the arm of peace,
He hurries to the distant house,
That is surrounded by tangled grape-vines
In front of the high steps. Beloved,
Let all of love's raptures flutter
About you in your dream,
May it be spun like fairy tales!—

Finale
But pale he came to this place
After only a few days,
To say farewell lamentingly
To love's sweet spell:
Already the bloody flame of dawn
Must consecrate itself to grave battle;
Our meaningful sensible life of love
Will be my final fairy tale.

I thought of the poetry as a theme for a sonata and 1 as Allegro, 2 Adagio, 3 Scherzo, 4 Trio, Finale Allegro. I do not know whether this is correctly thought out; but I believe that the poem could well function as a stimulus for a musical creation, and I would be glad to have approached you with it, highly esteemed sir, and to have shown you reverence. I could send you much that is similar, if you are inclined to pay attention to my work.

With infinite esteem

Yours
most humbly,
Louis du Rieux
Berlin February 19, [18]51.
Mittelstraße 45

It is unknown what influence this letter had on Schumann's *Märchenbilder*. The composition's movements obviously do not align with du Rieux's suggestions, and Armin Koch is skeptical of a correlation:

> Not least the layout in five stanzas—four stanzas are numbered, the fifth is headed "Finale," the second stanza is, moreover, a double stanza—makes a specific connection extremely improbable, even the proportions are against it. Furthermore, the musical progression of the movements does not indicate any parallel with the poetics of the poetry. If we were to link Schumann's *Märchenbilder* in any way whatsoever with du Rieux's poem, we would also expect the composer to at least allude accordingly to the poet.[18]

Despite Koch's reservations, possible connections between the two sources can be drawn. It would not take much imagination to detect similarities in the text of the third stanza with the music in the third movement: "But with a shudder, he seizes her, [And] wrenches her into the dance of life . . . The wild delight of the dancers intensifies." The first stanza conveys a mood that is similar to Schumann's music from the first movement, and other scholars have noted a parallel between the melancholy fifth (Finale) stanza and the fourth movement.[19] Given the proximity of the letter to the date of composition, along with the shared title, a connection between the two works is certainly plausible.

Märchenbilder is dedicated to Wilhelm Joseph von Wasielewski, Schumann's concertmaster in Düsseldorf:

> After Schumann had written his *Märchenbilder*, which, to my great pleasure, he dedicated to me, he had his wife play them through while I took the viola accompaniment. He then said with a smile: "Childish pranks! There's not much to them." By this he merely meant to intimate that the pieces belong to the genre of *Kleinkunst*. He made no objection when I called them delightful.[20]

The work dates from Schumann's late period, during which "the composer is often described as having 'withdrawn' from the world, and his music is accused of expressive emptiness."[21] His late works have benefited from a critical reappraisal in recent years: "A comparison between Schumann's late chamber music and his early piano pieces," notes Martin Geck, "reveals an identical impulse against a different background."[22] *Märchenbilder*, indeed, owes a debt to Schumann's earlier piano works, as well as to his lieder, as suggested by the reference to "Mährchenlieder" in the *Haushaltbücher* entry of March 15, 1851. The work also bears hallmarks of Schumann's overall Romantic style, as broadly described by Thomas Alan Brown: "The subjective, emotionally intoned nuances and differentiations of romantic thought are mirrored in Schumann's harmonic constructions, in his searching for delayed resolutions, and above all in the frequent application of shifting and complicated rhythmic patterns."[23]

The first movement, Nicht schnell (Not fast), is the most formally complex of the four movements, structured in a ternary (ABA) form (Chart 26.1) that bears traces of sonata form. The viola begins the movement with a lyrical eight-measure theme (Theme A; Unit 1.1), after which a double bar line appears. In m. 9 (all measure numbers refer to both the Henle and 2018 Schott editions), the piano introduces a new theme (Theme B; Unit 1.2), which is elaborated on more extensively than the first theme. The effect, both musically and visually (because of the double bar line), is that Theme A is intended to serve as a prologue to the first tale ("Once upon a time . . .").[24] The A section concludes in F major on the second beat of m. 29; the piano's subsequent sixteenth notes, starting *fp* on the

Zone	Thematic Areas/Snippet	Measures	Principal Tonal Areas/Function
A		1–29	
	Unit 1.1: Theme A	1–8	D minor
	Unit 1.2: Theme B	9–29	D minor; F major
B	Theme A and B material from A section	30–46	A minor
A		46–64	
	Unit 1.1: Theme B	46–58	D minor
	Unit 1.2: Theme A in viola (with Theme B in piano)	58–64	D minor
Coda		65–72	D minor

Chart 26.1 Schumann, *Märchenbilder for Viola and Piano*, op. 113: Structural analysis, first movement, Nicht schnell.

final beat, creates a sense of rhythmic displacement moving into the B section. In the following section (mm. 30–46), Schumann combines the two themes in a developmental manner while continuing with rhythmic complexities. For the return of the A section at m. 46, the piano begins with the second theme (Theme B), reinforcing the primacy of that melodic material. The viola returns to first-theme material (Theme A) at m. 58 in a rhythmically altered version over the piano's continuation of the second theme. Schumann shortens the statement of Theme A here to seven measures (mm. 58–64), avoiding a perfect authentic cadence and eliding into Theme B at m. 65 for the start of the dreamlike coda.[25]

Cast in a rondo form (Chart 26.2), the second movement, Lebhaft (Lively), is dominated by march-like dotted rhythms. After a triumphant opening fanfare establishes the key of F major (mm. 1–2), the viola galops through the A section with its raucous double stops in thirds. The piano comes to the fore in the B section (mm. 51–70), in the relative minor, with the viola offering ethereal comments, continuing with dotted rhythms. Another triumphant blast from the viola (mm. 67–70) segues to a repeat of the A section. Schumann offers more rhythmic and harmonic complexities in the C section (mm. 119–42): the piano

Zone	Thematic Areas/Snippet	Measures	Principal Tonal Areas/Function
Introduction		1–2	F major
A		3–51	F major
B		51–70	D minor
A		71–119	F major
C		119–42	B-flat major
A		143–90	F major
Coda		191–205	F major

Chart 26.2 Schumann, *Märchenbilder for Viola and Piano*, op. 113: Structural analysis, second movement, Lebhaft.

begins off-balance with its right-hand theme starting on the downbeat, seemingly in B♭ major, while the left hand is stuck on an F⁷ harmony (Ex. 26.1). The viola attempts to set things straight with its restatement of the piano's theme in the following measure, which now starts on beat two (firmly in B♭ major). But that just sets off a tussle between the two players for control of the melody, and they continue with an extended back and forth throughout the remainder of the section. After a final repeat of the A section (mm. 143–90), Schumann appends a brief coda that quietly closes out the movement.

Cast in an ABA form (Chart 26.3), the third movement, Rasch (Quickly), opens with dizzying triplet arpeggios in the viola, marked *Mit springendem Bogen* (with bouncing bow). Schumann makes dramatic use of dynamics in the opening section, with the frequent swells (e.g., m. 2 and mm. 18–19) and sharply alternating dynamics (mm. 28–32) creating a sense of danger or apprehension, as if a hidden threat were lurking in the woods, edging ever closer. The B section (mm. 37–61), set in the remote key of B major, is markedly calmer in mood, offering hope that

Example 26.1 Schumann, *Märchenbilder for Viola and Piano*, op. 113, movt. II, mm. 119–24.

Zone	Thematic Areas/Snippet	Measures	Principal Tonal Areas/Function
A		1–36	D minor
B		37–61	B major
A		62–91	Starts on dominant; D minor
Coda		91–107	D minor

Chart 26.3 Schumann, *Märchenbilder for Viola and Piano*, op. 113: Structural analysis, third movement, Rasch.

our story's hero has finally gotten to a point of safety. The texture also changes, with delicate pizzicato passages in the viola that lightly accentuate the pitter-patter of the piano. Schumann cunningly sneaks back into the A section in m. 62, starting on an A^7 chord and retaining the B section's dotted-quarter–eighth-note rhythm in the piano's left hand underneath the viola's *pp* triplet sixteenth notes. The tension quickly escalates with an extended *ff* section in the viola (mm. 74–91), after which the dynamic abruptly drops to *p* in m. 92. In the coda (mm. 91–107), the piano calmly revisits the dotted-quarter–eighth-note rhythm from the B section while the viola continues (quietly) with its triplet figures, emphasizing a repeated D pedal. This relaxed atmosphere suggests that the danger is finally receding and that the movement may end quietly, similar to the previous one. But Schumann provides a thrilling conclusion instead with the viola's *ff* pickup to m. 100 ushering in the movement's final spine-tingling moments.

The fourth movement, Langsam, mit melancholischem Ausdruck (Slowly, with a melancholy expression), is perhaps the most magical: a wistful reflection on lost youth, lost loves, lost hopes and dreams. To convey the melancholy mood, Schumann makes extensive use of the viola's lower register (mm. 42–45 is effectively the only spot that employs the A string). The movement, in an ABA form (Chart 26.4), opens with the piano doubling the viola's line, a characteristic trait found in Schumann's lieder.[26] At the start of the B section (mm. 31–62), the melody moves to the piano with the viola offering softly rippling remarks. The viola resumes a melodic function in mm. 40–51, once again doubled by the piano, before returning to its arpeggiated utterances. In the final section (mm. 63–94), Schumann repeats the opening twenty-eight measures—almost

Zone	Thematic Areas/Snippet	Measures	Principal Tonal Areas/Function
A		1–30	D major
B		31–62	F major
A		63–94	D major

Chart 26.4 Schumann, *Märchenbilder for Viola and Piano*, op. 113: Structural analysis, fourth movement, Langsam, mit melancholischem Ausdruck.

exactly—with one significant deviation in the viola in mm. 74–76. The music deviates again in m. 90 as Schumann wraps up his poignant tale.

It did not take long for violists to fall under *Märchenbilder*'s spell; the work enjoyed relatively widespread popularity during the nineteenth century, with documented performances by Henry Vieuxtemps in Belgium, Charles Baetens in the United States, and Emil Kreuz and Alfred Hobday in England. It remains a favorite among violists and audiences, who are enchanted not only by Schumann's marvelous music but also by the enigmatic stories contained within. The work has been orchestrated at least twice: by Max Erdmannsdörfer during the nineteenth century (published by Luckhardt in 1877–1878) and by Michael McLean during the twenty-first century (recorded by Roger Myers in 2012).[27]

27

Dmitry Shostakovich: Sonata for Viola and Piano, op. 147

I.   Moderato
II. Allegretto
III. Adagio

Date of Composition: April–July 5, 1975 (manuscript dated July 5, 1975)

First Edition: Dmitri Schostakowitsch, *Op. 147, Sonate für Viola und Klavier*, Hamburg: Musikverlag Hans Sikorski, 1975, Plate No. H. S. 2222

Dedication: Fjodor Druschinin gewidmet

Date/Place of First Private Performance: September 25, 1975, Fedor Druzhinin (viola), Mikhail Muntian (piano), home of Dmitry Shostakovich, Moscow

Date/Place of First Public Performance: October 1, 1975, Fedor Druzhinin (viola), Mikhail Muntian (piano), Glinka Hall, Leningrad

Introduction

"The Viola Sonata was not necessarily intended as Shostakovich's last work—but he was realistic enough about his health to have known that it might well turn out to be just that."[1] Shostakovich's sonata has earned a reputation as one of the most profound works in the viola repertoire. That reputation stems, in part, from its position as Shostakovich's final composition, which has fueled many "death-driven portrayals" of the work by performers and commentators who view it "as the composer's self-penned requiem."[2] The concept of self-requiem is reinforced by Shostakovich's incorporation of musical quotations into the sonata, which "create an atmosphere of elegiac contemplation in the veil of memories."[3]

Searching for quotations within the viola sonata (and attempting to decipher their meanings) has become almost a quest among listeners, who have put forth the names of numerous works that they have detected. The reference to Ludwig van Beethoven's "Moonlight" Sonata in the final movement is well-established, and many listeners have heard in the viola's opening pizzicato notes a

reference to Alban Berg's Violin Concerto.[4] Other works that listeners have identified include Shostakovich's Symphony No. 14, op. 135 and his Suite for Two
Pianos, op. 6.[5] And in one of the most extensive lists, Ivan Sokolov has identified quotations from all fifteen of Shostakovich's symphonies in the final movement.[6] But Viacheslav Dinerchtein advises caution when considering possible
quotations:

> The authenticity of many of the reported quotations, and in particular, self-
> quotations, can be questioned, for it is not always conclusive where the bor-
> rowing techniques end and the traits of . . . Shostakovich's [late] musical
> language begin.[7]

Ultimately, the use of quotations by Shostakovich is only one aspect of his final
masterpiece. There are many further avenues for exploration in the Sonata for
Viola and Piano, op. 147, and performers can devote a lifetime of study to this
epic work, constantly gaining new insights the more that they dig into it.

Biographical Sketch

Dmitry Dmitriyevich Shostakovich (1906–1975) was born in St. Petersburg,
Russia, the second of Sofya and Dmitry Boleslavovich Shostakovich's three children. His father served as an inspector in the Bureau of Weights and Measures,
and both parents enjoyed music-making in their home. When Shostakovich's
mother began teaching him piano at the age of eight, he immediately exhibited
perfect pitch and an exceptional musical memory. It was not long before he
started composing, and in the fall of 1915 he enrolled at Ignaty Glyasser's music
school, where he progressed rapidly on the piano. He later studied piano privately with Alexandra Rozanova, a teacher at the Petrograd Conservatory, before enrolling as a student in piano and composition at the conservatory in the
fall of 1919.[8] His teachers there included Nikolay Sokolov (counterpoint and
fugue) and Maximilian Steinberg (composition); after a year of piano studies
with Rozanova, Shostakovich transferred to Leonid Vladimirovich Nikolayev's
class. He also took violin and conducting lessons while at the school.[9]
Shostakovich's father died in 1922, straining the family's financial circumstances,
and Shostakovich himself fell ill with tuberculosis early in 1923. While recuper-
ating later that summer on the Crimean peninsula, he fell in love with Tatyana
Glivenko; the two would remain romantically involved for several years.[10]
    Shostakovich composed his First Symphony (1924–1925) as a requirement for
graduation at the conservatory (which by this time had been renamed Leningrad
Conservatory). The work was well-received when he played it in a two-piano

version at the exam on May 6, 1925, and the orchestral version—premiered on May 12, 1926—brought him international fame. In the following years, he accepted many commissions (particularly for film and theater projects), made solo and chamber appearances as a pianist, and continued for a period as a graduate student at the conservatory. In 1932, he married Nina Varzar, whom he had met five years earlier. Though the couple had agreed to an open marriage, one of Shostakovich's early affairs nearly derailed their union. The couple eventually reconciled and went on to have two children together.[11]

Shostakovich's early life coincided with a period of tremendous social upheaval in his homeland; the political climate grew more volatile after the establishment of the Union of Soviet Socialist Republics (USSR) in 1922 and the subsequent rise to power of Joseph Stalin. On January 28, 1936, Shostakovich found himself caught in the political crosshairs after the appearance of an unsigned editorial in the Communist newspaper *Pravda*, titled "Muddle Instead of Music," which lambasted his opera *Lady Macbeth of the Mtsensk District*:

> Apparently, the composer did not take the trouble to consider what the Soviet audience is looking for and expecting in music. It's as if he intentionally encoded his music and confused all of its resonances, in order to appeal to only those aesthete formalists who have lost a healthy sense of taste. He has overlooked the demands of Soviet culture that have expunged barbarity from all aspects of Soviet life.[12]

A second unsigned editorial, "Balletic Falsity," which criticized Shostakovich's ballet *The Limpid Stream*, appeared on February 6, 1936, sealing his fate; he was "toppled almost overnight from his position as the leading light of Soviet music."[13] While Shostakovich suffered hardships as a result of the controversy, he managed to weather the storm and was appointed to the faculty of the Leningrad Conservatory in 1937. Later that year he earned a triumphant success with his Symphony No. 5, op. 47, which "restored his name to favor and removed him, for the time being, from the roster of ideologically suspect artists."[14]

During World War II, Shostakovich volunteered with the Home Guard in Leningrad before being evacuated to Kuybïshev during the fall of 1941. He moved to Moscow in 1943 and started teaching at the Moscow Conservatory; although he resumed teaching at the Leningrad Conservatory after the war, Shostakovich continued to reside in Moscow until his death. Early in 1948, Shostakovich found himself embroiled in a sweeping investigation of composers by the Central Committee of the Communist Party, led by Andrey Zhdanov.[15] On February 10, 1948, the committee issued a decree in which Shostakovich and other composers "were accused of leading Soviet music astray and of other sins."[16] As punishment for his sins, Shostakovich was dismissed from his teaching positions at the Moscow and Leningrad conservatories and had a significant number of his works banned from performance and stricken from the repertory.[17]

Afterward, Shostakovich publicly toed the party line; he served as a Soviet representative to the Cultural and Scientific Congress for World Peace held in New York in 1949 and attended later national and international congresses. Restrictions on performances of his music in the USSR were gradually relaxed, and, bowing to prolonged coercion, he finally applied for membership in the Communist Party in 1960.[18] This was a turbulent period in Shostakovich's personal life: his wife died of cancer in 1954, and his mother died the following year. His second marriage, to Margarita Kainova in 1956, ended in divorce three years later. And in 1958 the early symptoms of a debilitating condition—later diagnosed as a form of polio—began to appear.[19]

In 1962, Shostakovich married Irina Antonovna Supinskaya, a literary editor. In the following years, he enjoyed further professional success at home and abroad, though a heart attack in 1966 put an end to his performing career. His health continued to worsen, and he suffered another heart attack in 1971 and was diagnosed with lung cancer in 1972. Shostakovich died on August 9, 1975, in a hospital at Kuntsevo, on the outskirts of Moscow.[20]

Shostakovich's Sonata for Viola and Piano, op. 147

For more than forty years, Shostakovich's Sonata for Viola and Piano, op. 147 (1975) was believed to be his only work for the instrument. Then, in 2017, the previously unknown *Impromptu for Viola and Piano* was discovered. The manuscript for that short, two-minute work, is dated May 2, 1931, and it bears the opus number 33—a number that Shostakovich subsequently assigned to the film score for *Counterplan* (1932).

Shostakovich composed the viola sonata for Fedor Druzhinin, who had served as violist in the Beethoven Quartet since 1964. The Beethoven Quartet, founded in the early 1920s, had a long association with Shostakovich, and Druzhinin played in the premieres of the composer's string quartets nos. 11 through 14 with that ensemble. While working with Shostakovich, Druzhinin periodically suggested that he compose a work for viola:

> More than a few times during these years I tried to delicately remind [Shostakovich] that his enormous catalogue still misses a composition for viola. He usually replied, "I don't know, I don't know, Fedya, I have to ponder it, I have to ponder it." But that was not the case in the course of [Shostakovich's]

very last years, when his health condition worsened and I did not feel comfortable bothering him with my requests any longer.[21]

It came as a surprise to Druzhinin, then, when Shostakovich phoned him about a new viola sonata during the summer of 1975:

> At nine in the morning on the 1st July 1975, the telephone rang and, picking up the receiver, I heard his beloved, if deafening, voice.
>
> "Fedya! Dmitry Dmitrievich Shostakovich speaking." He always introduced himself with his full name on the phone, even though I could recognize him in an instant.
>
> "I thought of writing a viola sonata."
>
> My heart leapt, knowing that when Dmitry Dmitrievich said he thought he might write something, it meant that the composition had actually matured to the extent that it was ready to be let loose; he would never have started talking about something he was only planning to write.[22]

In his memoirs, Druzhinin indicates that the two artists conversed numerous times via telephone over the next few days, discussing various aspects of the work. On July 5, another call from Shostakovich came:

> "Fedya, of course you will want a general idea of its structure."
>
> He never said anything about the contents of his compositions, at least in front of me. Instead, he would make comments such as: "This must sound sacred," or, "The walls should come crashing down here." . . .
>
> "The first part is a *novella*, the second is a *scherzo*, the finale is an *adagio* in memory of Beethoven. You mustn't mix them up: each section is distinct . . . distinct."
>
> Dmitry Dmitrievich evidently wanted to emphasize that his sonata was not a funeral march or anything of that sort.
>
> "It lasts about half an hour and it should have its own section of the concert programme."[23]

Later that evening, Shostakovich phoned Druzhinin, informing him that the score was finished and that he was sending it off to be transcribed.[24] Shostakovich continued working on the sonata until a few days before his death, correcting proofs on August 4 and 5 while in the hospital.[25] Druzhinin premiered the work with the pianist Mikhail Muntian on the composer's birthday, September 25, 1975, in a private performance at the composer's home; the official public premiere occurred on October 1 at the Glinka Hall in Leningrad.

The Sonata for Viola and Piano, op. 147 exhibits traits that are associated with Shostakovich's late works, including the prominent use of the perfect fourth and the semitone.[26] And, like other of his late works, it incorporates twelve-note compositional technique:

> Inwardly his thoughts and creative projects turned increasingly to the topic of death; at the same time he became interested in 12-note composition, still the subject of official disapproval. . . . He never applied the technique in the manner of the Second Viennese School; rather, themes of this kind took on symbolic associations with death or stasis.[27]

Given Shostakovich's designation of the first movement as a "novella," the following analysis labels the sections as "chapters" (Chart 27.1). The movement

Zone	Thematic Areas/Snippet	Measures
Chapter 1		1–70
Chapter 2		71–157
	Unit 1.1	71–119
	Unit 1.2	120–57
Chapter 3		157–221
	Unit 1.1	157–79
	Unit 1.2	180–221
Epilogue		222–61

Chart 27.1 Shostakovich, Sonata for Viola and Piano, op. 147: Structural analysis, first movement, Moderato.

opens with an accompanimental pizzicato motive in the viola, spanning its four strings. In m. 5, the piano enters with the twelve-note theme (Db–C–Bb–A–B–Ab–G–F#–D–Eb–F–E). Throughout the movement, Shostakovich uses portions of this twelve-note row, though he does not follow typical serial compositional techniques, preferring to transform the row through other means, including timbre and rhythm.[28] Shostakovich continues with fragments of this theme as well as variations of the accompanying opening motive until m. 70, after which a new idea is presented.

The triplet figurations and *f* dynamic at the beginning of Chapter 2 (Unit 1.1) bring an immediate sense of agitation and drama, in great contrast to the calm mood and spare texture that prevailed in Chapter 1. Shostakovich further heightens the sense of drama in m. 120 (Unit 1.2) with the viola playing an augmented version of the triplet figurations from mm. 71–72 over the piano's sixteenth notes. This rhythmic juxtaposition creates tension between the viola (which seems to be pulling back) and the piano (which, in introducing the first sixteenth notes of the movement, seems interested in moving forward). Shostakovich continues to transform the triplet figurations throughout the remainder of this section (e.g., inverting them in mm. 131–32). Calm begins to return around m. 139, and the first notes of the twelve-tone row reappear in m. 143, foreshadowing a return of the opening in m. 157 (Chapter 3; Unit 1.1). Here, the piano picks up the accompanimental motive with the viola playing the entire twelve-note theme *sul ponticello* and tremolo in mm. 161–63. Shostakovich returns to material from Chapter 2 in m. 180 (Unit 1.2), concluding the third chapter with a passage for viola alone (mm. 215–21) that segues into the novella's Epilogue. Here, Shostakovich brilliantly exploits different registers of the viola in an extended solo passage, interspersing accompanimental and melodic figurations, as if two different instruments were being used. In m. 242, the piano returns, with Shostakovich revisiting material from the end of the first chapter (see mm. 62–70). At the conclusion of the movement, the piano plays one last snippet of the triplet figurations in an inverted version (mm. 257–59).

The music for the second movement is largely taken from Shostakovich's unfinished opera *The Gamblers*, which the composer had started in 1941 but abandoned in 1942. The movement, which "jolts us by its radically different manner,"[29] thus transports us to a different time and place in the composer's life. Shostakovich describes this movement as a scherzo, and—despite its formal ambiguities—the movement can be viewed in a ternary form (Chart 27.2).[30] Section A (mm. 1–123) is derived from the opening of the opera. In this section, many of the viola's double stops result from Shostakovich's combining of orchestral parts. The movement opens with a rather drunken theme (Unit 1.1), with the viola staggering around all over the fingerboard. At m. 39, the viola introduces a new motive (Unit 1.2), which is then taken over by the piano at m. 48 with

Zone	Thematic Areas/Snippet	Measures
A		1–123
	Unit 1.1	1–38
	Unit 1.2	39–73
	Unit 1.3	73–123
B		124–201
	Unit 1.1	124–56
	Unit 1.2 pizz.	157–70
	Unit 1.3	171–93
	Unit 1.4: Transition	193–201
A		201–318
	Unit 1.1	201–22
	Unit 1.2	223–32
	Unit 1.3	233–80
	Unit 1.4	281–318
Coda	Pno.	319–35

Chart 27.2 Shostakovich, Sonata for Viola and Piano, op. 147: Structural analysis, second movement, Allegretto.

the viola introducing a new lyrical theme in the following measure. After the viola's dramatic climax on an e♭iii in m. 73, Shostakovich begins to deviate from the course of the opera in the following measures, though mm. 74–123 roughly corresponds to mm. 77–119 of *The Gamblers*.[31]

Shostakovich jumps ahead in the opera for the B section (mm. 124–201). At m. 124, an oscillating eighth-note figure (taken from *The Gamblers*) is introduced in the piano's bass line. After a short introductory passage (mm. 124–31), the viola plays a new theme (mm. 132–55) in its lowest register. The material for this section is taken from mm. 301–19 of the opera (where two bass singers, Alexei and Gavryushka, split the melody that is given to the viola). At m. 157 (Unit 1.2), Shostakovich once again jumps ahead in the opera (see m. 481 of *The Gamblers*) to a scene where Gavryushka sings a song to the accompaniment of a bass balalaika. The viola, with its pizzicato chords, initially takes the part of the bass balalaika while the piano takes Gavryushka's melody. At m. 171 (Unit 1.3), Shostakovich continues with music from this scene with a motive that appeared earlier in the movement at m. 39.[32] The B section concludes with a transitional passage for the viola (Unit 1.4; mm. 193–201), which scholars have identified as a quotation from the Prelude of Shostakovich's Suite for Two Pianos, op. 6.[33] At m. 201, the formal boundaries are blurred by a return of the motive that had appeared in both the A (at m. 39) and B (at m. 171) sections, but by m. 223 (Unit 1.2), we are firmly back to the A section. Shostakovich makes greater use of the lyrical theme from m. 49 in the final A section, frequently combining it with the oscillating half-step accompanimental figure that had opened the B section (see mm. 124–26). The movement winds down with a short coda (mm. 319–35), in which Shostakovich revisits thematic material from the B section (see mm. 157–63).

The third movement is dominated by the interval of a fourth, starting with the opening viola solo, in which Shostakovich revisits the transitory passage from the second movement (see movt. II, mm. 193–201). While Shostakovich uses the interval of a fourth in various manners throughout the remainder of the movement, he frequently revisits the descending fourth pattern that begins this passage. His designation of the movement as "an *adagio* in memory of Beethoven" becomes clear in the following measures, with the piano's right-hand arpeggios and the viola's dotted rhythms alluding to Beethoven's "Moonlight" Sonata. Druzhinin commented on the sublime merging of two creative geniuses in this movement:

> The shadow of Beethoven in the finale was astounding because the Moonlight Sonata theme was not used as a quotation but more as a shadowy image. Instead of the even triplets of Beethoven's *Sonata Quasi una Fantasia*, he had a quadruplet with a pause entering the sonata's finale with an astonishing harmony

and naturalness, all the while sounding purely Shostakovich. Many dream of achieving such a moment of spiritual unity between two great composers, so far apart from one another in time, but only a genius could bring it to fruition and give voice to such a thing on earth.[34]

The remainder of the fantasia-like movement has an almost improvisatory quality, as if the instrumentalists were extemporizing on the two ideas (the interval of a fourth and the "Moonlight" Sonata material) that are introduced in the first twenty or so measures. At m. 87, the viola's half-step eighth-note figure recalls the piano's oscillating accompanimental figure that opened the B section of the second movement. This gives way to an extended solo passage for the viola (mm. 93–114), which returns to material from the opening and escalates to the first *ff* of the movement in m. 104. Briefly quieting down at the end of its solo passage, the viola swiftly crescendos in m. 114, after which the piano joins in for an impassioned outburst in mm. 115–32. The anguish begins to subside with the return of the "Moonlight" Sonata material in m. 133, and Shostakovich continues to juxtapose the two principal ideas until the movement's final, serene moments of release, ending on a peaceful C major chord.

Performers and critics immediately embraced Shostakovich's Sonata for Viola and Piano, op. 147; a recording by Druzhinin was released within months of its premiere, and a string of performances and recordings soon followed. As of 2014, the work has been orchestrated at least five times; most well-known is the version for viola, strings, and celesta by Vladimir Mendelssohn.[35] Regardless of whether Shostakovich realized the work would be his last, it can truly "be regarded as a fitting requiem for a man who had lived through and chronicled the scourges of a cruel age."[36]

28

Carl Stamitz: Concerto for Viola and Orchestra in D Major

I. Allegro
II. Andante moderato
III. Rondo

Date of Composition: by 1774

First Edition: Carlo Stamitz, *N.º I Concerto Pour Alto Viola Principale, deux Violons, deux Clarinettes, deux Cors {ad-Libitum deux Alto Viola, contra-Basso Con Violoncello*, Paris: Heina, [c. 1773–1774] (Orchestral Parts)

Select Later Editions: Carlo Stamitz, *Concerto pour Alto Viola Principale, deux Violons, deux Clarinettes, deux Cors, deux Alto Viola et Basse, Oeuvre I*, Frankfurt am Main: W. N. Haueisen [c. 1775–1780] (Orchestral Parts); Karl Stamitz, Concerto for Viola and Orchestra, D Major, op. 1, ed. Clemens Meyer, London: Edition Peters, n.d., Plate No. 10434, No. 3816a (Piano Reduction); Carl Stamitz, *Concerto in D-dur für Viola und Orchester, op. 1*, ed. Ulrich Drüner, Winterthur: Amadeus, 1995, BP 750P (Score); Carl-Philipp Stamitz, *Concerto Pour Alto en Ré Majeur (c.a. 1744)* [*sic*] *(Éditions originales de Haueisen et Heina)*, Courlay, France: Éditions J. M. Fuzeau, 1997, No. 5397 (Orchestral Parts) [facsimiles of Haueisen and Heina editions]; Carl Stamitz, *Violakonzert Nr. 1 D-dur*, ed. Norbert Gertsch and Annemarie Weibezahn, Munich: Henle, 2003, HN 758 (Piano Reduction)

Date/Place of Early Public Performance: [December 17 and 20, 1772, Carl Stamitz (viola), Akademien der Tonkünstler-Societät, Vienna?]

Orchestral Instrumentation: Solo viola, 2 clarinets in A, 2 horns in D, strings (with 2 viola parts)

Introduction

"The most famous violist in Germany, and one of our most endearing composers. He deeply studied the peculiarities of the viola; therefore he plays this instrument with a gracefulness never heard before."[1] If not the first virtuoso viola soloist, Carl Stamitz was certainly the first to earn widespread prominence. Through his masterful playing, he brought unprecedented approval and respect to the viola as a solo instrument. Stamitz was particularly admired for his viola concertos, which were considered "as agreeable to listen to as they are difficult to play."[2] Today, the Concerto for Viola and Orchestra in D Major, with its combination of tender expression and pyrotechnical display, stands as a monument to Stamitz's status as the pre-eminent viola virtuoso of the eighteenth century.

Biographical Sketch

The eldest of five children born to the noted Mannheim court composer and violinist Johann Stamitz and his wife, Maria, Carl Philipp Stamitz (1745–1801) received his early musical training from his father. After Johann's death in 1757, Carl studied with other court musicians, including Christian Cannabich, Ignaz Holzbauer, and Franz Xaver Richter. He joined the ranks of the court orchestra as a violinist in 1762, remaining there for the next eight years. In 1770, he and his younger brother, Anton, left for Paris; by the following year Carl had accepted an appointment as court composer and conductor to Duke Louis de Noailles.[3] It was in Paris that Carl made the viola and viola d'amore his principal instruments at the suggestion of Baron de Bagge, an influential patron and amateur musician.[4] Both Carl and Anton (who also played violin and viola) met with success as performers and composers over the next few years, including appearances at the Concert Spirituel.[5] In the eyes of the public, the two brothers soon came to be linked—not only through their family name, but also through their shared artistry on the viola:

> But would anyone who has heard a Stamitz play the viola with a taste for majesty and tenderness, which appears to be peculiar only to him, not then declare himself for the viola, would he not then accept it among his favorite instruments?[6]

It was Carl, however, who would earn greater fame on the instrument, thanks to his extensive traveling as a virtuoso soloist. After leaving Paris in 1777, he proceeded to London, subsequently moving to the Hague and then to Hamburg. From 1787 to 1789, he appeared as a violist in several European cities, including Dresden, Halle, Prague, and Kassel.[7] By 1790, Stamitz had married Maria Josepha Pilz; the couple would have four children, none of whom would survive past childhood. Family obligations and financial difficulties curtailed his previously carefree, wandering existence, and he sought a more stable position with limited success.[8] By 1795, he was teaching at the university in Jena, though his debts continued to mount. Tragedy struck the Stamitz family in 1801, starting with the death of Carl's wife early in that year, followed by the death of one of their surviving children, and then, finally, by the death of Carl, himself, on November 9.[9]

Stamitz's Concerto for Viola and Orchestra in D Major

Stamitz's known compositions include at least sixty concertos and fifty symphonies, thirty-eight symphonies concertantes, and more than two hundred chamber works. Surviving compositions for the viola include three concertos: No. 1 in D Major (by 1774), No. 2 in B♭ Major (by 1774), and No. 3 in A Major (n.d.), as well as the Sonata in B♭ Major for Harpsichord (or Piano) and Viola (by 1778). Both the sonata and the B♭-major concerto use scordatura for the viola part with the instrument tuned up a half step. Several multi-instrument concertos and symphonies concertantes have solo viola parts, notably the Symphonie concertante in D Major for Violin, Viola, and Orchestra (n.d.). There are also a number of chamber works prominently involving the viola, including six duos for two violas and at least thirty duos for violin and viola.[10]

All three of Stamitz's viola concertos were presumably written for his own use and likely date to the early 1770s, after he had relocated to Paris. The numbering of the concertos does not necessarily reflect the order in which they were written. Stamitz undoubtedly performed the Concerto for Viola and Orchestra in D Major on occasion; he performed one of the concertos in Vienna at the end of 1772, though it is unknown which one.[11] The concerto was published in two editions during Stamitz's lifetime: first by François-Joseph Heina in Paris, around 1773–1774, and then by Wolfgang Nicolaus Haueisen in Frankfurt am Main, sometime later.[12]

Stamitz's compositions display characteristics typically associated with Mannheim, including dramatic dynamic effects and homophonic textures. But numerous formal, thematic, and harmonic elements bear the influence of Paris and London, giving his music "a more cosmopolitan context than that of Mannheim alone."[13] The orchestration of Stamitz's concertos reflects his symphonic background: tutti violas are often divided into two parts, and he does not restrict wind parts to tutti sections.[14] In the Concerto for Viola and Orchestra in D Major, the orchestration is even more advanced: winds also play in the slow movement, and clarinets are substituted for the standard oboes.

Many aspects of Stamitz's music are transitional from the older Baroque style to the newer Classical style. This is particularly true of his formal structures, which seem less coherent when compared to music cast in the Viennese Classical tradition. His sonata forms often have little development, and his recapitulations often start with secondary thematic material.[15] While it is possible to approach the first two movements of the Concerto for Viola and Orchestra in D Major from various formal perspectives, the following descriptions are intended to demonstrate how they correspond to (and deviate from) conventional Classical-era forms.

The first movement is in concerto (sonata) form (Chart 28.1), opening with a lengthy tutti, totaling seventy-one measures. The eight-measure primary

Zone	Thematic Areas/Snippet	Measures	Principal Tonal Areas/Function
Opening Ritornello		1–71	
	Theme Group 1	1–47	
	Unit 1.1	1–16	D major
	Unit 1.2	17–26	D major; ends on dominant
	Unit 1.3	27–47	Tonicizes A major
	Theme Group 2	48–71	D major
Solo Exposition		72–137	
	Theme Group 1	72–120	
	Unit 1.1	72–90	D major
	Unit 1.2	91–107	D major; tonicizes A major; moves to V/V
	Unit 1.3	108–20	Tonicizes A major
	Theme Group 2 (material from Ritornello Theme Group 2)	120–37	A major
Second Ritornello		137–65	
	Unit 1.1	137–48	A major
	Unit 1.2	149–65	A major

Chart 28.1 Stamitz, Concerto for Viola and Orchestra in D Major: Structural analysis, first movement, Allegro.

Zone	Thematic Areas/Snippet	Measures	Principal Tonal Areas/Function
Development		166–200	
	Solo	166–98	A major; begins sequence of fifths at m. 183
	Tutti retransition	198–200	Dominant
Recapitulation		201–50	
	Theme Group 1	201–30	
	Unit 1.1 (new material)	201–16	D major
	Unit 1.2 (new material)	217–30	D major
	Theme Group 2 (material from Ritornello Theme Group 2)	230–50	D major
Closing Ritornello & Cadenza		250–71	D major

Chart 28.1 (continued) Stamitz, Concerto for Viola and Orchestra in D Major: Structural analysis, first movement, Allegro.

theme (Unit 1.1) is stated twice, which is followed by a theme that will appear in each of the orchestral ritornellos only (Unit 1.2; Ex. 28.1). A transitional section tonicizing A major (Unit 1.3) leads to the second theme group at m. 48. The music crescendos in a characteristically Mannheim fashion starting at m. 55, building to a *ff* passage in the violins at m. 63 that closes the section out with dramatic style.

Maintaining a sense of drama, the viola enters with a bold statement of the primary theme in m. 72 (Unit 1.1). From the outset, Stamitz emphasizes virtuosity with chords, double stops, and arpeggiated figures that ascend to a high d^{iii} in m. 88. A contrasting lyrical theme is introduced at m. 91 (Unit 1.2), set against a drone. After a short tutti (mm. 105–7), the violist's technical capabilities are further demonstrated in Unit 1.3 with a passage of string crossings. The second theme group starts at m. 120 in A major, also set against a drone.

At m. 137, the second orchestral ritornello starts with the primary theme, now in A major, followed by Unit 1.2 material (see Ex. 28.1). The viola begins

Example 28.1 Stamitz, Concerto for Viola and Orchestra in D Major, movt. I, mm. 16–18, violin I.

the development at m. 166 with a lyrical passage. Next is a virtuosic passage of bariolage and arpeggios at m. 183 that works its way through a sequence of descending fifths. After a brief orchestral retransition (mm. 198–200), the recapitulation begins at m. 201 with the viola playing new melodic material in thirds (Unit 1.1). Stamitz introduces another new melodic idea with the pickups to m. 217 (Unit 1.2) followed by a return of the second theme group at m. 230, now in D major. A final virtuosic passage (mm. 240–50) leads into the closing ritornello and cadenza.

In the second movement, Stamitz employs the winds (restricting them to the tuttis), with the clarinets adding a sublime touch of melancholy. The movement follows an Aria or Ariette form as described by the German music theorist Heinrich Koch (Chart 28.2).[16] After an opening ritornello in D minor, the viola enters with its first theme (Unit 1.1) at m. 14. Stamitz reduces the accompaniment to divided orchestral violas at m. 23 (Unit 1.2), as the music shifts to F major, with the rest of the strings returning for the solo viola's final thematic area at m. 31 (Unit 1.3).

The viola starts the second main period at m. 54 (Ex. 28.2) with material related to both the opening (Ex. 28.3) and the viola's Unit 1.2 material from mm. 23–26 (Ex. 28.4). Rather than bringing back the solo viola's initial thematic statement after the development at m. 70, Stamitz restates material from m. 31, which originally appeared in F major but now appears in D minor. A short, two-measure orchestral retransition (mm. 77–78) leads us to the cadenza at m. 79 followed by a lengthy orchestral closing.

The third movement is in rondo form with three episodes (Chart 28.3), following a pattern found in Stamitz's other concertos:

These are routine Parisian rondos, almost completely predictable in their design. Refrains consist of eight measures solo, with repetition by orchestra; there are no extensions, no variations on the returns. The first episode moves to the dominant; the second is in the tonic minor, with a brief turn to the flat mediant; and the final episode remains usually in the tonic.[17]

Starting with an upbeat, the eight-measure solo refrain is accompanied only by violins; the rest of the orchestra enters for the refrain's restatement in mm. 9–16.

Zone	Thematic Areas/Snippet	Measures	Principal Tonal Areas/Function
Opening Ritornello		1–13	D minor
First Main Period		14–44	
	Unit 1.1	14–23	D minor
	Unit 1.2	23–30	F major
	Unit 1.3	31–44	F major
Second Ritornello		44–53	F major
Second Main Period		54–77	
	Fragmentation/development	54–69	F major; moves to dominant function
	Unit 1.1 (return of Unit 1.3 material from First Period)	70–77	D minor
Closing Ritornello & Cadenza		77–91	D minor

Chart 28.2 Stamitz, Concerto for Viola and Orchestra in D Major: Structural analysis, second movement, Andante moderato.

Example 28.2 Stamitz, Concerto for Viola and Orchestra in D Major, movt. II, mm. 54–59, solo viola.

Example 28.3 Stamitz, Concerto for Viola and Orchestra in D Major, movt. II, mm. 1–4, violin I (opening).

Andante moderato

Example 28.4 Stamitz, Concerto for Viola and Orchestra in D Major, movt. II, mm. 23–26, solo viola (First Main Period Unit 1.2 material).

The first episode (mm. 17–37) starts in D major but moves to A major at m. 20, when the bass drops out, leaving the solo viola, once again, accompanied only by the violins.

The second episode (mm. 54–93) begins with a lyrical theme in D minor moving to F major at m. 62 for a new thematic area (Unit 1.2). This episode incorporates an interesting technique: left-hand pizzicato, from mm. 78–83, which is notated by an "o" symbol in both the Heina and Haueisen editions. Early twentieth-century editions omitted the symbol, and it took decades for this technique to reappear. Ernst Wallfisch was an early adopter, using the pizzicato when he recorded the work in 1967,[18] and Janusz Zathey and Jerzy Kosmala included it in their edition published by Polskie Wydawnictwo Muzyczne in 1979.[19] Ulrich Drüner expounded on this technique (and the "o" notation) in his 1995 edition for Amadeus, referencing Pierre Baillot's L'art du violon. Baillot illustrates this technique with a passage similar to mm. 78–83, indicating that "in the Solos, Stamitz sometimes used this kind of Pizzicato."[20]

The third episode (mm. 110–65) starts with rapid arpeggios and runs designed to showcase the violist's technical ability. A contrasting middle section (mm. 125–42) tonicizes A major and features a drone in the solo part. Resuming six-teenth-note runs at m. 143, the viola ascends to a high d^{iii} at m. 156 for a final lyrical passage in its upper register before the final statement of the rondo refrain.

Eighteenth-century music critics expressed their admiration for Stamitz's concerto-writing skills: "This excellent symphonist put in all his openings and in his *tutti* a strength and a majesty worthy of Tartini. . . . His solos have fire, originality."[21] Stamitz's Concerto for Viola and Orchestra in D Major exhibits these and many other qualities: attractive melodies, imaginative orchestration,

Zone	Thematic Areas/Snippet	Measures	Principal Tonal Areas/Function
A		1–16	
	Solo	1–8	D major
	Tutti	9–16	D major
B		17–37	D major; A major
A		38–53	D major
C		54–93	
	Unit 1.1	54–61	D minor
	Unit 1.2	62–85	F major; ends on dominant
	Closing	86–93	D minor
A		94–109	D major
D		110–65	
	Unit 1.1	110–24	D major; moves to dominant
	Unit 1.2	125–42	A major
	Unit 1.3	143–65	D major
A		166–81	D major

Chart 28.3 Stamitz, Concerto for Viola and Orchestra in D Major: Structural analysis, third movement, Rondo.

and brilliant solo writing. Most impressive is the sheer virtuosity of the solo part, which was nothing short of revolutionary in its day. The concerto was taken up by violists early in the twentieth century thanks to the publication of a modern edition by Clemens Meyer in 1900.[22] Many other editions have since been produced, several of which substantially alter Stamitz's music (Vadim Borisovsky's "freely transposed" edition is the most outlandish).[23] Clemens Meyer composed cadenzas for his edition, as did Paul Klengel for his edition published in 1932;[24] both sets of cadenzas have proved popular among violists. Franz Beyer's cadenzas, composed later in the twentieth century, have also been exceptionally popular, appearing on numerous recordings.[25]

29

Igor Stravinsky: *Élégie for Viola or Violin Unaccompanied*

Date of Composition: 1944

First Edition: Igor Stravinsky, *Élégie for Viola or Violin unaccompanied*, New York: Chappell & Co. (Associated Music Publishers), 1945, Plate No. A.C. 19454

Dedication: composée à l'intention de Germain Prévost, pour être jouée à la mémoire de Alphonse Onnou, fondateur du Quatuor Pro Arte

Date/Place of First Public Performance: January 26, 1945, Germain Prévost (viola), Coolidge Auditorium, Library of Congress, Washington, DC

Introduction

"I was much drawn to the study of counterpoint, though that is generally considered a dry subject, useful only for pedagogical purposes. From about the age of eighteen I began to study it alone, with no other help than an ordinary manual. The work amused me, even thrilled me, and I was never tired of it. This first contact with the science of counterpoint opened up at once a far vaster and more fertile field in the domain of musical composition than anything that harmony could offer me. And so I set myself with heart and soul to the task of solving the many problems it contains."[1] Writing a work for a solo string instrument offers many problems for a composer to solve, notably how to best evoke harmony using a blend of monophonic and polyphonic textures. In the *Élégie for Viola or Violin Unaccompanied*, Stravinsky's only contribution to the solo-string literature, he avoids this problem altogether by setting himself a different problem: how to write a fully two-voiced work for a single string instrument.

Biographical Sketch

On June 5, 1882, Anna Kirillovna Stravinskaya and Fyodor Ignat'yevich Stravinsky welcomed the birth of their third son, Igor Fyodorovich Stravinsky

(1882–1971), in the small resort town of Oranienbaum (now Lomonosov), Russia.[2] Fyodor was a leading operatic bass singer at the Mariinsky Theatre in the nearby city of St. Petersburg, where Igor was raised. Though surrounded by music during his youth, Igor did not begin studies on the piano until around the age of nine.[3] In 1901, he entered St. Petersburg University as a law student but devoted much time to music, studying harmony and counterpoint privately with Fyodor Akimenko and then with Vasily Kalafati. The following year he secured a meeting with Nikolay Rimsky-Korsakov, who encouraged him in his musical pursuits. He began frequenting public concerts and gatherings of musicians, coming more under Rimsky-Korsakov's direct influence.[4]

The 1905 Russian Revolution closed St. Petersburg University, preventing Stravinsky from taking his law finals; he never graduated but did receive a half-course diploma.[5] In January 1906, Stravinsky married his first cousin Yekaterina (Katya) Nosenko. The couple would have four children together, remaining married until Katya's death in 1939. Stravinsky's public debut as a composer occurred on December 27, 1907, when Yelizaveta Petrenko sang two of his songs at an Evenings of Contemporary Music concert.[6] Interest was soon aroused in the young composer, most fortuitously by the ballet impresario Serge Diaghilev, who was in the audience for the premiere of Stravinsky's *Scherzo fantastique* on January 24, 1909. The two men soon formed a creative partnership that "would change not only the course of Stravinsky's career but the face of twentieth-century art for good."[7] Stravinsky produced three ballets in quick succession for Diaghilev's *Ballets Russes*, which launched him to international fame: *The Firebird* (1909–1910), *Petrushka* (1910–1911), and *Le Sacre du printemps* (*The Rite of Spring*) (1911–1913). The premiere of *Le Sacre du printemps*, in Paris at the Théâtre des Champs-Élysées on May 29, 1913, caused a riot that has entered classical music lore.

During World War I, Stravinsky was exempted from service on medical grounds and went into exile with his family in Switzerland. After six financially lean years in Switzerland, the Stravinskys moved to France in 1920, with Igor setting up base in a studio provided by the Pleyel piano company in their Paris factory. While in France, Igor was involved in several romantic affairs, the most substantial one being with Vera Sudeykina, whom he would eventually marry in 1940. This period marks the beginning of Stravinsky's neo-classical phase, which would last until the early 1950s. Over the following years, a number of high-profile works solidified his status as one of the leading composers of the early twentieth century, including the Octet, for winds (1922–1923); *Oedipus rex* (1926–1927); and *Symphonie de psaumes* (1930).

Stravinsky suffered devastating personal losses in the late 1930s with the deaths of his daughter Lyudmila, his wife, and his mother all within the span of a year. The outbreak of World War II brought more strife, and Stravinsky fled to America in September 1939.[8] He settled in Hollywood, California, with his new wife, Vera, in the spring of 1941, becoming an American citizen four years later. In 1944, Stravinsky began corresponding with a young admirer, Robert Craft, who would play an influential role in Stravinsky's life after the two met in person in 1948. Craft moved into Stravinsky's house the following year, serving as assistant, confidant, promoter, and "quasi-adoptive son" until the composer's death.[9] It was Craft who helped Stravinsky through a compositional crisis in the early 1950s, leading him to experiment with serialism.[10] After Stravinsky suffered a stroke in 1956, his time was increasingly occupied by medical concerns, limiting his compositional output. In 1969, Stravinsky moved to New York City, where he lived out his final years, dying early on the morning of April 6, 1971, at the age of eighty-eight.

Stravinsky's *Élégie for Viola or Violin Unaccompanied*

Stravinsky's sole work for viola, *Élégie for Viola or Violin Unaccompanied*, was written in memory of the violinist Alphonse Onnou, who had founded the renowned Pro Arte Quartet in 1912 and played with that ensemble until his death in 1940. While Stravinsky had a minor connection to Onnou, the work was written as an apology of sorts to the quartet's founding violist, Germain Prévost. The story begins on January 23, 1944, when Stravinsky visited Edgewood College, a private Dominican institution in Madison, Wisconsin.[11] One of Nadia Boulanger's former students, Sister Edward Blackwell, was teaching at the college. Boulanger, a close friend of Stravinsky's, had taught at Edgewood the previous summer and helped arrange his visit. At the college, Stravinsky performed his *Duo concertante*, for violin and piano, with Antonio Brosa, the Pro Arte Quartet's new first violinist. Brosa took the opportunity to bad-mouth Prévost to Stravinsky, who repeated these comments to Boulanger.

 Later that summer, Boulanger returned to teach at Edgewood and called on Prévost to take her to Onnou's grave. During the visit, Prévost suggested that they read through some music together; Boulanger initially put him off but agreed to meet with him the following day. While playing through Brahms's F-minor sonata, she exclaimed: "You play well . . . Stravinsky told me that you couldn't play anymore."[12] The full story came out, and Boulanger decided to include Prévost in a couple of concerts at Edgewood. On the August 2 concert, they premiered Darius Milhaud's second viola sonata, which the violist had recently commissioned in memory of Onnou.[13] The next part of the story is detailed in a letter that Boulanger wrote to Stravinsky on August 21, 1944:

Germain Prévost (violist Pro Arte), a *good* musician, a good man, charged me with a request for you that he does not dare ask himself.

He took part in my lectures in Madison. Sister E. gave him a small cheque of $100 as a stipend. He at first refused, then said: "I'll accept it, since I just had a vision for this money."

"Would you, he said to me, explain this story to Mr. Strawinsky, and tell him that I permit myself one truly audacious but very humble [request]. I know it's ridiculous to dare offer him $100. I know, but I know he will understand that this is all I can part with at the moment (his wife and his daughters are in Belgium, he has a *very difficult life*, mentally, practically, because, the quartet is here . . .). Would you, if you judge that you can pass along such a request, see if he might write me a small piece dedicated to the memory of Alphonse Onnou, or to you? I am not worth the trouble. I would be so happy, so proud."

He reminded me of the day when you gave them [the Pro Arte Quartet] the manuscript for the *Concertino*. So here you are, I have passed along his request. If you had seen his devotion to your entire body of work and his enthusiasm for the *Sonata [for Two Pianos]*, you would understand why I feel obliged to share this with you.[14]

Boulanger's meaning was undoubtedly clear to Stravinsky, and over the following weeks he composed the *Élégie*, refusing the payment that had been offered.[15] Prévost premiered the work at the Library of Congress on January 26, 1945, playing "it with warm tone and clear musical diction."[16]

Stravinsky's *Élégie* has been described as "above all else an essay in two-part counterpoint."[17] The work exhibits characteristic traits from his neo-classical phase: "precision, simplicity, clarity, order, [and] gracefulness."[18] It shares similarities with other works written during the same period, notably the Sonata for Two Pianos, whose contrapuntal complexities include a Theme and Variations that "seem to hint at the keyboard writing of Bach."[19] Writers have often described the *Élégie* as a "two-part invention," suggesting a connection to Bach's keyboard writing in this work, as well.[20] The surviving manuscripts housed in the Library of Congress include a version written on two separate staves, which presumably allowed Stravinsky to work out the two-voice writing. On the first page of the published score, Stravinsky noted that "the fingerings have been chosen with a view to underlining the counterpoint, and not for technical facility."[21] There are no time signatures in the music, and the viola plays muted throughout.

Élégie is in an ABA form, opening with a fifteen-measure section centered on C minor. In this quiet section, Stravinsky deftly uses a mixture of consonance and dissonance (including the recurring juxtaposition of c and d$\flat^i$) to create an aura of mourning. The B section (mm. 16–44) is a fugue in two

Zone	Measure Numbers
First Statement of Subject	16–20
Second Statement of Subject	21–26
First Episode	27–29
Third Statement of Subject	30–35
Second Episode	36–39
Fourth (Final) Statement of Subject	40–43
Transition	44

Chart 29.1 Structure of the fugal B section of Stravinsky's *Élégie for Viola or Violin Unaccompanied.*

voices (Chart 29.1); the subject starts in the lower voice with the upper voice entering in m. 21. Stravinsky takes advantage of the lack of time signatures to alter the rhythm in the subject over the course of the fugue (so the first statement of the subject spans twelve quarter notes over five measures, while the second statement spans fifteen quarter notes over six measures). For the final statement (mm. 40–43), the upper voice plays the subject, and the lower voice enters with an inverted version of the subject in m. 41. The subject breaks off in m. 43 with Stravinsky using a series of narrowing intervals in the following measure (starting with a minor sixth and ending with an augmented second) to transition back to the opening A section. Stravinsky ends the work (mm. 56–59) in a more harmonically ambiguous manner than the close of the opening section (mm. 12–15), denying a sense of closure for the grief-stricken listener.

Stravinsky's *Élégie for Viola or Violin Unaccompanied* was quickly embraced by violists after its premiere. The violin version also garnered interest from violinists and has remained popular, making it a rare example of an original viola composition that has been frequently programmed and recorded as a transcription for violin. *Élégie* also gained the attention of George Balanchine, who choreographed the work as a *pas de deux* in 1945. Initially performed on November 5 of that year at Carnegie Hall by students of the School of American Ballet, the ballet received its official premiere on April 28, 1948, at the Ballet Society in New York with Emanuel Vardi playing the solo. In discussing his choreography for *Élégie*, Balanchine wrote:

> With the limited sound values of one viola (it's a great mistake to perform it with more instruments) all the possibilities of a two-voiced fugue are exploited.

In the dance I composed to this score (1945) I tried to reflect the flow and concentrated variety of the music through the interlaced bodies of two dancers rooted to a central spot of the stage.[22]

Balanchine choreographed *Élégie* again on two later occasions: in 1966 and 1982, both times as a work for a solo dancer.[23]

30

Tōru Takemitsu: *A Bird came down the Walk*, for viola and piano

Date of Composition: 1994

First Edition: Toru Takemitsu, *A Bird came down the Walk: for viola accompanied by piano*, Tokyo: Schott Music Co., 1995, SJ 1092

Dedication: Dedicated to Nobuko Imai

Date/Place of First Public Performance: October 29, 1995, Nobuko Imai (viola), Roger Vignoles (piano), Konzerthaus, Vienna

Introduction

"I love gardens. They do not reject people. There one can walk freely, pause to view the entire garden, or gaze at a single tree. Plants, rocks, and sand show changes, constant changes."[1] The Japanese composer Tōru Takemitsu often transmitted his love of nature and gardens into his music (Fig 30.1). Expressing the influence that gardens had on his compositions, he remarked: "What I do is to translate an extremely specific plan of a garden into music. The point is that there are many different 'times' in a garden . . . the movement of vegetation, the 'time' of vegetation growing, the fast changes of elements like grass . . . there are rocks . . . and sand."[2] *A Bird came down the Walk*, one of Takemitsu's final compositions, displays this fascination with gardens and natural elements, including the ever-changing aspects of time, space, and colors.

Biographical Sketch

Tōru Takemitsu (1930–1996) was born in Tokyo, Japan, but spent his early years in China, where his father, Takeo Takemitsu, worked as an official of the Japanese government. At the age of seven, he returned to Tokyo to attend school, living with an aunt and uncle. His aunt played and taught the *koto*, and Takemitsu was surrounded by traditional Japanese music, though it did not appeal to him at the time.[3] In 1944, Takemitsu was conscripted by the Japanese military. While living

Figure 30.1 One of the many gardens illustrated in Shunkō Nakajima's 1896 guide to Japanese garden design, *Kokon hiden tsukiyama teizōhō*.

in the barracks, an officer played a recording of the French chanson *Parlez-moi d'amour*, which left a deep impression on Takemitsu. After the war, he eagerly listened to Western music on the newly established American radio station and discovered works by leading American composers at a local library.[4] Captivated by this music, Takemitsu was inspired to compose; he soon joined an amateur choir and began working at a US Army PX (post exchange), where he was permitted to use their piano after hours.[5]

In 1948, Takemitsu was accepted as a student by the composer Yasuji Kiyose; two years later he was granted admission to the group Shin-Sakkyokuha Kyōkai (New Composers' Association), receiving his first public performance as a composer at one of the group's concerts on December 7, 1950. The following year, he co-founded the interdisciplinary artists' group Jikken Kōbō (Experimental Workshop), which was devoted to avant-garde experiments across multiple media, including music, painting, poetry, and photography. For the remainder of his career, Takemitsu would enjoy close friendships and productive working relationships with artists in various media.[6] In 1954, he married Asaka Wakayama, an actress; they would have one daughter together. Over the next few years, Takemitsu experimented with music in a variety of genres, including *musique concrète*, instrumental compositions, and works for radio and film.

Takemitsu's international profile was greatly raised in 1959 when Igor Stravinsky, while touring Japan, publicly expressed admiration for the young composer's *Requiem*, for strings (1957). During the 1960s, Takemitsu continued with avant-garde experiments while further refining his use of timbres and sonorities in his compositions.[7] He also became interested in Japanese instruments, earning acclaim for his integration of the *biwa* and *shakuhachi* into the symphony orchestra in *November Steps* (1967), written for the 125th anniversary of the New York Philharmonic Orchestra. In the 1980s, Takemitsu's style began to change, becoming more tonal and less experimental.[8] The stylistic change did not diminish his reputation, and he solidified his status as Japan's leading composer over the following years, earning many international honors and awards. On February 20, 1996, after battling cancer for several months, Takemitsu died at the age of sixty-five.

Takemitsu's *A Bird came down the Walk*, for viola and piano

Early in his career, Takemitsu was influenced by the music of Claude Debussy and Olivier Messiaen; later, John Cage would prove a significant influence. He was also inspired by visual artists, including Joan Miró and Jasper Johns. An avid lover of films, Takemitsu composed more than one hundred film scores that helped popularize his music among Western audiences. Takemitsu became fascinated with the viola after hearing Nobuko Imai perform at the 1984 Aldeburgh Festival.[9] He composed two works for her: *A String around Autumn*, for viola and orchestra (1989) and *A Bird came down the Walk*, for viola and piano (1994), both dating from his late, post-experimental period. Imai recalled her first encounter with *A Bird came down the Walk* in a letter written to the composer after his death:

> Seven years ago, you gave me a treasured gift: the piece called *A String Around Autumn*, which I first played in 1989. And then, two-and-a-half years ago, you presented me with another such gift. It was at the reception following my recital at the 1994 Yatsugatake Music Festival. I remember your coming up to me, clutching a large score. "Can you tell what this is?" you asked me, "... but I can't give it to you yet." It was your manuscript for a new piece for viola and piano called *A Bird came down the Walk*. Still holding onto it, you let me take a peek and, pointing to one passage, you said: "This part is really beautiful..."[10]

Takemitsu provided further insight into the work's origin:

> *A Bird came down the Walk* was composed as an expression of friendship and respect for the eminent viola player Nobuko Imai and it is my personal gift to her. The viola, expressing the bird of the title, repeatedly plays the theme, based on the bird theme of my orchestral work *A Flock Descends into the Pentagonal Garden*. As subtle changes occur in tone colour, the bird theme goes walking through the motionless, scroll painting like a landscape, a garden hushed and bright with daylight.[11]

As these comments suggest, the work demonstrates Takemitsu's love of nature, words, art, and instrumental colors. The title, *A Bird came down the Walk*, comes from a poem by Emily Dickinson, first published in 1891. While a connection can be drawn between the general atmosphere of both works, there is no indication that Takemitsu was attempting to convey the specific actions of the poem in his composition:

> A Bird came down the walk:
> He did not know I saw;
> He bit an angle-worm in halves
> And ate the fellow, raw.
>
> And then he drank a dew
> From a convenient grass,
> And then hopped sidewise to the wall
> To let a beetle pass.

He glanced with rapid eyes
That hurried all abroad,—
They looked like frightened beads, I thought;
He stirred his velvet head

Like one in danger; cautious,
I offered him a crumb,
And he unrolled his feathers
And rowed him softer home

Than oars divide the ocean,
Too silver for a seam,
Or butterflies, off banks of noon,
Leap, plashless, as they swim.[12]

Takemitsu borrowed the principal theme in *A Bird came down the Walk* from an earlier orchestral work, *A Flock Descends into the Pentagonal Garden* (1977). In the Japanese titles for these two compositions, he used the same word, *tori*, for both "flock" and "bird."[13] With these musical and verbal connections, an impression is created within *A Bird came down the Walk* that we are encountering a single bird from the flock while walking through the pentagonal garden. There are many features in the work that evoke the bird theme of the title: "A notable melodic feature is the use of tremolo to suggest bird song; at one point Takemitsu employs the descriptive marking 'as a bird's calling' in the piano part [m. 26]."[14] Certain harmonics are suggestive of short bird chirps (e.g., m. 5, m. 32, and m. 45), while rapid string crossings suggest the fluttering of wings (e.g., m. 22, m. 24, and m. 46).[15]

A characteristic aspect of Takemitsu's music is the manipulation of instrumental colors and sonorities to great effect. In *A Bird came down the Walk*, numerous techniques are used, including harmonics, *sul ponticello, sul tasto*, glissandos, and left-hand pizzicato. Detailed instructions regarding the amount of vibrato to use and which string to play on are also provided. Since Takemitsu's music relies on subtle changes in color, it is critical to observe these markings while not losing sight of the bigger picture.[16] The careful selection and arrangement of sounds and textures in *A Bird came down the Walk* is in keeping with Takemitsu's ideas about translating a specific plan of a garden into his music:

There are similarities in the approach to the construction of both a Japanese Garden and Takemitsu's compositions to achieve a "natural" result. Contrary to the aesthetic objective of recreating undisciplined nature, a highly disciplined and concentrated artistic thought goes into the placement of every element in order for the garden to mirror nature as effortlessly as possible. Similarly, Takemitsu's scores are so detailed that almost every note has a specific instruction, but the intent is that upon hearing his music it seems almost improvisatory.[17]

Another significant element in Takemitsu's music is silence:

> In the flow of Japanese music, for example, short fragmented connections of sounds are complete in themselves. Those different sound events are related by silences that aim at creating a harmony of events. Those pauses are left to the performer's discretion. In this way there is a dynamic change in the sounds as they are constantly reborn in new relationships.[18]

Nobuko Imai emphasized the importance of silence and connections between notes in *A Bird came down the Walk*:

> The most important pieces of advice [Takemitsu] gave were about timing. He said to always think about the next note while playing the previous one—if there's a pause, you can wait a long time while you think about the next note—and to remember the importance of silence: Takemitsu's music needs space around it.[19]

Space, nature, and colors are integral components of Takemitsu's delightful morsel *A Bird came down the Walk,* for viola and piano—components that contribute to an understanding of the work's overall form. Time also plays an important role in Takemitsu's concept of form:

> Westerners, especially today, consider time as linear and continuity as a steady and unchanging state. But I think of time as circular and continuity as a constantly changing state. These are important assumptions in my concept of musical form. Sometimes my music follows the design of a particular existing garden. At times it may follow the design of an imaginary garden I have sketched. Time in my music may be said to be the duration of my walk through these gardens.[20]

At roughly five to six minutes in length, *A Bird came down the Walk* is just a brief excursion into the garden, but there is still time to marvel at the wondrous sights and sounds that await.

Delve Deeper into *A Bird came down the Walk*

Readers interested in exploring further analyses of *A Bird came down the Walk* are referred to the following sources:

Green, Phoebe. "The Influence of Nature on Two Works for the Viola by Toru Takemitsu and Ross Edwards." Master's thesis, University of Queensland, 2010.
Michael, Julie. "Zen in the Art of Viola Playing: Takemitsu's *A Bird came down the Walk.*" *Journal of the American Viola Society* 30, no. 1 (Spring 2014): 29–38.

31

Georg Philipp Telemann: Concerto in G Major for Viola, Strings, and Basso continuo, TWV 51:G9

I.   Largo
II. Allegro
III. Andante
IV. Presto

Date of Composition: c. 1716–1721

First Edition: G. Ph. Telemann, *Konzert G-Dur für Bratsche und Streichorchester (mit Generalbass)*, ed. Hellmuth Christian Wolff, Kassel: Bärenreiter, [c. 1941], BA 1743 (Score and Parts); Telemann, *Concerto in G major for Viola and Piano*, ed. Milton Katims, New York: International Music, 1948, No. 401 (Piano Reduction)

Select Later Editions: Telemann, *Konzert in G-Dur für Viola, Streicher und Basso continuo, TWV 51:G9*, ed. Wolfgang Hirschmann, Kassel: Bärenreiter, 2002, BA 5878 (Score); BA 5878a (Piano Reduction); Georg Philipp Telemann, *Violakonzert G-dur*, ed. Phillip Schmidt, Munich: Henle, 2014, HN 1217 (Piano Reduction)

Orchestral Instrumentation: Solo viola, 2 violins, viola, and basso continuo

Introduction

"Telemann was not only an innovative composer of 'fluent' and 'tasteful' music, but also an original—and at times even revolutionary—creator of concertos, sonatas, and suites, more than a few of which rank among the eighteenth century's finest."[1] During his lifetime, Telemann was held in great esteem, producing a vast amount of tasteful music for an eager public. But his reputation declined significantly over the course of the nineteenth and early twentieth centuries, with critics viewing him as "a fluent, popular, highly prolific, but not very original composer."[2] Scholars began to seriously re-examine Telemann's music toward the middle of the twentieth century, developing a better appreciation for his style and making his compositions more widely available. One of the great rediscoveries during this period was his Concerto in G Major for Viola, Strings, and Basso continuo, TWV 51:G9, the earliest surviving concerto for the instrument. Violists quickly embraced the concerto, giving it a place of honor in the repertoire. Tasteful, original, and revolutionary, Telemann's viola concerto has deservedly become "one of his most famous works."[3]

Biographical Sketch

Georg Philipp Telemann (1681–1767) was born in Magdeburg to Heinrich Telemann, a deacon at the Heilig-Geist-Kirche, and his wife, Maria. Heinrich's death in 1685 left Maria with the responsibility of raising their children. Their younger son, Georg Philipp, displayed a disposition for music, teaching himself to play the violin, recorder, and zither. His formal music education, which began at the age of ten, was limited to singing lessons from a cantor, Benedikt Christiani, and a few keyboard lessons from a local organist. Teaching himself composition by transcribing scores, Telemann was soon writing vocal and instrumental works, completing an opera at the age of twelve.[4] Telemann's mother attempted to curtail her son's musical activities, sending him to Zellerfeld in late 1693 or early 1694 to study with the theologian Caspar Calvör. But Calvör was supportive of his pupil's musical talents, and Telemann continued composing works, which were performed by the town's musicians. In 1697, he advanced to the Gymnasium Andreanum in Hildesheim, excelling at his general studies while finding time to learn the rudiments of several more instruments.[5]

After four years in Hildesheim, Telemann's mother insisted that he "take up the study of law for his livelihood and 'leave music.' "[6] Accordingly, he entered Leipzig University in 1701, planning to devote himself to the study of law. But his musical talents were soon uncovered by a roommate, who organized a performance of one of Telemann's vocal works at the Thomaskirche (St. Thomas's Church). The mayor of Leipzig, who was in attendance and obviously liked what he heard, commissioned Telemann to regularly compose music for the city's two main churches. Telemann soon became entrenched in Leipzig's musical life, founding a student *collegium musicum* and taking over as director of the Opernhaus auf dem Brühl.[7]

Telemann left Leipzig in 1705 to serve as Kapellmeister to Count Erdmann II of Promnitz in Sorau (now Żary, Poland). From there he went to Eisenach, where he served as Konzertmeister and then Secretary and Kapellmeister at the court of Duke Johann Wilhelm of Saxe-Eisenach.[8] In 1709, he married Amalie Louise Juliane Eberlin, who died fifteen months later, shortly after giving birth to their daughter. Telemann next went to Frankfurt in 1712, where he served as the city's director of municipal music. His responsibilities included directing music activities at the Barfüsserkirche (Church of the Barefoot Friars) and the Katharinenkirche (St. Catherine's Church), supervising music education at the city's school, and composing music for civic functions. He also became involved with the Frauenstein society, a group of patricians who played music for enjoyment, serving as director of their *collegium musicum*. The weekly concerts that he organized for this group marked "the beginning of Frankfurt's regular concert life."[9] In 1714, he married his second wife, Maria Catharina Textor, with whom he would have nine children.

Telemann was lured to Hamburg in 1721, accepting a prestigious position as Kantor of the Johanneum Lateinschule and music director for the city's five principal churches. As part of his duties, Telemann was required to compose a substantial amount of sacred music. Yet he still found time to direct other local musical organizations, including the city's *collegium musicum* and opera theater. In Hamburg, Telemann's marriage began to deteriorate: his wife had an affair with a Swedish military officer, and by 1736 she had left him.[10] Despite his domestic misfortunes, "Telemann passed the last decades of his long life at Hamburg, loaded with honours and living in relatively secure economic circumstances."[11] He died of a "chest ailment" on June 25, 1767, at the age of eighty-six.[12]

Telemann's Concerto in G Major for Viola, Strings, and Basso continuo, TWV 51:G9

During his lengthy career, Telemann composed more than 3,000 works, including around 125 concertos. Surviving works for viola include the Concerto in G Major for Viola, Strings, and Basso continuo, TWV 51:G9 (c. 1716–21) and the Sonata (in Canon) in B♭ Major for Viola or Gamba and Basso continuo, TWV 41:B3 (published 1728–1729). Additionally, sources record a Concerto in A Major for Two Violas, Strings, and Basso continuo, TWV 52:A3 (n.d.), which is presumed to be lost.[13] There are also several works by Telemann that include a violetta part; the term "violetta" has a complicated history but commonly meant viola in the seventeenth and eighteenth centuries.[14] Surviving works for the violetta include the Concerto in A Major for Violetta, Strings, and Basso continuo, TWV 51:A5 (c. 1725–1735) and the Concerto in G Major for 2 Violettas, Strings, and Basso continuo, TWV 52:G3 (n.d.).[15] Telemann's viola works achieved some renown during his lifetime; in 1738, Johann Philipp Eisel wrote:

> One employs [the viola] in harmonious concertos not only as a mere middle voice, in order to fill in the alto or tenor [parts], but also as a concertante voice, of which the concertos and *Concert-Ouverturen* of the famous Kapellmeister Telemann give ample evidence.[16]

The Concerto in G Major for Viola, Strings, and Basso continuo, TWV 51:G9 survives in a single manuscript source: a score in the hand of Christoph Graupner, likely dating between 1724 and 1727.[17] Stylistic evidence suggests that the concerto was written during Telemann's time in Frankfurt, probably between 1716 and 1721.[18] It may have been intended for performance at the "Weekly Grand Concert of the Frauenstein," which played to an invited audience of music lovers.[19] The work was first published during the middle of the twentieth century.[20]

Telemann's concertos demonstrate variety in their styles and formal layouts, though he favored the four-movement *sonata da chiesa* pattern (slow–fast–slow–fast) based on Italian models. He also favored ritornello forms, which constitute the largest category of his concerto movements:

> The broadest definition of a ritornello is a passage which recurs at various points during a movement or complex of movements. In a concerto, the ritornello is that recurring tutti passage with which the movement begins and which lasts until the beginning of the first solo episode. . . . While there is no problem in identifying the first and last statements of the ritornello, the number and exact position of the middle statements is not always so sharply defined.[21]

The difficulty in determining the exact placement of ritornello statements is owing to its flexible structure:

> Unlike the refrain of a rondo, a ritornello is a highly flexible structure amenable to modification on any restatement. It can be shortened by losing its beginning, middle or end; its units can be shuffled around or presented in new forms; it can be supplemented by newly introduced material.[22]

In analyzing ritornello structures, some scholars have emphasized the importance of tonal centers:

> Above all the ritornello movement unfolds as a succession of discrete events that delineate a process of departure from the tonic and arrival at several intermediate tonal centres, before the inescapable re-establishment of the home key.[23]

Telemann employed ritornello form in each movement of the viola concerto. While the ritornello structures in the slow movements are fairly straightforward, the exact positions of the ritornellos in the fast movements are, as Pippa Drummond suggested, "not always so sharply defined." The following analyses are influenced by the tonal plan for each movement as well as the manner in which the soloist and orchestra interact.

With its slow triple meter and dotted rhythms, the first movement (Chart 31.1) resembles a sarabande. At its entrance in m. 9, the viola takes up material from the opening ritornello (mm. 1–9), making its way to D major at m. 19 for the second ritornello (mm. 19–22). The second solo episode demonstrates Telemann's inventive harmonic treatment of the material: In mm. 25–26, the viola plays the same material as mm. 16–17, now raised by a second, creating an expectation that this episode

Example 31.1 Telemann, Concerto in G Major for Viola, Strings, and Basso continuo, TWV 51:G9, movt. I, mm. 16–19, solo viola.

Example 31.2 Telemann, Concerto in G Major for Viola, Strings, and Basso continuo, TWV 51:G9, movt. I, mm. 25–30, solo viola.

Zone	Thematic Areas/Snippet	Measures	Principal Tonal Areas/Function
Ritornello 1	Vln. 1	1–9	G major
Solo Episode 1		9–19	G major to D major
Ritornello 2	Vln. 1	19–22	D major
Solo Episode 2		22–30	D major to A major
Ritornello 3	Vln. 1	30–34	A major to D major
Solo Episode 3		34–48	Starts on V^7; moves immediately to G major
Ritornello 4	Vln. 1	48–57	G major

Chart 31.1 Telemann, Concerto in G Major for Viola, Strings, and Basso continuo, TWV 51:G9: Structural analysis, first movement, Largo.

will conclude in the relative minor (Exs. 31.1 and 31.2). But rather than cadencing, Telemann extends the phrase, dramatically inserting an f♯ in m. 27. This then leads to an E⁷ harmony in the following measure, setting up a move to A major in m. 30 for the start of the third ritornello. Telemann exploits the viola's lowest register in the third solo episode, ending on the open C string in m. 45, providing an opportunity for embellishment before the viola's final solo statement in mm. 46–48.

In the second movement, the soloist and orchestra engage in many playful interactions that blur the lines between ritornello statements and solo episodes (Chart 31.2). This movement "represents the simplest type of ritornello form used by Telemann. The opening ritornello is short, consisting of a head-motif and sequential section alone"[24] (Ex. 31.3). After the opening ritornello, the viola begins its first episode in m. 7, getting no farther than two measures before the orchestra interrupts, repeating the ritornello's sequential section (mm. 9–13). The viola starts again in m. 13, making its way through a complete statement and cadencing on C major in m. 19. Here, the orchestra begins an orchestral ritornello, which the viola—demonstrating that two can play the game—interrupts in m. 20. Feeling that equity has been restored after its cadence on D major in m. 25, the viola allows the orchestra to play a full statement of the opening ritornello (mm. 25–31). The viola and orchestra continue their playful interactions during the following solo episode: at m. 40, a sequence begins with the soloist playing the first four notes of the ritornello, which is then taken over by the orchestra. After three measures of this dialogue, the viola returns with a statement of the ritornello's head motif and sequential section at m. 43. The remainder of this episode is devoted to fancy passagework for the soloist, punctuated by outbursts from the orchestra (mm. 52–57). At m. 70, the orchestra plays a final complete statement of the ritornello to close out the movement.

Example 31.3 Telemann, Concerto in G Major for Viola, Strings, and Basso continuo, TWV 51:G9, movt. II, mm. 1–7, violin I, full ritornello statement.

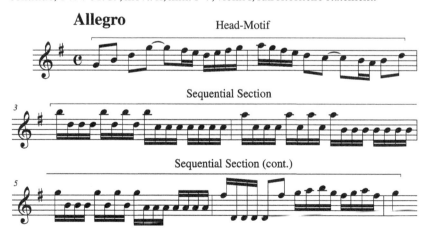

Zone	Thematic Areas/Snippet	Measures	Principal Tonal Areas/Function
Ritornello 1	Full ritornello Vln. 1	1–7	G major
Solo Episode 1		7–19	
	Unit 1.1: Solo episode 1a	7–8	G major
	Unit 1.2: Tutti ritornello interruption (sequential passage)	9–13	G major
	Unit 1.3: Solo episode 1b	13–19	G major to C major
Ritornello 2	Head-motif only	19–20	C major
Solo Episode 2		20–25	C major to D major
Ritornello 3	Full ritornello	25–31	D major
Solo Episode 3		31–70	
	Unit 1.1	31–43	D major to G major
	Unit 1.2	43–52	G major
	Unit 1.3	52–60	G major
	Unit 1.4	60–70	G major
Ritornello 4	Full ritornello	70–76	G major

Chart 31.2 Telemann, Concerto in G Major for Viola, Strings, and Basso continuo, TWV 51:G9: Structural analysis, second movement, Allegro.

For the third movement (Chart 31.3), Telemann varies his approach: rather than assigning the viola material derived from the ritornello at its entrance in m. 4, he provides it with thematically independent material. He also demonstrates his harmonic inventiveness in this movement: In m. 9, the viola introduces a b♭^{i}, setting the stage for a cadence on G minor. The anticipated cadence follows in m. 10, but it is not a definitive one. Instead, the b♭^{i} is repeated, which now functions as a respelled a♯^{i}, moving the tonality to B minor for the definitive cadence in m. 11

(Ex. 31.4).[25] The viola and orchestra engage in a bit of dialogue in the next solo episode, with the viola returning to its opening melody in m. 20. Telemann exploits the viola's lowest register before pausing on a dissonant f♯¹ in m. 25, where he uses the same harmonic trick from m. 10: the f♯¹ subsequently serves as a respelled e♯¹ for a resolution to C♯ major in m. 26, from which Telemann deftly makes his way back to E minor in the following measure for the final ritornello.

The fourth movement merges ritornello and binary forms (Chart 31.4). Here, Telemann writes the lengthiest ritornello statement: twelve measures, which can be divided into three units (Ex. 31.5). In this movement, the soloist and orchestra once again interact in interesting ways; after completing its solo episode in m. 31, the violist plays double-stopped unisons (resembling a horn call) over Unit A of the orchestral ritornello. After a scalar passage (mm. 34–38), the viola closes the first half out with Unit B and Unit C (slightly altered) from the ritornello, concluding on D major. The second section opens with a varied statement of Unit A by the orchestra in D major, which the viola then restates in E minor (mm.

Example 31.4 Telemann, Concerto in G Major for Viola, Strings, and Basso continuo, TWV 51:G9, movt. III, mm. 9–12, orchestral reduction showing the function of the B♭ in m. 10 as a respelled A♯.

Zone	Thematic Areas/Snippet	Measures	Principal Tonal Areas/Function
Ritornello 1	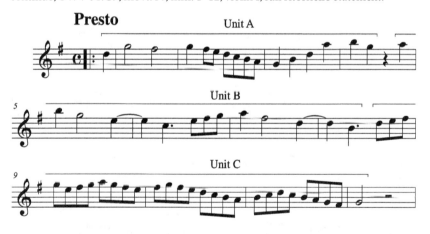 Vln. 1	1–4	E minor
Solo Episode 1		4–11	E minor to B minor
Ritornello 2	Vln. 1	11–15	B minor
Solo Episode 2		15–27	
	Unit 1.1	15–20	B minor to dominant
	Unit 1.2	20–27	E minor
Ritornello 3	Vln. 1	27–30	E minor

Chart 31.3 Telemann, Concerto in G Major for Viola, Strings, and Basso continuo, TWV 51:G9: Structural analysis, third movement, Andante.

Example 31.5 Telemann, Concerto in G Major for Viola, Strings, and Basso continuo, TWV 51:G9, movt. IV, mm. 1–12, violin I, full ritornello statement.

Presto   Unit A

Unit B

Unit C

51–54). After traversing through multiple harmonic areas, the music makes its way back to G major at m. 85 for another ritornello statement that parallels mm. 31–34, complete with the viola's "horn calls." Once again, the viola plays a scalar passage followed by Unit B and Unit C from the ritornello, suggesting that

Zone		Thematic Areas/Snippet	Measures	Principal Tonal Areas/Function
First Section (Repeated)	Ritornello 1	Complete (Units A, B, & C)	1–12	G major
	Solo Episode 1		13–31	G major to D major
	Ritornello 2	Unit A	31–34	D major
	Solo Episode 2		34–46	D major
Second Section (Repeated)	Ritornello 3	Unit A	47–50	D major
	Solo Episode 3		51–67	E minor to A minor
	Ritornello 4	Unit A	67–70	A minor
	Solo Episode 4		71–85	D major to G major
	Ritornello 5	Unit A	85–88	G major
	Solo Episode 5		88–99	G major
	Ritornello 6	Units B & C	99–106	G major

Chart 31.4 Telemann, Concerto in G Major for Viola, Strings, and Basso continuo, TWV 51:G9: Structural analysis, fourth movement, Presto.

the second half will conclude in the same manner as the first. But the orchestra interrupts the viola's statement in m. 98 with the pickup to the final ritornello, playing Unit B and Unit C while the soloist fills out the harmony.

Violists hold dear Telemann's Concerto in G Major for Viola, Strings, and Basso continuo, TWV 51:G9. It is the first concerto that many violists learn and one that can be returned to time and again for performance or pleasure. The work demonstrates Telemann's harmonic ingenuity and skill at instrumental writing: "No contemporary of Bach except Handel and Rameau had Telemann's sense of the character of instruments, singly and in groups."[26] Effectively show-casing different aspects of the viola within its four short movements, Telemann's engaging viola concerto is one of the true gems of the repertoire.

Learn More about Ritornello Form and Telemann's Concerto in G Major for Viola, Strings, and Basso continuo, TWV 51:G9

Readers interested in learning more about ritornello form and its application to Telemann's viola concerto are referred to the following sources:

DeBolt, Katharine Gerson. "Information and Imagination as Sources of Interpretation: The Performer's Procedures Applied to Telemann's Viola Concerto in G Major." MA Thesis, Ohio State University, 1965.

Trygstad, Alexander. "Ritornello Form and the Dynamics of Performance in Telemann's Viola Concerto in G Major." *Journal of the American Viola Society* 31, no. 2 (Fall 2015): 11–25.

32

Ralph Vaughan Williams: Suite for Viola and Small Orchestra

Group I.   1. Prelude
            2. Carol
            3. Christmas Dance
Group II.   1. Ballad
            2. Moto Perpetuo
Group III. 1. Musette
            2. Polka Melancolique
            3. Galop

Date of Composition: Completed 1934

First Edition: R. Vaughan Williams, *Suite for Viola and Orchestra (Pianoforte)*, 3 vols., London: Oxford University Press, 1936 (Piano Reduction); R. Vaughan Williams, *Suite for Viola and Small Orchestra*, London: Oxford University Press, 1966 (Score)

Dedication: To Lionel Tertis

Date/Place of First Public Performance: November 12, 1934, Lionel Tertis (viola), London Philharmonic Orchestra, Malcolm Sargent (conductor), Courtauld-Sargent Concerts, Queen's Hall, London

Orchestral Instrumentation: Solo viola, 2 flutes (2nd also piccolo), oboe, 2 clarinets, 2 bassoons, 2 horns in F, 2 trumpets in C, timpani, percussion (side drum, triangle), celesta, harp, strings

Introduction

"The fact that he appreciated the virtues of English folk music, that he studied it so thoroughly and absorbed its essence into his own music should not cause us to lose sight of the equally important fact that folk-song was the spring that finally released his true musical personality, not a substitute for genuine style and inspiration."[1] Vaughan Williams drew inspiration from wide-ranging sources, admiring all types of music. Decrying elitist distinctions between "classical" and "popular" music, he asserted that "all music should be classical and all music should be popular."[2] He participated in musical activities of every kind, some of which "many lesser composers would have considered beneath them."[3] And through his compositions, lectures, and writings, he extolled the virtues of folk song as representative of society's finest artistic contributions.

Biographical Sketch

Hailing from the village of Down Ampney, Gloucestershire, Ralph Vaughan Williams (1872–1958) was the youngest of three children born to the Reverend Arthur Vaughan Williams and his wife, Margaret. After his father's death in 1875, he moved with his mother, a descendent of Josiah Wedgwood who was also related to Charles Darwin, to her family's home in Surrey. The young Vaughan Williams enjoyed playing piano, organ, and violin, eventually turning to the viola while a student at Charterhouse. He grew to love the viola, playing it later in many settings.[4]

While the family had been tolerant of Vaughan Williams's pursuit of music as a hobby, they did not consider it suitable as a profession. Despite their objections, he entered the Royal College of Music (RCM) in 1890. After two years of study there, he entered Trinity College, Cambridge, where he would go on to receive degrees in history and music. In 1895, he returned to the RCM for further studies. His composition studies during his college years were with Hubert Parry, Charles Wood, and Charles Villiers Stanford. Vaughan Williams left the RCM in 1896 and married his first wife, Adeline Fisher, the following year; they remained married until her death in 1951. The newly wed couple went to Berlin, where Vaughan Williams pursued additional studies with Max Bruch. After returning to England, he occupied himself with various musical activities, including teaching, lecturing, and composing.

The early 1900s would be a period of discovery for Vaughan Williams, as he started collecting folk songs and editing a hymn book—two undertakings that would significantly influence the direction of his career.[5] Performances of his works from this period, including *Songs of Travel* and *Toward the Unknown Region*, were favorably received, and Vaughan Williams started more ambitious projects, drafting a large-scale work that would eventually become *A Sea Symphony*. But by 1907, he was feeling "lumpy and stodgy" and decided that "a little French polish would be of use."[6] Three months of lessons with Maurice Ravel in Paris provided the needed stimulus, and soon his "personal voice fully emerged."[7]

Though he was past conscription age, Vaughan Williams entered service during the First World War, initially serving as a wagon orderly and later as director of music, First Army, British Expeditionary Force in France.[8] In 1919, he was invited to teach composition at the RCM, and he received an honorary Doctor of Music degree from Oxford University that same year. Vaughan Williams was, by this time, a well-respected musical figure, and he cemented his status as one of England's great modern composers in subsequent years. In 1938, he met Ursula Wood, a young poet and writer. The two began an affair, eventually marrying in 1953 after the death of his first wife.[9] Composing and traveling filled Vaughan Williams's final years until his death on August 26, 1958.

Vaughan Williams's Suite for Viola and Small Orchestra

Vaughan Williams produced a large number of compositions in the major genres (including music for films and radio). His works for viola include *Flos Campi* (1925), Suite for Viola and Small Orchestra (1934), and the *Romance for Viola and Piano* (n.d.; published posthumously in 1962). Additionally, his *Six Studies in English Folk Song for Cello* (1926) includes an alternate part for viola.

The Suite for Viola and Small Orchestra was written for the great English violist Lionel Tertis, who had previously premiered *Flos Campi*. Work on it was underway by 1933, with Vaughan Williams writing to a cousin in October: "My viola suite is not finished & I do not know if it ever will be."[10] He did manage to complete it the following year, and the work was first performed at a pair of Courtauld-Sargent Concerts held at Queen's Hall on November 12 and 13, 1934. An example of "sophisticated 'original' music" derived from Vaughan Williams's interest in folk music,[11] the suite consists of eight short movements broken into three groups. Each group was individually published in a piano reduction in 1936 with the indication that "the Suite may also be played with pianoforte accompaniment."[12] Since the groups were first published separately, each "may be regarded as reasonably detachable,"[13] and violists have often programmed single groups with piano accompaniment on recitals. There are a couple of humorous accounts of Vaughan Williams playing the piano part for the suite; one comes from composer Gordon Jacob:

> One of my most cherished memories was his performance of the *Moto Perpetuo* from his Suite for Viola and Orchestra in which the solo part was represented by a continuous buzzing through his teeth whilst he played the irregularly rhythmed chords of the accompaniment not always with complete accuracy.[14]

And another account from Vaughan Williams's speech at a 1937 retirement dinner for Tertis:

> [Vaughan Williams] told the story of how, having written a few small pieces for Tertis, he invited him down to play them over. Unable to find an accompanist, he had to play himself. As though this were not bad enough, they found that his miserable piano was half a tone flat. Tertis tuned down, set to work and after following the accompanist right through apologised for his own shortcomings.[15]

With its unusual arrangement of short movements interspersing songs, dances, and character pieces, the suite seems akin to Vaughan Williams's masques or pageants. These festive works were intended for performance by amateurs and often included miming, dancing, singing, and spoken text as well as elaborate scenery and costumes. Vaughan Williams composed several different sorts of these over his career. *Job: A Masque for Dancing* (1930) is effectively a ballet in nine scenes with no vocal parts. *The Bridal Day* masque (1938) is in eleven scenes with a baritone soloist, speaker, dancers, mimers, and chorus. While composing the Suite for Viola and Small Orchestra, Vaughan Williams was also working on music for the *Abinger Pageant* (1934). This pageant, consisting of six "episodes" for which Vaughan Williams supplied seventeen musical selections, was "rural rather than historical" and attempted "to show the continuity of country life."[16] Instead of elaborate ceremony, the pageant featured "understated episodes from everyday country life," and emphasized "vernacular practices over cultivated idioms."[17] Considered in this context, the Suite for Viola and Small Orchestra can be viewed as a pageant in three scenes with the viola protagonist in the role of "everyman," singing, dancing, and toiling through life in England:

Scene I: Prelude; A Christmas Celebration

Scene II: Two contrasting views: the bucolic tale of the English country farmer (in the major mode) and the frenzied tale of the city dweller (in the minor mode)

Scene III: An evening of dances for every taste

The "Prelude," in C major, uses three interspersed motives: First is the opening series of sixteenth notes, calling to mind preludes to J. S. Bach's instrumental works. At m. 7, the second motive briefly appears (Ex. 32.1) before being subsumed by a return of the sixteenth notes (all measure numbers and rehearsal letters refer to the Oxford University Press edition with repeated sections in the piano reduction counted twice; there are no repeats in the score). The third figure appears at m. 19 (Letter B) in a new key (A major) and time signature ($\frac{6}{8}$). This motive breaks off at the end of m. 25, after which the opening sixteenths return,

Example 32.1 Vaughan Williams, Suite for Viola and Small Orchestra, Group I, No. 1. "Prelude," mm. 7–10, solo viola.

Zone	Thematic Areas/Snippet	Measures	Principal Tonal Areas/Function
Verse 1		1–9	E-flat major
Verse 2		10 (Let. A)–18	E-flat major
Verse 3		19 (Let. B)–27	C minor
Verse 4		28 (Let. C)–39	E-flat major

Chart 32.1 Vaughan Williams, Suite for Viola and Small Orchestra: Structural analysis, Group I, No. 2, "Carol."

now starting from the top string and working their way downward. At m. 32 (Letter C), the second motive appears in inversion. The movement continues alternating motives, traversing through assorted key areas before settling back into C major at m. 48 (Letter E).

The "Carol" is a strophic song consisting of four verses (Chart 32.1); in the first verse, the solo viola states the nine-measure tune accompanied by cellos, flutes, and clarinets. For the second verse, the viola weaves lovely figures around the tune, which is played by the first violins. The viola resumes the tune in the third verse—now varied and in C minor—largely accompanied by the same orchestral forces as in the first verse. And for the final verse, Flute I presents the tune while the viola follows in canon an octave below.

Fluctuating between $\frac{3}{4}$ and $\frac{6}{8}$, the "Christmas Dance" is in an ABA form (Chart 32.2). The work opens with a rustic, fiddle-like tune in G major, contrasted by a lyrical melody (Unit 1.2) at m. 17 (Letter B). As the oboe takes over this melody at m. 29 (Letter C), the solo viola seems intent on resurrecting the boisterous opening. The B section (mm. 38–81) features shifting tonalities with the first theme (Unit 1.1) beginning over a B♭ major harmony with E♭s in the cellos and basses. At m. 47 (Letter E), the second theme (Unit 1.2) starts in the G Aeolian mode (natural minor) and is repeated at m. 59 (Letter F) in the D Phrygian mode. Vaughan Williams returns to the B section's opening material at

Zone	Thematic Areas/Snippet	Measures	Principal Tonal Areas/Function
A		1–37	
	Unit 1.1	1–16	G major
	Unit 1.2	17 (Let. B)–37	G major
B		38 (Let. D)–81 (Let. H)	
	Unit 1.1	38 (Let. D)–46	B-flat major/E-flat major
	Unit 1.2	47 (Let. E)–68	Modal
	Unit 1.3 (return of Unit 1.1 material)	69 (Let. G)–81 (Let. H)	G minor
A		81 (Let. H)–108	
	Unit 1.1	81 (Let. H)–86	G major
	Unit 1.2	87 (Let. K)–96 (Let. L)	E major
	Unit 1.3 (return of Unit 1.1 material)	96 (Let. L)–108	G major

Chart 32.2 Vaughan Williams, Suite for Viola and Small Orchestra: Structural analysis, Group I, No. 3, "Christmas Dance."

m. 69, this time harmonized in G minor. The movement closes out with a return of material from the A section, alternating between G major and E major.

The second group opens with a "Ballad," "a short popular or traditional song that normally frames a narrative element."[18] Cast in a ternary form, the movement is built on two different pentatonic modes commonly found in English folk music. The opening theme (Ex. 32.2), in $\frac{3}{4}$, uses a two-gapped pentatonic mode lacking the fourth and seventh degrees of the C major scale.[19] The

Example 32.2 Vaughan Williams, Suite for Viola and Small Orchestra, Group II, No. 1. "Ballad," mm. 2–7, solo viola.

Example 32.3 Vaughan Williams, Suite for Viola and Small Orchestra, Group II, No. 1. "Ballad," mm. 48–51, oboe.

contrasting middle section, Allegro ma non troppo (mm. 48–71), begins in $\frac{6}{8}$ and uses a pentatonic mode lacking the third and sixth degrees of the A minor scale (Ex. 32.3; this theme and mode is foreshadowed by the principal flute at m. 20).[20] At m. 67 (Letter C), the music shifts to C minor and $\frac{3}{4}$, preparing for a return of the opening at m. 72. But rather than the opening theme, this section starts with melodic material that initially appeared at m. 19. The opening theme finally returns at the Largamente (m. 86; Letter D), punctuated by two quasi cadenza statements in the viola. Vaughan Williams's use of the folk idiom seems most conspicuous in this movement, so it is rather surprising that it was originally titled "Romance" in the manuscript, which has been marked out and replaced by the title "Ballad."[21]

The virtuosic "Moto Perpetuo" features a stream of challenging sixteenth notes in the solo viola. Cast in a sonata form (Chart 32.3), the movement opens with alternating consonance and dissonance, emphasizing the intervals of a second and seventh within the first six measures. At m. 73 (Letter E), slurred sixteenths and a *pp* dynamic impart a more subdued mood for the start of the second theme group. Vaughan Williams begins the development at m. 111 (Letter G) by recalling the material from the first three measures in an inverted form (mm. 111–16). The remainder of the development makes extensive use of open strings in double-stop and bariolage passages. After the recapitulation (mm. 181–251), the movement culminates in a coda that begins with a C major chord but quickly moves to C minor. Throughout the coda, the viola reinforces the interval of the second, ending with an inverted version of the double stops that opened the movement.

Zone	Thematic Areas/Snippet	Measures	Principal Tonal Areas/Function
Exposition		1–111 (Let. G)	
	Theme Group 1	1–72	
	Unit 1.1	1–34 (Let. B)	C minor
	Unit 1.2	34 (Let. B)–72	G minor
	Theme Group 2	73 (Let. E)–111 (Let. G)	G major
Development		111 (Let. G)–81 (Let. M)	Begins G major; modulates
Recapitulation		181 (Let. M)–251	
	Theme Group 1	181 (Let. M)–212	C minor
	Theme Group 2	213–51	C major
Coda		251–74	Begins C major chord; C minor

Chart 32.3 Vaughan Williams, Suite for Viola and Small Orchestra: Structural analysis, Group II, No. 2, "Moto Perpetuo."

The final group consists entirely of dances, none of which fully conforms to standard expectations. The odd character of the dance forms has often been commented on: "At a first hearing the two final movements, a Polka and a Galop, did not quite get hold of us. Perhaps the composer was not very wise to give them those titles: these set up connotations in us that are alien to the whole cast of Vaughan Williams's mind."[22] Extended tutti passages occur in each of these movements, a major textural change from the first two groups, where the solo viola is a nearly constant presence.

Beginning this group is a "Musette," which is typically "a dance-like piece of pastoral character whose style is suggestive of the sound of the musette or

Zone	Thematic Areas/Snippet	Measures	Principal Tonal Areas/Function
A		1–45	E-flat major
B	Vln. 1	46–69	G major; modulates
A		70–95	E-flat major

Chart 32.4 Vaughan Williams, Suite for Viola and Small Orchestra: Structural analysis, Group III, No. 1, "Musette."

bagpipe. The bass part generally has a drone (*bourdon*) on the tonic and the upper voice or voices consist of melodies in conjunct motion."[23] The movement begins with a drone in the bass line, which is implied over the course of the movement but "not rigidly maintained."[24] Cast in an ABA form (Chart 32.4), the "Musette" is delicate in tone and texture, with the muted strings, celesta, and opening harp ostinato creating "an orchestral atmosphere reminiscent of Ravel."[25] After two introductory measures, the viola states the principal theme in E♭ major. At m. 18, the viola transitions to accompanimental eighth notes with the theme given over to the celesta and a single first violin at m. 22 (Letter A). An orchestral tutti starts the B section at m. 46 with a theme that is related to material from the A section: the first five notes follow the contour of the opening harp ostinato (and the first eight notes match the intervals and rhythms of the solo viola's line in mm. 11–14). This section fluctuates between major and minor harmonies before returning to the movement's opening theme at m. 70. The orchestral texture in the final A section is sparse and ethereal with lovely use of harmonics, first in the harp and finally in the solo viola.

"Polka Melancolique" was originally titled "Polka" in both the manuscript and the program for the premiere.[26] "A lively couple-dance in $\frac{2}{4}$ time," the polka originated in Bohemia.[27] Vaughan Williams presumably added "melancolique" in response to comments regarding the dance's uncharacteristic features: "The next piece has the true rhythm of the Polka, but otherwise little to associate it with the dance said to have been invented by a Czech serving-maid. For one thing it clings to the minor mode."[28] While this movement can be considered in various forms, it is anchored by three appearances of the principal theme separated by two episodes, resulting in an ABACA form with coda (Chart 32.5). Vaughan Williams emphasizes the solo viola's low d during the initial presentation of the theme (mm. 3–17). The d♭ that begins the first episode at m. 18 (Letter B) thus

Zone	Thematic Areas/Snippet	Measures	Principal Tonal Areas/Function
A		1–17	D minor
B		18 (Let. B)–38	B-flat minor; C-sharp minor
A		39 (Let. D)–49	D minor
C		50 (Let. E)–77	D major; modulates
A		78 (Let. H)–88	D major/D minor
Coda		89 (Let. K)–101	D minor

Chart 32.5 Vaughan Williams, Suite for Viola and Small Orchestra: Structural analysis, Group III, No. 2, "Polka Melancolique."

comes as a jarring change. Making its way through B♭ minor and C♯ minor, the episode ends with cadenza-like material (mm. 34–38) as a setup for a return of the A theme at m. 39 (Letter D). The second episode (mm. 50–77), which starts in D major but quickly modulates through several keys, includes a sizable central tutti section (mm. 61–69) in E♭ major. At m. 70 (Letter G), the viola returns with a passage that culminates in a "quasi cadenza" from mm. 76–77, which once again sets up a return of the A section. The viola lets loose at m. 78 (Letter H) with a double-stop presentation of the A theme, mixing D major and D minor. A brief coda (incorporating yet another cadenza) closes the movement.

The suite concludes with a "Galop," "a quick, lively dance in ²⁄₄ time," which "derived its name from the galloping movement of horses."[29] This is not a Galop for the ballroom, but one for the open countryside with its "cheeky rhythmic cross currents and engaging contrapuntal flippancies."[30] Cast in an ABA form, the movement opens in F♯ minor, briefly changing key at m. 23 (Letter B) with the introduction of a new theme in ⁶⁄₈ (Ex. 32.4). The B section starts at m. 56 (Letter E) in E♭ major with a "theme that one might find in a score for a western film. The theme is transformed into a saloon dance through an increase in orchestration and rhythmic emphasis on the second beat of each measure."[31] At m. 112 (Letter L), the A section returns, with a brief statement by the solo viola giving way to

Example 32.4 Vaughan Williams, Suite for Viola and Small Orchestra, Group III, No. 3. "Galop," mm. 23–26, solo viola.

an orchestral tutti (mm. 126–38). After the orchestra comes to a screeching halt in m. 139, the viola takes off in one mad dash for the finish line, abruptly halting itself in m. 142 before launching into the rather unexpected Largamente ending.

Vaughan Williams's Suite for Viola and Small Orchestra was favorably received upon its premiere, though aspects of the work puzzled reviewers. The critic William McNaught offered the most astute observations regarding the work's character:

> The viola's dusky tone and gift of plaintiveness do not necessarily cast it for tragic parts: they are part of its homely nature and are fit for homely thoughts. Its voice, unlike that of the aristocratic violin, is the voice of lowly humanity, with its simplicities and humours as well as its dumps. Its candle-light is that of the cottage. . . . The lowering of the brow does not in the least lower the style. In fact, Vaughan Williams has never written a work more crowded with points of musical interest, sudden gleams of beauty, inspired simplicities, and telling subtleties.[32]

While the references to "homely nature" and "lowly humanity" may sound unduly negative to modern readers, they strike at the heart of Vaughan Williams's egalitarian beliefs about music and humanity. By using the viola to represent the "common man," Vaughan Williams is not only emphasizing the expressive, vocal, and inherently human qualities of the instrument, he is also demonstrating his admiration and respect for it.

Continued reception of the work has been mixed: its unusual gathering of miniature movements, full of contradictory forms, has proved challenging for many critics. Edmund Rubbra considered the viola suite, along with the piano concerto, to be "experimental essays rather than solid achievements,"[33] while Hugh Ottaway considered it an "unsuccessful work" and an "unsatisfactory piece of writing," in which "both the overall conception of the work and the content of some of the movements . . . leave an impression that is inconsequential, almost casual."[34] Other critics have recognized that the suite's "apparent small scale indicates the concentration of a great mind relaxing rather than the triviality of a small mind turning out elegant trifles."[35]

There is nothing trivial about Vaughan Williams's Suite for Viola and Small Orchestra; each movement is a finely crafted work of art. Superb orchestrations, beautiful tunes, intriguing harmonies—and inventive approaches to traditional forms—merge to form a piece that is simultaneously simple and complex. Like many great works of art, it can be difficult to appreciate without repeated exposure. But those who invest time listening to or performing it will discover the many wonders that lurk within.

33

Henry Vieuxtemps: *Élégie for Viola and Piano*, op. 30

Date of Composition: c. 1848

First Edition: H. Vieuxtemps, *Élégie pour Alto ou Violoncelle avec accompagnement de Piano, op. 30,* Offenbach: Jean André, [1854], Plate No. 7430

Select Later Edition: Henry Vieuxtemps, *Élégie Opus 30 für Viola und Klavier*, ed. Peter Jost, Munich: Henle, 2014, HN 1229

Dedication: À Son Excellence Le Comte Mathieu Wielhorsky

Date/Place of First Public Performance: March 1, 1848, Henry Vieuxtemps (viola), St. Petersburg

Introduction

"We are therefore faced with two fundamentally distinct compositions: the composition *for* the violin and the composition *by* the violin. Beethoven is *for*; Vieuxtemps is *by*."[1] To the casual observer, Ysaÿe's assessment of Henry Vieuxtemps's violin concertos—compared to the superlative one by Ludwig van Beethoven—may seem suspect. But admirers of Vieuxtemps will recognize the validity of Ysaÿe's statement. Yes, Vieuxtemps's solo works were written as vehicles to showcase his virtuosic technique; but they were never solely about technique. Instead, Vieuxtemps aimed for a synthesis of musicality and technique that was unique to the violin, resulting in "an original violinistic vocabulary that remained valid for the entire 19th century."[2] His music was lauded by composers of the day, including Hector Berlioz and Pyotr Tchaikovsky, and his seven violin concertos, with their ingenuity of form and expansive role for the orchestra, are considered a cut above those of his fellow virtuoso violinist-composers.

Vieuxtemps also played viola, writing a sizable number of works for the instrument. While the technical demands in these works are suitably impressive, the virtuoso devices employed are more modest than those in his compositions for violin.[3] Since Vieuxtemps composed these works for himself, the reduced technical demands cannot be attributed to a lack of technique on the violist's part. Rather, Vieuxtemps was aware that the character and technique of the viola is distinct from that of the violin. Thus, just as Ysaÿe asserted that Vieuxtemps's violin works were written *by* the violin, it may also be said that his viola works were written *by* the viola.

Biographical Sketch

Henry Vieuxtemps (1820–1881) was born in Verviers. His father, Jean François, was a textile worker and amateur violinist who taught Henry to play the violin at age four. The young Vieuxtemps performed Pierre Rode's Fifth Violin Concerto with an orchestra at the age of six; shortly afterward he embarked on a tour of neighboring cities, including Liège, Brussels, Antwerp, and Amsterdam. The family moved from Verviers to Brussels in 1828 so that Henry could study with Charles de Bériot. When de Bériot left for Italy three years later, he counseled Vieuxtemps's father to entrust the young violinist's further education to "no one! Your son should prepare his way himself by his own intelligence, and also by hearing foreign artists which he should do as much as possible."[4] Vieuxtemps never had another violin lesson,[5] but he continued touring: performing in London, Paris, Mannheim, and other European cities to critical acclaim while meeting prominent musicians, including Louis Spohr and Nicolò Paganini.

He did, however, pursue lessons in composition, studying with Simon Sechter in Vienna and with Antoine Reicha in Paris. The studies with Reicha, in 1835–1836, would prove significant, inspiring Vieuxtemps to experiment with concerto form.[6] Over the next few years, he performed widely throughout Europe, firmly establishing a reputation as a pre-eminent violin soloist:

> M. Vieuxtemps, in his playing, unites the perfections of style, intonation, execution, and, beyond all, expression. Although a pupil of De Beriot, he is not of the school of De Beriot; nor is he of the school of any other violinist we have ever heard. Assuming the prerogative of genius, he has made a school for himself.[7]

Not content with merely conquering Europe, Vieuxtemps traveled west, touring America in 1843–1844, including trips to Mexico and Cuba. In America, he was embraced by the public and fellow musicians alike; the recently founded New York Philharmonic Society elected him as their first Honorary Member.[8] Later in 1844, Vieuxtemps married the pianist Josephine Eder, who would routinely accompany her husband in recital and would also manage many of his professional business affairs.

Weary from his extensive travels, Vieuxtemps accepted an offer in 1846 to serve as violinist to Emperor Nicholas I and the Imperial Theaters in St. Petersburg, Russia. He remained there for the next six years, also serving as a professor at the School of Music.[9] After resigning over a contract dispute, Vieuxtemps resumed an exhausting tour schedule while residing in his country estate outside of Frankfurt am Main. Political events surrounding the Austro-Prussian War forced a relocation to Paris in 1866, where his wife contracted cholera. She succumbed to a recurrence of the disease two years later, dying in her husband's arms.[10] To alleviate his grief, Vieuxtemps embarked on more tours, including trips to Scandinavia and a third, and final, trip to the United States.

In 1871, Vieuxtemps accepted a position as professor of violin at the Brussels Conservatory. Just two short years later he suffered a stroke that paralyzed his entire left side.[11] Though his condition slowly improved, he would never regain enough dexterity in his left hand to resume concertizing. Instead, the once-great virtuoso took solace in the continued ability to compose. He briefly returned to teaching at the end of the decade but was compelled to resign from the conservatory in 1879, moving to Algeria to be near his daughter and son-in-law. On June 3, 1881, he suffered another stroke—his fourth—and died three days later.[12]

Vieuxtemps's *Élégie for Viola and Piano*, op. 30

Though more widely known for his violin playing, Vieuxtemps also earned critical acclaim for his viola playing: "M. Vieuxtemps' command of the viola is as complete and absolute as his mastery of all the secrets of the cognate instrument with which his name is associated."[13] He was "singularly fond of the low and gentle tone" of the viola and played works by other composers, "especially Schumann's *Fairy-Tale Pictures* (*Märchenbilder*)."[14]

Vieuxtemps primarily composed string music, including solo, chamber, and concertante works. His five original works for viola have been problematic to date: *Élégie for Viola and Piano*, op. 30 (c. 1848; published 1854); *Étude*, for viola and piano (c. 1850?);[15] Sonata for Viola and Piano, op. 36 (1860; published 1862); Capriccio, op. 55, no. 7 (published posthumously in 1883); and two movements of an incomplete sonata for viola and piano, consisting of an Allegro con fuoco and Scherzo (published posthumously in 1884). Additionally, his *Duo Brillant*, for violin, cello, and orchestra, op. 39 (published 1864) has an alternate viola part in place of the cello, and he arranged *La Nuit*, from Félicien David's ode-symphonie *Le désert*, for viola and piano (published 1846) and W. A. Mozart's Clarinet Quintet, K. 581 for viola and piano in an edition titled *Grand Duo* (published 1855–1856).

The *Élégie* is dedicated to Count Mathieu Wielhorsky, the nobleman who had persuaded Vieuxtemps to accept his position in St. Petersburg. Vieuxtemps premiered the work on a concert that included Felix Mendelssohn's Violin Concerto in E Minor, op. 64, and he performed it on several subsequent occasions. A showstopper of a work, it seems to have been influenced by his violin technique to a greater degree than his later viola compositions.[16]

Élégie is cast in an ABA form with coda (Chart 33.1). Highly operatic in style, the solo part brims with long cantilena lines, forceful declamatory statements, and florid passages. Vieuxtemps firmly establishes the elegiac atmosphere by setting the work in F minor, a key noted for its "deep depression, funereal lament, groans of misery and longing for the grave."[17] The piano's insistent, plodding eighth notes in the opening section add to the sense of gloom. At its entrance in m. 7, the viola immediately introduces the interval of a half step, which dominates the piece. Here, the half step functions as a neighboring tone, producing an elegiac sighing effect. Elsewhere, accentuated appoggiaturas (e.g., m. 15 and m. 28) and chromatic passages (e.g., mm. 79–81) create dramatic intensity. In m. 28, Vieuxtemps ventures into the most remote tonal area, tonicizing F♯ minor (a half step above the tonic). The adventure is brief, and the work returns to the flat side of the spectrum at m. 32, steadily building tension until the viola's climactic c[iii] in m. 40, followed by a rapid descent to its lowest register. The

Zone	Thematic Areas/Snippet	Measures	Principal Tonal Areas/Function
Introduction		1–6	F minor
A	*[musical notation]*	7–49	F minor (tonicizes F-sharp minor, mm. 28–31)
B		50–88	
	Unit 1.1 *[musical notation]*	50–61	A-flat major
	Unit 1.2 *[musical notation]*	61–71	E-flat major
	Unit 1.3 (return of Unit 1.1 material) *[musical notation]*	72–88	A-flat major
A	*[musical notation]*	89–110	F minor
Coda	*[musical notation]*	111–23	F minor

Chart 33.1 Vieuxtemps, *Élégie for Viola and Piano*, op. 30: Structural analysis.

tension resolves in m 43, where the viola stalls on an f while the piano takes over the melody before giving way to the viola's languid cadenza in mm. 48–49.

The B section turns to the relative major, though the opening *molto espressivo* theme (Unit 1.1) bears resemblances to the principal theme from the A section. After a contrasting *dolce* section (Unit 1.2), the *molto espressivo* theme returns at m. 72 (Unit 1.3). Sextuplets appear almost constantly throughout the B section, both as an accompanimental figure as well as in the viola's embellishments. The piano's sextuplets begin at the duration of a half note in m. 50 but change to the duration of a quarter note at m. 72. This gradual quickening of the subdivision at the quarter-note level (eighth at m. 1; triplet at m. 50; sextuplet at m. 72) creates a sense of agitation, driving the music forward. The viola takes up the piano's sextuplets in mm. 86–88, gradually unwinding on a half step in m. 88 to smoothly transition back to the A section.

Vieuxtemps continues building momentum in the return of the A section: in the piano, triplets replace the earlier repeated eighth notes while rising sextuplet figures crescendo in the bass line (given the frequent triplet subdivision, the piano part is written in $\frac{12}{8}$ in mm. 89–109, while the viola part is written in common time). At m. 108, the viola once again ascends to a climactic c[iii] before descending to a low c in the following measure. Rather than resolving calmly as he did in m. 43, Vieuxtemps instead adds a virtuosic coda, with the viola's torrent of sextuplets propelling the work to its dramatic conclusion.

The *Élégie for Viola and Piano, op. 30* was favorably reviewed upon publication in 1854: "Like all that M. Vieuxtemps composes, this *Elégie* is full of musical feeling and remarkable for ingenuity. We prefer it on the *alto*, the instrument for which, we presume, it was originally intended."[18] Just a few years after publication, the *Musical World* reported that "every violinist is acquainted with the *Elégie* of M. Vieuxtemps,"[19] and the work remained popular during the nineteenth century in both its viola and violin versions. The work fell out of favor during the early twentieth century as critical appreciation for Vieuxtemps declined, and it was not until 1980 that it received its first commercial recording.[20] Kim Kashkashian's later recording, released in 1986,[21] helped revive the work, and it has since been embraced by performers and audiences as a stellar example of Romantic virtuosic writing *by* the viola.

34

William Walton: Concerto for Viola and Orchestra

I.   Andante comodo
II. Vivo, con molto preciso[1]
III. Allegro moderato

Date of Composition: 1928–1929

First Edition: William Walton, *Concerto for Viola and Orchestra*, London: Oxford University Press, 1930 (Score and Piano Reduction)

Select Later Editions: William Walton, *Concerto for Viola and Orchestra*, London: Oxford University Press, [1964], © 1930, Plate No. O.U.P. 160 (Piano Reduction); *William Walton Edition*, vol. 12, *Concerto for Viola and Orchestra*, ed. Christopher Wellington, Oxford: Oxford University Press, 2002 (1929 and 1962 Scores); William Walton, *Concerto for Viola and Orchestra*, ed. Christopher Wellington, Oxford: Oxford University Press, 2002 (Piano Reduction)

Dedication: To Christabel [McLaren]

Date/Place of First Public Performance (1929 Version): October 3, 1929, Paul Hindemith (viola), Henry J. Wood Symphony Orchestra, William Walton (conductor), Promenade Concert, Queen's Hall, London

Date/Place of First Public Performance (1962 Version): January 18, 1962, John Coulling (viola), London Philharmonic Orchestra, Malcolm Sargent (conductor), Royal Festival Hall, London

Orchestral Instrumentation (1929 Version): Solo viola, piccolo, 2 flutes, 2 oboes, English horn, 2 clarinets, bass clarinet in B♭, 2 bassoons, contrabassoon, 4 horns in F, 3 trumpets in C, 3 trombones, tuba, timpani, strings

Orchestral Instrumentation (1962 Version): Solo viola, 2 flutes (second also piccolo), oboe, English horn, 2 clarinets in B♭ (second also bass clarinet in B♭), 2 bassoons, 4 horns in F, 2 trumpets in C, 3 trombones, timpani, harp, strings

Introduction

"It took me time to realize what a tower of strength in the literature of the viola was this concerto, and how deep would be the gratitude we who play the viola should feel toward the composer—with gratitude, too, to Beecham for having suggested to Walton the composition of a viola concerto."[2] The story behind Walton's viola concerto is legendary: In 1928, at the suggestion of the conductor Thomas Beecham, Walton began work on a concerto for the great English violist Lionel Tertis. After completing the concerto the following year, Walton "sent it to Tertis, who turned it down sharply by return of post."[3] Edward Clark, who was in charge of music production at the British Broadcasting Corporation (BBC), suggested Paul Hindemith as an alternate soloist. Hindemith agreed to premiere the work, saving it from being turned into a violin concerto. After attending the premiere, Tertis realized his mistake and went on to champion the work. Legions of violists have since recognized Walton's concerto as a "tower of strength" in the viola repertoire. And we all, indeed, owe a debt of gratitude not only to Walton and Beecham, but to all of the key participants who helped guide the concerto through its rocky start.

Biographical Sketch

William Turner Walton (1902–1983) was the second of four children born to Charles and Louisa Walton in the industrial town of Oldham, England. Both of Walton's parents were singers; his father taught music and directed a church choir, which Walton sang in as a boy. During his youth, Walton played piano and organ; he also took violin lessons for a period.[4] In 1912, he won a scholarship to Christ Church Cathedral School, a preparatory school in Oxford. Despite his family's financial hardships during the war, Walton was able to remain at Christ Church for six happy years, excelling at sports and trying his hand at composing. The organists Henry Ley and Hugh Allen were his principal music instructors, but it was Thomas Strong—Dean of Christ Church—who served as Walton's most important musical mentor, introducing him to works by Arnold Schoenberg and other contemporary composers.[5]

In 1918, Walton entered Oxford University, spending many hours at the Ellis Library in the Radcliffe Camera poring over scores by Igor Stravinsky, Claude Debussy, and Maurice Ravel at the expense of his other studies.[6] While at Oxford, Walton developed several important friendships, most significantly with the cultured, aristocratic Sitwell siblings—Edith, Sacheverell, and Osbert. Walton became an "adopted, or elected, brother" to the trio,[7] moving into their house after failing his exams in 1919 and living with them for nearly fifteen years. The Sitwells exerted considerable influence over Walton's cultural development, introducing him to their literary friends and enabling him to attend concerts of contemporary music: "We were able to keep him in touch with the vital works of the age," recalled Osbert.[8] Financial support from the Sitwells, and from other friends, proved invaluable to Walton during his early career; a gift from Thomas Strong allowed Walton to make his first trip to Italy with the Sitwells in the spring of 1920, an experience that Walton indicated "changed my whole attitude about life and music."[9]

Walton enjoyed early successes with *Façade* (1921–1928) and the *Sinfonia concertante*, for orchestra with piano (1926–1927), but it was the Concerto for Viola and Orchestra (1928–1929) that put him on the map. In 1929, he met the Baroness Imma von Doernberg, beginning a tumultuous relationship that lasted until 1934, when she left him for a Hungarian doctor. Quickly bouncing back, he next began an affair with Alice, Viscountess Wimborne, who was more than twenty years his senior—and married. Despite the turmoil in his personal life, Walton's musical reputation (and financial security) greatly increased during the 1930s with the completion of several works, including his first symphony and his first film score, *Escape Me Never*, for which he was paid the tremendous sum of £300.[10]

In April 1948, Walton's longtime companion, Alice Wimborne, died.[11] During a trip to Buenos Aires in October of that year, he met twenty-two-year-old Susana Gil Passo, to whom he promptly proposed marriage. For weeks, Walton persisted with his proposal; Susana finally accepted, and they married on December 13.[12] The couple lived for a few years in London, but they also spent several months each year on the island of Ischia, eventually making it their permanent home.[13] During the post–World War II years, Walton's critical reputation diminished; his style seemed old-fashioned compared to modern currents, and his position as the golden boy of English music had been supplanted by Benjamin Britten. Yet Walton was still in high demand and received many honors, including a knighthood in 1951 and the Order of Merit in 1967. He also enjoyed major celebrations to mark his seventieth and eightieth birthdays. After years of declining health, Walton died early on the morning of March 8, 1983, just as a doctor was writing out a prescription for a cylinder of oxygen to help him breathe.[14]

Walton's Concerto for Viola and Orchestra

Walton was a slow and careful composer who worked on one composition at a time, often with great difficulty: "It's always been a nightmare for me," he remarked about composing, "and the more I go on, the more difficult it seems to become."[15] He was also "an inveterate reviser,"[16] and "hardly a major score of his escaped the most rigorous revision."[17] Walton's sole work for viola, the Concerto for Viola and Orchestra (1928–1929), was begun late in the fall of 1928 in Amalfi, Italy.[18] On December 5, 1928, Walton mentioned the concerto in a letter to Siegfried Sassoon, a friend from Oxford and financial supporter:

> I have been working hard at a Viola Concerto suggested by Beecham & designed for Lionel Tertis. It may be finished by Xmas and is I think by far my best effort up to now.[19]

An attack of flu delayed work on the concerto, and Walton wrote again to Sassoon on February 2, 1929, providing details about his progress:

> I finished yesterday the second movement of my Viola Concerto. At the moment, I think it will be my best work, better than the "Sinfonia [concertante]," if only the third and last movement works out well—at present I am in the painful position of starting it, which is always full of trials and disappointments, however I hope to be well away with it in a day or two.[20]

Walton provided another brief update in a letter to Sassoon on February 12:

> Otherwise I have no news, except that I have started on the 3rd movement & hope to complete it soon.[21]

Over the next months, Walton continued working on the concerto, playing it for a number of friends.[22] He sent the completed score to Tertis after returning to England in the spring, which was promptly returned by post:

> With shame and contrition I admit that when the composer offered me the first performance I declined it. I was unwell at the time; but what is also true is that I had not learnt to appreciate Walton's style. The innovations in his language, which now seem so logical and so truly in the main stream of music, struck me as farfetched.[23]

Walton considered turning the work into a violin concerto until Edward Clark, a conductor and music producer for the BBC, said that he could get Paul Hindemith to premiere the work.[24] On July 3, 1929, Walton joyfully wrote to Sassoon:

> There is very good news about my [Viola] concerto. Hindemith is playing it on Oct 3rd, myself with the "baton." . . .

I have more or less got to go to Germany to see Hindemith about the V.C. but how I am going to go, I can't think. He is going to be at the Baden-Baden Festival on the 25th & I hope to meet him there as it will be better than going to Berlin.[25]

Sassoon provided the money for Walton to go to the Baden-Baden Festival, where the composer was able to meet with Hindemith and secure his participation as soloist.[26] The performance would mark Hindemith's debut as a featured soloist in England, much to the chagrin of his publisher, Willy Strecker, who was negotiating Hindemith's appearance at a Courtauld-Sargent Concert. Strecker wrote to Hindemith's wife, Gertrud:

> I want your husband, appearing there for the first time before the larger public, to do it in a worthy setting, and as a composer, not just as a soloist. An appearance with [Henry] Wood to play a concerto by a moderately gifted English composer—and that is what Walton is—is not as I see it a début.[27]

Despite Strecker's objections, Hindemith premiered Walton's viola concerto on October 3, 1929, at a Promenade Concert in Queen's Hall with the composer conducting.[28] Hindemith was unhappy with the limited rehearsal time and state of the orchestra, as he wrote in a letter to his wife on October 2:

> I have just come from the rehearsal (evening around 7); it should have been early this morning but wasn't because other things were being rehearsed. In this way—because I stayed to listen—I at least got to know the famous Sir Wood and now know for certain that he cannot do my viola concerto. I shall talk to Clark about it tomorrow. Walton is conducting his concerto himself. It won't be up to much. So far he has had only one rehearsal in which he managed to play the first movement just once. The orchestra is bad, consists mainly of women, and English ones at that. . . . I shall play as decently as I can, but not much—I believe—will come of it.[29]

Bernard Shore, who played principal viola in the orchestra, recalled the disarray surrounding the premiere:

> Feverish was the activity that went on behind the scenes to get the orchestral parts ready. Up till seven o'clock on the night, the artists' room was full of copyists, while an anxious Walton and an irritated Hindemith (who wanted more rehearsal) paced up and down, debating over the score and agreeing upon various vital code-signs. Wood, very indignant, was meanwhile heard to

mutter: "These young composers! I can't even get into my own artists' room! What next?"[30]

Nevertheless, the premiere went well with reviewers raving about the work:

> The Concerto is a very live work in three movements—an Andante, an animated and piquant Scherzo, and a final Allegro. Eccentricity has little or no place in it, and the classical influence is strong, though mixed amusingly with an occasional Elgarian phraseology and a fair spice of jazz. But out of these various influences it is clear that Mr. Walton is developing a very real power of personal expression. The composer conducted, and with Herr Hindemith was recalled to the platform many times.[31]

Reviewers were less impressed with Hindemith's performance but gratefully acknowledged his willingness to perform a work by a young English composer: "Frankly, he did not shine particularly as a solo player, but it was gracious of him to place what must now be a secondary activity at the disposal of a new English work."[32] Walton later commented about Hindemith's style of playing: "His technique was marvellous, but he was rough—no nonsense about it. He just stood up and played."[33]

Walton admitted that his viola concerto had been influenced by Hindemith's own *Kammermusik No. 5*, op. 36, no. 4: "I was surprised he played it," Walton remarked to Hindemith's biographer Geoffrey Skelton, "one or two bars are almost identical."[34] Many similarities between the two works can be found, including florid runs (Exs. 34.1 and 34.2) and, more important, the use of cross-relations (Exs. 34.3 and 34.4).

During a March 17, 1972, BBC radio interview with John Amis, Walton admitted that Sergey Prokofiev's Violin Concerto No. 1, op. 19 had also served

Example 34.1 Hindemith, *Kammermusik No. 5*, op. 36, no. 4, movt. III, mm. 33–36, solo viola.

Example 34.2 Walton, Concerto for Viola and Orchestra, movt. III, mm. 98–99, solo viola.

Example 34.3 Hindemith, *Kammermusik No. 5*, op. 36, no. 4, movt. II, mm. 56–59, solo viola.

Example 34.4 Walton, Concerto for Viola and Orchestra, movt. I, mm. 162–65, solo viola.

as a conscious model, "up to a point."[35] A resemblance to Prokofiev's concerto is evident from the outset (Exs. 34.5 and 34.6), and scholars have noted extensive similarities between the two works: "Walton's Viola Concerto, a work so pervasively modelled on Prokofiev's First Violin Concerto that one suspects Walton had a copy of Prokofiev's score open in front of him while composing, illustrates the conservative streak in the post-war English concerto."[36]

Walton ultimately dedicated his concerto to Christabel McLaren (Lady Aberconway), a friend and financial supporter. The work is greatly admired for

Example 34.5 Prokofiev, Violin Concerto No. 1, op. 19, movt. I, mm. 3–7, solo violin.

Example 34.6 Walton, Concerto for Viola and Orchestra, movt. I, mm. 3–6, solo viola.

its overt lyricism, modern harmonic language (including elements of jazz), virtuosic solo writing, and superb orchestration. There are, however, many spots where the viola has difficulty competing against Walton's thick orchestration (Walton provided instructions to reduce the number of string players during the solo passages, which helps some). Over the years, Walton made revisions to the work, completely re-orchestrating it in 1961, reducing the number of winds and adding a harp. Walton considered the new orchestration to be an improvement over the original, though he did not withdraw the earlier version:

> In 1962 [*sic*] the composer rescored this work for a reduced orchestra and authorized that both the original and the new orchestration may be used: however, the composer strongly prefers the new version.[37]

The revised orchestration has since overtaken the original in popularity; it is the version that is now most often heard in performances and recordings. Walton was not the only person to alter the concerto; several violists have also tinkered with it, introducing their own changes. Despite initially rejecting the work, Lionel Tertis quickly put his personal stamp on it, and Walton permitted publication in 1931 of a separate solo part edited by Tertis that includes numerous alterations.[38] Not everyone was partial to Tertis's version: while preparing for a performance at the University of Edinburgh in 1935 with the violist John Fairbairn, Donald Tovey wrote:

> Please tell Mr Walton that the reason why I cannot come to hear his symphony is that I am producing his viola concerto here with a local viola player (he had to be born somewhere and why not here?). Incidentally, he is following the

printed text, as he shares my feeling that Tertis is a little too anxious to turn the viola into a violin.[39]

A performance by William Primrose in 1936 with Thomas Beecham included a note in the program that "Mr. Primrose's rendering of the solo viola part diverges occasionally from the published version."[40] And Frederick Riddle introduced further changes when he made the premiere recording in 1937 with the composer conducting. Walton was pleased enough with Riddle's changes to allow another new version of the solo part to be published incorporating those changes. Yet Walton still permitted Primrose to include his own changes when the pair recorded the work in 1946, creating the aura of authoritativeness for this interpretation:

> While preparing the Concerto for my début performance with Beecham, I contrived to rewrite some passages in the scherzo-like second movement and certain sections of the other two. But, I do assure you, not without the full approval of the composer—or so it seemed to me. For thirty-five years I pursued my way, many performances taking place under Walton's direction, to say nothing of one recording in 1946 with him conducting, and another under Sir Malcolm Sargent in his hearing. All this time nary a peep of protest from the composer. . . .
>
> Time passed, and much later I learned from an obscure source, a young player from New Zealand, or from some other antipodean outpost of the Empire as it used to be, that in a local performance of the work when Walton was present, the soloist had enquired in his own behalf the right or wrong of the matter and elicited the authoritative word that the composer indeed preferred his original conceptions to the emendations I had presumed to insert.[41]

In all, at least six different versions of the solo viola part have been published by Oxford University Press (OUP) (Chart 34.1).[42] This is to say nothing of the different versions of the published scores and piano reductions. For violists interested in sorting out the many differences, there are three sources that should be consulted: the full score published as volume 12 of the William Walton Edition (2002), the 1964 piano reduction (Plate No. O.U.P. 160 with a copyright date of 1930; renewed 1958), and the 2002 piano reduction (see Select Later Editions at the head of this chapter).

Most useful among these sources is the William Walton Edition (WWE), edited by Christopher Wellington, which includes both the 1929 and 1962 orchestrations. This edition is important for its inclusion of Walton's original solo line from 1929 (printed as a separate line below Wellington's edition). It is highly worthwhile for violists to read through this line to discover Walton's

Date of Publication	Price	Copyright Date	Responsibility	Note
1930	7s. 6d.	1930	William Walton (uncredited)	
1931	1s. 6d.	1930	Lionel Tertis (credited)	Price of viola part, which was available separately
1938	10s. 6d. (price of 1947 printing)	1930	Frederick Riddle (uncredited)	Viola part inserted in existing piano reduction in 1938; new piano reduction published in 1947
1958	12s. 6d.	1930; 1958 renewed	Mixture of Walton's 1930 original with select changes from Tertis's and Riddle's editions (uncredited)	
1964	18s.	1930; 1958 renewed	William Walton (uncredited)	
2002		2002	Christopher Wellington (editor); based on Frederick Riddle's revision (credited)	

Chart 34.1 Walton, Concerto for Viola and Orchestra, six known viola parts that have been published by Oxford University Press.

original conception of the solo part. In preparing this edition, Wellington concluded that Riddle's edition from 1938 was preferred by the composer, and the WWE gives preference to that version. While Wellington admires the numerous changes that Riddle made, primarily to articulations and bowings, many violists do not. And while Wellington makes a plausible case for Walton's preference of Riddle's edition, the composer's continued willingness to allow violists to alter his original music argues against Riddle's version as "authoritative."

Sifting through the sources and making sense of the many changes that Walton made—or permitted to be made—was obviously a challenge in producing the WWE. While Wellington has done an admirable job, this edition is not without its problems. For example, Wellington writes that Riddle's version "remained the only version of the solo line available with the piano reduction until the appearance of the revised orchestration in 1962."[43] This ignores the 1958 edition, which

Example 34.7 Walton, Concerto for Viola and Orchestra, movt. II, mm. 53–55, solo viola, comparing Tertis's edition to Walton's original.

Example 34.8 Walton, Concerto for Viola and Orchestra, movt. II, mm. 90–94, solo viola, comparing Tertis's edition (this alteration also appears in Riddle's edition) to Walton's original.

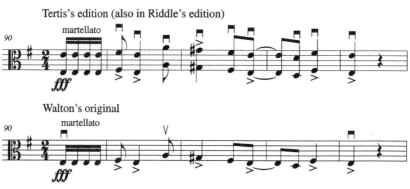

reverts in many places to Walton's original solo line (published in 1930) while retaining various changes that appeared in Tertis's and Riddle's editions.[44] There are also many instances where documentation is lacking in the WWE's Textual Notes. For example, there are more than two dozen spots with modifications in Tertis's edition (not counting changes of articulation), of which only seven are recorded in the Textual Notes.[45] Some of these changes are unique to Tertis's edition (Ex. 34.7), but many also appear in Riddle's edition (Ex. 34.8), indicating that Riddle adopted them from Tertis. There are also instances where Wellington's edition deviates from both the 1930 original solo line and Riddle's edition with no explanation.[46] Most significant among these instances is the well-known discrepancy that occurs in m. 155 of the first movement (Ex. 34.9). The trill in this measure is to an f♯ii in all of the early sources, including Riddle's edition, yet Wellington begins with a trill to an f♯ii, changing to an f♮ii, with no explanation

Example 34.9 Walton, Concerto for Viola and Orchestra, movt. I, mm. 155–56, solo viola, comparing Wellington's edition to Walton's original.

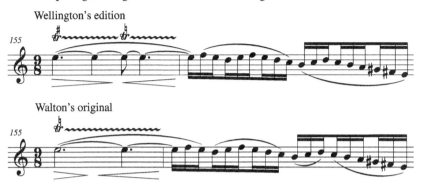

for the change. This specific change originates from the 1964 edition, when the trill was accidentally changed to an f♯ii throughout the entire measure in both the score and piano reduction. The viola scholar Donald Maurice wrote to OUP in 1972 asking for clarification. They consulted Walton, who indicated that he wanted the note to begin by trilling to an f♯ii and then to change to an f♮ii on the final eighth note of the second beat, at the point when the cellos play an f♮i.[47] So, Walton was still revising the work at such a late date. The publisher changed the trill to Walton's specifications in later printings of the score, and Wellington included this change in the WWE, providing no note.[48] The lack of a note creates the impression that this change was made by Riddle, when it originates from Walton, himself. Given the intense interest that violists have in this concerto (including the origins for the many changes to the viola line), it is disappointing to see such incomplete documentation.

The two other sources worth consulting are both piano reductions. In the 1964 edition (Plate No. O.U.P. 160), the solo viola line—through a rather fortunate accident—largely reverted to Walton's original version. This edition remains popular among violists and is useful for performers who prefer urtext editions (it is the closest to an urtext viola part that is easily available, either through libraries or on the second-hand market). Lastly, for performers who prefer Riddle's changes, the 2002 piano reduction, edited by Christopher Wellington from the WWE, would be the edition of choice.

Though Walton's concerto is in three movements, it is unusual in that the second movement is the fastest of the three (one of the similarities that it shares with Prokofiev's Violin Concerto No. 1). The first movement is in sonata form (Chart 34.2), opening with a short orchestral introduction from which the viola emerges with its *cantabile espressivo* theme with the pickup to m. 4 (measure numbers and rehearsal numbers apply to all of the OUP editions). Within these first few

Zone	Thematic Areas/Snippet	Measures	Principal Tonal Areas/Function
Exposition		1–45	
	Introduction	1–3	A minor
	Theme Group 1	4–33 (No. 4)	A minor
	Theme Group 2	33 (No. 4)–45	D minor; moves to a tonality centered on F-sharp
Development		46–142	
	Unit 1.1: Solo	46–69 (No. 8)	Modulatory
	Unit 1.2: Transition/Tutti	69 (No. 8)–81 (No. 9)	Modulatory; ends centered on B-flat
	Unit 1.3: Solo	81 (No. 9)–108	Begins centered on B major; modulates
	Unit 1.4: Tutti	108–42	Begins centered on F-sharp; modulates; ends on dominant function
Recapitulation		143 (No. 14)–65	
	Introduction: Solo	143 (No. 14)–49 (No. 15)	Dominant
	Theme Group 1	149 (No. 15)–58 (No. 16)	A minor
	Theme Group 2/Closing	158 (No. 16)–65	A minor

Chart 34.2 Walton, Concerto for Viola and Orchestra: Structural analysis, first movement, Andante comodo.

measures, Walton introduces the cross-relationship element that is integral to the entire concerto. The cross-relation in m. 4, where the solo viola's c^{ii} is pitted against a c♯ in the orchestra, establishes a conflict between A minor and A major that exists even in the final measures of the third movement.[49] In addition to the vertical cross-relations, there are also frequent horizontal cross-relations in the melodic line (see Ex. 34.4). At m. 11 (No. 1), the viola turns to accompanimental figures as Oboe I takes over the melody. The viola continues with its eighth-note figures until m. 19 (No. 2), when it resumes the melody. A dramatic bridge section featuring sixteenth notes and double stops (mm. 26–31) leads to the lyrical second theme group at m. 33 (No. 4). Walton contrasts this lyrical melody with a more animated figure at m. 46, which begins the development section.[50] After the orchestra's altered version of Theme Group 1 material at m. 52 (No. 6), virtuosic viola writing follows, culminating with energetic *martellato* multiple stops at m. 69 (No. 8). The viola plays a double-stopped version of Theme Group 2 material in sixths at m. 81 (No. 9), which is followed by a motive at m. 93 (No. 10) that reinforces the cross-relation concept with the viola's c♯^{ii}s set against the second violins' c♯^{i}s.[51] A majestic orchestral tutti (mm. 108–42) leads to a return of the introduction (mm. 143–49), now played by the viola in an extended version set over a tremolo E pedal. Walton continues to reverse roles from the opening, giving the viola murmuring sixteenth notes as an accompaniment to the orchestra's statement of Theme Group 1 material (mm. 149–58). The viola's accompanimental figurations give way to Theme Group 2 material at m. 158 (No. 16), which functions here as the closing section. Walton revisits material from mm. 30–31 in the final measures, once again emphasizing cross-relations with a mixture of C♮s and C♯s.

The second movement is a scherzo in E minor with a rather interesting form, which is typically described as either a rondo or a modified sonata form.[52] Built around three main themes, the movement has a substantial development section and strong return of the opening material at m. 216 (No. 33), tying it closely to sonata form, which is reflected in the following analysis (Chart 34.3). Regardless of how you analyze the movement, a major feature is the continual elongation (and elaboration) of each Theme A statement, giving an organic feel to the movement while demonstrating Walton's ingenuity at making the most of a small amount of material. The opening theme is built on a rising fourth in the viola (Theme A; Unit 1.1a). At m. 17, Theme A—starting from the second measure—is repeated a fifth higher in the viola, with a third appearance of the theme starting at m. 35 (No. 19) in the orchestra. Muted brass introduce a subsidiary theme at m. 60 (Theme B; Unit 1.2), punctuated by the viola's continuation of Theme A material (mm. 64–66) in a section that serves as a transition to Theme Group 2.[53] After introducing Theme Group 2 at m. 74 (Theme C; Unit 2.1), the viola revisits Theme B at m. 90, brilliantly fleet and jazzy in Walton's original version (see Ex. 34.8).[54] At m. 94, woodwinds echo the viola's Theme A punctuations from mm. 64–66, leading back to Theme A in the viola (m. 96), which serves as closing material for the exposition. After a bold tutti (mm. 127–41), the viola develops Theme A material from m. 142 through m. 174, giving way to another substantial orchestral tutti at m. 176. In this section, Walton inserts a stunning modulation: after three iterations of Theme C material using an A Locrian scale (mm. 203–8), he abruptly shifts to E minor at m. 209 (No. 32), with the orchestra then cascading downward in mm. 214–15 in preparation for the return of the opening at m. 216 (No. 33). For the viola's final statement of Theme A, Walton pulls out all the stops with harmonic double stops and whirlwind passages that climb into the viola's upper

Zone	Theme	Thematic Areas/Snippet	Measures	Principal Tonal Areas/Function
Exposition			1–126	
		Theme Group 1	1–73	
	Theme A	Unit 1.1a	1–17	E minor
	Theme A	Unit 1.1b	17–35 (No. 19)	B minor; moves to a tonality centered on F
	Theme A	Unit 1.1c Vln. 1 & 2	35 (No. 19) –60 (No. 21)	E minor; modulates
	Theme B	Unit 1.2 Tpt. 1	60 (No. 21) –73	A major
		Theme Group 2	74 (No. 22) –96	
	Theme C	Unit 2.1	74 (No. 22) –90 (No. 24)	Starts centered on F major; modulates
	Theme B	Unit 2.2: Transition	90 (No. 24) –96	E major
	Theme A	Closing (Theme Group 1 material)	96–126	E minor; modulates

Chart 34.3 Walton, Concerto for Viola and Orchestra: Structural analysis, second movement, Vivo, con molto preciso.

Zone	Theme	Thematic Areas/Snippet	Measures	Principal Tonal Areas/Function
Development			127 (No. 26) –216 (No. 33)	
	Theme C mixed with Theme B	Unit 1.1: Tutti introduction Vln. 1	127 (No. 26) –41	D major; B minor
	Theme A	Unit 1.2: Solo	141– 76 (No. 30)	Starts C-sharp⁷; modulates
	Theme C mixed with Theme B & Theme A material	Unit 1.3: Tutti	176 (No. 30) –216 (No. 33)	Starts F-sharp major; modulates
Recapitulation	Theme A	Theme Group 1	216 (No. 33) –61 (No. 36)	E minor; modulates; ends on dominant function
Closing			261 (No. 36) –73	
	Theme B	Unit 1.1 Cl. 1	261 (No. 36) –68	Starts E major; modulates
	Theme A	Unit 1.2	268–73	E major

Chart 34.3 (continued) Walton, Concerto for Viola and Orchestra: Structural analysis, second movement, Vivo, con molto preciso.

register. After the viola finishes its pyrotechnics in m. 261 (No. 36), the orchestra plays a modified version of Theme B. Here, the ascending scalar passage in m. 267 recalls m. 73 and suggests a return of Theme Group 2 material, but instead the viola playfully closes out the movement with fragments of Theme A.

With its intricately developed and interwoven themes, the final movement is a melodic and contrapuntal *tour de force*. Set in A major, it opens with a touch of the previous scherzo: a grotesque theme (Theme Group 1) in the bassoon, whose first three pitches (E–B–F♯, in rising fifths) are a retrograde version of the first three notes of the scherzo's Theme A (F♯–B–E, in rising fourths).[55] The viola enters with this first theme, a fifth higher, at m. 8, followed by a third statement of the theme in the orchestra at m. 21 (No. 38), yet another fifth higher, so that the first notes of these three statements (E–B–F♯) parallels the opening rising-fifth motive. A transitional theme featuring triplets (mm. 28–40) leads to the second theme group, starting with a lyrical melody played by the viola in sixths (mm. 41–49), which is followed by a motive that emphasizes wide intervals (mm. 49–58). Both ideas are similar in design to the first movement's Theme Group 2 material, creating a "point at which first and third movements come to grips."[56] At m. 58 (No. 42), a developmental section begins, during which Walton produces a heart-wrenching *cantabile* melody at m. 89 by augmenting earlier material (see mm. 59–60). After an orchestral tutti (mm. 105–20), the viola emerges with the transitional triplet theme, leading to a soaring descant statement set over Theme Group 2 material in the orchestra (mm. 125–29). At m. 130, the viola then takes up material from the second theme group. Starting around m. 144, the music gradually morphs into Theme Group 1 material. The solo viola attempts to assert Theme Group 2 again at m. 162 but is thwarted and returns to the first theme in earnest at m. 177 (No. 54), giving way to the orchestra for an expansive fugal tutti at m. 193. For the final coda (mm. 265–301), Walton combines material from the concerto's outer movements starting with a sublime return of the first movement's Theme Group 1 material in the viola, set over an ostinato built from the third movement's Theme Group 1 material in the orchestra. The cross-relations from the first movement return in the final measures, with the solo viola's c♯ in m. 301 set against the orchestra's C♮s.[57] Walton's biographer Michael Kennedy wrote that "this eloquent epilogue remains the single most beautiful and moving passage in all Walton's music, sensuous yet full of uncertainty, with additional poignancy added by the oboes. There is, underlying the music, a sense of frustrated longing as the predominant emotion. Whatever the hidden personal programme of the concerto, it was something Walton could never repeat."[58]

In reviewing the premiere performance of Walton's Concerto for Viola and Orchestra, Eric Blom wrote:

> Mr. Walton has style, form, invention, and, above all, simplicity. There is no nonsense, no pose about his music, but fancy in abundance. One thought this work of his in many ways comparable, if such comparisons serve any purpose, to that of Virginia Woolf in literature. Everything is lucidly and economically said with no studied oddity, yet with an effect that is unlike anything else ever achieved before.[59]

Stylish, daring, and profound, Walton's concerto brilliantly captured the essence of the postwar jazz age. It inspired a new generation of violists and composers, helping to usher in a golden age for the viola concerto as a genre. The work continues to impress critics and audiences, and it remains one of the most highly regarded compositions for the instrument.

35

Carl Maria von Weber: *Andante e Rondo ungarese for Viola and Orchestra,* J. 79

Andante
Allegretto ungarese

Date of Composition: Completed October 18, 1809

First Edition: Carl Maria von Weber, *Andante und Rondo ungarese für Viola und Orchester,* ed. Georg Schünemann, Mainz: B. Schott's Söhne, 1938, Plate No. B·S·S 35340, Edition Schott 3303 (Score); Plate No. B·S·S 35342, Edition Schott 2645 (Piano Reduction)

Dedication: Für Bruder Fritz [Fridolin Weber]

Date/Place of Early Public Performance: April 10, 1823, Franz Xaver Semler (viola), Berlin

Orchestral Instrumentation: Solo viola, 2 flutes, 2 oboes, 2 bassoons, 2 horns in C, 2 trumpets in C, timpani, strings

Introduction

"He soaked himself in German folk-songs as a young man, singing them to his own guitar accompaniment and allowing them to sink deep into his consciousness."[1] Considered one of the founders of the German Romantic school, Weber wielded considerable influence over the direction of Western classical music, particularly the genre of German opera through his landmark *Der Freischütz.* Based on a traditional German legend with mystical themes, *Der Freischütz* exemplifies Weber's fascination with folklore and the exotic. But this interest was not limited to Germanic sources, and Weber composed music in a variety of cultural styles, often incorporating traditional melodies, harmonies, and orchestral techniques to great effect.

Biographical Sketch

Carl Maria von Weber (1786–1826) was born into a musical family in Eutin, the son of composer and violinist Franz Anton Weber and his second wife, Genovefa. His early musical training was at the hands of his domineering father and older half-brothers; he subsequently studied with Michael Haydn in Salzburg, producing his first composition at the age of eleven.[2] In 1803, Weber traveled to Vienna, where he studied with Georg Joseph Vogler. Here, the teenaged Weber discovered that his beautiful singing voice and lithe frame caught the attention of women, and he wandered through the city, reveling in "wine, women, and song."[3] Vogler managed to secure his young protégé a conducting post at the theater in Breslau, located in Middle Silesia (now Wrocław, Poland). Weber resigned that post following an illness (he accidentally drank acid that was stored in a wine bottle) and afterward worked for Duke Eugen Friedrich Heinrich of Württemberg-Öls, in Carlsruhe, located in Upper Silesia.

Weber next served as private secretary to Duke Ludwig Friedrich Alexander of Württemberg in Stuttgart. Misfortunes plagued Weber in this post, and he was jailed for multiple offenses, most significantly for the misappropriation of the duke's funds, which were used to cover personal debts. Weber escaped severe punishment for the crime, but he and his father—who was also involved in the scheme—were escorted out of town on February 26, 1810, and permanently exiled from Württemberg.[4]

After a period of travel, Weber settled in Prague in 1813, where he took over as director of a struggling opera company at the Estates Theatre. Though he initially ran into resistance from the musicians, he managed to improve the standards of the orchestra and reorganize the theater system.[5] But Weber's personal life turned chaotic, as he began an affair with Therese Brunetti, the wife of a dancer in the theater.[6] A visiting singer, Caroline Brandt, next caught Weber's eye, and for a while he was torn between the two women. Brandt won out, but she proved highly temperamental, causing Weber much anguish. They became engaged in November 1816 —shortly after Weber left Prague—and married a year later. Work and relationship woes took their toll, and Weber suffered through numerous illnesses while in Prague, already showing early signs of tuberculosis.[7]

In early 1817, Weber arrived in Dresden, where he "had the mandate to create a royal company for German-language opera."[8] Troubles persisted, and Weber endured ill health, musical politics, and personal tragedy; his first child died in 1819, only a few months after her birth. But tragedy mixed with triumph, for it was during this period that he composed the seminal *Der Freischütz*. The opera premiered to immediate success in Berlin in 1821, catapulting him to fame. Continued illness greatly reduced his compositional output, but he managed to complete two more works that would cement his stature as a major opera composer: *Euryanthe* and *Oberon*. While in London for the premiere of *Oberon*, Weber died on June 5, 1826, at the age of thirty-nine.

Weber's *Andante e Rondo ungarese for Viola and Orchestra*, J. 79

Weber composed more than three hundred works covering the major genres, including two concertante works for viola: the *Sechs Variationen for Viola and Orchestra*, J. 49 (1806) and the *Andante e Rondo ungarese for Viola and Orchestra*, J. 79 (1809). The latter work was composed for his elder half-brother Fridolin "Fritz" Weber, who studied with Joseph Haydn and played viola in various orchestras, including the orchestra of the Hamburg Stadt-Theater from 1819 until his death in 1833.[9] In 1813, Weber prepared an arrangement for bassoon and orchestra (J. 158) at the request of Georg Friedrich Brandt, which was published around 1816 as opus 35. This version became widely known, and the work is still sometimes erroneously considered to be an original piece for bassoon. For many years the manuscript of the viola version was in the possession of Franz Xaver Semler, a prominent viola soloist in Berlin during the early part of the nineteenth century.[10] Semler performed the work on at least one occasion, in 1823.[11]

Completed when he was twenty-two, the *Andante e Rondo ungarese* is the earliest of Weber's works written in the *style hongrois*, a "specific musical language used by Western composers from the mid-eighteenth to the twentieth centuries to evoke the performances of Hungarian Gypsies."[12] The work begins with an Andante, in variation form (Chart 35.1; measure numbers and rehearsal numbers refer to the Schott edition with the two repeated sections, mm. 103–10 and

Zone	Thematic Areas/Snippet	Measures	Principal Tonal Areas/Function
Theme		1–21	C minor; G minor; C minor
Variation I		22–39	C minor; G minor; C minor
Variation II		40–55	A-flat major
Variation III		56 (No. 3)–78	C minor; G minor; C minor; moves to dominant

Chart 35.1 Weber, *Andante e Rondo ungarese for Viola and Orchestra*, J. 79: Structural analysis, Andante section.

mm. 199–206, each counted only once in the numbering). The Andante theme, played by the viola over pizzicato strings, is in sectional binary form, consisting of two eight-measure periods, with the second period starting in G minor. Weber appends a four-measure orchestral tag to this initial thematic statement. For the first variation (mm. 22–39), the first violins restate the theme while the viola plays sixteenth-note accompanimental material, and the orchestral tag is shortened to two measures. In the second variation (mm. 40–55), the viola presents an altered version of the theme, now in A♭ major and in a rounded binary form. Dispensing with the orchestral tag, Weber launches directly into the third variation in m. 56 (No. 3).[13] The orchestra restates the theme while the viola vigorously leaps around the fingerboard with a barrage of thirty-second notes. At the end of this variation, the orchestral tag reappears, now extended to six measures (mm. 72–77). But the viola obliviously carries on with its thirty-second notes, finally cluing in that it has intruded into the orchestra's territory and apologetically uttering the tag material in mm. 77–78 before moving into the rondo.[14]

The distinctive Hungarian style of the rondo portion is termed *verbunkos*, a traditional "dance music originally used for recruiting."[15] Duple meter, dotted rhythms, and extensive ornamentation (including grace notes, trills, and chromatic runs) are standard characteristics of the *verbunkos* style.[16] These, and other rhythmic, melodic, harmonic, and accompanimental features relating to *verbunkos* style, appear throughout the rondo.

Weber is known to have incorporated existing folk materials into his works; the opera *Euryanthe* uses Turkish and Egyptian melodies that he found in the Royal Library in Dresden.[17] The primary rondo refrain of the *Andante e Rondo ungarese* (Ex. 35.1) bears similarities to several early sources, including a tune that appears in German song books—identified as Hungarian in origin—to the words *Die Hussiten zogen vor Naumberg* (Ex. 35.2),[18] as well as a tune appearing

Example 35.1 Weber, *Andante e Rondo ungarese for Viola and Orchestra*, J. 79, rondo refrain, mm. 79–90, solo viola.

Example 35.2 *Die Hussiten zogen vor Naumberg*, mm. 1–6 (melody only).

Example 35.3 *Tańcowała ryba z rakiem*, mm. 1–6 (melody only).

Example 35.4 Weber, *Grande polonaise*, J. 59, mm. 21–24.

in Silesian/Polish sources (Ex. 35.3) to the words *Tańcowała ryba z rakiem*.[19] In considering a possible Silesian connection, it is worth noting that the dotted rhythms in the rondo refrain are similar to material in the *Alla Polacca* section of Weber's *Grande polonaise*, J. 59 (Ex. 35.4), written in 1808. Such dotted rhythms are frequently identified with Hungarian music, but not exclusively so, and intermingling of styles has been common across cultures. And Weber did not always delineate specific national styles when incorporating exotic elements into his music.[20] Regardless of the exact sources and influences of the rondo, it demonstrates a "thorough knowledge of the verbunkos style since the Hungarian influence is demonstrable with consistency . . . almost to the end."[21]

From a formal perspective, Weber's rondos have widely diverse structures, with some critics finding fault with his form.[22] Here, the *rondo ungarese* generally follows a typical rondo form, though it still diverges from the norm (Chart 35.2), with the

Zone	Thematic Areas/Snippet	Measures	Principal Tonal Areas/Function
A		79–134	
	Unit 1.1	79–102	C major; E minor; C major; E minor
	Unit 1.2	103–10 (repeated)	C major
	Unit 1.3	111 (No. 4)–18	A minor
	Transition (Unit 1.1 material)	119–34	C major
B		135 (No. 5)–70	C major; G major
A		171–90	
	Unit 1.1	171–82	C major; E minor
	Unit 1.2: Tutti	183–90	C major
C		191–261	
	Unit 1.1	191–252	F major; modulates
	Retransition (Section A Unit 1.1 material)	252–61	Starts E-flat major; moves to dominant
A		262–80	C major; F minor; C major
Coda		281–319	C major

Chart 35.2 Weber, *Andante e Rondo ungarese for Viola and Orchestra*, J. 79: Structural analysis, Allegretto ungarese section.

formal construction primarily serving as a means for Weber to introduce *verbunkos* elements rather than conforming to standard melodic or key relationships. This is evident from the opening rondo refrain (see Ex. 35.1), which begins in C major but ends in E minor. Such a shift would be peculiar in most Classical rondos, but here it "enhances the Hungarian flavour."[23] Adding to the formal complexity, Weber blurs the lines between starting and ending points of sections. This is especially true of the opening A section (mm. 79–134): After the orchestra restates the rondo refrain (mm. 91–102), it sounds as if m. 103 (Unit 1.2) will start the first episode, a notion reinforced with the reappearance of the refrain in m. 119. But as this refrain statement changes, the listener realizes that the rondo is only now transitioning to the true start of the first episode in m. 135 (No. 5).

The viola's *cantabile* melody at m. 135 provides a change in mood. Though the first episode (mm. 135–70) begins in the tonic, it settles into the more customary dominant key (G major) at m. 142. Weber once again blurs the line between sections at m. 167 (No. 6) as the principal flute and principal oboe anticipate the refrain, playing the beginning of the theme in C minor before the viola takes over the proper return in m. 171. Weber toys with us again in this section by including the Unit 1.2 material from the first A section as an orchestral tutti (mm. 183–90), leaving us to wonder if we will hear the A section repeated in its entirety. Instead, he abruptly shifts to the second episode in m. 191.

The second episode begins in the subdominant (F major) and is developmental in nature, two common characteristics at this point in a rondo. Further *verbunkos* attributes appear in this episode, including "rhythmic differentiation, pointed dancing gestures," and "sweeping melodic writing."[24] As the viola climaxes with its highest note of the piece in m. 252 ($e\flat^{iii}$), the orchestra once again presents the refrain material, but it is clear that we are merely retransitioning to the next appearance of the A section at m. 262. After the viola presents the full refrain (mm. 262–73), Weber cuts short the orchestral restatement (mm. 274–80), forgoing the E minor portion and settling for a quick G^7 chord resolving to C major at the start of the coda in m. 281. Snippets of earlier motives appear in the coda while the viola raucously plays virtuosic arpeggios to close out the piece with a flourish.

Much of the literature devoted to the *Andante e Rondo ungarese* focuses on the bassoon version, with critics remarking about Weber's capable writing for that instrument. Though Weber did make many changes when adapting the work for bassoon, such critical attention to that version obscures the effectiveness of his original concept. A primary concern for Weber in his instrumental music "was to maximize the technical, sonic, and expressive potential of the forces."[25] The viola version showcases Weber's skill in this respect, with highly idiomatic and bravura solo writing for the viola. It is also masterfully and sympathetically orchestrated; the sparse orchestration in the Andante section's first variation (consisting of the solo viola and the first and second violins only) is a particularly brilliant example. String instruments (including violas) were popular for Hungarian dancing occasions and feasts,[26] making his original choice of solo instrument (versus the bassoon) apt. Though the viola version has lagged behind the bassoon version in terms of popularity (owing to its belated publication in 1938), it has earned its rightful place as a standard of the repertoire.

Notes

Chapter 1

1. Malcolm Boyd, *Bach: The Brandenburg Concertos* (Cambridge: Cambridge University Press, 1993), vii.
2. Corinne Ramey, "Bach's Baroque Gem Offers (Grateful) Violists the Spotlight," *Strings* 27, no. 6 (January 2013): 29.
3. Michael Talbot, "Purpose and Peculiarities of the *Brandenburg Concertos*," in *Bach und die Stile: Bericht über das 2. Dortmunder Bach-Symposion 1998*, ed. Martin Geck and Klaus Hofmann (Dortmund, Germany: Klangfarben Musikverlag, 1999), 267.
4. Talbot, "Purpose and Peculiarities," 267.
5. David Ledbetter, "Instrumental Chamber and Ensemble Music," in *The Routledge Research Companion to Johann Sebastian Bach*, ed. Robin A. Leaver (London: Routledge, 2017), 344–45.
6. Peter Williams, *Bach: A Musical Biography* (Cambridge: Cambridge University Press, 2016), 222.
7. Williams, *Bach: A Musical Biography*, 224. For examples of other works that forgo violins and employ the instrumentation of pairs of violas and gambas, see Ares Rolf, *J. S. Bach: Das sechste Brandenburgische Konzert; Besetzung, Analyse, Entstehung* (Dortmund, Germany: Klangfarben Musikverlag, 2002), 27–31, 145–68.
8. For more on the idea that the concerto may have been borrowed from an earlier trio sonata, see Martin Geck, "Gattungstraditionen und Altersschichten in den Brandenburgischen Konzerten," *Die Musikforschung* 23, no. 2 (April/June 1970): 147–48.
9. See, in particular, Michael Marissen, *The Social and Religious Designs of J. S. Bach's Brandenburg Concertos* (Princeton, NJ: Princeton University Press, 1995), 35–62; and Peter Schleuning, "Bachs sechstes *Brandenburgisches Konzert*—eine Pastorale," in *Bachs Orchesterwerke: Bericht über das 1. Dortmunder Bach-Symposion 1996*, ed. Martin Geck and Werner Breig (Witten, Germany: Klangfarben Musikverlag, 1997), 203–21.
10. Boyd, *Bach: The Brandenburg Concertos*, 96.
11. "List of Musicians: Johann Ambrosius Bach (11)," in *The New Grove Bach Family*, by Christoph Wolff et al. (New York: W. W. Norton, 1983), 8.
12. "Johann Sebastian Bach (24)," in *New Grove Bach Family*, 46.
13. [Carl Philipp Emanuel Bach and Johann Friedrich Agricola], "Denkmal dreyer verstorbenen Mitglieder [. . .] Johann Sebastian Bach [. . .]," *Musikalische Bibliothek* 4, no. 1 (1754): 160; translation from *The Bach Reader: A Life of Johann Sebastian Bach in Letters and Documents*, ed. Hans T. David and Arthur Mendel (New York: W. W. Norton, 1945), 216. This important obituary of J. S. Bach is often referred to as the Nekrolog.

14. Christoph Wolff, *Johann Sebastian Bach: The Learned Musician* (New York: W. W. Norton, 2000), 53–68.

15. Wolff, *Bach: The Learned Musician*, 119; and "Bach (24)," in *New Grove Bach Family*, 59.

16. "Bach Receives His Dismissal: Excerpt from the Court Secretary's Reports," in *Bach Reader*, 75.

17. Wolff, *Bach: The Learned Musician*, 192. Bach seems to have enjoyed a good relationship with his new employer; Prince Leopold was named godfather to Bach's short-lived son Leopold Augustus, who was baptized on November 17, 1718; see ibid., 199.

18. "Bach (24)," in *New Grove Bach Family*, 82.

19. "Bach (24)," in *New Grove Bach Family*, 93.

20. "Bach (24)," in *New Grove Bach Family*, 113. Christoph Wolff indicates that the stroke occurred on July 20; see *Bach: The Learned Musician*, 449.

21. "Letters from C. P. E. Bach to [Johann Nicolaus] Forkel: On Bach's Personal and Artistic Traits," in *Bach Reader*, 277.

22. J. S. Bach, *Konzert Es-Dur für Viola, Streicher und Basso continuo: Rekonstruktion nach BWV 169, 49, 1053* (Kassel: Bärenreiter, 1996). For more information about this concerto, its reconstruction, and the selection of instrument, see Wilfried Fischer, "Hat Bach ein Bratschenkonzert geschrieben? Neue Überlegungen zur Vorlage von BMV [*sic*] 1053, 169 und 49," in *Dortmunder Bach-Symposion 1996*, 249–56. Several violists have since made their own reconstructions of the work (often favoring the key of D major instead of E♭ major); for more details, see Elias Goldstein, "'J. S. Bach Viola Concerto in E Flat Major': A Reconstruction of BWV 169, 49, and 1053; Merits and Shortcomings" (DMA diss., University of Wisconsin–Madison, 2011).

23. Boyd, *Bach: The Brandenburg Concertos*, 5.

24. Heinrich Besseler, "Zur Chronologie der Konzerte Joh. Seb. Bachs," in *Festschrift Max Schneider: Zum achtzigsten Geburtstage*, ed. Walther Vetter (Leipzig: Deutscher Verlag für Musik, 1955), 118–19.

25. Erik Smith, liner notes to *Six "Brandenburg Concertos,"* by Johann Sebastian Bach, with Academy of St. Martin-in-the-Fields, Neville Marriner (director), Philips 6880 004–005, 33-1/3 rpm. In these liner notes, Smith references notes that Dart had prepared for a BBC broadcast on February 22, 1971, of concertos nos. 3, 4, and 6.

26. Boyd, *Bach: The Brandenburg Concertos*, 15.

27. Boyd, *Bach: The Brandenburg Concertos*.

28. See, for example, Ruth Tatlow, *Bach's Numbers: Compositional Proportion and Significance* (Cambridge: Cambridge University Press, 2015), 266–74.

29. S. W. Dehn, preface to *Sixième Concerto pour deux Altos, deux Violes da gamba, avec Violoncelle et Basse*, by Jean Sebastien Bach, ed. S. W. Dehn (Leipzig: Au Bureau de Musique de C. F. Peters, [1852]), 3; translation from Felix Borowski, program note to *Concerto No. 6, B Flat Major*, by Johann Sebastian Bach, Chicago Symphony Orchestra, Thirty-Second Season, Sixteenth Program, January 26 and 27, 1923, 7.

30. Boyd, *Bach: The Brandenburg Concertos*, 22.

31. Pippa Drummond, *The German Concerto: Five Eighteenth-Century Studies* (Oxford: Clarendon Press, 1980), 52–53.

32. Various analyses may differ as to the exact starting and ending points of some episodes; see, for example, Rolf, *Das sechste Brandenburgische Konzert*, 43; *Bachs Orchestermusik: Entstehung, Klangwelt, Interpretation; Ein Handbuch*, ed. Siegbert Rampe and Dominik Sackmann (Kassel: Bärenreiter, 2000), 222; and Boyd, *Bach: The Brandenburg Concertos*, 93.

33. Rolf, *Das sechste Brandenburgische Konzert*, 47–48; translation by Edward Klorman.

34. Rudolf Kloiber describes this as a fugue; see *Handbuch des Instrumentalkonzerts*, vol. 1, *Vom Barock bis zur Klassik* (Wiesbaden: Breitkopf & Härtel, 1972), 55; Ares Rolf describes it as resembling a passacaglia; see *Das sechste Brandenburgische Konzert*, 73; and Peter Schleuning describes it as a chaconne; see "*Brandenburgisches Konzert*—eine Pastorale," 212–15.

35. From a historical perspective, the terms "chaconne" and "passacaglia" have proved problematic. Nineteenth-century composers took the ostinato bass line in Bach's Passacaglia for organ to be a "defining feature" of that genre, and though "some writers attempted to define a distinction between the passacaglia and the chaconne based primarily on the examples by Bach . . . no consensus was ever reached and for the most part the terms continued to be used interchangeably." *Grove Music Online*, s.v. "Passacaglia," by Alexander Silbiger, accessed April 12, 2019, https://doi.org/10.1093/gmo/9781561592630.article.21024; and "Chaconne," by Alexander Silbiger, accessed April 12, 2019, https://doi.org/10.1093/gmo/9781561592630.article.05354.

36. Drummond, *German Concerto*, 66.

37. Boyd, *Bach: The Brandenburg Concertos*, 96.

38. My analysis here corresponds with that in *Bachs Orchestermusik: Ein Handbuch*, 222. For other perspectives, see Rolf, *Das sechste Brandenburgische Konzert*, 96; and Gregory G. Butler, "J. S. Bach's Reception of Tomaso Albinoni's Mature Concertos," in *Bach Studies 2*, ed. Daniel R. Melamed (Cambridge: Cambridge University Press, 1995), 25.

39. Drummond, *German Concerto*, 58.

40. David Yearsley, "The Concerto in Northern Europe to c. 1770," in *The Cambridge Companion to the Concerto*, ed. Simon P. Keefe (Cambridge: Cambridge University Press, 2005), 58–59.

Chapter 2

1. Peter Laki, "Violin Works and the Viola Concerto," in *The Cambridge Companion to Bartók*, ed. Amanda Bayley (Cambridge: Cambridge University Press, 2001), 148.

2. Donald Maurice, Csaba Erdélyi, and Peter Bartók (in conjunction with Nelson Dellamaggiore) have all made attempts; see Donald Maurice, *Bartók's Viola Concerto: The Remarkable Story of His Swansong* (Oxford: Oxford University Press, 2004), chap. 6. Maurice also references contributions by Atar Arad, who "did not produce a substantive revision" but "was most likely the first violist to make significant departures from the Serly version in public performances." Ibid., 99.

3. Maurice, *Bartók's Viola Concerto*, 33–34.

4. Paul Griffiths, *Bartók* (London: J. M. Dent & Sons, 1984), 2.

5. David Cooper, *Béla Bartók* (New Haven, CT: Yale University Press, 2015), 10.

6. *Grove Music Online*, s.v. "Bartók, Béla," by Malcolm Gillies, accessed April 13, 2019, https://doi.org/10.1093/gmo/9781561592630.article.40686.

7. Paul Griffiths notes that "by 1918 he had collected something in the region of 2,700 Hungarian, 2,500 Slovak and 3,500 Romanian melodies." *Bartók*, 26.

8. *Grove Music Online*, s.v. "Bartók, Béla."

9. *Grove Music Online*, s.v. "Bartók, Béla."

10. *Grove Music Online*, s.v. "Bartók, Béla."

11. Béla Bartók Jr., "Béla Bartók's Diseases," *Studia Musicologica Academiae Scientiarum Hungaricae* 23, nos. 1–4 (1981): 438–40; and Cooper, *Béla Bartók*, 372–73.

12. Ernő Lendvai, *Béla Bartók: An Analysis of His Music*, rev. reprint ed. (London: Kahn & Averill, 1979), 96.

13. Béla Bartók, *Viola Concerto: Facsimile Edition of the Autograph Draft* (Homosassa, FL: Bartók Records, 1995).

14. Maurice, *Bartók's Viola Concerto*.

15. Primrose to Bartók, Ellensburg, WA, January 22, 1945. The text of the full letter may be found in László Somfai, commentary to *Viola Concerto: Autograph Draft*, 24; a facsimile of the letter may be found in Maurice, *Bartók's Viola Concerto*, 12–13. Hans Heinsheimer was a representative of Boosey & Hawkes, Bartók's publisher.

16. Bartók to Primrose, Saranac Lake, NY, August 5, 1945. The text of the full letter may be found in Somfai, commentary to *Viola Concerto: Autograph Draft*, 24–25; a facsimile of the letter may be found in Maurice, *Bartók's Viola Concerto*, 15.

17. Bartók to Primrose, New York, September 8, 1945. The text of the full letter may be found in Somfai, commentary to *Viola Concerto: Autograph Draft*, 25; a facsimile of the letter may be found in Maurice, *Bartók's Viola Concerto*, 17–19.

18. Tibor Serly to Victor Bator, New York, December 19, 1947. A facsimile of the complete letter may be found in Maurice, *Bartók's Viola Concerto*, 161.

19. For more details, see Maurice, *Bartók's Viola Concerto*, chap. 3.

20. "Bartók's Finale," *Newsweek* 34, no. 24 (December 12, 1949): 80.

21. Halsey Stevens, *The Life and Music of Béla Bartók* (New York: Oxford University Press, 1953), 253–54.

22. Tibor Serly, "A Belated Account of the Reconstruction of a 20th Century Masterpiece," *College Music Symposium* 15 (Spring 1975): 7–25.

23. Peter Bartók, "Correcting Printed Editions of Béla Bartók's Viola Concerto and Other Compositions," in *Bartók Perspectives: Man, Composer, and Ethnomusicologist*, ed. Elliott Antokoletz, Victoria Fischer, and Benjamin Suchoff (Oxford: Oxford University Press, 2000), 249–50.

24. "Panel Discussion: The Bartók Viola Concerto; From the 1997 International Viola Congress in Austin, Texas," *Journal of the American Viola Society* 14, no. 1 (1998): 28. The author was fortunate to have attended this lively panel discussion.

25. Csaba Erdélyi (viola), *Viola Concerto (The Erdélyi Restoration and Orchestration 2001)*, by Béla Bartók and *Harold en Italie*, by Hector Berlioz, with the New Zealand Symphony Orchestra, Marc Taddei (conductor), Concordance CCD03, 2002, compact disc.

26. Csaba Erdélyi, foreword to *Viola Concerto*, by Béla Bartók, critical restoration and orchestration by Csaba Erdélyi (Wellington, NZ: Promethean Editions, 2004), iv.

27. Although Donald Maurice's completion dates from the late twentieth century, it remains unpublished as of 2019; see Maurice, *Bartók's Viola Concerto*, chap. 6. The author was fortunate to attend Maurice's June 27, 1993, lecture ("New Light on the Bartók Concerto") at the Twenty-First International Viola Congress in Evanston, IL, and he found certain of Maurice's solutions compelling (including the omission of the Lento parlando material).

28. Stephanie Ames Asbell, "Béla Bartók's *Viola Concerto*: A Detailed Analysis and Discussion of Published Versions" (DMA treatise, University of Texas at Austin, 2001).

29. Cooper, *Béla Bartók*, 371.

30. Asbell, "Bartók's *Viola Concerto*: A Detailed Analysis," 33.

31. Maurice, *Bartók's Viola Concerto*, 89.

32. Asbell, "Bartók's *Viola Concerto*: A Detailed Analysis," 59.

33. Bartók to Primrose, Saranac Lake, NY, August 5, 1945; see Somfai, commentary to *Viola Concerto: Autograph Draft*, 25; and Maurice, *Bartók's Viola Concerto*, 15. In this letter, Bartók described the four movements as "a serious Allegro, a Scherzo, a (rather short) slow movement, and a finale beginning Allegretto and developping [*sic*] the tempo to an Allegro molto." Peter Bartók notes: "It seems that my father, some time after having set down the beginning of the four movements, abandoned the idea of the Scherzo in second place and designed a bridge that attached it to the ritornello following the slow movement. The Scherzo and Finale thus become, together, the last movement." Peter Bartók, "Correcting Printed Editions," 253.

34. The revised edition by Dellamaggiore and Bartók and the restoration by Erdélyi both, indeed, label this section as "Ritornello."

35. This approach follows that of Ames Asbell; see "Bartók's *Viola Concerto*: A Detailed Analysis," 44; and Mosco Carner, "Béla Bartók (1881–1945)," in *The Concerto*, ed. Ralph Hill (Westport, CT: Greenwood, 1978), 355. The movement has an overarching ABA form, which is how Donald Maurice presents it; see *Bartók's Viola Concerto*, 88, 93. Elliott Antokoletz views this as an ABCBA form; see "Pitch Organization in the Finale of Bartók's Viola Concerto," in *Bartók's Viola Concerto*, by Donald Maurice, 134; and "Bartók's Viola Concerto Manuscript: Some Questions and Speculations," *Studia Musicologica* 53, nos. 1–3 (2012): 83.

36. Cooper, *Béla Bartók*, 371.

37. "Panel Discussion: The Bartók Viola Concerto," 46.

Chapter 3

1. Spelling as it appears in the manuscript and first published edition; frequently spelled "Abruzzes" in other sources.

2. Thomas Austenfeld, " 'But, Come, I'll Set Your Story to a Tune': Berlioz's Interpretation of Byron's *Childe Harold*," *Keats-Shelley Journal* 39 (1990): 84.

3. Hector Berlioz, "*Symphonie fantastique*: The Symphony's Programme (1845 and 1855 versions)," trans. Michel Austin, The Hector Berlioz Website, accessed September 24, 2018, http://www.hberlioz.com/Scores/fantas.htm.

4. David Cairns, *Berlioz*, [vol. 1], *1803–1832: The Making of an Artist* (London: André Deutsch, 1989), 80–84.

5. *Autobiography of Hector Berlioz, Member of the Institute of France: From 1803 to 1865, Comprising His Travels in Italy, Germany, Russia, and England*, trans. Rachel Scott Russell Holmes and Eleanor Holmes (London: Macmillan, 1884), 1:14–15.

6. Cairns, *Making of an Artist*, 94.

7. Peter Bloom, *The Life of Berlioz* (Cambridge: Cambridge University Press, 1998), 13.

8. Peter Raby, "Smithson, Harriet ('Henriette') Constance," in *The Cambridge Berlioz Encyclopedia*, ed. Julian Rushton (Cambridge: Cambridge University Press, 2018), 310.

9. The Prix de Rome, initially awarded to painters and sculptors, was established in 1663 and discontinued in 1968. The conditions for the music prize, which was added in 1803, have changed over time; the details here are largely taken from Rainer Schmusch, "Prix de Rome (1)," trans. Louisa Tsougaraki, in *Berlioz Encyclopedia*, 262–63.

10. *The Memoirs of Hector Berlioz*, trans. and ed. David Cairns (New York: Alfred A. Knopf, 2002), 154. Berlioz was excused from the required stay in Germany and Austria altogether.

11. Hugh Macdonald, *Berlioz* (London: J. M. Dent & Sons, 1982), 31.

12. *Autobiography of Hector Berlioz*, 1:282.

13. D. Kern Holoman, "Conducting (1). Berlioz Conducting His Own Works," in *Berlioz Encyclopedia*, 79.

14. Catherine Massip, "Bibliothèque du Conservatoire," in *Berlioz Encyclopedia*, 55.

15. Peter Bloom, "Recio [Récio], Marie," in *Berlioz Encyclopedia*, 272.

16. *Grove Music Online*, s.v. "Berlioz, (Louis-)Hector," by Hugh Macdonald, accessed September 3, 2018, https://doi.org/10.1093/gmo/9781561592630.article.51424.

17. *Grove Music Online*, s.v. "Idée fixe," by Hugh Macdonald, accessed September 27, 2018, https://doi.org/10.1093/gmo/9781561592630.article.13701.

18. *Grove Music Online*, s.v. "Berlioz, (Louis-)Hector."

19. *Autobiography of Hector Berlioz*, 1:279.

20. "Nouvelles," *Gazette musicale de Paris* 1, no. 4 (January 26, 1834): 34; translation by Deborah Harter. For additional sources that published this announcement, see Paul Banks and Hugh Macdonald, foreword to *New Edition of the Complete Works*, vol. 17, *Harold en Italie*, by Hector Berlioz, ed. Paul Banks and Hugh Macdonald (Kassel: Bärenreiter, 2001), viiin4.

21. Berlioz to Joseph d'Ortigue, Paris, January 24, 1834, in *Correspondance générale*, ed. Pierre Citron, vol. 2, *1832–1842*, ed. Frédéric Robert (Paris: Flammarion, 1975), no. 378, 159; translation by Deborah Harter.

22. Paganini to Luigi Germi, London, October 29, 1833, in Arturo Codignola, *Paganini intimo* (Genoa: Edito a Cura del Municipio, 1935), 390; translation from G. I. C. de Courcy, *Paganini: The Genoese* (New York: Da Capo, 1977), 2:134.

23. "Signor Paganini Gave a Concert Last Night at the Hanover-Square Rooms," *Times* (London), April 29, 1834.

24. Berlioz to Nanci Pal, Rome, February 23, 1832, in *Correspondance générale*, vol. 1, *1803–1832*, ed. Pierre Citron (Paris: Flammarion, 1972), no. 263, 534. The two opera projects were *Richard en Palestine* (based on Scott's *The Talisman*) and *Robin Hood*.

25. Walter Scott, *The Abbot*, ed. Christopher Johnson (Edinburgh: Edinburgh University Press, 2000), 187.

26. Scott, *The Abbot*, 74.

27. Oliver Vogel, "*Harold en Italie*," trans. Gillian Andrews, in *Berlioz Encyclopedia*, 157.

28. *Autobiography of Hector Berlioz*, 1:279–80.

29. Berlioz to Humbert Ferrand, Paris, March 19, 1834, in *Correspondance générale*, vol. 2, no. 384, 164; translation by Deborah Harter.

30. Berlioz to Adèle Berlioz, Paris, March 20, 1834, in *Correspondance générale*, vol. 2, no. 385, 166; translation by Paul Engle.

31. Berlioz to Adèle Berlioz, Montmartre, April 29, 1834, in *Correspondance générale*, vol. 2, no. 394, 176; translation by Paul Engle.

32. Berlioz to Humbert Ferrand, Montmartre, May 15 or 16, 1834, in *Correspondance générale*, vol. 2, no. 398, 185; translation by Paul Engle.

33. Berlioz to Joseph d'Ortigue, Montmartre, May 31, 1834, in *Correspondance générale*, vol. 2, no. 399, 185; translation by Paul Engle.

34. Berlioz to Édouard Rocher, Montmartre, July 31, 1834, in *Correspondance générale*, vol. 2, no. 401, 188; translation by Edward Klorman.

35. Early manuscript sources also refer to this as *Harold* or *Harold* Symphonie; see, for example, the autograph cello part reproduced in Berlioz, *New Edition of the Complete Works*, vol. 17, *Harold en Italie*, 211.

36. Berlioz to Humbert Ferrand, Montmartre, August 31, 1834, in *Correspondance générale*, vol. 2, no. 408, 196; translation by Paul Engle.

37. Banks and Macdonald, foreword to *Harold en Italie*, ix.

38. D. Kern Holoman, *Berlioz* (Cambridge, MA: Harvard University Press, 1989), 164.

39. "Second concert de M. Berlioz," *Gazette musicale de Paris* 1, no. 49 (December 7, 1834): 394; translation by Paul Engle.

40. *Autobiography of Hector Berlioz*, 1:314.

41. H. Berlioz, "Concert de M. Berlioz au Théatre-Italien," *Revue et Gazette musicale de Paris* 11, no. 19 (May 12, 1844): 168; translation by Paul Engle.

42. *Memoirs of Hector Berlioz*, 289. On this occasion, Berlioz found the orchestra weak in violins, and as the trombones were "manifestly unequal" to the final movement, he only programmed the first three movements. Ibid., 288–89.

43. H. Earle Johnson, *Symphony Hall, Boston* (Boston: Little, Brown, 1950), 320.

44. "Classical Records . . . for Week Ending January 10," *Billboard* (January 17, 1953): 50.

45. Liszt to Berlioz, Milan, c. December 8–10, 1837, in *Correspondance générale*, vol. 2, no. 525, 387–88; translation by Paul Engle.

46. "Vermischtes: Literarische Notizen," *Neue Zeitschrift für Musik* 8, no. 19 (March 6, 1838): 76.

47. Berlioz to Liszt, Paris, July 3 or 4, 1852, in Hector Berlioz, *Correspondance générale*, ed. Pierre Citron, vol. 4, *1851–1855*, ed. Pierre Citron, Yves Gérard, and Hugh

J. Macdonald (Paris: Flammarion, 1983), no. 1501, 183–84; translation from Adrienne Kaczmarczyk and Eszter Mikusi, preface to *Neue Ausgabe sämtlicher Werke*, supplement no. 9, *Harold en Italie (Berlioz) und andere Werke*, by Franz Liszt, ed. Adrienne Kaczmarczyk and Eszter Mikusi, trans. Lorna Dunbar (Budapest: Editio Musica Budapest, 2009), xxxiii.

48. For additional details about the specific changes, see Kaczmarczyk and Mikusi, preface to *Harold en Italie*, xxxiv.

49. Hugh Macdonald, foreword to *Harold en Italie: Symphonie en 4 parties avec un alto principal*, by [Hector] Berlioz, piano reduction by Hugh Macdonald (Kassel: Bärenreiter, 2001), iii.

50. Holoman, *Berlioz*, 243–45.

51. *Grove Music Online*, s.v. "Berlioz, (Louis-)Hector."

52. Julian Rushton, *The Musical Language of Berlioz* (Cambridge: Cambridge University Press, 1983), 196.

53. Rushton, *Musical Language of Berlioz*, 197; and Hermann Danuser, "Symphonisches Subjekt und Form in Berlioz' Harold en Italie," *Melos/NZ* 3, no. 3 (May/June 1977): 205–7. In his analysis, Danuser numbers the second ending as 197 rather than 192.

54. Donald Francis Tovey, "Berlioz: 'Harold in Italy,' Symphony with Viola Obbligato, op. 16," in *Essays in Musical Analysis*, vol. 4, *Illustrative Music* (London: Oxford University Press, 1948), 76.

55. David Aaron Carpenter (viola), Overture to *Béatrice et Bénédict*, op. 27 and *Harold in Italy*, op. 16, by Hector Berlioz and *Sonata per la Gran Viola e Orchestra*, op. 35, by Nicolò Paganini, with Vladimir Ashkenazy (conductor) and the Helsinki Philharmonic Orchestra, Ondine ODE 1188-2, 2011, compact disc. This material can be found in Berlioz, *New Edition of the Complete Works*, vol. 17, *Harold en Italie*, 219–20 and as an *ossia* on pp. 2–3 of the solo viola part in Bärenreiter's piano reduction.

56. *Memoirs of Hector Berlioz*, 216.

57. *Memoirs of Hector Berlioz*, 155–57.

58. Jeffrey Langford, "The Symphonies," in *The Cambridge Companion to Berlioz*, ed. Peter Bloom (Cambridge: Cambridge University Press, 2000), 58–59.

59. Julian Rushton, *The Music of Berlioz* (Oxford: Oxford University Press, 2001), 36–37; and Edward T. Cone, "Inside the Saint's Head: The Music of Berlioz," in *Music: A View from Delft; Selected Essays*, ed. Robert P. Morgan (Chicago: University of Chicago Press, 1989), 240.

60. *Autobiography of Hector Berlioz*, 1:220–21.

61. *Autobiography of Hector Berlioz*, 1:206–7.

62. Langford, "The Symphonies," 59.

63. Langford, "The Symphonies," 59–60.

64. *Autobiography of Hector Berlioz*, 1:234–35.

65. *Autobiography of Hector Berlioz*, 2:81.

66. Donald McInnes, "Berlioz's Harold in Italy," *Strad* 123, no. 1469 (September 2012): 84.

Chapter 4

1. Olin Downes, "Ernest Bloch, the Swiss Composer, on the Influence of Race in Composition," *Musical Observer* 15, no. 3 (March 1917): 11.

2. David Z. Kushner, *The Ernest Bloch Companion* (Westport, CT: Greenwood, 2002), 4.

3. Alexander Knapp, "Ernest Bloch's *Suite Hébraïque* and *Meditation and Processional*: Historical Overview and Analysis of Traditional Musical Materials," *Journal of the American Viola Society* 33, no. 2 (Fall 2017): 19.

4. Alexander Knapp, "From Geneva to New York: Radical Changes in Ernest Bloch's View of Himself as a 'Jewish Composer' during His Twenties and Thirties," in *Ernest Bloch Studies*, ed. Alexander Knapp and Norman Solomon (Cambridge: Cambridge University Press, 2016), 13–14.

5. Alexander Knapp, "The Jewishness of Bloch: Subconscious or Conscious?," *Proceedings of the Royal Musical Association* 97 (1970–1971): 100.

6. Knapp, "From Geneva to New York," 16. Sources vary as to the exact number of compositions that make up the "Jewish Cycle"; here, Knapp includes seven works in the cycle.

7. Ruth Rafael, "Ernest Bloch at the San Francisco Conservatory of Music," *Western States Jewish Historical Quarterly* 9, no. 3 (April 1977): 198.

8. Rafael, "Ernest Bloch at the San Francisco Conservatory," 207–9; and Kushner, *Ernest Bloch Companion*, 80.

9. *Grove Music Online*, s.v. "Bloch, Ernest," by David Z. Kushner, accessed February 16, 2019, https://doi.org/10.1093/gmo/9781561592630.article.03287.

10. Alex Cohen and Suzanne Bloch, "Ernest Bloch—A Biography," in *Ernest Bloch: Creative Spirit; A Program Source Book*, prepared by Suzanne Bloch with Irene Heskes (New York: Jewish Music Council of the National Jewish Welfare Board, 1976), 7–8.

11. Scott Woolley, "Milton Preves: A Remarkable Musical Career," *Journal of the American Viola Society* 5, no. 1 (Spring 1989): 9–11.

12. Bloch to Alfred Pochon, Agate Beach, OR, February 19, 1951, in *Ernest Bloch (1880–1959): Sa vie et sa pensée suivi du catalogue de l'œuvre*, ed. Joseph Lewinski and Emmanuelle Dijon, vol. 4, *Le Havre de Paix en Oregon (1939–1959)* (Geneva: Slatkine, 2005), 432; translation by the author.

13. In the manuscript housed at the University of California at Berkeley, the order of the movements is *Rhapsodie hébraïque*, Processional II, and Processional III, and the date of March 10, 1951, appears at the end of the second movement (page 30); Ernest Bloch collection, ARCHIVES BLOCH 1, Music Library, University of California, Berkeley. On March 11, 1951, Bloch wrote to his sister Loulette: "I'm going to finish the 40-page orchestration of my new *Suite hébraïque* for viola and orchestra dedicated to my friends in Chicago." Bloch to Loulette Bloch, Agate Beach, OR, March 11, 1951, in *Le Havre de Paix*, 433; translation by the author.

14. Bloch to Lillian Hodghead and Ada Clement, Agate Beach, OR, December 14, 1950, in *Le Havre de Paix*, 416–17. In this letter, and others, Bloch writes about how moved

he was by the outpouring of support from everyone in Chicago and how pleased he was with the performance of his Suite for Viola and Orchestra. The Covenant Club was only a minor sponsor of the Chicago festival, and other writers have questioned why Bloch dedicated the *Suite hébraïque* specifically to this group; for those discussions, see Knapp, "Ernest Bloch's *Suite Hébraïque*," 23; and Rachel Heimovics Braun, "Ernest Bloch and His Chicago Jewish Colleagues," *Chicago Jewish History* 35, no. 2 (Spring 2011): 4–7.

15. Liner notes to *Five Jewish Pieces*, by Ernest Bloch, with Milton Preves (viola) and Helene Brahm (piano), Covenant Club of Illinois E2-CL-3628–3629, [1952], 33-1/3 rpm.
16. Bloch [to Covenant Club of Illinois], Agate Beach, OR, n.d., cited in liner notes to *Five Jewish Pieces*.
17. Musicale Program, The Covenant Club, March 3, 1952, courtesy of Spertus Institute, Chicago.
18. Chicago Symphony Orchestra, Fourteenth Program, January 1 and 2, 1953, 3, 27.
19. See note 13; it is unknown why the order of movements for the premiere performance and recording of *Five Jewish Pieces* and the premiere of the orchestral version of *Suite hébraïque* differed from the manuscript and final published version.
20. Isidore Singer, ed., *The Jewish Encyclopedia*, 12 vols. (New York: Funk and Wagnalls, 1901–1906). Bloch, fortunately, wrote down the exact tunes that he used in *Suite hébraïque* on an undated sheet of notepaper, which is reproduced in Knapp, "Ernest Bloch's *Suite Hébraïque*," 24.
21. Knapp, "Ernest Bloch's *Suite Hébraïque*," 19–33.
22. Kushner, *Ernest Bloch Companion*, 127; and *Grove Music Online*, s.v. "Rhapsody," by John Rink, accessed February 24, 2019, https://doi.org/10.1093/gmo/9781561592630.article.23313.
23. Knapp, "Ernest Bloch's *Suite Hébraïque*," 26.
24. *Oxford English Dictionary*, s.v. "processional (*n.*)," accessed February 24, 2019, http://www.oed.com/view/Entry/151803.
25. *The Jewish Encyclopedia* includes multiple themes under the entry for "kerobot" (prayers of approach). Bloch used the third melody under "Kerobot (Melodies for Kaliric Strophic Hymn)"; see *The Jewish Encyclopedia* (1901–1906), s.v. "kerobot."
26. *The Jewish Encyclopedia* includes three themes under the heading of "geshem" (rain). Bloch used the third version, labeled "Geshem (C)"; see *The Jewish Encyclopedia* (1901–1906), s.v. "geshem."
27. Knapp, "Ernest Bloch's *Suite Hébraïque*," 28–29.
28. Abram Loft, review of *Suite Hébraïque for Viola (or Violin) and Piano*, by Ernest Bloch, *Notes*, 2nd ser., 11, no. 2 (March 1954): 273.

Chapter 5

1. Donald Brook, "York Bowen," in *Composers' Gallery: Biographical Sketches of Contemporary Composers* (London: Rockliff, 1946), 37.
2. Monica Watson, *York Bowen: A Centenary Tribute* (London: Thames, 1984), 15.

3. Watson, *York Bowen*, 9–10.

4. Kaikhosru Shapurji Sorabji, *Mi Contra Fa: The Immoralisings of a Machiavellian Musician* (London: Porcupine, 1947), 237. Bowen is now frequently referred to as the "English Rachmaninoff."

5. Watson, *York Bowen*, 20–23; and Brook, "York Bowen," 36.

6. Watson, *York Bowen*, 35–37.

7. Watson, *York Bowen*, 69.

8. Watson, *York Bowen*, 82–86.

9. Multiple sources also list a *Romance for Viola and Organ*; see Watson, *York Bowen*, 94; and Lionel Tertis, *My Viola and I: A Complete Autobiography* (London: Paul Elek, 1974), 173. No such work exists in the Bowen Archives at the RAM (email message from Amy Foster, Library Assistant, to the author, January 9, 2018), and the *Romance* is likely an alternative title for the *Fantasia*.

10. John White, "The Viola Music of York Bowen," in *An Anthology of British Viola Players*, comp. and ed. John White (Colne, UK: Comus, 1997), 19.

11. Tertis, *My Viola and I*, 33–34.

12. "Mr. York Bowen," *Musical Herald*, no. 769 (April 1, 1912): 99.

13. "London Concerts: Viola Recital," *Musical Times* 46, no. 748 (June 1, 1905): 403–4.

14. "Comments and Opinions: Opera and Two Concerts," *Musical Standard* 23, no. 595 (May 27, 1905): 319.

15. *Cobbett's Cyclopedic Survey of Chamber Music*, 2nd ed. (1963), s.v. "Bowen, York," by T[homas] F. Dunhill. Dunhill's comments first appeared in the 1929 edition of this work.

Chapter 6

1. Michael Musgrave, *The Music of Brahms* (London: Routledge & Kegan Paul, 1985), 252.

2. Brahms to Fritz Simrock, Frankfurt am Main, February 17, 1895, in *Johannes Brahms Briefe an P. J. Simrock und Fritz Simrock*, ed. Max Kalbeck ([Tutzing]: Hans Schneider, 1974), 4:165; translation by Harald Krebs.

3. *Cobbett's Cyclopedic Survey of Chamber Music*, 2nd ed. (1963), s.v. "Brahms, Johannes," by Donald F. Tovey.

4. Malcolm MacDonald, *Brahms* (New York: Schirmer, 1990), 3–9.

5. *Grove Music Online*, s.v. "Brahms, Johannes," by George S. Bozarth and Walter Frisch, accessed August 10, 2019, https://doi.org/10.1093/gmo/9781561592630.article.51879.

6. Berthold Litzmann, *Clara Schumann: An Artist's Life*, trans. Grace E. Hadow (London: Macmillan, 1913), 2:42–43.

7. MacDonald, *Brahms*, 50.

8. For more information about their relationship and separation, see Hans Küntzel, *Brahms in Göttingen: Mit Erinnerungen von Agathe Schütte, geb. von Siebold* (Göttingen: Edition Herodot, 1985), which includes Agathe's memoir (*Allerlei aus meinem Leben*; 89–98) and a fictionalized version of their relationship (*In memoriam J. B.*; 99–105). See also Peter Clive, *Brahms and His World: A Biographical Dictionary* (Lanham, MD: Scarecrow, 2006), s.v. "Siebold, (Sophie Luise Bertha) Agathe von."

9. MacDonald, *Brahms*, 132–36.

10. *Grove Music Online*, s.v. "Brahms, Johannes."

11. *Grove Music Online*, s.v. "Brahms, Johannes"; and MacDonald, *Brahms*, 234.

12. Clive Brown, preface to *Sonaten in f und Es für Viola und Klavier, op. 120*, by Johannes Brahms, ed. Clive Brown and Neal Peres Da Costa (Kassel: Bärenreiter, 2016), iii; see also Johannes Behr, preface to *Sonaten Opus 120 für Klarinette und Klavier, Fassung für Viola*, by Johannes Brahms, ed. Egon Voss and Johannes Behr (Munich: Henle, 2013), v.

13. Brahms to Joachim, Vienna, October 14, 1894, in *Johannes Brahms im Briefwechsel mit Joseph Joachim*, ed. Andreas Moser (Berlin: Deutschen Brahms-Gesellschaft, 1908), 2:275; translation by Edward Klorman.

14. Brahms to Joachim, Vienna, October 17, 1894, in *Briefwechsel mit Joseph Joachim*, 2:277; translation by Edward Klorman.

15. See, for example, Paul Silverthorne, "Brahms Viola Sonata Op. 120 No. 2," *Strad* 127, no. 1518 (October 2016): 69; and Bruno Giuranna, "Brahms' 'Viola' Sonata in E Flat," *Strad* 104, no. 1238 (June 1993): 552.

16. Brown, preface to *Sonaten in f und Es*, iii–ix.

17. Johannes Brahms, *Neue Ausgabe sämtlicher Werke*, Serie II: *Kammermusik*, vol. 9, *Violoncello- und Klarinettensonaten*, ed. Egon Voss and Johannes Behr (Munich: Henle, 2010). The Stichvorlage for the viola part is housed at the Brahms Archive, Staats- und Universitätsbibliothek Hamburg, shelf mark: BRA: Ab7, https://www.sub.uni-hamburg.de/en/sammlungen/musiksammlung/brahms-archiv.html. The *Neue Ausgabe* edition also provides a convenient comparison (in score format) of instances where the clarinet and viola versions deviate.

18. Brown, preface to *Sonaten in f und Es*, viii.

19. Robin Stowell, *The Early Violin and Viola: A Practical Guide* (Cambridge: Cambridge University Press, 2001), 164.

20. Giuranna, " 'Viola' Sonata in E Flat," 552.

21. Schuberth also issued Vieuxtemps's arrangement in a version for viola and piano titled *Grand Duo*, which used the same viola part that was issued with the full quintet version.

22. René de Boisdeffre, *Trois pièces pour clarinette (en la) ou alto avec accompagnement de piano, op. 40* (Paris: J. Hamelle, [1888]).

23. Walter Rabl, *Quartett (Es dur) für Pianoforte, Violine, Clarinette (oder Bratsche) und Violoncell, op. 1* (Berlin: Simrock, 1897), https://imslp.org/wiki/Quartet_for_Piano%2C_Violin%2C_Clarinet%2C_and_Cello%2C_Op.1_(Rabl%2C_Walter).

24. Brown, preface to *Sonaten in f und Es*, ix.

25. Daniel Gregory Mason, *The Chamber Music of Brahms*, reprint ed. (Ann Arbor, MI: Edwards Brothers, 1950), 257.

26. See, in particular, Giuranna's critical comments regarding this passage, " 'Viola' Sonata in E Flat," 553.

27. For more details regarding the prominence of these quarter notes, see Edwin Evans, *Handbook to the Chamber & Orchestral Music of Johannes Brahms*, vol. 2, *Second Series Op. 68 to the End* (London: William Reeves, 1935), 320–24.

28. Mason, *Chamber Music of Brahms*, 263.

29. Kelly Dean Hansen, "Clarinet (or Viola) Sonata No. 2 in E-Flat Major, Op. 120, No. 2," *Listening Guides to the Works of Johannes Brahms*, http://www.kellydeanhansen.com/opus120-2.html.

30. Mason, *Chamber Music of Brahms*, 263–64.

31. MacDonald, *Brahms*, 371.

32. Eduard Hanslick, "Feuilleton: Concerte," *Neue freie Presse*, no. 10918 (January 15, 1895): 2, Morgenblatt edition; translation by John Daverio from "Hanslick on Brahms's Chamber Music with Clarinet," *American Brahms Society Newsletter* 13, no. 1 (Spring 1995): 7.

33. Renate Hofmann and Kurt Hofmann, *Johannes Brahms: Zeittafel zu Leben und Werk* (Tutzing: Hans Schneider, 1983), 267.

34. "Yesterday's Concerts," *Standard* (London), November 30, 1899.

35. MacDonald, *Brahms*, 369.

Chapter 7

1. "Benjamin Britten," in *British Composers in Interview*, by Murray Schafer (London: Faber and Faber, 1963), 118.

2. "Sir Michael Tippett," in *Remembering Britten*, ed. Alan Blyth (London: Hutchinson, 1981), 65.

3. "Peter Schidlof," in *Remembering Britten*, 47.

4. David Dalton, *Playing the Viola: Conversations with William Primrose* (Oxford: Oxford University Press, 1988), 206.

5. Neil Powell, *Benjamin Britten: A Life for Music* (London: Hutchinson, 2013), 6.

6. *Grove Music Online*, s.v. "Britten, (Edward) Benjamin: 1. Childhood, adolescence, 1913–30," by Philip Brett, rev. Heather Wiebe, accessed October 16, 2018, https://doi.org/10.1093/gmo/9781561592630.article.46435.

7. Humphrey Carpenter, *Benjamin Britten: A Biography* (New York: Charles Scribner's Sons, 1992), 17.

8. "Did You Hear That? How to Become a Composer," *Listener* 36, no. 930 (November 7, 1946): 624. The text of this article is drawn from a BBC broadcast featuring Britten.

9. Michael Kennedy notes that Britten had briefly met Pears in 1934; see *Britten* (Oxford: Oxford University Press, 2001), 23. Neil Powell writes of their 1937 meeting: "Although they had almost certainly been in the same room before, this was his first proper meeting with Peter Pears." *A Life for Music*, 129.

10. Carpenter, *Benjamin Britten: A Biography*, 124–33.

11. "Sir Peter Pears," in *Remembering Britten*, 21. Britten had received Frank Bridge's 1843 Giussani viola from his former teacher immediately prior to sailing for America; see Carpenter, *Benjamin Britten: A Biography*, 128.

12. Carpenter, *Benjamin Britten: A Biography*, 174.

13. Elizabeth Sweeting, "The First Festival and Its Background: 1948," in *Time & Concord: Aldeburgh Festival Recollections*, comp. and ed. Jenni Wake-Walker (Saxmundham, UK: Autograph Books, 1997), 1–2.

14. Carpenter, *Benjamin Britten: A Biography*, 576–82.

15. For a complete list, see the *Britten Thematic Catalogue*, http://www.brittenproject. org/. Britten also arranged compositions by other composers for the viola; his arrangement of Frank Bridge's orchestral work *There Is a Willow Grows Aslant a Brook* for viola and piano from 1932 was published in 1990 by Thames.

16. William Primrose to Britten, Westport, CT, October 24, 1949, ©Britten-Pears Foundation.

17. Britten to Elizabeth Sweeting, New York, November 4, 1949, in *Letters from a Life: The Selected Letters of Benjamin Britten, 1913–1976*, vol. 3, *1946–1951*, ed. Donald Mitchell, Philip Reed, and Mervyn Cooke (Berkeley: University of California Press, 2004), 549–50.

18. *The Complete Programme Book, The Third Aldeburgh Festival of Music and the Arts,* June 17–25, 1950, 30.

19. *The Complete Programme Book, The Fifth Aldeburgh Festival of Music and the Arts*, June 14–22, 1952, 36–37. © Britten-Pears Foundation. While Britten's name is not credited as author of the program note here, it was credited when the note was reprinted for the 1984 festival; see *Festival Programme Book, Thirty-Seventh Aldeburgh Festival of Music and the Arts*, June 8–24, 1984, 92.

20. Philip Reed, introduction to *Letters from a Life: The Selected Letters of Benjamin Britten, 1913–1976*, vol. 4, *1952–1957*, ed. Philip Reed, Mervyn Cooke, and Donald Mitchell (Woodbridge, UK: Boydell Press, 2008), 6.

21. The designation of motives *x, x′, y,* and *y′* correspond here to the references in David Sills, "Benjamin Britten's *Lachrymae*: An Analysis for Performers," *Journal of the American Viola Society* 13, no. 3 (1997): 17–34. Peter Evans preferred to label the four-note motives as *x* and *y*, marking the three-note versions as incomplete; see *The Music of Benjamin Britten* (Minneapolis: University of Minnesota Press, 1979), 303–6.

22. Nicola Aronowitz, "Cecil Aronowitz," in *An Anthology of British Viola Players*, comp. and ed. John White (Colne, UK: Comus, 1997), 4. The manuscript for this alternative section is dated June 1970.

23. *Letters from a Life: The Selected Letters of Benjamin Britten, 1913–1976*, vol. 6, *1966–1976*, ed. Philip Reed and Mervyn Cooke (Woodbridge, UK: Boydell Press, 2012), 392–93n3. As of 2018, this alternative variation has not yet appeared in the viola part, only in the piano score.

24. Cecil Aronowitz to Britten, London, April 22, 1976, *Selected Letters of Britten*, vol. 6, *1966–1976*, 715n2.

25. *Selected Letters of Britten*, vol. 6, *1966–1976*, 715n2.

26. "Aldeburgh Festival: New Work by Britten," *Times* (London), June 22, 1950.

27. *Letters from a Life: The Selected Letters of Benjamin Britten, 1913–1976*, vol. 5, *1958–1965*, ed. Philip Reed and Mervyn Cooke (Woodbridge, UK: Boydell Press, 2010), 515n8.

Chapter 8

1. Arthur M. Abell, *Talks with Great Composers* (New York: Philosophical Library, 1955), 144.

2. Christopher Fifield, *Max Bruch: His Life and Works* (London: Victor Gollancz, 1988), 18–21.

3. Fifield, *Bruch: His Life and Works*, 62–79.

4. Fifield, *Bruch: His Life and Works*, 93.

5. Fifield, *Bruch: His Life and Works*, 138–45.

6. Fifield, *Bruch: His Life and Works*, 171.

7. Fifield, *Bruch: His Life and Works*, 170, 232.

8. *Grove Music Online*, s.v. "Bruch, Max (Christian Friedrich)," by Christopher Fifield, accessed February 20, 2017, https://doi.org/10.1093/gmo/9781561592630. article.04122.

9. Fifield, *Bruch: His Life and Works*, 324.

10. Bruch to Maurice Vieux, Friedenau, February 23, 1911, private collection; translation by Paul Engle.

11. Fifield, *Bruch: His Life and Works*, 170.

12. *Grove Music Online*, s.v. "Romance: 3. The Vocal Romance in Other Countries. (ii) Germany," by Roger Hickman, accessed February 20, 2017, https://doi.org/10.1093/ gmo/9781561592630.article.23725.

13. *Grove Music Online*, s.v. "Romance: 4. The Instrumental Romance," by Roger Hickman, accessed February 20, 2017, https://doi.org/10.1093/gmo/9781561592630. article.23725.

14. Fifield, *Bruch: His Life and Works*, 296.

15. For more information on this topic, see Nicholas Hardisty, "Studies of Vocality in the Music of Max Bruch: Instrumental Recitative," in *Max Bruch: Neue Perspektiven auf Leben und Werk*, ed. Fabian Kolb (Kassel: Merseburger, 2016), 161–82. Hardisty does not specifically examine the *Romanze* but mentions "a number of unmarked passages in the … *Romanze* for viola, Op. 85 (1911), and the Double Concerto for clarinet and viola, Op. 88 (1911), which similarly show qualities consistent with models of both vocal and instrumental types of recitative." Ibid., 163n6.

16. Fifield, *Bruch: His Life and Works*, 307.

17. The work was first programmed by the Philadelphia Orchestra in 1990, when Joseph de Pasquale coupled it with the Concerto in B Minor for Viola and Orchestra by Henri Casadesus (attributed to G. F. Handel). As of 2016, it has yet to be programmed by the New York Philharmonic (http://archives.nyphil.org/) or by the Boston Symphony Orchestra (http://archives.bso.org/).

Chapter 9

1. Abraham Veinus, "George Frederick Handel: Concerto for Viola and Orchestra in B Minor," in *Victor Book of Concertos* (New York: Simon and Schuster, 1948), 187.

2. Patricia Cohen, "A Real Pollock? On This, Art and Science Collide," *New York Times*, November 25, 2013.

3. [William J.] Gatens, review of *Bach: Apocryphal Cantatas II: 15, 141, 142, 160*, with I Febiarmonici and the Alsfeld Vocal Ensemble, Wolfgang Helbich (conductor), cpo 999985, *American Record Guide* 67, no. 6 (November/December 2004): 53.

4. *Casadesus: A Century of Artistic Excellence*, http://www.casadesus.com/UK/famille/luis-casadesus.html; and Régina Patorni-Casadesus, *Souvenirs d'une claveciniste: Ma famille Casadesus* (Paris: La Ruche Ouvriere, 1962).

5. E. van der Straeten, "The Viola: Part IV; Noted Players of the Viola and Viole D'amour," *Strad* 24, no. 280 (August 1913): 134.

6. Alfredo Casella, *Music in My Time*, trans. and ed. Spencer Norton (Norman: University of Oklahoma Press, 1955), 72.

7. John Canarina, *Pierre Monteux, maître* (Pompton Plains, NJ: Amadeus, 2003), 89.

8. Walter Lebermann, "Apokryph, Plagiat, Korruptel oder Falsifikat?," *Die Musikforschung* 20, no. 4 (October/December 1967): 422.

9. See Noah Charney, *The Art of Forgery: The Minds, Motives, and Methods of Master Forgers* (London: Phaidon, 2015).

10. Jean-Claude Casadesus, *La partition d'une vie* (Paris: Écriture, 2012), 27–28.

11. Lawrence Gilman, "Notes on the Program," Tenth Pair of Concerts, Twenty-Seventh Season, The Philadelphia Orchestra, December 10 and 11, 1926, 463.

12. Casadesus to Samuel Lifschey, October 12, 1926, reproduced in Louise Rood, "The Viola as Solo Instrument" (MA thesis, Smith College, 1942), 121; translation by Robert Estep.

13. Henri Casadesus, "Handel concerto en si mineur pour alto avec accompagnement d'orchestre," *Notes*, no. 1 (July 1934): 9; translation by Robert Estep. This letter was presumably written in response to a request by Yale music librarian Eva J. O'Meara, who was responsible for most, if not all, of the content of this issue.

14. "The renowned French violist H. Casadesus was enormously successful. . . . [in] a superior execution of the concerto for viola by Handel." "Correspondances: Anvers," *Le Guide musical* 58, no. 2 (January 14, 1912): 36; translation by the author.

15. Stanley Sadie, *Handel Concertos*, BBC Music Guides (Seattle: University of Washington Press, 1972), 5.

16. A representative comment appears in the liner notes for the premiere recording: "[Casadesus] has retained the Handelian feeling very convincingly, and it might well be taken for an original work." Liner notes to *Concerto in B Minor for Viola and Chamber Orchestra*, by [G. F.] Handel (arr. Casadesus), with William Primrose (viola) and unidentified chamber orchestra, conducted by Walter Goehr, Columbia 68975D–S68977D, 1937, 78 rpm.

17. Veinus, "George Frederick Handel," 187.

Chapter 10

1. "Contingencies," *Sackbut* 1, no. 3 (July 1920): 109.

2. Rebecca Clarke, program note to *Viola Sonata*, by Rebecca Clarke, Toby Appel (viola) and Andrew Willis (piano) recital, April 2, 1977, *Lincoln Center for the Performing Arts Stagebill* 4, no. 8 (April 1977): [31].

3. W. H. Haddon Squire, "Rebecca Clarke Sees Rhythm as Next Field of Development," *Christian Science Monitor*, December 9, 1922.

4. Rebecca Clarke, "I Had a Father Too, or The Mustard Spoon" (unpublished manuscript, n.d. [c. 1967–77]), 10. Copyright © 2004, Christopher Johnson. Reproduced by permission.

5. Clarke, "I Had a Father Too," 107, 114–15.

6. In her autobiography, Clarke indicates that the proposal occurred when she was seventeen, which would place it between August 27, 1903, and August 26, 1904, yet she remained at the RAM through the Midsummer term of 1905; see "I Had a Father Too," 117. She did obtain a Licentiate of the Royal Academy of Music for teaching in 1906; Amy Foster, Royal Academy of Music Library, email message to author, January 8, 2019; see also Clarke, "I Had a Father Too," 151.

7. Charles Villiers Stanford to Joseph Clarke, January 1, 1908, London, private collection. Transcribed by Christopher Johnson. Reproduced by permission.

8. Clarke, "I Had a Father Too," 158.

9. Clarke, "I Had a Father Too," 178.

10. Arthur Jacobs, *Henry J. Wood: Maker of the Proms* (London: Methuen, 1994), 142. Wood selected six women—four violinists and two violists—from 137 applicants to join the orchestra.

11. H[erbert] F. P[eyser], "Gifted Artists Join in Unique Recital," *Musical America* 27, no. 17 (February 23, 1918): 10.

12. Michael Ponder, "Rebecca Clarke," *Journal of the British Music Society* 5 (1983): 84.

13. Calum MacDonald, [introduction] to *Trio for Violin, Violoncello and Piano*, by Rebecca Clarke (London: Winthrop Rogers, 1994), [i].

14. Christopher Johnson, introduction to *Trio: For Piano, Violin, and Cello*, by Rebecca Clarke (New York: Da Capo, 1980), vii.

15. "Radio: 10:06–Noon, WQXR; The Listening Room," *New York Times*, August 30, 1976.

16. Clarke, program note to *Viola Sonata*, [31].

17. Rebecca Clarke, Diaries (1919–1933), 3 vols., unpublished. Copyright © 2004, Christopher Johnson. Reproduced by permission.

18. Clarke, Diaries.

19. Clarke, Diaries.

20. Clarke, Diaries.

21. *Berkshire Festivals of Chamber Music: 1918–1938* (Pittsfield, MA: Eagle Printing & Binding, [1938]), ii–1.

22. Translation by Christopher Johnson.

23. "Gives Her Own Sonata: Rebecca Clarke, Viola, Plays with Winifred Christie, Pianist," *New York Times*, January 27, 1920. "La nuit de Mai" is structured as an exchange between "The Poet" and "The Muse" and deals with themes of inspiration and suffering for one's art; see James Robert Hewitt, "The Tropes of Self in the Poetry of Alfred de Musset" (PhD diss., New York University, 1973), 53, 197–99, 233–37. Clarke's selection of this poem may have reflected her own experience in composing the sonata. Much of Clarke's sonata (notably the final movement) was written during the month of May, which she may also have been alluding to with this inscription. Clarke later told Christopher Johnson that she had added the Musset verses on the

manuscript so that hers would be readily identifiable among the submitted entries in the competition; email message to author, January 22, 2019.

24. For an extensive discussion of Orientalism in Clarke's viola sonata, see Daphne Cristina Capparelli Gerling, "Connecting Histories: Identity and Exoticism in Ernest Bloch, Rebecca Clarke, and Paul Hindemith's Viola Works of 1919" (DMA thesis, Rice University, 2007).

25. It is possible to interpret the opening mode in various ways; Clarke's later harmonic settings in mm. 23–31 and mm. 74–78 suggest either a hexatonic mode centered on D (which lacks the 6th degree) or a pentatonic mode centered on D (which lacks the 2nd and 6th degrees but includes two 2nd degrees in m. 5). Both modes correspond to Mode 2 as described by Cecil J. Sharp; see introduction to *English Folk Songs from the Southern Appalachians*, collected by Olive Dame Campbell and Cecil J. Sharp (New York: G. P. Putnam's Sons, 1917), xvii.

26. M. M. S., "On Some Second Thoughts: Rebecca Clarke's Concert," *Christian Science Monitor*, November 13, 1925.

27. Christopher Johnson, email message to author, January 22, 2019.

Chapter 11

1. Noel Malcolm, "The Universality of George Enescu," in *Celebrating George Enescu: A Symposium* (Washington, DC: Education for Peace, 1997), 31.

2. Bernard Gavoty, *Les Souvenirs de Georges Enesco* (Bucharest: Curtea Veche, 2005), 76–78.

3. *Grove Music Online*, s.v. "Enescu, George," by Noel Malcolm and Valentina Sandu-Dediu, accessed March 20, 2018, https://doi.org/10.1093/gmo/9781561592630.article.08793.

4. *Grove Music Online*, s.v. "Enescu, George."

5. Boris Schwarz, *Great Masters of the Violin: From Corelli and Vivaldi to Stern, Zukerman and Perlman* (New York: Simon & Schuster, 1983), 361.

6. Bernard Gavoty, *Yehudi Menuhin and Georges Enesco* (Geneva: René Kister, 1955), 10.

7. Robert Magidoff, *Yehudi Menuhin: The Story of the Man and the Musician*, 2nd ed. (London: Robert Hale, 1973), 67.

8. Noel Malcolm, *George Enescu: His Life and Music* ([London]: Toccata, 1990), 174–76.

9. Malcolm, *Enescu: His Life and Music*, 253.

10. Malcolm, *Enescu: His Life and Music*, 13.

11. Yehudi Menuhin, *Unfinished Journey* (New York: Alfred A. Knopf, 1977), 70.

12. Grove Music Online, s.v. "Enescu, George."

13. The surnames of the violists can be found in multiple sources; see, for example, "Au Conservatoire: Concours de Contrebasse, Alto et Violoncelle," *Le Radical* (Paris), July 5, 1908. The full names of the six students at the beginning of this chapter have been taken from Frédéric Lainé, "Petit dictionnaire des élèves de la classe d'alto de Théophile Laforge au Conservatoire," *Les Amis de l'alto* (blog), February 12, 2013, http://amisdelalto.over-blog.fr/article-petit-dictionnaire-des-eleves-de-la-clas-115294896.html.

14. This recording has appeared on several LP albums and compact discs, including *The Recorded Viola*, vol. 2, Pearl GEMM CDS 9149, 1995, 2 compact discs.

15. Lory Wallfisch, translator's preface to *Masterworks of George Enescu: A Detailed Analysis*, by Pascal Bentoiu, trans. Lory Wallfisch (Lanham, MD: Scarecrow, 2010), viii.

16. Gavoty, *Souvenirs de Georges Enesco*, 158; translation by Paul Engle.

17. B. Kotlyarov, *Enesco: His Life and Times*, trans. B. Kotlyarov and E. D. Pedchenko (Neptune City, NJ: Paganiniana, 1984), 210.

18. Bentoiu, *Masterworks of George Enescu*, 104.

19. "Au Conservatoire," *Le Radical*; translation by the author.

20. "Les Concours du Conservatoire: Alto," *Le Ménestrel* 74, no. 28 (July 11, 1908): 219; translation by the author.

Chapter 12

1. T[homas] F. D[unhill], "Obituary: Cecil Forsyth," *RCM Magazine* 38, no. 2 (June 1942): 65.

2. Ralph Vaughan Williams, "A Musical Autobiography," in *National Music: And Other Essays* (London: Oxford University Press, 1963), 186.

3. David M. Bynog, "The Vocal Music of Cecil Forsyth," *British Music* 30 (2008): 6–7.

4. "Promenade Concerts," *Observer* (London), September 13, 1903.

5. David M. Bynog, "Cecil Forsyth: The Forgotten Composer?," *Journal of the American Viola Society* 24, no. 1 (Spring 2008): 14.

6. Cecil Forsyth, *Orchestration* (London: Macmillan, 1914), 395–96.

7. Bynog, "Vocal Music," 12.

8. William Primrose, *Walk on the North Side: Memoirs of a Violist* (Provo, UT: Brigham Young University Press, 1978), 4.

9. "Obituary: Mr. Cecil Forsyth," *Times* (London), January 30, 1942.

10. Bynog, "Cecil Forsyth," 15–16.

11. "Promenade Concerts," *Times* (London), September 14, 1903.

12. Hazel Davis, "Lawrence Power," *Strad* 118, no. 1405 (May 2007): 27.

Chapter 13

1. David Sills, "The Viola Music of Lillian Fuchs," *American String Teacher* 35, no. 2 (Spring 1985): 60.

2. Amédée Daryl Williams, *Lillian Fuchs: First Lady of the Viola*, 2nd rev. ed. (New York: iUniverse, 2004), 1–2.

3. Williams, *Lillian Fuchs*, 9.

4. Williams, *Lillian Fuchs*, 25.

5. Oscar Thompson, "Fuchs and Sister Play with Barzin," *New York Sun*, March 13, 1945.

6. Dennis Rooney, "Traditional Values," *Strad* 96, no. 1149 (January 1986): 677.

7. Bernard Zaslav, *The Viola in My Life: An Alto Rhapsody* (Palo Alto, CA: Science & Behavior Books, 2011), 126.

8. Jessie Ash Arndt, "Family in Tune: Lillian Fuchs, Violist, Heads Noted Clan," *Christian Science Monitor*, November 1, 1961.

9. Williams, *Lillian Fuchs*, 117.

10. Lillian Fuchs, "In Reverence to the Viola," *American String Teacher* 29, no. 2 (Spring 1979): 5. Fuchs espoused similar sentiments elsewhere: "Viola teaching . . . is very much different from violin teaching. Students have to be taught individually, and much of the teaching is related to the size of the pupil as well as to the size of the viola." "Lillian Fuchs," in *The Way They Play: Book 2*, by Samuel Applebaum and Sada Applebaum (Neptune City, NJ: Paganiniana, 1973), 223.

11. Williams, *Lillian Fuchs*, 116–23.

12. For a fuller account of the importance that Rosalie Leventritt—and her husband, Edgar—played in Fuchs's professional and personal life, see Williams, *Lillian Fuchs*, chap. 3.

13. The program for a July 6, 1961, recital that Ms. Fuchs gave at the University of Michigan School of Music lists the movements as Maestoso, Pastorale, and Allegro. The *attacca* indication in m. 72 of the second movement suggests that the Allegro at m. 73 should be the proper start of a third movement rather than the energico.

14. Fuchs to Robert Oppelt, March 30, 1956, cited in Robert Lloyd Oppelt, "A Study of Contemporary American Viola Solos" (DMA diss., University of Rochester, 1956), 83.

15. Sills, "Viola Music of Fuchs," 60.

16. "Musicians Concert Offers New Sonata," *New York Times*, March 10, 1953.

Chapter 14

1. *Testimony: The Memoirs of Dmitri Shostakovich*, as related to and ed. Solomon Volkov, trans. Antonina W. Bouis (New York: Harper & Row, 1979), 165. Dmitri Shostakovich, who benefited greatly from Glazunov's benevolence while a student at the conservatory, maintained a high regard for Glazunov, which has been expressed in multiple sources. However, *Testimony* has generated intense debate as to the accuracy and authenticity of the views that are attributed to Shostakovich; see, for example, Malcolm Hamrick Brown, ed., *A Shostakovich Casebook* (Bloomington: Indiana University Press, 2004); and Allan B. Ho and Dmitry Feofanov, *Shostakovich Reconsidered* ([London]: Toccata, 1998). Documentary evidence exists regarding a meeting between Shostakovich and Solomon Volkov in the form of a photograph, which includes an inscription by Shostakovich: "To dear Solomon Moiseyevich Volkov in fond remembrance. D. Shostakovich. 13 XI 1974. A reminder of our conversations about Glazunov, Zoshchenko, Meyerhold. D. S." *Memoirs of Dmitri Shostakovich*, [iii]; and Laurel E. Fay, "Shostakovich versus Volkov: Whose *Testimony*? (1980)," in *A*

Shostakovich Casebook, 18. Regarding this book, Mstislav Rostropovich remarked: "I have to say that I consider that Volkov's book is not a balanced account. It is like a series of anecdotes; or rather, as basically everything that is stated there is true, one might say a series of 'interesting little stories.'" Elizabeth Wilson, *Shostakovich: A Life Remembered* (Princeton, NJ: Princeton University Press, 1994), 188.

2. Boris Schwarz, *Music and Musical Life in Soviet Russia*, enlarged ed. (Bloomington: Indiana University Press, 1983), 34–35.

3. *Memoirs of Dmitri Shostakovich*, 166.

4. Simon Mundy, *Alexander Glazunov: Russia's Great Musical Conciliator* (London: Thames, 1987), 13.

5. Nikolay Andreyevich Rimsky-Korsakoff, *My Musical Life*, ed. Carl van Vechten, trans. Judah A. Joffe, 2nd ed., rev. (New York: Alfred A. Knopf, 1928), 194.

6. Richard Beattie Davis, *The Beauty of Belaieff*, 2nd ed. (Bedford, England: G-Clef, 2009), 43–46.

7. See, for example, *Memoirs of Dmitri Shostakovich*, 68; and Donald J. Venturini, *Alexander Glazounov: His Life and Works* (Delphos, OH: Aero Printing, 1992), 13.

8. Venturini, *Alexander Glazounov*, 28–31.

9. *Memoirs of Dmitri Shostakovich*, 69.

10. Venturini, *Alexander Glazounov*, 41.

11. Mundy, *Alexander Glazunov*, 14.

12. Davis, *The Beauty of Belaieff*, 43; and M. Ganina, *Aleksandr Konstantinovich Glazunov: Zhizn' i tvorchestvo* (Leningrad: Gosudarstvennoe muzykal'noe izdatel'stvo, 1961), 357–60.

13. Povl Engelstoft and Svend Dahl, eds., *Dansk biografisk Leksikon* (Copenhagen: J. H. Schultz, 1933–1944), s.v. "Hildebrand, Frants Paulin."

14. In a letter from Glazunov to Rimsky-Korsakov dated August 4, 1886, Glazunov indicated that he had written "a slow piece for Belyayev, perhaps not the best one, although its beginning is not bad." A. K. Glazunov, *Pis'ma, stat'i, vospominaniia: Izbrannoe*, comp. M. A. Ganina (Moscow: Gos. muzykal'noe izd-vo, 1958), 80–81; translation by Elena Artamonova. In this source, Maria Ganina indicates that the slow piece referred to is the *Élégie*; see 81n3.

15. Barcarolles are "pieces that imitate or suggest the songs (*barcarole*) sung by Venetian gondoliers as they propel their boats through the water" and are typically in ⁶⁄₈. *Grove Music Online*, s.v. "Barcarolle," by Maurice J. E. Brown and Kenneth L. Hamilton, accessed January 1, 2018, https://doi.org/10.1093/gmo/9781561592630.article.02021. Barcarolles appear in other meters; Gabriel Fauré's Barcarolle No. 9, op. 101, for piano solo is a notable example in ⁶⁄₈. During the 1880s, Glazunov composed two works for piano solo that bear the title Barcarolle: *Barcarolle sur des touches noires* (1887) and the first movement of his 2 Morceaux, op. 22 (1889).

16. Boris Vladimirovich Asaf'yev [Igor Glebov, pseud.], "Pathways into the Future," *Melos* 2 (1918): 50–96, reprinted in *Russians on Russian Music, 1880–1917: An Anthology*, ed. and trans. Stuart Campbell (Cambridge: Cambridge University Press, 2003), 247.

Chapter 15

1. "Zum zweiten Kammermusikfest in Donaueschingen: Paul Hindemith," *Neue Musik-Zeitung* 43, no. 20 (1922): 329; translation from Ian Kemp, *Hindemith* (London: Oxford University Press, 1970), 7. Hindemith would go on to provide details of his musical approach in later theoretical writings, including *The Craft of Musical Composition* (published 1937–1939).

2. Paul Hindemith, lecture, Berlin, October 1927; translation from Willi Reich, "Paul Hindemith," *Musical Quarterly* 17, no. 4 (October 1931): 486.

3. *Grove Music Online*, s.v. "Hindemith, Paul," by Giselher Schubert, accessed June 23, 2019, https://doi.org/10.1093/gmo/9781561592630.article.13053.

4. Geoffrey Skelton, *Paul Hindemith: The Man behind the Music* (London: Victor Gollancz, 1975), 33–35.

5. Hindemith to Frau Ronnefeldt, August 20, 1918, in *Selected Letters of Paul Hindemith*, ed. and trans. Geoffrey Skelton (New Haven, CT: Yale University Press, 1995), 21.

6. *Grove Music Online*, s.v. "Hindemith, Paul."

7. Skelton, *Paul Hindemith*, 58; and *Grove Music Online*, s.v. "Hindemith, Paul."

8. Stephen Hinton, "Aspects of Hindemith's Neue Sachlichkeit," *Hindemith-Jahrbuch* 14 (1985): 35.

9. Walton's concerto, originally intended for Lionel Tertis, was premiered by Hindemith in London on October 3. Milhaud's first viola concerto, which was dedicated to Hindemith, was premiered in Amsterdam on December 15. Hindemith subsequently dedicated his *Konzertmusik*, op. 48 (1930) to Milhaud and his wife.

10. David Neumeyer, *The Music of Paul Hindemith* (New Haven, CT: Yale University Press, 1986), 5; see also Hindemith to Otto Ernst Sutter, Frankfurt, January 5, 1927, in *Selected Letters*, 47–49.

11. Hindemith to Elizabeth Sprague Coolidge, Berlin, May 8, 1930, in *Selected Letters*, 59.

12. *Grove Music Online*, s.v. "Gebrauchsmusik," by Stephen Hinton, accessed July 13, 2019, https://doi.org/10.1093/gmo/9781561592630.article.10804.

13. Paul Hindemith, preface to *A Composer's World: Horizons and Limitations* (Garden City, NY: Anchor Books, 1961), x–xi.

14. Kemp, *Hindemith*, 15.

15. G. F. Hartlaub, circular letter, May 18, 1923; translation from Hinton, "Hindemith's Neue Sachlichkeit," 26.

16. Skelton, *Paul Hindemith*, 54.

17. Hindemith to Emmy Ronnefeldt, September 28, 1918, in *Selected Letters*, 22.

18. A draft of the first movement as well as the Theme and Variation I from the second movement appear in sketchbooks labeled 1914–1916; for more details, see Peter Cahn, Einleitung to *Sämtliche Werke*, vol. 5, no. 6, *Streicherkammermusik III*, by Paul Hindemith, ed. Peter Cahn (Mainz: B. Schott's Söhne, 1976), xi, xiv; and Luitgard Schader, "Hindemiths Skizzenbücher Nr. 1 bis 41: Entstehungszusammenhang und Inhalt einer Quellengruppe," *Hindemith-Jahrbuch* 30 (2001): 232, 238.

19. Walter Bruno Hilse, "Hindemith and Debussy," *Hindemith-Jahrbuch* 2 (1972): 67.

20. Note to *Sonata for Viola and Piano, Opus 11, No. 4*, by Paul Hindemith (New York: Associated Music Publishers, 1922), 2.

21. Siglind Bruhn, *Hindemiths große Instrumentalwerke* (Waldkirch, Germany: Edition Gorz, 2012), 59.

22. Hilse, "Hindemith and Debussy," 77.

23. My analysis here corresponds to that of Walter Bruno Hilse, "Factors Making for Coherence in the Works of Paul Hindemith, 1919–1926" (PhD diss., Columbia University, 1971), 436; and Daejin Whang, "Observations of Paul Hindemith's Approach to Form and Tonal Language: The Three Sonatas for Viola and Piano" (DMA diss., The Hartt School, University of Hartford, 2005), 9. David Neumeyer considers Variations V and VI as a "substitute for a development section." *Music of Paul Hindemith*, 116.

24. Joel Christian Haney, "The Emergence of a Postwar Musical Outlook: Hindemith's 'Hard-Edged Simplicity,' 1919–1922" (PhD diss., Yale University, 2006), 239–44.

25. Stanley E. Saxton, "Hindemith Presents Own Work on Viola," *Saratogian* (Saratoga Springs, NY), March 10, 1939.

26. Neumeyer, *Music of Paul Hindemith*, 115.

Chapter 16

1. Paul Hindemith, [preface] to *Der Schwanendreher: Konzert nach alten Volksliedern für Bratsche und kleines Orchester* (Mainz: B. Schott's Söhne, 1936), [i]; translation from Lawrence Gilman, program note to *Der Schwanendreher: Concerto on Old Folk-Melodies, for Viola and Small Orchestra*, by Paul Hindemith, The Philharmonic-Symphony Society of New York (Ninety-Fifth Season, 3314th and 3315th Concerts), April 15 and 16, 1937, [4].

2. Willy Strecker to Hindemith, April 5, 1933, cited in Geoffrey Skelton, *Paul Hindemith: The Man behind the Music* (London: Victor Gollancz, 1975), 106.

3. Skelton, *Paul Hindemith*, 122–23.

4. Skelton, *Paul Hindemith*, 128–33; see also Hindemith to Willy Strecker, Berlin-Charlottenburg, June 29, 1936, in *Selected Letters of Paul Hindemith*, ed. and trans. Geoffrey Skelton (New Haven, CT: Yale University Press, 1995), 92.

5. Skelton, *Paul Hindemith*, 134.

6. Skelton, *Paul Hindemith*, 139–40. The resignation was effective September 30, 1937.

7. Paul Hindemith to Gertrud Hindemith, April 10, 1937, in *Selected Letters*, 101.

8. Luther Noss, *Paul Hindemith in the United States* (Urbana: University of Illinois Press, 1989), chap. 6.

9. Skelton, *Paul Hindemith*, 175–79.

10. Skelton, *Paul Hindemith*, 237; and "Hindemith Gives Germans New Outlook on Music," *Information Bulletin*, no. 157 (March 22, 1949): 11–12, 23; see also Hindemith to Bruce Simonds, Palermo, November 15, 1948, in *Selected Letters*, 208–10.

11. Louise Lansdown, "Paul Hindemith's *Der Schwanendreher*: A Biographical Landmark," *Journal of the American Viola Society* 28, no. 2 (Fall 2012): 33–51.

12. Hans Kohlhase, "Paul Hindemiths Bratschenkonzert 'Der Schwanendreher,'" in *2. Viola-Symposium 1990: Dokumentation*, ed. Rolf Fritsch (Trossingen, Germany: Bundesakademie für musikalische Jugendbildung, 1991), 49.

13. Hindemith to Willy Strecker, Berlin-Charlottenburg, June 15, 1935, in *Selected Letters*, 89.

14. Lansdown, "A Biographical Landmark," 34.

15. Giselher Schubert, preface to *Der Schwanendreher: Concerto after Old Folksongs for Viola and Small Orchestra*, by Paul Hindemith, trans. Penelope Souster (London: Ernst Eulenburg, 1985), vii. The original ending may be found in Paul Hindemith, *Sämtliche Werke*, series III, vol. 4, *Bratschenkonzerte*, ed. Hans Kohlhase (Mainz: Schott, 1997), 227–34.

16. Kohlhase, "Paul Hindemiths Bratschenkonzert," 55; translation by the author.

17. David Neumeyer, *The Music of Paul Hindemith* (New Haven, CT: Yale University Press, 1986), 24.

18. For more information, see Giselher Schubert, "Vorgeschichte und Entstehung der *Unterweisung im Tonsatz. Theoretischer Teil*," *Hindemith-Jahrbuch* 9 (1980): 16–64. Hindemith incorporated parts of "Komposition und Kompositionslehre" into *The Craft of Musical Composition*, Part I (1937) and Part II (1939); see Neumeyer, *Music of Paul Hindemith*, 25; and Simon Desbruslais, *The Music and Music Theory of Paul Hindemith* (Woodbridge, UK: Boydell Press, 2018), 18–19.

19. Paul Hindemith, *Unterweisung im Tonsatz: Theoretischer Teil* (Mainz: B. Schott's Söhne, 1937), 251; translation from Desbruslais, *Music and Theory of Hindemith*, 2. Readers interested in an application of Hindemith's theories from *The Craft of Musical Composition* to *Der Schwanendreher* may wish to consult Christine Cheng, "On Approaching a Performance of Paul Hindemith's *Der Schwanendreher*" (master's thesis, University of Queensland, 2016), chap. 2.

20. Ralph Winett, "Interviewing Paul Hindemith: Some Engaging—Some Disturbing—Qualities Shown," *Brooklyn Daily Eagle*, April 18, 1937.

21. Neumeyer, *Music of Paul Hindemith*, 187.

22. Skelton, *Paul Hindemith*, 129–30.

23. There are also slight differences among published editions of *Der Schwanendreher* related to each movement's exact title, including the use of quotation marks; the inclusion of a colon after Variationen; the ending punctuation for "Nun laube, Lindlein, laube" and "Seid ihr nicht der Schwanendreher"; and the full title of the second movement. The author's choice of movement titles in this chapter was determined after consulting many sources and was largely influenced by the forms in Hindemith's *Sämtliche Werke* and his *Verzeichnis aller fertigen Kompositionen, 1913–1938* (unpublished manuscript).

24. Analyses of this movement vary widely; my analysis here most closely aligns with Ian Kemp, "Some Thoughts on Hindemith's Viola Concertos," *Hindemith-Jahrbuch* 35 (2006): 107–12. Giselher Schubert views mm. 96–123 as the exposition's closing theme, with mm. 124–207 functioning as a developmental reprise; see preface to *Der Schwanendreher*, v.

25. Schubert, preface to *Der Schwanendreher*, v–vi.

26. Kemp, "Some Thoughts," 111–12.
27. Kemp, "Some Thoughts," 113.
28. The variation designations in Chart 16.4 come from Hindemith's sketches.
29. Gilman, program note to *Der Schwanendreher*, [4]. The meaning of the term *Schwanendreher* and the reason why Hindemith selected it as the title of the concerto have aroused much interest since the work premiered. For more on the subject, see Kemp, "Some Thoughts," 101–7; and Lansdown, "A Biographical Landmark," 44–46, which summarizes Kemp's points.
30. Paul H. Apel, *The Message of Music* (New York: Vantage, 1958), 336.
31. *Grove Music Online*, s.v. "Variations," by Elaine Sisman, accessed September 19, 2019, https://doi.org/10.1093/gmo/9781561592630.article.29050. For an extended discussion of Hindemith's combination of strict and free variations in this movement, see Neumeyer, *Music of Paul Hindemith*, 189–95.
32. Kemp, "Some Thoughts," 115.
33. Neumeyer, *Music of Paul Hindemith*, 193.
34. Kemp, "Some Thoughts," 116.
35. Hindemith to Gertrud Hindemith, April 15, 1937, in *Selected Letters*, 103.

Chapter 17

1. Louise Rood, "A Welcome Viola Concerto," *Repertoire* 1, no. 1 (October 1951): 49. Rood is referencing here the edition by Paul Doktor, published by International Music (No. 1075).
2. Ulrich Drüner, [preface] to *Konzert für Viola und Orchester D dur*, by Franz Anton Hoffmeister, ed. Ulrich Drüner (Adliswil, Switzerland: Kunzelmann, 1982), [i].
3. Ernst Ludwig Gerber, *Neues historisch-biographisches Lexikon der Tonkünstler* [. . .] (1812–1814), s.v. "Hoffmeister (Franz Anton)." Translation from Dianne James and Allan Badley, foreword to *Viola Concerto in B♭*, by Franz Anton Hoffmeister, ed. Allan Badley (Wellington, NZ: Artaria, 2002), iii.
4. *Die Musik in Geschichte und Gegenwart: Allgemeine Enzyklopädie der Musik*, 2nd, rev. ed. (1994–2007), s.v. "Hoffmeister, Franz Anton," by Axel Beer.
5. "An die Musikliebhaber," *Wiener Zeitung*, January 24, 1784, 152; translation by the author.
6. *Grove Music Online*, s.v. "Hoffmeister, Franz Anton," by Alexander Weinmann, accessed January 1, 2018, https://doi.org/10.1093/gmo/9781561592630.article.13162.
7. Alexander Weinmann, *Die Wiener Verlagswerke von Franz Anton Hoffmeister* (Vienna: Universal Edition, 1964), 1–2.
8. *Grove Music Online*, s.v. "Hoffmeister, Franz Anton."
9. *Musik in Geschichte und Gegenwart*, s.v. "Hoffmeister, Franz Anton."
10. J. P. Larsen, "Some Observations on the Development and Characteristics of Vienna Classical Instrumental Music," *Studia Musicologica Academiae Scientiarum Hungaricae* 9, nos. 1–2 (1967): 131.

11. Housed at the Sächsische Landesbibliothek—Staats- und Universitätsbibliothek Dresden, Mus.3944-O-5 (Signatur: Mus.2358-N-1a), http://digital.slub-dresden.de/id367732491.

12. Traeg's catalogue can be found in Alexander Weinmann, *Johann Traeg: Die Musikalienverzeichnisse von 1799 und 1804 (Handschriften und Sortiment)*, vol. 1 (Vienna: Universal Edition, 1973). Seventeen viola concertos appear in this catalogue, including Hoffmeister's concerto in B♭ major.

13. "Concert Hall," *Columbian Centinel* (Boston), September 25, 1805. Hagen and his father, who also played viola, were early music retailers and publishers in the United States and would have had the means to obtain this concerto through Johann Traeg or some other source.

14. Larsen, "Vienna Classical Instrumental Music," 135.

15. Chappell White, *From Vivaldi to Viotti: A History of the Early Classical Violin Concerto* (Philadelphia: Gordon and Breach, 1992), 46.

16. Heinrich Christoph Koch, *Versuch einer Anleitung zur Composition*, vol. 3 (Leipzig: Böhme, 1793), 241–47, 340 (sections 84 and 126). The chart is based on the form as presented in White, *From Vivaldi to Viotti*, 39.

17. Rood, "A Welcome Viola Concerto," 49.

Chapter 18

1. Joel Sachs, *Kapellmeister Hummel in England and France*, Detroit Monographs in Musicology 6 (Detroit: Information Coordinators, 1977), 9.

2. Mark Kroll, *Johann Nepomuk Hummel: A Musician's Life and World* (Lanham, MD: Scarecrow, 2007), xi–xii.

3. *Grove Music Online*, s.v. "Hummel, Johann Nepomuk," by Joel Sachs and Mark Kroll, accessed April 14, 2018, https://doi.org/10.1093/gmo/9781561592630.article.13548.

4. Kroll, *Hummel: A Musician's Life*, 4–5.

5. Kroll, *Hummel: A Musician's Life*, 12–13.

6. *Grove Music Online*, s.v. "Hummel, Johann Nepomuk."

7. *Grove Music Online*, s.v. "Hummel, Johann Nepomuk." Records indicate that Hummel had likely entered the Prince's employ by the end of 1803.

8. *Thayer's Life of Beethoven*, rev. and ed. Elliot Forbes (Princeton, NJ: Princeton University Press, 1967), 1:369. These observations were made by Beethoven's protégé Carl Czerny.

9. *Grove Music Online*, s.v. "Hummel, Johann Nepomuk."

10. Kroll, *Hummel: A Musician's Life*, 171–85.

11. Hummel had previously published a mixed grouping of three works (Opus 2a) consisting of a trio for piano, flute or violin, and cello; a sonata for flute or violin and piano; and a sonata for piano.

12. "Ankündigung," *Wiener Zeitung*, January 3, 1798, 16; translation by Edward Klorman.

13. The decline of the viola as a solo instrument among professional musicians coincided with a decline in Hummel's popularity toward the middle of the nineteenth century, so the lack of documented public performances is not surprising.

14. *Grove Music Online*, s.v. "Hummel, Johann Nepomuk."

15. Noting the formal ambiguity of this movement, Jacek Dumanowski views it as either a two-part form (AA', with the division at the Tempo I in m. 25) or as an ABA' form, with the B section starting at m. 18 (where the music shifts to F major) instead of m. 13. *Sonaty altówkowe Carla Stamitza, Johanna Baptisty Vanhala i Johanna Nepomuka Hummla: Studium klasycznej stylistyki wykonawczej* (Kraków: Akademia Muzyczna w Krakowie, 2013), 65.

16. William E. Caplin, *Classical Form: A Theory of Formal Functions for the Instrumental Music of Haydn, Mozart, and Beethoven* (Oxford: Oxford University Press, 1998), 239.

17. Potpourris typically gather strings of melodies from operas; Hummel's *Potpourri for Viola and Orchestra*, op. 94 uses melodies from multiple operas, including ones by W. A. Mozart and Gioachino Rossini.

18. John A. Rice, "The Musical Bee: References to Mozart and Cherubini in Hummel's 'New Year' Concerto," *Music & Letters* 77, no. 3 (August 1996): 401–24.

19. Dumanowski, *Sonaty altówkowe*, 69–73.

20. Gerald Abraham, *Chopin's Musical Style* (London: Oxford University Press, 1939), 5.

21. "Kurze Anzeigen: Trois Sonates p. le Pianoforte, ded. à M. la Pr. roy. de Danemark, p. Jean Nep. Hummel. Oeuv. 3 [*sic*]. Bey Ebend. (3 Fl. 30 Xr.)," *Allgemeine musikalische Zeitung* 1, no. 10 (December 5, 1798): col. 157; translation by the author.

22. "Kurze Anzeigen: Sonate pour le Pianoforte, av. accomp. d'Alto ou (de) Violon, comp. par J. N. Hummel. Oeuvr. 19. Leipzig, chez Peters. (Pr. 20 Gr.)," *Allgemeine musikalische Zeitung* 20, no. 31 (August 5, 1818): cols. 563–64; translation by the author.

Chapter 19

1. Miloš Šafránek, *Bohuslav Martinů: The Man and His Music*, trans. Božena Linhartová (New York: Alfred A. Knopf, 1944), xiv.

2. F. James Rybka, *Bohuslav Martinů: The Compulsion to Compose* (Lanham, MD: Scarecrow, 2011), 187.

3. Rybka, *Compulsion to Compose*, 20, 109–10.

4. Miloš Šafránek, *Bohuslav Martinů: His Life and Works*, trans. Roberta Finlayson-Samsourová (London: Allan Wingate, 1962), 25. Šafránek is quoting here from a privately published work: Bohuslav Martinů, *Reminiscences* (Polička: Popelka, 1945).

5. Šafránek, *Martinů: His Life*, 26

6. Brian Large, *Martinů* (New York: Holmes & Meier, 1976), 2–3.

7. Šafránek, *Martinů: His Life*, 43–44.

8. Šafránek, *Martinů: His Life*, 48.

9. Šafránek, *Martinů: The Man*, 14; and Rybka, *Compulsion to Compose*, 27.

10. Šafránek, *Martinů: His Life*, 66–67.

11. Šafránek, *Martinů: His Life*, 80–88.

12. Šafránek, *Martinů: His Life*, 91.

13. Šafránek, *Martinů: His Life*, 253–54.

14. George H. L. Smith, historical and analytical note to *Rhapsody-Concerto for Viola and Orchestra*, by Bohuslav Martinu, The Cleveland Orchestra (Fifteenth Program), February 19 and 21, 1953, 459. The instrument that inspired the *Rhapsody-Concerto* is Gasparo da Salò's "Harshman, Sandeman" viola, dating from around 1590. See "Gasparo Bertolotti 'da Salò,' Brescia, c. 1590, the 'Harshman, Sandeman,'" The Cozio Archive, Tarisio Fine Instruments & Bows, accessed October 6, 2018, https://tarisio.com/cozio-archive/property/?ID=44671; and Maurice W. Riley, *The History of the Viola*, vol. 1 (Ann Arbor, MI: Braun-Brumfield, 1980), 32–34.

15. Donald Rosenberg, *The Cleveland Orchestra Story: "Second to None"* (Cleveland: Gray & Company, 2000), 639.

16. Gdal Saleski, *Famous Musicians of Jewish Origin* (New York: Bloch, 1949), 409; and "Symphony Viola Soloist Risks Key Finger on Radio," *Pittsburgh Post-Gazette*, December 10, 1953.

17. Jirka Kratochvíl and Michael Beckerman, "A Talk around Martinů," in *Martinů's Mysterious Accident: Essays in Honor of Michael Henderson*, ed. Michael Beckerman (Hillsdale, NY: Pendragon, 2007), 176.

18. For more information about his concept of cellules, see John Clapham, "Martinů's Instrumental Style," *Music Review* 24, no. 2 (May 1963): 158–67; Michael Crump, *Martinů and the Symphony* ([London]: Toccata, 2010), chap. 4; Bohuslav Martinů, *Domov, hudba a svět: Deníky, zápisníky, úvahy a články* (Prague: Státní Hudební, 1966), 205–6; and Šafránek, *Martinů: His Life*, 127.

19. Clapham, "Martinů's Instrumental Style," 160–61; see also Crump, *Martinů and the Symphony*, 103.

20. Herbert Elwell, "Martinu Rhapsody Excellent as Orchestra Returns Here," *Plain Dealer* (Cleveland, OH), February 20, 1953. Arthur Loesser similarly wrote that the *Rhapsody-Concerto* "proved to be pleasant music, with long flowing melodic lines and a rather bland flavor of harmony." "Violist Jascha Veissi Pleases at Severance," *Press* (Cleveland, OH), February 20, 1953.

21. M[ichael] T[ilmouth], review of *Rhapsody-Concerto*, by Bohuslav Martinů, *Music & Letters* 54, no. 4 (October 1973): 520.

22. David Cope, review of *Rhapsody-Concerto*, by Bohuslav Martinů, *Notes*, 2nd ser., 36, no. 3 (March 1980): 745.

23. Bohuslav Martinů, descriptive note to *Symphony No. 1*, by Bohuslav Martinů, *Concert Bulletin of the Boston Symphony Orchestra* (Sixty-Second Season, Sixth Programme), November 13 and 14, 1942, 230.

Chapter 20

1. Greg Vitercik, *The Early Works of Felix Mendelssohn: A Study in the Romantic Sonata Style* (Philadelphia: Gordon and Breach, 1992), 1.

2. *Grove Music Online*, s.v. "Mendelssohn(-Bartholdy), (Jacob Ludwig) Felix," by R. Larry Todd, accessed May 20, 2018, https://doi.org/10.1093/gmo/9781561592630.article.51795.

3. Benedict Taylor, *Mendelssohn, Time and Memory: The Romantic Conception of Cyclic Form* (Cambridge: Cambridge University Press, 2011), 45. Taylor suggests that "it is also possible that there was simply not a sufficient market for the solo viola to justify having such a work engraved." Ibid., 45n.

4. Linda Shaver-Gleason, "Felix Mendelssohn: Violist," *Journal of the American Viola Society* 27, no. 2 (Fall 2011): 21.

5. *Grove Music Online*, s.v. "Mendelssohn(-Bartholdy), (Jacob Ludwig) Felix."

6. *Carl Friedrich Zelters Darstellungen seines Lebens*, ed. Johann-Wolfgang Schottländer (Weimar: Verlag der Goethe-Gesellschaft, 1931), 155–56. Fasch's method was based on Johann Philipp Kirnberger's *Die Kunst des reinen Satzes in der Musik*. Kirnberger "regretted that Bach left no didactic or theoretical works and tried through his own teaching and writing to propagate 'Bach's method.'" *Grove Music Online*, s.v. "Kirnberger [Kernberg], Johann Philipp," by Howard Serwer, accessed May 30, 2018, https://doi.org/10.1093/gmo/9781561592630.article.15061.

7. R. Larry Todd, *Mendelssohn's Musical Education: A Study and Edition of His Exercises in Composition* (Cambridge: Cambridge University Press, 1983), 2.

8. *Grove Music Online*, s.v. "Mendelssohn(-Bartholdy), (Jacob Ludwig) Felix."

9. R. Larry Todd, *Mendelssohn: A Life in Music* (Oxford: Oxford University Press, 2003), 123, 195–98.

10. Todd, *Mendelssohn: A Life*, 303.

11. Todd, *Mendelssohn's Musical Education*, 3.

12. *Grove Music Online*, s.v. "Mendelssohn(-Bartholdy), (Jacob Ludwig) Felix."

13. "Feuilleton," *Neue Zeitschrift für Musik* 18, no. 31 (April 17, 1843): 126; translation from Todd, *Mendelssohn: A Life*, 451.

14. Peter Mercer-Taylor, *The Life of Mendelssohn* (Cambridge: Cambridge University Press, 2000), 189.

15. Georgii Bezrukov (viola), *Sonaty dlia al'ta i fortepiano*, with Anatolii Spivak (piano), Melodiia D 023785/023786, 1968, 33-1/3 rpm.

16. Robert Schumann considered the viola to be Mendelssohn's "main instrument, excepting the organ and piano." "Zweiter Quartett-Morgen," *Neue Zeitschrift für Musik* 8, no. 49 (June 19, 1838): 194; translation by the author. For more information regarding Mendelssohn's activities as a violist, see Shaver-Gleason, "Felix Mendelssohn: Violist," 19–27; and Franz Krautwurst, "Felix Mendelssohn Bartholdy als Bratschist," in *Gedenkschrift Hermann Beck*, ed. Hermann Dechant and Wolfgang Sieber (Laaber, Germany: Laaber-Verlag, 1982), 151–60.

17. Felix Diergarten, "Sonate c-moll für Viola und Klavier, MWV Q 14," in *Felix Mendelssohn Bartholdy: Interpretationen seiner Werke*, ed. Matthias Geuting (Laaber, Germany: Laaber-Verlag, 2016), 1:125; translation by the author.

18. Shaver-Gleason, "Felix Mendelssohn: Violist," 23. Benedict Taylor and Felix Diergarten also make brief allusions to other relationships among the movements; see Taylor, *Mendelssohn, Time and Memory*, 45; and Diergarten, "Sonate c-moll," 126.

19. Delaying the arrival of the new key area in the second theme group was a maneuver that Mendelssohn employed in other works; see Erez Rapoport, *Mendelssohn's Instrumental Music: Structure and Style* (Hillsdale, NY: Pendragon, 2012), 107–9;

and Vitercik, *Early Works of Mendelssohn*, 46. For more information regarding key relationships in Mendelssohn's sonata forms, see Paul Wingfield and Julian Horton, "Norm and Deformation in Mendelssohn's Sonata Forms," in *Mendelssohn Perspectives*, ed. Nicole Grimes and Angela R. Mace (Farnham, UK: Ashgate, 2012), 83–112.

20. Todd, *Mendelssohn: A Life*, 130.
21. R. Larry Todd, "The Chamber Music of Mendelssohn," in *Nineteenth-Century Chamber Music*, ed. Stephen E. Hefling (New York: Schirmer Books, 1998), 179.
22. Taylor, *Mendelssohn, Time and Memory*, 45.
23. David M. Brin, "Sonata in C Minor for Viola and Piano: A Neglected Work by a Master Composer," *Strings* 5, no. 6 (May/June 1991): 28–31. Shaver-Gleason also addresses the issue of cuts, providing suggestions for judicious ones; see "Felix Mendelssohn: Violist," 24–25.

Chapter 21

1. Paul Collaer, *Darius Milhaud*, trans. and ed. Jane Hohfeld Galante (San Francisco: San Francisco Press, 1988), 2.
2. Darius Milhaud, *Notes without Music: An Autobiography*, trans. Donald Evans and ed. Rollo H. Myers (New York: Alfred A. Knopf, 1953), 9–22.
3. Milhaud, *Notes without Music*, 97.
4. Milhaud, *Notes without Music*, 14–16.
5. Collaer, *Darius Milhaud*, 33.
6. Milhaud, *Notes without Music*, 62–63.
7. Milhaud, *Notes without Music*, 65–66.
8. Roger Nichols, *Conversations with Madeleine Milhaud* (London: Faber and Faber, 1996), 13.
9. Henri Collet, "La Musique chez soi: Un livre de Rimsky et un livre de Cocteau— Les cinq Russes, les six Français et Erik Satie," *Comœdia* (Paris), January 16, 1920. The other composers were Georges Auric, Louis Durey, Arthur Honegger, Francis Poulenc, and Germaine Tailleferre.
10. For an account of the performance, see Milhaud, *Notes without Music*, 105–7. Multiple accounts compare the bedlam to that which greeted Stravinsky's *Le Sacre du printemps* in 1913; see, for example, Jean Wiéner, *Allegro Appassionato* (Paris: Pierre Belfond, 1978), 48; and "Théatres: Aux Concerts-Colonne," *Le Temps* (Paris), October 26, 1920.
11. "Prevost to Present Work Honoring Wisconsin Girls," *Wisconsin State Journal*, January 9, 1944.
12. Milhaud, *Notes without Music*, 302.
13. Kenneth Martinson, "The Music for Viola of Milhaud," *Journal of the American Viola Society* 15, no. 1 (1999): 27.
14. Nichols, *Conversations with Madeleine Milhaud*, 100.
15. Martinson, "The Music for Viola," 27.

16. The manuscript is dated 1943, and the dates of composition listed at the beginning of this chapter, November 16–December 1, 1943, come from Georges Beck, *Darius Milhaud: Etude suivie du Catalogue chronologique complet de son oeuvre* (Paris: Heugel, 1949), 110–11. John W. Barker indicates that Prévost sent Milhaud a check for $400 "as a commission for a piece for him. The response came an amazing five days later, in the form of a set of *Quatre Visages*, op. 238, for viola and piano." *The Pro Arte Quartet: A Century of Musical Adventure on Two Continents* (Rochester, NY: University of Rochester Press, 2017), 101–2. Barker seems to be confusing the dates of composition for *Quatre Visages* with the Sonata No. 2 for Viola and Piano, op. 244, which Prévost indicated had been written in five days in a 1979 audio interview; see Norman Paulu and Catherine Paulu, "Germain Prévost: A Reminiscence of the Pro Arte Quartet," WHA radio broadcast; and Beck, *Catalogue chronologique complet*, 112–13.

17. Milhaud, *Notes without Music*, 284.

18. Martinson, "The Music for Viola," 28–29. *La Brabançonne* is presented in the version that appears in *National Anthems of the World*, 8th ed. (1993), s.v. "Belgium"; it has been transposed from B♭ major to A♭ major for ease of comparison with Example 21.4.

19. Collaer, *Darius Milhaud*, 35–36.

20. Donald Fuller, "Forecast and Review: Russian and American Season, 1945," *Modern Music* 22, no. 4 (May–June 1945): 257.

Chapter 22

1. Eric Blom, *Mozart* (New York: Pellegrini and Cudahy, 1949), 95–96. The other work in E♭ major written in 1779 that Blom references is the Concerto for Two Pianos and Orchestra, K. 365 (316a).

2. W. A. Mozart to Abbé Joseph Bullinger, Paris, August 7, 1778, in *Mozart's Letters, Mozart's Life: Selected Letters*, ed. and trans. Robert Spaethling (New York: W. W. Norton, 2000), 180.

3. Cliff Eisen and Stanley Sadie, *The New Grove Mozart* (London: Macmillan, 2002), 17–18.

4. Simon McVeigh, "Concerto of the Individual," in *The Cambridge History of Eighteenth-Century Music*, ed. Simon P. Keefe (Cambridge: Cambridge University Press, 2009), 597.

5. Eisen and Sadie, *New Grove Mozart*, 1–3.

6. Konrad Küster, *Mozart: A Musical Biography*, trans. Mary Whittall (Oxford: Clarendon Press, 1996), 24.

7. Eisen and Sadie, *New Grove Mozart*, 12.

8. Eisen and Sadie, *New Grove Mozart*, 14.

9. W. A. Mozart to Leopold Mozart, Vienna, June 9, 1781, in *Mozart's Letters*, 261.

10. Eisen and Sadie, *New Grove Mozart*, 19–20.

11. Mozart requested financial assistance from Michael Puchberg, a Masonic brother, in more than twenty letters written between 1788 and 1791; see *Mozart's Letters*, 397.

Other major creditors that Mozart turned to included Heinrich Lackenbacher, Franz Anton Hoffmeister, and Prince Karl Lichnowsky; see John Rosselli, *The Life of Mozart* (Cambridge: Cambridge University Press, 1998), 127–28.

12. Eisen and Sadie, *New Grove Mozart*, 36.

13. The Viennese banker Joseph Henickstein recalled that "Mozart played the Violin very well and the viola still better, he [Henickstein] often heard him play that part in pieces of his own writing." *A Mozart Pilgrimage: Being the Travel Diaries of Vincent & Mary Novello in the Year 1829*, transc. and comp. Nerina Medici di Marignano, ed. Rosemary Hughes (London: Novello, 1955), 144.

14. Philip G. Downs, *Classical Music: The Era of Haydn, Mozart, and Beethoven* (New York: W. W. Norton, 1992), 321.

15. See, for example, Charles Rosen, *The Classical Style: Haydn, Mozart, Beethoven* (New York: W. W. Norton, 1972), 214; and Louis Biancolli, "*Sinfonia Concertante* for Violin, Viola, and Orchestra in E Flat Major (K. 364)," in *The Mozart Handbook: A Guide to the Man and His Music*, comp. and ed. Louis Biancolli (Cleveland: World Publishing, 1954), 440.

16. Christoph-Hellmut Mahling, foreword to *Neue Ausgabe sämtlicher Werke*, Serie V, *Konzerte*, Werkgruppe 14, *Konzerte für ein oder mehrere Streich-, Blas- und Zupfinstrumente und Orchester*, vol. 2, *Concertone, Sinfonia concertante*, by Wolfgang Amadeus Mozart, ed. Christoph-Hellmut Mahling (Leipzig: VEB Deutscher Verlag für Musik, 1975), xiin35.

17. Christoph-Hellmut Mahling indicates that this edition appeared "shortly after 1800, probably in 1802," and it has frequently been assigned a publication date of 1802. Foreword to *Concertone, Sinfonia concertante*, xiii. In the sixth edition of Köchel's catalogue, it is assigned a publication date of 1801; see Ludwig Ritter von Köchel, *Chronologisch-thematisches Verzeichnis sämtlicher Tonwerke Wolfgang Amade Mozarts: Nebst Angabe der verlorengegangenen, angefangenen, übertragenen, zweifelhaften und unterschobenen Kompositionen*, 6th ed., ed. Alfred Einstein (Leipzig: VEB Breitkopf & Härtel, 1969), 410. In 1801, Makarius Falter's Munich shop advertised the edition as being newly available; see "Musikalien-Anzeige," *Kurpfalzbaierischer Münchner Anzeiger*, no. 40 (October 7, 1801): [7].

18. "II. Instrumentalmusik," *Allgemeine musikalische Zeitung* 10, no. 31 (April 27, 1808): col. 496.

19. "Mr. C. Halle's Grand Concerts," *Manchester Guardian*, January 17, 1868.

20. *Grove Music Online*, s.v. "Symphonie concertante," by Barry S. Brook and Jean Gribenski, accessed March 16, 2019, https://doi.org/10.1093/gmo/9781561592630. article.27252.

21. *Grove Music Online*, s.v. "Symphonie concertante."

22. Leonard G. Ratner, *Classic Music: Expression, Form, and Style*, paperback ed. (New York: Schirmer, 1985), 291.

23. The viola was a relatively popular choice as a solo instrument in symphonies concertantes, typically in combination with one or two solo violins. Given the small percentage that are available in modern editions, it is difficult to accurately compare Mozart's treatment of the viola to that of other composers.

24. Maurice W. Riley, "Scordatura for the Viola," in *The History of the Viola*, vol. 2 (Ann Arbor, MI: Braun-Brumfield, 1991), 139.

25. H. C. Robbins Landon, "The Concertos: (2) Their Musical Origin and Development," in *The Mozart Companion*, ed. H. C. Robbins Landon and Donald Mitchell (New York: W. W. Norton, 1956), 255.

26. Ratner, *Classic Music*, 291.

27. A. Hyatt King, *Mozart Wind and String Concertos*, BBC Music Guides (London: British Broadcasting Corporation, 1978), 48.

28. Küster, *Mozart: A Musical Biography*, 113.

29. Heather K. Scott, "Living in Alto Clef: 11 Top Players Pick the Best Loved, and Most Overlooked, Viola Works of All Time," *Strings* 22, no. 5 (December 2007): 61–68. Atar Arad and Carol Cook are the two violists who selected Mozart's Sinfonia concertante.

Chapter 23

1. Krzysztof Penderecki, "The Tree Inside," in *Labyrinth of Time: Five Addresses for the End of the Millennium*, ed. Ray Robinson, trans. William Brand (Chapel Hill, NC: Hinshaw Music, 1998), 16.

2. Krzysztof Penderecki and Ray Robinson, "Krzysztof Penderecki's 'Labyrinth of Time': Conversations at the End of the Millennium," in *Labyrinth of Time*, 83.

3. Penderecki and Robinson, "Conversations," 89.

4. Wolfram Schwinger, *Krzysztof Penderecki: His Life and Work*, trans. William Mann (London: Schott, 1989), 16–17.

5. Schwinger, *Krzysztof Penderecki*, 22.

6. Penderecki, *Labyrinth of Time*, 114. The State Higher School of Music became the Academy of Music in 1979 during Penderecki's tenure as rector. After serving as a visiting professor at Yale's School of Music from 1973 to 1978, he served as an adjunct professor of composition there from 1978 to 1981.

7. Schwinger, *Krzysztof Penderecki*, 69–70.

8. Ray Robinson, *Krzysztof Penderecki: A Guide to His Works* (Princeton, NJ: Prestige, 1983), 7.

9. Ates Orga, "Penderecki: Composer of Martyrdom," *Music and Musicians* 18, no. 1 (September 1969): 35.

10. Schwinger, *Krzysztof Penderecki*, 187. A live recording of that performance is available: Krzysztof Penderecki, *Concerto for Viola and Orchestra / Symphony No. 2*, Grigori Zhislin (viola), Leningrad Philharmonia Orchestra, Krzysztof Penderecki (conductor), Melodiia C10 23281 002, ©1985, 33-1/3 rpm. Zhislin recorded the concerto again on later occasions but did not record *Cadenza*.

11. Erica Amelia Reiter, "Krzysztof Penderecki's Cadenza for Viola Solo as a Derivative of the Concerto for Viola and Orchestra: A Numerical Analysis and a Performer's Guide" (DMA thesis, University of Arizona, 1997), 24. Readers interested in a more in-depth analysis of *Cadenza*, including the manner in which its construction parallels the Concerto for Viola and Orchestra, may wish to consult this source.

12. Schwinger, *Krzysztof Penderecki*, 113.

13. The editorial manuscript (Redaktionsvorlage) from which Schott engraved the music clearly has a courtesy natural before this note, which did not make it into the printed edition. A courtesy natural appears in the edition by Polskie Wydawnictwo Muzyczne as well as the comparable spot in the violin version; see Krzysztof Penderecki, *Cadenza per viola sola: Fassung für Violine solo*, arr. Christiane Edinger (Mainz: B. Schott's Söhne, 1989), 6.

14. Music publishers frequently make slight changes in later printings, and it can be difficult to differentiate among these printings. Schott's first printing of *Cadenza* is printed on fold-out pages that are numbered 3–6. This printing also lacks the dedication to Zhislin. Most (if not all) of Schott's later printings that incorporate the changes in Chart 23.1 are printed on standard pages that are numbered 4–7 and include the dedication to Zhislin on the verso of the title page (Grigorij Zyslin gewidmet). Some, but not all, of these changes appear in the PWM edition as well as the violin version published in 1989; see Penderecki, *Cadenza per viola sola*, arr. Edinger. The first change listed in the chart corrects a transcription error from the Redaktionsvorlage, while the second adds a courtesy natural for clarity, but the basis for each of the other changes is unknown.

15. *Grove Music Online*, s.v. "Penderecki, Krzysztof," by Adrian Thomas, accessed July 28, 2018, https://doi.org/10.1093/gmo/9781561592630.article.21246.

16. Michael Newman, review of *Cadenza for Solo Viola*, by Krzysztof Penderecki, *Strad* 99, no. 1182 (October 1988): 817.

17. David L. Sills, review of *Concerto per viola ed orchestra* and *Cadenza per viola solo*, by Krzysztof Penderecki, *Notes*, 2nd ser., 46, no. 1 (September 1989): 231.

18. Newman, review of *Cadenza*, 817.

Chapter 24

1. Howard Boatwright, "Quincy Porter (1897–1966)," *Perspectives of New Music* 5, no. 2 (Spring–Summer 1967): 163.

2. Howard Boatwright, "Quincy Porter," *Bulletin of American Composers Alliance* 6, no. 3 (1957): 4.

3. Herbert Elwell, "American Composers, XXIV: Quincy Porter," *Modern Music* 23, no. 1 (Winter 1946): 22.

4. Willard Kent Hall, "Quincy Porter: His Life and Contributions as a Composer and Educator (1897–1966)" (DMA thesis, University of Missouri–Kansas City, 1970), 1.

5. Nadia Boulanger to Porter, Paris, February 19, 1931, quoted in Hall, "Quincy Porter," 8.

6. Boatwright, "Quincy Porter (1897–1966)," 162.

7. From the organization's bylaws, cited in James Browning, "The American Music Center," *Notes*, 2nd ser., 21, no. 4 (Autumn 1964): 511.

8. *Grove Music Online*, s.v. "Porter, (William) Quincy," by Howard Boatwright and Jonas Westover, accessed February 20, 2017, https://doi.org/10.1093/gmo/9781561592630.article.A2259127.

9. MSS 15, The Quincy Porter Papers in the Irving S. Gilmore Music Library of Yale University, Series X: Porter's Works, 1914–1966, http://hdl.handle.net/10079/fa/music.mss.0015.

10. For more details regarding early performances of the suite, see Aaron Daniel Conitz, "(Re)Examining Narratives: Personal Style and the Viola Works of Quincy Porter (1897–1966)" (DMA thesis, Rice University, 2019), chap. 3.

11. Quincy Porter, *Suite for Viola Alone*, with Quincy Porter (viola), New Music Recordings 1512, 1939, 78 rpm.

12. Louise Rood, "Quincy Porter: Suite for Solo Viola," *Repertoire* 1, no. 2 (November 1951): 110.

13. Judson Griffin, "A Guide to American Viola Music" (DMA thesis, The Juilliard School, 1977), 114.

14. Allan Kozinn, "A Violist and His Friends, Assertive and Collaborative," *New York Times*, November 28, 2007.

15. Eliesha Nelson (viola), *Quincy Porter: Complete Viola Works*, with John McLaughlin Williams (violin, piano, harpsichord, and conductor), Douglas Rioth (harp), and Northwest Sinfonia, Dorian Sono Luminus DSL-90911, 2009, compact disc.

Chapter 25

1. Walter Frisch, "Reger's Bach and Historicist Modernism," *19th Century Music* 25, nos. 2–3 (Fall/Spring 2001–2002): 300.

2. Susanne Popp and Susanne Shigihara, *Max Reger: At the Turning Point to Modernism* (Bonn: Bouvier, 1988), 52.

3. Christopher Anderson, "Reger in Bach's Notes: On Self-Image and Authority in Max Reger's Bach Playing," *Musical Quarterly* 87, no. 4 (Winter 2004): 754.

4. Max Reger, "[Was ist mir Johann Sebastian Bach und was bedeutet er für unsere Zeit?]," *Die Musik* 5, no. 1 (October 1905): 74; translation from Frisch, "Reger's Bach," 299. This special issue of *Die Musik* published responses from more than eighty artists and scholars to the question: "What is Johann Sebastian Bach to me, and what does he mean for our time?"

5. Paul Rosenfeld, *Musical Portraits: Interpretations of Twenty Modern Composers* (New York: Harcourt, Brace, 1920), 223.

6. Rosenfeld, *Musical Portraits*, 229.

7. Adalbert Lindner, *Max Reger: Ein Bild seines Jugendlebens und künstlerischen Werdens* (Stuttgart: J. Engelhorns Nachf., 1922), 43. Reger later destroyed this work.

8. *Grove Music Online*, s.v. "Reger, (Johann Baptist Joseph) Max(imilian)," by John Williamson, accessed August 14, 2018, https://doi.org/10.1093/gmo/9781561592630.article.23064.

9. *Grove's Dictionary of Music and Musicians*, 5th ed. (1954), s.v. "Reger, Max."

10. Reger to Karl Straube, Jena, April 7, 1915, in *Max Reger: Briefe an Karl Straube*, ed. Susanne Popp (Bonn: Ferd. Dümmlers, 1986), 249; translation by the author.

11. Walther served as a board member of the Giessen Konzertverein and had offered lodging to Reger while the composer was in town for performances; see Susanne

Popp, ed., *Thematisch-chronologisches Verzeichnis der Werke Max Regers und ihrer Quellen: Reger-Werk-Verzeichnis (RWV)* (Munich: Henle, 2010), 1:768; and Wilhelm Lotz and Heinrich Walther, "Die Gießener Musikgeschichte," in *Giessen, 1248–1948: Siebenhundert Jahre Gießen in Wort und Bild* (Giessen, Germany: Brühlsche Universitätsdruckerei Gießen, 1948), 86. Reger also dedicated his Piano Quartet No. 2, op. 133 to Walther.

12. Popp, *Thematisch-chronologisches Verzeichnis*, 1:753. The violinist Else Mendel-Oberüber premiered the second and third suites on an October 9, 1917, recital in Berlin; she had performed the first suite in Berlin earlier that year; see Bruno Schrader, "Musikbrief: Aus Berlin," *Neue Zeitschrift für Musik* 84, no. 11 (March 15, 1917): 89.

13. Paul Doktor, [preface] to *Suite für Viola Solo*, by Adolf Busch (Winterthur: Amadeus, 1980), [2].

14. The first published edition of the complete cello suites transcribed for viola did not appear until 1916; see Johann Sebastian Bach, *Six Suites for Violoncello*, adapted, rev., and fingered for viola by Louis Svečenski (New York: G. Schirmer, 1916). The pioneering German violist Hermann Ritter had previously published an edition of the first four suites only; see Joh. Seb. Bach, *Sonaten für die Altgeige (Viola alta) allein*, transcribed by Hermann Ritter (Leipzig: Carl Merseburger, [c. 1885]).

15. The published version of the first suite is even scaled back from the sole extant manuscript: a fair copy in Reger's hand that belonged to Heinrich Walther, which has additional music in the first, second, and fourth movements; see Max Reger, *Sämtliche Werke*, vol. 24, *Werke für Streicher: I*, ed. Hermann Grabner (Wiesbaden: Breitkopf & Härtel, 1957), ix.

16. Daniel Harrison, "Max Reger's Motivic Technique: Harmonic Innovations at the Borders of Atonality," *Journal of Music Theory* 35, nos. 1/2 (Spring–Fall 1991): 70.

17. Karl Straube to Oskar Söhngen, Leipzig, November 15, 1946, in *Karl Straube: Briefe eines Thomaskantors*, ed. Wilibald Gurlitt and Hans-Olaf Hudemann (Stuttgart: K. F. Koehler, 1952), 211; translation by Paul Engle. Straube was a close friend of Reger's.

18. Tully Potter, "Max Reger Explores the Alto Clef," *Mitteilungen* [Internationale Max-Reger-Gesellschaft], no. 16 (2008): 30.

19. Compare this movement to the third of Reger's Six Preludes and Fugues for Solo Violin, op. 131a, which includes a similar *perpetuum mobile* as the prelude.

20. Frédéric Lainé, *L'alto: Histoire, facture, interprètes, répertoire, pédagogie* (Bressuire, France: Anne Fuzeau, 2010), 183; translation by the author.

Chapter 26

1. Tempo marking as it appears in the first edition and most later editions. Langsam mit melancholischem Ausdruck (without the comma) in Robert Schumann, *Neue Ausgabe sämtlicher Werke*, Serie II, *Kammermusik*, Werkgruppe 3, *Werke für verschiedene Instrumente und Klavier*, ed. Michael Beiche et al. (Mainz: Schott, 2015), 132; and Robert Schumann, *Märchenbilder für Viola (Violine) und Klavier opus 113*, ed. Armin Koch (Mainz: Schott, 2018) (piano score and viola part).

2. "The Hen-Roost," in *The Complete Illustrated Works of the Brothers Grimm* (London: Chancellor, 1984), 698.

3. John Daverio, *Robert Schumann: Herald of a "New Poetic Age"* (New York: Oxford University Press, 1997), 469.

4. *Grove Music Online*, s.v. "Schumann, Robert," by John Daverio and Eric Sams, accessed January 26, 2019, https://doi.org/10.1093/gmo/9781561592630.article.40704; and Martin Geck, *Robert Schumann: The Life and Work of a Romantic Composer*, trans. Stewart Spencer (Chicago: University of Chicago Press, 2013), 8.

5. Michael Musgrave, *The Life of Schumann* (Cambridge: Cambridge University Press, 2011), 11.

6. Daverio, *Robert Schumann*, 62.

7. Daverio, *Robert Schumann*, 77.

8. Musgrave, *Life of Schumann*, 48.

9. Musgrave, *Life of Schumann*, 67.

10. *Grove Music Online*, s.v. "Schumann, Robert."

11. *Grove Music Online*, s.v. "Schumann, Robert"; and Musgrave, *Life of Schumann*, 104–5.

12. [Wilhelm Joseph] Von Wasielwski, *Life of Robert Schumann*, trans. A. L. Alger (Boston: Oliver Ditson, 1871), 179.

13. Berthold Litzmann, *Clara Schumann: An Artist's Life*, trans. Grace E. Hadow (London: Macmillan, 1913), 2:55–56.

14. Robert Schumann, *Tagebücher*, vol. 3, pt. 2, *Haushaltbücher, 1847–1847 [sic]*, ed. Gerd Nauhaus (Leipzig: VEB Deutscher, 1982), 554–55.

15. Schumann, *Haushaltbücher, 1847–1847*, 556; and Andrew H. Weaver, "Crafting the Fairy Tales: Schumann's Autograph Manuscript of *Märchenbilder*, Op. 113," *Journal of the American Viola Society* 34, no. 1 (Spring 2018): 35.

16. Armin Koch, "Kritischer Bericht: Märchenbilder. Four Pieces for Piano and Viola (*Ad Libitum* Violin), Op. 113," in Schumann, *Werke für verschiedene Instrumente*, 329–71.

17. Louis du Rieux to Schumann, Berlin, February 19, 1851; Kraków, Biblioteka Jagiellońska, *Schumann-Correspondenz*, Band 26/1, Nr. 4133; translation by Edward Klorman, with contributions by Harald Krebs, Sharon Krebs, Alexandra Moellmann, and Liza Stepanova. The German text can be found in Klaus Martin Kopitz and Torsten Oltrogge, "Ein Dichter namens Louis du Rieux und Schumanns 'Märchenbilder' op. 113," *Denkströme: Journal der Sächsischen Akademie der Wissenschaften zu Leipzig* 11 (2013): 114–15, http://www.denkstroeme.de/heft-11/s_112-140_kopitz-oltrogge.

18. Koch, "Kritischer Bericht: Märchenbilder," 330.

19. Kopitz and Oltrogge, "Louis du Rieux und Schumanns 'Märchenbilder,'" 117.

20. Wilh. Josef v. Wasielewski, *Robert Schumann: Eine Biographie*, ed. Waldemar v. Wasielewski (Leipzig: Breitkopf und Härtel, 1906), 417n2; translation from Wiltrud Haug-Freienstein, preface to *Märchenbilder für Klavier und Viola Opus 113*, by Robert Schumann, ed. Wiltrud Haug-Freienstein (Munich: Henle, 2000), iv.

21. Laura Tunbridge, *Schumann's Late Style* (Cambridge: Cambridge University Press, 2007), 7.

22. Geck, *Robert Schumann: Romantic Composer*, 236.

23. Thomas Alan Brown, *The Aesthetics of Robert Schumann* (New York: Philosophical Library, 1968), 123.

24. For more on the concept of Theme A as a prologue, see Peter H. Smith, "*Hausmusik* for Cognoscenti: Some Formal Characteristics of Schumann's Late-Period Character Pieces for Instrumental Ensemble," *Music Theory Spectrum* 37, no. 1 (Spring 2015): 58–59. Henle's edition, unfortunately, does not include this double bar line at the end of m. 8, but it appears in many other editions.

25. For more on the lack of a perfect authentic cadence at the end of this movement and its effect, see Weaver, "Crafting the Fairy Tales," 40.

26. Ronald Taylor, *Robert Schumann: His Life and Work* (New York: Universe, 1982), 191–92.

27. Roger Myers (viola), *Fantasy and Farewell: Music for Viola and Orchestra*, with London Symphony Orchestra, conducted by Michael Francis, Delos DE 3441, 2013, compact disc.

Chapter 27

1. Malcolm MacDonald, "'I Took a Simple Little Theme and Developed It': Shostakovich's String Concertos and Sonatas," in *The Cambridge Companion to Shostakovich*, ed. Pauline Fairclough and David Fanning (Cambridge: Cambridge University Press, 2008), 142.

2. Viacheslav Dinerchtein, "Shostakovich's Viola Sonata: A Historical Survey" (DMA thesis, Northwestern University, 2008), 54–55.

3. Manashir Jakubov, "A Bridge over the Past into the Future," trans. David Babcock, in *Sonate für Viola und Klavier, op. 147*, by Dmitri Schostakowitsch, facsimile edition ([Hamburg]: Sikorski, n.d. [c. 2001]), 5.

4. See, for example, Jakubov, "A Bridge over the Past," 5.

5. Dinerchtein, "Shostakovich's Viola Sonata," 63–65.

6. Ivan Sokolov, "Moving towards an Understanding of Shostakovich's Viola Sonata," trans. Elizabeth Wilson, in *Contemplating Shostakovich: Life, Music and Film*, ed. Alexander Ivashkin and Andrew Kirkman (Burlington, VT: Ashgate, 2012), 79–94.

7. Dinerchtein, "Shostakovich's Viola Sonata," 61.

8. Laurel E. Fay, *Shostakovich: A Life* (Oxford: Oxford University Press, 2000), 7–15. The Petrograd Conservatory was formerly named the St. Petersburg Conservatory.

9. *Grove Music Online*, s.v. "Shostakovich, Dmitry (Dmitriyevich)," by Laurel Fay and David Fanning, accessed April 27, 2019, https://doi.org/10.1093/gmo/9781561592630.article.52560; and Fay, *Shostakovich: A Life*, 18–19.

10. *Grove Music Online*, s.v. "Shostakovich, Dmitry (Dmitriyevich)."

11. *Grove Music Online*, s.v. "Shostakovich, Dmitry (Dmitriyevich)."

12. "Sumbur vmesto muzyki: Ob opere 'Ledi Makbet Mtsenskogo uezda,'" *Pravda* (Moscow), January 28, 1936; translation from "The Official Denunciation of Shostakovich's *Lady Macbeth of Mtsensk District*," in *Epic Revisionism: Russian*

History and Literature as Stalinist Propaganda, ed. Kevin M. F. Platt and David Brandenberger (Madison: University of Wisconsin Press, 2006), 138. This editorial appeared two days after Joseph Stalin attended a performance of the opera.

13. *Grove Music Online*, s.v. "Shostakovich, Dmitry (Dmitriyevich)."

14. Fay, *Shostakovich: A Life*, 107.

15. The investigation was prompted by Vano Muradeli's opera *The Great Friendship*, which Stalin and other party officials had seen at a dress rehearsal on January 5, 1948; see Fay, *Shostakovich: A Life*, 154.

16. *Grove Music Online*, s.v. "Shostakovich, Dmitry (Dmitriyevich)." An English translation of the committee's decree, "On the Opera *The Great Friendship* by V. Muradeli," may be found in Andrey Olkhovsky, *Music under the Soviets: The Agony of an Art* (New York: Frederick A. Praeger, 1955), 280–85.

17. Fay, *Shostakovich: A Life*, 162. Many other composers also had their works banned as fallout from the committee's decree.

18. Elizabeth Wilson, *Shostakovich: A Life Remembered* (Princeton, NJ: Princeton University Press, 1994), 260.

19. *Grove Music Online*, s.v. "Shostakovich, Dmitry (Dmitriyevich)."

20. *Grove Music Online*, s.v. "Shostakovich, Dmitry (Dmitriyevich)"; and "Dmitri Shostakovich Dead at 68 after Hospitalization in Moscow," *New York Times*, August 11, 1975.

21. Victor Yuzefovich, "Posledneye sochineniye Shostakovicha" ["Shostakovich's Last Work"], *Muzykal'naia zhizn'*, no. 21 (November 1975): 4; translation from Dinerchtein, "Shostakovich's Viola Sonata," 26–27.

22. Fedor Druzhinin, *Memoirs: Pages from the Life and Works*, ed. Elena Skripka, trans. Emily Finer (Moscow: Museum Graeco-Latinum, 2015), 145–46.

23. Druzhinin, *Memoirs*, 147.

24. Druzhinin, *Memoirs*, 147–49.

25. Derek C. Hulme, *Dmitri Shostakovich Catalogue: The First Hundred Years and Beyond*, 4th ed. (Lanham, MD: Scarecrow, 2010), 557.

26. Laurel Elizabeth Fay, "The Last Quartets of Dmitrii Shostakovich: A Stylistic Investigation" (PhD diss., Cornell University, 1978), 80.

27. *Grove Music Online*, s.v. "Shostakovich, Dmitry (Dmitriyevich)."

28. Leslie Faye Johnson, "The Shostakovich Viola Sonata: An Analytical Performer's Guide" (DMA diss., University of Washington, 1991), 11–12.

29. MacDonald, "'I Took a Simple Little Theme,'" 141.

30. For alternative analyses, see Johnson, "The Shostakovich Viola Sonata," chap. 3; and Dwayne Steven Milburn, "The Use of Quotation in *Sonata for Viola and Piano* and *Symphony No. 15* as Examples of Late Style in Shostakovich" (PhD diss., University of California, Los Angeles, 2009), 73–82.

31. The first seventy-six measures of this movement correspond to mm. 3–79 of *The Gamblers*, comprising the orchestral introduction and the first two measures of Alexei's entrance. (Alexei, a bass, is the innkeeper's servant.) Shostakovich curiously omits m. 61 from *The Gamblers* in this passage, which explains the discrepancy in the measure numbers between the opera and the sonata. In the remainder of this

section, the largest deviation is in mm. 110–18 of the sonata, which is effectively an extended virtuosic passage that Shostakovich inserted between m. 114 and m. 115 of *The Gamblers*.

32. An opera's overture or introductory material often uses themes found within the opera itself. Shostakovich's recycling of this theme from both the opera's introduction and from the scene in which it appears results in formal ambiguities in this movement.

33. Jakubov, "A Bridge over the Past," 5.

34. Druzhinin, *Memoirs*, 151–52.

35. *Dmitri Shostakovich* [*Work List*], 2nd ed. (Hamburg: Sikorski Musikverlage, 2011, updated 2014), 218, accessed August 1, 2019, https://www.sikorski.de/336/en/shostakovich_dmitri.html. Other orchestrations have been made by Bernhard Barth, Michaël Kugel, Dmitri Smirnov, and Mikhail Zinman.

36. Wilson, *Shostakovich: A Life Remembered*, 469.

Chapter 28

1. Christ[ian] Fried[rich] Dan[iel] Schubart, *Ideen zu einer Ästhetik der Tonkunst*, ed. Ludwig Schubart (Vienna: Bey J. V. Degen, 1806), 140; translation by the author.

2. [Jean-Benjamin Laborde], *Essai sur la musique ancienne et moderne* (Paris: Pierres, 1780), 1:304; translation from Maurice W. Riley, *The History of the Viola*, vol. 1 (Ann Arbor, MI: Braun-Brumfield, 1980), 120.

3. *Grove Music Online*, s.v. "Stamitz family: (2) Carl (Philipp) Stamitz," by Fritz Kaiser, rev. Eugene K. Wolf, accessed May 6, 2018, https://doi.org/10.1093/gmo/9781561592630.article.40302.

4. Ernst Ludwig Gerber, *Historisch-biographisches Lexicon der Tonkünstler* [. . .] (1790–1792), s.v. "Stamitz (Carl)." See also C. Sanford Terry, "Baron Bach," *Music & Letters* 12, no. 2 (April 1931): 135.

5. *Grove Music Online*, s.v. "Carl (Philipp) Stamitz."

6. *Musikalischer Almanach auf das Jahr 1782* (Alethinopel: self-pub, 1782), 90; translation from Ann M. Woodward, "Observations on the Status, Instruments, and Solo Repertoire of Violists in the Classical Period," *Journal of the Violin Society of America* 9, no. 2 (1988): 88.

7. *Grove Music Online*, s.v. "Carl (Philipp) Stamitz."

8. *Grove Music Online*, s.v. "Carl (Philipp) Stamitz."

9. Ulrich Drüner, "Glanz und Elend eines Musikers der Empfindsamkeit: Carl Stamitz zum 250. Geburtstag," *Das Orchester* 43, no. 12 (1995): 21.

10. For a detailed listing of Stamitz's viola works, see Michael Jappe and Dorothea Jappe, *Viola Bibliographie: Das Repertoire für die historische Bratsche von 1649 bis nach 1800* (Winterthur: Amadeus, 1999), 366–80. The listing does not include works for three or more solo instruments with orchestra, of which Stamitz composed many involving the viola.

11. Eduard Hanslick, *Geschichte des Concertwesens in Wien*, vol. 1 (Vienna: Wilhelm Braumüller, 1869), 30.

12. Heina's editions of the D-major and B♭-major concertos appeared in supplement IX of Breitkopf's Thematic Catalogue from 1774; see Barry S. Brook, *The Breitkopf Thematic Catalogue: The Six Parts and Sixteen Supplements, 1762–1787* (New York: Dover, 1966), col. 538. Both concertos also appear in a catalogue accompanying Stamitz's *Six Duo Pour un Violon et un Alto, Oeuvre X* (Paris: Heina, [c. 1773]), which multiple sources date to 1773: http://gallica.bnf.fr/ark:/12148/btv1b90575722.

13. *Grove Music Online*, s.v. "Carl (Philipp) Stamitz."

14. Chappell White, *From Vivaldi to Viotti: A History of the Early Classical Violin Concerto* (Philadelphia: Gordon and Breach, 1992), 279.

15. *Grove Music Online*, s.v. "Carl (Philipp) Stamitz."

16. Heinrich Christoph Koch, *Versuch einer Anleitung zur Composition*, vol. 3 (Leipzig: Böhme, 1793), 241–47, 340 (sections 84 and 126). The chart is based on the form as presented in White, *From Vivaldi to Viotti*, 39.

17. White, *From Vivaldi to Viotti*, 282. Most editions use the spelling Rondo for the third movement. The Heina edition uses the French spelling Rondeaux in the solo viola and Violin I parts with variant spellings (Rondeau and Rondau) in the other parts. The Henle edition uses the spelling Rondeaux in the piano score and viola part and the spelling Rondo in the comments.

18. Karl Stamitz, *Concerto in D Major for Viola and Orchestra, Op. 1; Sinfonia concertante for Violin and Viola with Orchestra*, with Ernst Wallfisch (viola); Susanne Lautenbacher (violin); Württemberg Chamber Orchestra, Heilbronn, conducted by Jörg Faerber; and Stuttgart Soloists, Turnabout TV 34221, [1968], 33-1/3 rpm.

19. Karel Stamic, *Koncert D-dur nr 1 na altówkę i orkiestrę*, ed. Janusz Zathey and Jerzy Kosmala, [3rd ed.] (Kraków: Polskie Wydawnictwo Muzyczne, 1979). This edition uses the + symbol for the pizzicato.

20. P[ierre] Baillot, *L'art du violon: Nouvelle méthode* (Paris: Depot Central de la Musique, [1834]), 222; translation from Ulrich Drüner, [preface] to *Concerto in D-dur für Viola und Orchester, op. 1*, by Carl Stamitz, ed. Ulrich Drüner, score (Winterthur: Amadeus, 1995), [i].

21. [Nicolas Etienne] Framery and [Pierre-Louis] Ginguené, eds., *Encyclopedie méthodique: Musique*, vol. 1 (Paris: Panckoucke, 1791), 320; translation by the author.

22. Clemens Meyer, ed., *Sammlung auserlesener und seltener Werke (aus d. 18. Jahrhundert) für Viola und Clavier*, 2 vols. (Leipzig: J. Rieter-Biedermann, 1900).

23. K[arl] Stamitz, *Kontsert dlia al'ta s orkestrom*, ed. Vadim Borisovsky (Moscow: Muzgiz, 1962).

24. Karl Stamitz, *Konzert in D Dur für Viola und Klavier, Op. 1*, ed. Paul Klengel (Leipzig: Breitkopf & Härtel, 1932). Klengel made numerous changes to Stamitz's music in his edition.

25. Franz Beyer, *Kadenzen zu Viola-Konzerten von Stamitz, Zelter und Hoffmeister* (Adliswil, Switzerland: Kunzelmann, [1991], © 1971). Beyer provides two versions of cadenzas for the first and second movements, and it is the second version of his first-movement cadenza that is exceptionally popular. For more information on cadenzas to the concerto and editorial changes among editions, see David M. Bynog, "A Catalogue of Cadenzas for Carl Stamitz's Concerto in D Major for Viola and Orchestra, 1900–2015," *Journal of the American Viola Society* 34, online issue (2018): 18–39.

Chapter 29

1. Igor Stravinsky, *An Autobiography* (New York: M. & J. Steuer, 1958), 14–15.
2. Stravinsky was born on June 5 in the Old Style (OS) Julian calendar (in use at the time in Russia), equating to June 17 in the New Style (NS) Gregorian calendar. Anna and Fyodor's fourth and final son, Gury, was born in 1884.
3. Stravinsky recalled that "when I was nine my parents gave me a piano mistress." *An Autobiography*, 5. Stephen Walsh notes that while there are records of a few casual piano lessons from a governess when Stravinsky was nine, his first piano mistress, Aleksandra Snetkova, did not start prior to the fall of 1893; see *Stravinsky: A Creative Spring; Russia and France, 1882–1934* (New York: Alfred A. Knopf, 1999), 26.
4. Walsh, *Stravinsky: A Creative Spring*, 57–71.
5. *Grove Music Online*, s.v. "Stravinsky, Igor (Fyodorovich)," by Stephen Walsh, accessed January 12, 2019, https://doi.org/10.1093/gmo/9781561592630.article.52818.
6. Walsh, *Stravinsky: A Creative Spring*, 108.
7. Jonathan Cross, *Igor Stravinsky* (London: Reaktion, 2015), 33; see also Walsh, *Stravinsky: A Creative Spring*, 122.
8. *Grove Music Online*, s.v. "Stravinsky, Igor (Fyodorovich)."
9. *Grove Music Online*, s.v. "Stravinsky, Igor (Fyodorovich)."
10. Cross, *Igor Stravinsky*, 159–63; and Stephen Walsh, *Stravinsky: The Second Exile; France and America, 1934–1971* (New York: Alfred A. Knopf, 2006), 279–84.
11. This story is drawn from Norman Paulu and Catherine Paulu, "Germain Prévost: A Reminiscence of the Pro Arte Quartet," WHA radio broadcast. John W. Barker also relays details in *The Pro Arte Quartet: A Century of Musical Adventure on Two Continents* (Rochester, NY: University of Rochester Press, 2017), 102–3.
12. Paulu and Paulu, "Germain Prévost: A Reminiscence."
13. Their first concert, on July 30, consisted solely of viola and piano works, with the pair playing Brahms's Sonata for Viola and Piano, op. 120, no. 1 and J. S. Bach's Sonata V, arranged for viola and piano. The first part of the August 2 concert included Prévost and was dedicated "In Memoriam Alphonse Onnou, *Founder of the Pro Arte Quartet.*" *Edgewood Convent Annals II*, 117–18, Edgewood College Archives; and Mary Paynter, *Phoenix from the Fire: A History of Edgewood College* (Madison, WI: Edgewood College, 2002), 55–56.
14. Boulanger to Stravinsky, Lake Arrowhead, CA, August 21, 1944, in *Nadia Boulanger and the Stravinskys: A Selected Correspondence*, ed. Kimberly A. Francis (Rochester, NY: University of Rochester Press, 2018), 115–16. This letter has been translated from the French; the text of the original French version (alongside the English translation) may be found at: https://digex.lib.uoguelph.ca/exhibits/show/boulangerandstravinskys/item/2352. The Pro Arte Quartet did not have a significant connection to Stravinsky but had performed his *Concertino* and *Three Pieces* in Europe in the 1920s; see Walsh, *Stravinsky: A Creative Spring*, 363, 368, 383. Boulanger also references Stravinsky's Sonata for Two Pianos, which she premiered with Richard Johnston at the Edgewood College concert on August 2, 1944; see *Edgewood Convent Annals II*, 118; and Paynter, *Phoenix from the Fire*, 56.

15. Paulu and Paulu, "Germain Prévost: A Reminiscence."

16. Glenn Dillard Gunn, "Pro Arte Group Concert Honors Onnou's Memory," *Times Herald* (Washington, DC), January 27, 1945.

17. Virginia Rose Fattaruso Strauss, "The Stylistic Use of the Violin in Selected Works by Stravinsky" (DMA treatise, University of Texas at Austin, 1980), 103.

18. Cross, *Igor Stravinsky*, 103.

19. Walsh, *Stravinsky: The Second Exile*, 155.

20. See, for example, Eric Walter White, *Stravinsky: The Composer and His Works*, 2nd ed., paperback (Berkeley: University of California Press, 1984), 427; and Paul Griffiths, *Stravinsky* (New York: Schirmer, 1992), 132.

21. Igor Stravinsky, *Élégie for Viola or Violin Unaccompanied* (New York: Chappell, 1945), 1.

22. George Balanchine, "The Dance Element in Stravinsky's Music," in *Stravinsky in the Theatre*, ed. Minna Lederman (New York: Da Capo, 1975), 77.

23. *Choreography by George Balanchine: A Catalogue of Works* (New York: Viking, 1984), 182, 249, 286.

Chapter 30

1. Toru Takemitsu, "Mirror and Egg: 2. The Garden of Music," in *Confronting Silence: Selected Writings*, trans. and ed. Yoshiko Kakudo and Glenn Glasow (Berkeley, CA: Fallen Leaf, 1995), 95.

2. "Roger Reynolds and Toru Takemitsu: A Conversation," *Musical Quarterly* 80, no. 1 (Spring 1996): 65.

3. Tōru Takemitsu, "Contemporary Music in Japan," *Perspectives of New Music* 27, no. 2 (Summer 1989): 200. The *koto* is a plucked, zither-like instrument with thirteen strings stretched over thirteen movable bridges; see *Grove Music Online*, s.v. "koto," by W. Adriaansz, accessed December 9, 2018, https://doi.org/10.1093/gmo/9781561592630.article.15420.

4. Takemitsu, "Contemporary Music in Japan," 199–200.

5. Peter Burt, *The Music of Tōru Takemitsu* (Cambridge: Cambridge University Press, 2001), 24.

6. Burt, *Music of Tōru Takemitsu*, 39.

7. Burt, *Music of Tōru Takemitsu*, 80–82.

8. Burt, *Music of Tōru Takemitsu*, 175.

9. Asaka Takemitsu, *A Memoir of Tōru Takemitsu*, trans. Tomoko Isshiki with David Pacun and Mitsuko Ono (Bloomington, IN: iUniverse, 2010), 76. At the festival, Imai appeared as soloist in W. A. Mozart's Sinfonia concertante, K. 364 (June 16), Stravinsky's *Élégie* (June 20), and Benjamin Britten's *Lachrymae*, op. 48 and *Elegy* (June 22); Takemitsu met Imai after the concert he attended on June 22. See Nobuko Imai, "Tōru Takemitsu's *A Bird came down the Walk*," *Strad* 124, no. 1477 (May 2013): 86.

10. "A Letter to Tōru Takemitsu, from Nobuko Imai," trans. Peter Grilli, Switzerland, February 25, 1997, in liner notes to *A Bird came down the Walk: Original Works for*

Viola and Piano, with Nobuko Imai (viola) and Roland Pöntinen (piano), BIS CD-829, 1997, compact disc, 8.

11. Liner notes to Imai and Pöntinen, *A Bird came down the Walk*, 6.

12. Emily Dickinson, *Poems*, second ser., ed. T. W. Higginson and Mabel Loomis Todd (Boston: Roberts Brothers, 1891), 140–41. While this poem is now generally titled "A Bird came down the Walk," it was originally published with the title "In the Garden."

13. Burt, *Music of Tōru Takemitsu*, 225, 266chap.11n15.

14. Timothy Koozin, review of *A Bird came down the Walk for Viola Accompanied by Piano*, by Toru Takemitsu, *Notes*, 2nd ser., 54, no. 1 (September 1997): 279–80.

15. Given its similarity to the piano's *leggiero* motive in m. 21 (and the *leggiero* motive labeled "as a bird's calling" in m. 26), it is possible to view these rapid string-crossing passages as a bird call instead of fluttering wings. Takemitsu's music is open to many possible interpretations, which is part of its allure.

16. Imai, "Takemitsu's *A Bird*," 86.

17. Phoebe Green, "The Influence of Nature on Two Works for the Viola by Toru Takemitsu and Ross Edwards" (master's thesis, University of Queensland, 2010), 24.

18. Takemitsu, "Notes on *November Steps*," in *Confronting Silence*, 84.

19. Imai, "Takemitsu's *A Bird*," 86.

20. Takemitsu, "Dream and Number," in *Confronting Silence*, 119.

Chapter 31

1. Steven Zohn, *Music for a Mixed Taste: Style, Genre, and Meaning in Telemann's Instrumental Works* (Oxford: Oxford University Press, 2008), xi.

2. William S. Newman, *The Sonata in the Baroque Era* (Chapel Hill: University of North Carolina Press, 1959), 288.

3. Zohn, *Mixed Taste*, 168.

4. *Grove Music Online*, s.v. "Telemann, Georg Philipp," by Steven Zohn, accessed October 21, 2018, https://doi.org/10.1093/gmo/9781561592630.article.27635.

5. Richard Petzoldt, *Georg Philipp Telemann*, trans. Horace Fitzpatrick (New York: Oxford University Press, 1974), 11–13.

6. Petzoldt, *Georg Philipp Telemann*, 14.

7. *Grove Music Online*, s.v. "Telemann, Georg Philipp."

8. Petzoldt indicates that the contract for Telemann's employment is dated March 11, 1707; see *Georg Philipp Telemann*, 26–27. Zohn writes that "precisely when Telemann entered the service of Duke Johann Wilhelm of Saxe-Eisenach remains unclear. On 24 December 1708 he was appointed Konzertmeister of the newly formed court musical establishment, becoming Secretary and Kapellmeister the following August." *Grove Music Online*, s.v. "Telemann, Georg Philipp."

9. *Grove Music Online*, s.v. "Telemann, Georg Philipp."

10. *Grove Music Online*, s.v. "Telemann, Georg Philipp."

11. Petzoldt, *Georg Philipp Telemann*, 60.

12. *Grove Music Online*, s.v. "Telemann, Georg Philipp."

13. This work is recorded in the same early source as the Concerto in G Major for Viola, Strings, and Basso continuo, TWV 51:G9: Part II of Breitkopf's catalogue from 1762; see Barry S. Brook, *The Breitkopf Thematic Catalogue: The Six Parts and Sixteen Supplements, 1762–1787* (New York: Dover, 1966), col. 73.

14. *Grove Music Online*, s.v. "Violetta," by Howard Mayer Brown and Stephen Bonta, accessed October 19, 2018, https://doi.org/10.1093/gmo/9781561592630.article.29459. For more information about the term "violetta," see Andrew Filmer, introduction to *Concerto for Two Violettas, TWV 52:G3*, by Georg Philipp Telemann, ed. Andrew Filmer and David M. Bynog ([Dallas, TX]: American Viola Society, 2013), 1–13.

15. The Concerto in A Major for Violetta, Strings, and Basso continuo, TWV 51:A5 presents particular problems regarding the intended solo instrument, and it is assigned as a work for viola da gamba in Telemann's Thematic Catalogue. For further details, see Wolfgang Hirschmann, "Telemanns Konzertschaffen im Beziehungsfeld von Quellenforschung—Edition—Interpretation," in *Historische Aufführungspraxis im heutigen Musikleben: Konferenzbericht der XVII. Wissenschaftlichen Arbeitstagung Michaelstein, 8.–11. Juni 1989*, vol. 1, ed. Eitelfriedrich Thom and Frieder Zschoch (Michaelstein, Germany: Institut für Aufführungspraxis–Kultur- und Forschungsstätte Michaelstein, 1990), 91.

16. [Johann Philipp Eisel], *Musicus Autodidaktos, Oder Der sich selbst informirende Musicus* [. . .] (Erfurt: Johann Michael Funcken, 1738), 37; translation from Zohn, *Mixed Taste*, 43.

17. Wolfgang Hirschmann, preface to *Konzert in G-Dur für Viola, Streicher und Basso continuo, TWV 51:G9*, by [Georg Philipp] Telemann, ed. Wolfgang Hirschmann, score (Kassel: Bärenreiter, 2002), ix. The manuscript is housed in the Universitäts- und Landesbibliothek Darmstadt; a digital version is available at: http://tudigit.ulb.tu-darmstadt.de/show/Mus-Ms-1033-47.

18. Hirschmann, preface to *Konzert in G-Dur*, vii.

19. Franz Beyer, [introduction] to *Konzert in G-dur für Viola und Orchester*, by Georg Philipp Telemann, ed. Franz Beyer (Berg am Irchel, Switzerland: Amadeus, 1974), [i]; translation and further details taken from Petzoldt, *Georg Philipp Telemann*, 33.

20. The initial date of publication for the viola concerto remains uncertain. Bärenreiter's edition (BA 1743), edited by Hellmuth Christian Wolff, was likely released around 1941 and no later than 1942, when it was advertised on the back cover of *Deutsche Musikkultur* 6, no. 6 (February/March 1942).

21. Pippa Drummond, *The German Concerto: Five Eighteenth-Century Studies* (Oxford: Clarendon Press, 1980), 53, 201.

22. Michael Talbot, "The Italian Concerto in the Late Seventeenth and Early Eighteenth Centuries," in *The Cambridge Companion to the Concerto*, ed. Simon P. Keefe (Cambridge: Cambridge University Press, 2005), 45.

23. Simon McVeigh and Jehoash Hirshberg, *The Italian Solo Concerto, 1700–1760: Rhetorical Strategies and Style History* (Woodbridge, UK: Boydell Press, 2004), 6.

24. Drummond, *The German Concerto*, 202.

25. This example is drawn from Alexander Trygstad, "Ritornello Form and the Dynamics of Performance in Telemann's Viola Concerto in G Major," *Journal of the American Viola Society* 31, no. 2 (Fall 2015): 18–19.

26. Arthur Hutchings, *The Baroque Concerto*, rev. ed. (New York: Charles Scribner's Sons, 1979), 240.

Chapter 32

1. James Day, *Vaughan Williams*, 3rd ed. (Oxford: Oxford University Press, 1998), 27.

2. Ralph Vaughan Williams, "British Music," in *Vaughan Williams on Music*, ed. David Manning (Oxford: Oxford University Press, 2008), 47.

3. *Grove Music Online*, s.v. "Vaughan Williams, Ralph," by Hugh Ottaway and Alain Frogley, accessed December 14, 2017, https://doi.org/10.1093/gmo/9781561592630. article.42507.

4. Ursula Vaughan Williams, *R. V. W.: A Biography of Ralph Vaughan Williams* (London: Oxford University Press, 1964), 30.

5. Michael Kennedy, *The Works of Ralph Vaughan Williams* (London: Oxford University Press, 1964), 59.

6. Ralph Vaughan Williams, "A Musical Autobiography," in *National Music: And Other Essays* (London: Oxford University Press, 1963), 191.

7. *Grove Music Online*, s.v. "Vaughan Williams, Ralph."

8. Ursula Vaughan Williams, *R. V. W.*, 116–31.

9. Keith Alldritt, *Vaughan Williams: Composer, Radical, Patriot—A Biography* (London: Robert Hale, 2015), 243–300.

10. Vaughan Williams to Peter Montgomery, Dorking, England, October 19, [1933], http://vaughanwilliams.uk/letter/vwl1104. Ursula Vaughan Williams dates this letter to 1933; see *R. V. W.*, 203.

11. Kennedy, *Works of Vaughan Williams*, 268–69.

12. Note to *Suite for Viola and Orchestra (Pianoforte)*, by R. Vaughan Williams, 3 vols. (London: Oxford University Press, 1936), [i].

13. A. E. F. Dickinson, *Vaughan Williams* (London: Faber and Faber, 1963), 429.

14. Gordon Jacob, "[Remembrance of Ralph Vaughan Williams]," *RCM Magazine* 55, no. 1 (February 1959): 31.

15. Lionel Tertis, *Cinderella No More* (London: Peter Nevill, 1953), 97.

16. E. M. Forster, "The Abinger Pageant," in *Abinger Harvest* (London: Edward Arnold, 1936), 338.

17. Eric Saylor, *English Pastoral Music: From Arcadia to Utopia, 1900–1955* (Urbana: University of Illinois Press, 2017), 129.

18. *Grove Music Online*, s.v. "Ballad," by James Porter et al., accessed February 6, 2018, https://doi.org/10.1093/gmo/9781561592630.article.01879.

19. Mode 3 of the pentatonic modes as described by Cecil J. Sharp, introduction to *English Folk Songs from the Southern Appalachians*, collected by Olive Dame Campbell and Cecil J. Sharp (New York: G. P. Putnam's Sons, 1917), xvii.

20. Mode 4 of the pentatonic modes from Sharp, introduction to *English Folk Songs*, xvii.

21. William E. Everett, "Ralph Vaughan Williams's Suite for Viola and Orchestra," *Journal of the American Viola Society* 13, no. 2 (1997): 15.

22. Ernest Newman, "The Week's Music: The Courtauld-Sargent Concert," *Sunday Times* (London), November 18, 1934.

23. *Grove Music Online*, s.v. "Musette (i)," by Robert A. Green, Anthony C. Baines, and Meredith Ellis Little, accessed February 6, 2018, https://doi.org/10.1093/gmo/9781561592630.article.19398.

24. Frank Howes, *The Music of Ralph Vaughan Williams* (London: Oxford University Press, 1954), 114.

25. Everett, "Ralph Vaughan Williams's Suite," 12.

26. Everett, "Ralph Vaughan Williams's Suite," 15.

27. *Grove Music Online*, s.v. "Polka," by Gracian Černušák, Andrew Lamb, and John Tyrrell, accessed February 6, 2018, https://doi.org/10.1093/gmo/9781561592630.article.22020.

28. Edwin Evans, analytical note to *Suite for Viola and Orchestra*, by Ralph Vaughan Williams, Courtauld-Sargent Concerts (6th Series), November 12 and 13, 1934, [17].

29. *Grove Music Online*, s.v. "Galop," by Andrew Lamb, accessed March 16, 2018, https://doi.org/10.1093/gmo/9781561592630.article.10589.

30. Percy M. Young, *Vaughan Williams* (London: Dobson, 1953), 135.

31. Everett, "Ralph Vaughan Williams's Suite," 12.

32. [William] McN[aught], "London Concerts: Courtauld-Sargent Concert," *Musical Times* 75, no. 1102 (December 1934): 1128.

33. Edmund Rubbra, "The Later Vaughan Williams," *Music & Letters* 18, no. 1 (January 1937): 4.

34. Hugh Ottaway, "English Orchestral," review of *Suite for Viola and Small Orchestra*, by Ralph Vaughan Williams, *Musical Times* 107, no. 1482 (August 1966): 708.

35. Day, *Vaughan Williams*, 230.

Chapter 33

1. Eugène Ysaÿe, *Henri Vieuxtemps: Mon maître*, Les cahiers Ysaÿe, no. 1 (Brussels: Éditions Ysaÿe, 1968), 15; translation by the author.

2. *Grove Music Online*, s.v. "Vieuxtemps Family: (1) Henry Vieuxtemps," by Boris Schwarz and Sarah Hibberd, accessed December 14, 2017, https://doi.org/10.1093/gmo/9781561592630.article.29341.

3. L. Ginsburg, *Vieuxtemps*, ed. Herbert R. Axelrod, trans. I. Levin (Neptune City, NJ: Paganiniana, 1984), 97.

4. J. T. Radoux, *Henry Vieuxtemps: His Life and Works*, trans. Samuel Wolf (Linthicum Heights, MD: Swand, 1983), 9.

5. "The Autobiography of Henry Vieuxtemps," in Radoux, *Henry Vieuxtemps: His Life and Works*, 60.

6. "Autobiography of Vieuxtemps," 62.

7. "Musical Examiner: Philharmonic Concerts," *Examiner* (London), April 25, 1841.

8. Vera Brodsky Lawrence, *Strong on Music: The New York Music Scene in the Days of George Templeton Strong, 1836–1875*, vol. 1, *Resonances: 1836–1850* (New York: Oxford University Press, 1988), 246.

9. "Autobiography of Vieuxtemps," 63.

10. Maurice Kufferath, *Henri Vieuxtemps: Sa vie et son oeuvre* (Brussels: J. Rozez, 1882), 130.

11. "Autobiography of Vieuxtemps," 65.

12. Radoux, *Henry Vieuxtemps*, 54.

13. "Monday Popular Concerts," *Players* 3, no. 57 (January 26, 1861): 235.

14. Kufferath, *Henri Vieuxtemps*, 82; translation by Paul Engle.

15. Marie Cornaz, preface to *Sonate B-dur Opus 36 für Klavier und Viola*, by Henry Vieuxtemps, ed. Peter Jost (Munich: Henle, 2013), v.

16. The manuscript for the *Élégie* has not survived, and at least one account of the premiere indicates that the work originally had an orchestral accompaniment: "Vieuxtemps . . . played . . . an Elegie for viola with orchestra" (eine Elegie für die Viola mit Orchester). "Notizen: St. Petersburg," *Allgemeine Wiener Musik-Zeitung* 8, no. 42 (April 6, 1848): 168; translation by the author. If the *Élégie* was originally conceived as a concertante work, it may explain its high degree of virtuosity.

17. Christ[ian] Fried[rich] Dan[iel] Schubart, *Ideen zu einer Ästhetik der Tonkunst*, ed. Ludwig Schubart (Vienna: Bey J. V. Degen, 1806), 378; translation from Rita Steblin, *A History of Key Characteristics in the Eighteenth and Early Nineteenth Centuries*, 2nd ed. (Rochester, NY: University of Rochester Press, 2002), 116.

18. "Reviews: 'Elegie'—for Alto, Violin, or Violoncello, with Accompaniment for the Pianoforte. By H. Vieuxtemps, Op. 30, Ewer & Co.," *Musical World* 32, no. 26 (July 1, 1854): 439.

19. "Reviews: 'Elégie,' pour alto, ou violoncelle, ou violon, avec accompagnement de piano—par H. Vieuxtemps, Op. 30 (Ewer & Co.)," *Musical World* 37, no. 26 (June 25, 1859): 403.

20. Else Krieg (violin and viola), *Romantic Recital*, with Frédéric Meinders (piano), Young Artists YA 1021, 1980, 33-1/3 rpm.

21. Kim Kashkashian (viola), *Elegies*, with Robert Levin (piano), ECM 1316, 1986, compact disc.

Chapter 34

1. Tempo marking as it appears in the original autograph manuscript score, original program, and many published editions of the 1929 version. Sources related to the 1962 version, including the autograph manuscript score, published study score (1964), and piano reduction (1964) also have the marking Vivo, con molto preciso. Vivo, e molto preciso on Contents page and at head of the second movement of the 1962 version (189) in the 2002 *William Walton Edition*; this marking also appears in other sources, including Stewart R. Craggs, *William Walton: A Catalogue*, 3rd ed. (Oxford: Oxford

University Press, 2015), 28. Vivo e molto preciso (without the comma) in the Textual Notes (xv, xviii–xx) and at head of the second movement of the 1929 version (41) in the 2002 *William Walton Edition*. This tempo marking also appears in some printings of the 1929 version, including copies of the 1947 piano reduction (priced at 10s. 6d.) and the 1958 piano reduction (priced at 12s. 6d.)—see Chart 34.1—as well as the first printing of the 2002 piano reduction edited by Christopher Wellington. Regarding this tempo change, Wellington writes: "Alteration first made in final version of miniature score," though it is unclear to which printing/version he is referring. "Textual Notes," in *William Walton Edition*, vol. 12, *Concerto for Viola and Orchestra*, by William Walton, ed. Christopher Wellington (Oxford: Oxford University Press, 2002), xv.

2. Lionel Tertis, *Cinderella No More* (London: Peter Nevill, 1953), 38.

3. William Walton, "My Life in Music," *Sunday Telegraph* (London), March 25, 1962.

4. Michael Kennedy, *Portrait of Walton* (Oxford: Oxford University Press, 1990), 4–5.

5. Stephen Lloyd, *William Walton: Muse of Fire* (Woodbridge, UK: Boydell Press, 2001), 5–6.

6. "William Walton," in *British Composers in Interview*, by Murray Schafer (London: Faber and Faber, 1963), 74; and Susana Walton, *William Walton: Behind the Façade* (Oxford: Oxford University Press, 1988), 45.

7. Osbert Sitwell, *Laughter in the Next Room* (Boston: Little, Brown, 1948), 194.

8. Sitwell, *Laughter in the Next Room*, 192.

9. Harold Anson, *T. B. Strong: Bishop, Musician, Dean, Vice-Chancellor* (London: SPCK, 1949), 117.

10. Kennedy, *Portrait of Walton*, 76.

11. Alice offered to marry Walton after her husband's death in 1939, but "after a lifetime of being the exquisite Lady Wimborne, he could not allow her to become Mrs Walton." Susana Walton, *Behind the Façade*, 80.

12. Susana Walton, *Behind the Façade*, 1–12; and Kennedy, *Portrait of Walton*, 143.

13. Lloyd, *Muse of Fire*, 214–15, 235.

14. Susana Walton, *Behind the Façade*, 231.

15. "Sir William Walton's 70th Birthday: All Week, BBC2 and Radio 3," *Radio Times* 194, no. 2524 (March 23, 1972): 15.

16. David Lloyd-Jones, "Violin and Cello Concertos *(Vol. 11)*," in *The William Walton Reader: The Genesis, Performance, and Publication of His Works*, ed. David Lloyd-Jones (Oxford: Oxford University Press, 2018), 163.

17. Lloyd, *Muse of Fire*, 259.

18. In a 1968 BBC interview, Walton remarked that "in fact I started the Viola Concerto [in Amalfi]." "Sir William Walton Talks to John Warrack," *Listener* 80, no. 2054 (August 8, 1968): 177.

19. Walton to Siegfried Sassoon, Amalfi, December 5, 1928, in *The Selected Letters of William Walton*, ed. Malcolm Hayes (London: Faber and Faber, 2002), 44.

20. Walton to Siegfried Sassoon, Amalfi, February 2, 1929, in *Selected Letters of Walton*, 45.

21. Walton to Siegfried Sassoon, Amalfi, February 12, 1929, in *Selected Letters of Walton*, 46.

22. Multiple sources indicate that Walton was continuing to work on the concerto while staying at Haus Hirth in Bavaria in April; see, for example, Max Egremont, *Siegfried Sassoon: A Biography* (London: Picador, 2005), 339. Basil Maine and Angus Morrison both later recounted that Walton had played the work for them after his return to England; Maine recalled: "When I was living in Chelsea, I had a telephone call early one evening from William Walton, who lived near. He said he had just completed a concerto for viola and would like to come round and play some of it from the manuscript. He arrived soon after, and, in the indescribable idiom of his pianoforte-playing, gave me some idea of the orchestral score, and occasionally a sketchy *vocalise* of the viola part." Basil Maine, *Twang with Our Music* (London: Epworth, 1957), 112. For Morrison's recollections, see Lloyd, *Muse of Fire*, 91.

23. Tertis, *Cinderella No More*, 38.

24. "Walton Talks to Warrack," 177.

25. Walton to Siegfried Sassoon, London, July 3, 1929, in *Selected Letters of Walton*, 47.

26. Lloyd, *Muse of Fire*, 92.

27. Willy Strecker to Gertrud Hindemith, July 8, 1929, cited in Geoffrey Skelton, *Paul Hindemith: The Man behind the Music* (London: Victor Gollancz, 1975), 97. While Hindemith's performance of Walton's concerto is generally regarded as his first appearance as a featured soloist in England, he had previously performed his Sonata for Solo Viola, op. 25, no. 1 during a concert with the Amar Quartet on April 3, 1929; see Jennifer Doctor, *The BBC and Ultra-Modern Music, 1922–1936: Shaping a Nation's Tastes* (Cambridge: Cambridge University Press, 1999), 373.

28. Hindemith was able to secure another engagement during the London trip where he performed his own music for viola and viola d'amore on October 7 at the Arts Theatre Club as part of the BBC Contemporary Chamber Music series. On this concert, he played his Sonata for Viola and Piano, op. 11, no. 4; Kleine Sonata for Viola d'amore and Piano, op. 25, no. 2; and Trio for Viola, Heckelphone, and Piano, op. 47; see Doctor, *BBC and Ultra-Modern Music*, 375.

29. Paul Hindemith to Gertrud Hindemith, London, October 2, 1929, in *Selected Letters of Paul Hindemith*, ed. and trans. Geoffrey Skelton (New Haven, CT: Yale University Press, 1995), 54.

30. Bernard Shore, *Sixteen Symphonies* (London: Longmans, Green, 1949), 367.

31. H. H., "London Concerts: New English Works at the 'Prom': William Walton's Concerto," *Daily Telegraph* (London), October 4, 1929.

32. E[ric] B[lom], "Field-Day for British Music: William Walton's New Work," *Manchester Guardian*, October 4, 1929.

33. Skelton, *Paul Hindemith*, 98.

34. Skelton, *Paul Hindemith*, 98.

35. BBC Radio 3 Interview with John Amis, March 17, 1972, https://genome.ch.bbc.co.uk/f1ae65d8f97c416d9918d1f675f6481c, cited in Lloyd, *Muse of Fire*, 94.

36. David E. Schneider, "Contrasts and Common Concerns in the Concerto, 1900–1945," in *The Cambridge Companion to the Concerto*, ed. Simon P. Keefe (Cambridge: Cambridge University Press, 2005), 149. For further details regarding the similarities, see ibid., 148–51; and Atar Arad, "Walton as Scapino," *Strad* 100, no. 1186 (February 1989): 137–41.

37. [Preface] to *Concerto for Viola and Orchestra*, by William Walton, piano score (Oxford: Oxford University Press, [1964], © 1930), [1]. While the new orchestration was largely (if not entirely) completed in 1961, a label on the cover of the manuscript reads: "<u>REVISED</u> 1962," and this orchestration is widely referred to as the 1962 orchestration.

38. Christopher Wellington writes that "in 1931 or 1932 OUP also published separately Lionel Tertis's edition of the solo viola part, as an alternative to the standard version. It was priced 1s 6d." "Sources," in *William Walton Edition, Concerto for Viola*, xiii. An ad accompanying a performance by Tertis of Walton's concerto in 1931 lists as available the "Viola Concerto—Piano Score (with solo viola parts, edited by Lionel Tertis) 7s. 6d." and notes that "of special interest is the performance of this masterly work to-night, since not only is it the first time Mr. Tertis has played it in England, but also he has himself edited the solo viola part, which is issued to-day with his valuable markings." "The Works of William Walton in the Oxford Catalogue," The Royal Philharmonic Society (Hundred and Nineteenth Season, Eighth Concert), March 26, 1931, 6

39. Mary Grierson, *Donald Francis Tovey: A Biography Based on Letters* (London: Oxford University Press, 1952), 290.

40. E[dwin] E[vans], analytical program note to *Concerto for Viola and Orchestra*, by William Walton, The Royal Philharmonic Society (124th Season, Ninth Concert, Series A), February 27, 1936, 14.

41. David Dalton, *Playing the Viola: Conversations with William Primrose* (Oxford: Oxford University Press, 1988), 197.

42. Despite the publication of alternate solo parts, the original 1930 piano reduction remained in circulation until the 1947 printing (10s. 6d.), which incorporated changes from Riddle's viola part. Tertis's changes were never published in an accompanying piano part. At least one non-OUP piano reduction exists, published by Muzyka in 1974, with [Yevgeny] Strakhov identified as the editor of the viola part.

43. Christopher Wellington, preface to *William Walton Edition, Concerto for Viola*, ix.

44. Wellington does not list this 1958 renewal edition among the sources consulted; see "Sources," in *William Walton Edition, Concerto for Viola*, xiii.

45. "Textual Notes," in *William Walton Edition, Concerto for Viola*, xx.

46. For example, in m. 48 of the second movement Wellington's edition has a unison double-stopped a^i (with a fingered and open string), which does not appear in Walton's original 1930 edition nor in any of the copies of Riddle's edition that the author consulted. This double stop does appear in Tertis's edition, but there is no explanation why Wellington included this here.

47. Christopher Morris to Donald Maurice, London, May 31, 1972, private collection.

48. Related to the Study Score for the 1962 version, Wellington does mention that "this score was reprinted in September 1976, with minor corrections made to pp. 33 and 59," but provides no further details. "Sources," in *William Walton Edition, Concerto for Viola*, xiii. The "minor correction" on page 33 is presumably the change that Walton made to this trill.

49. In the 1929 orchestration, the c♯ is given to the second violins and violas. In the 1962 orchestration, it is given to Bassoon I and the violas.

50. Many violists consider the exposition, particularly for purposes of auditions, to extend until m. 81 (No. 9). From an analytical perspective, the development traditionally has been considered to begin at m. 46.
51. In the 1962 orchestration, the second violins' notes in mm. 93–99 are enharmonically respelled as d♭'s (originally c♯'s) and f♭'s (originally e♮'s).
52. Donald Francis Tovey was a leading proponent of analyzing the movement in rondo form; see *Essays in Musical Analysis*, vol. 3, *Concertos* (London: Oxford University Press, 1948), 223–25. Frank Howes was a leading proponent of the modified sonata form approach; see *The Music of William Walton*, 2nd ed. (London: Oxford University Press, 1974), 83–86.
53. Several analyses view the introduction of Theme B at m. 60 as the start of the second theme group; see, for example, Howes, *Music of Walton*, 85. I view Theme C as the start of the second theme group, which is the approach taken by the author of the original program notes, D[avid] M[illar] C[raig], descriptive note to *Concerto for Viola and Orchestra*, by William Walton, Promenade Concerts, British Composers Concert, October 3, 1929, [18].
54. Lawrence Power plays this on his recording using Walton's original 1929 orchestration; see *Viola Concertos*, by William Walton and Edmund Rubbra, with BBC Scottish Symphony Orchestra, conducted by Ilan Volkov, Hyperion CDA67587, 2007, compact disc.
55. Howes, *Music of Walton*, 86–87. Walton asserted that he was not consciously aware of this pitch connection to the second movement; see ibid., 87. In the 1929 orchestration, this theme is played by Bassoon I and II; in the 1962 orchestration, it is a solo for Bassoon I.
56. Howes, *Music of Walton*, 87.
57. In the 1929 orchestration, a c♯ is given to the violas. In the 1962 orchestration, C♯s are given to harp, violas, and cellos.
58. Kennedy, *Portrait of Walton*, 51.
59. B[lom], "William Walton's New Work."

Chapter 35

1. John Warrack, *Carl Maria von Weber*, 2nd ed. (Cambridge: Cambridge University Press, 1976), 369.
2. Warrack, *Carl Maria von Weber*, 31.
3. Max Maria von Weber, *Carl Maria von Weber: The Life of an Artist*, trans. J. Palgrave Simpson (London: Chapman and Hall, 1865), 1:52.
4. Max Maria von Weber, *Carl Maria von Weber*, 93, 117–28.
5. John Tyrrell, *Czech Opera* (Cambridge: Cambridge University Press, 1988), 17.
6. William Saunders, *Weber* (London: J. M. Dent and Sons, 1940; reprint, New York: Da Capo, 1970), 81–82.
7. *Grove Music Online*, s.v. "Weber Family: (9) Carl Maria (Friedrich Ernst) von Weber," by Michael C. Tusa, accessed December 21, 2017, https://doi.org/10.1093/gmo/9781561592630.article.40313.

8. *Grove Music Online*, s.v. "Carl Maria von Weber."

9. *Grove Music Online*, s.v. "Weber Family: (5) Fridolin (Stephan Johann Nepomuk Andreas Maria) [Fritz] Weber (ii)," by Joachim Veit, accessed December 17, 2017, https://doi.org/10.1093/gmo/9781561592630.article.40313; and E. van der Straeten, *The History of the Violin: Its Ancestors and Collateral Instruments from Earliest Times* (New York: Da Capo, 1968), 1:358–59. It is unknown why Weber composed the work for Fritz, and no performances by Fritz have yet been identified; see Friedr[ich] Wilh[elm] Jähns, *Carl Maria von Weber in Seinen Werken: Chronologisch-thematisches Verzeichniss seiner sämmtlichen Compositionen* [. . .] (Berlin: Verlag der Schlesinger'schen Buch- und Musikhandlung, 1871; Berlin-Lichterfelde: Robert Lienau, 1967), 92; and Christoph Schwandt, *Carl Maria von Weber in seiner Zeit: Eine Biografie* (Mainz: Schott, 2014), 95.

10. Carl Freiherrn von Ledebur, *Tonkünstler-Lexicon Berlin's von den ältesten Zeiten bis auf die Gegenwart* (Berlin: Ludwig Rauh, 1861), s.v. "Semler (Franz Xaver)."

11. "Nachrichten: Berlin. Uebersicht des April," *Allgemeine musikalische Zeitung* 25, no. 21 (May 1823): col. 337.

12. Jonathan Bellman, *The Style Hongrois in the Music of Western Europe* (Boston: Northeastern University Press, 1993), 11.

13. In the bassoon version, Weber added a four-measure orchestral tutti at the end of the second variation (with different material than the other orchestral tags), undoubtedly to give the bassoonist a short rest period before tackling the final variation.

14. In the bassoon version, Weber provided another rest period for the bassoonist, eliminating the solo part altogether in this tag (thereby shortening it by one measure).

15. *Grove Music Online*, s.v. "Verbunkos," by Jonathan Bellman, accessed January 1, 2018, https://doi.org/10.1093/gmo/9781561592630.article.29184.

16. Bálint Sárosi, *Gypsy Music*, trans. Fred Macnicol (Budapest: Corvina, 1978), 85–119; and Bellman, *Style Hongrois*, 18.

17. *Grove Music Online*, s.v. "Carl Maria von Weber."

18. Major Ervin, *Fejezetek a magyar zene történetéből: Válogatott tanulmányok*, ed. Bónis Ferenc (Budapest: Zeneműkiadó, 1967), 59. The melody for this example is taken from *Erk's Deutscher Liederschatz: Eine Auswahl der beliebtesten Volks-, Vaterlands-, Soldaten-, Jäger-, und Studenten-Lieder für eine Singstimme mit Pianofortebegleitung* (Leipzig: C. F. Peters, [1880s]), 1:190. In Ervin's example, the third note of m. 2 is an a^i, and the second note of m. 6 is a d^{ii}.

19. Anna Wojatycka, "Śląski motyw w 'Andante e rondo ungarese' Karola Marii Webera," *Prace Archiwum Śląskiej Kultury Muzycznej przy Bibliotece Głównej Akademii Muzycznej w Katowicach*, no. 8 (1979): 67; and Juliusz Roger, *Pieśni ludu polskiego w Górnym Szląsku z muzyką* (Wrocław: H. Skutsch, 1863), 222. Lujza Tari provides a number of additional sources that resemble the rondo theme; see "Unterhaltungsmusik als Quelle für das 'Ungarische' im 'Andante e Rondo Ungarese' op. 35 von Carl Maria von Weber," in *Kulturelle Identität durch Musik?: Das Burgenland und seine Nachbarn*, ed. Klaus Aringer, Ulrike Aringer-Grau, and Bernhard Habla (Vienna: Kliment, 2009), 83–93.

20. Csilla Pethő, "*Style Hongrois*. Hungarian Elements in the Works of Haydn, Beethoven, Weber and Schubert," *Studia Musicologica Academiae Scientiarum Hungaricae* 41, nos. 1–3 (2000): 229–30.

21. Pethő, "*Style Hongrois*," 236.

22. In examining the finale from the Piano Sonata No. 3 in D Minor, J. 206, Ebenezer Prout declared that "this rondo is very faulty in its form" and "we do not recommend it for imitation" because of its "peculiarities of construction." *Applied Forms: A Sequel to "Musical Form"* (London: Augener, 1895), 228–29.

23. Pethő, "*Style Hongrois*," 236.

24. Pethő, "*Style Hongrois*," 238.

25. *Grove Music Online*, s.v. "Carl Maria von Weber."

26. Sárosi, *Gypsy Music*, 53–54.

Bibliography

Abell, Arthur M. *Talks with Great Composers*. New York: Philosophical Library, 1955.

Abraham, Gerald. *Chopin's Musical Style*. London: Oxford University Press, 1939.

Alldritt, Keith. *Vaughan Williams: Composer, Radical, Patriot—A Biography*. London: Robert Hale, 2015.

Anderson, Christopher. "Reger in Bach's Notes: On Self-Image and Authority in Max Reger's Bach Playing." *Musical Quarterly* 87, no. 4 (Winter 2004): 749–70.

Anson, Harold. *T. B. Strong: Bishop, Musician, Dean, Vice-Chancellor*. London: SPCK, 1949.

Antokoletz, Elliott. "Bartók's Viola Concerto Manuscript: Some Questions and Speculations." *Studia Musicologica* 53, nos. 1–3 (2012): 69–84.

Antokoletz, Elliott. "Pitch Organization in the Finale of Bartók's Viola Concerto." In Donald Maurice, *Bartók's Viola Concerto: The Remarkable Story of His Swansong*, 132–35. Oxford: Oxford University Press, 2004.

Apel, Paul H. *The Message of Music*. New York: Vantage, 1958.

Arad, Atar. "Walton as Scapino." *Strad* 100, no. 1186 (February 1989): 137–41.

Aronowitz, Nicola. "Cecil Aronowitz." In *An Anthology of British Viola Players*, compiled and edited by John White, 1–6. Colne, UK: Comus, 1997.

Asbell, Stephanie Ames. "Béla Bartók's *Viola Concerto*: A Detailed Analysis and Discussion of Published Versions." DMA treatise, University of Texas at Austin, 2001.

Austenfeld, Thomas. " 'But, Come, I'll Set Your Story to a Tune': Berlioz's Interpretation of Byron's *Childe Harold*." *Keats-Shelley Journal* 39 (1990): 83–94.

[Bach, Carl Philipp Emanuel, and Johann Friedrich Agricola]. "Denkmal dreyer verstorbenen Mitglieder [. . .] Johann Sebastian Bach [. . .]." *Musikalische Bibliothek* 4, no. 1 (1754): 158–73.

Bach, J. S. *Konzert Es-Dur für Viola, Streicher und Basso continuo: Rekonstruktion nach BWV 169, 49, 1053*. Kassel: Bärenreiter, 1996.

Bach, Joh. Seb. *Sonaten für die Altgeige (Viola alta) allein*. Transcribed by Hermann Ritter. Leipzig: Carl Merseburger, [c. 1885].

Bach, Johann Sebastian. *Six Suites for Violoncello*. Adapted, revised, and fingered for viola by Louis Svećenski. New York: G. Schirmer, 1916.

Baillot, P[ierre]. *L'art du violon: Nouvelle méthode*. Paris: Depot Central de la Musique, [1834].

Balanchine, George. *Choreography by George Balanchine: A Catalogue of Works*. New York: Viking, 1984.

Balanchine, George. "The Dance Element in Stravinsky's Music." In *Stravinsky in the Theatre*, edited by Minna Lederman, 75–84. New York: Da Capo, 1975.

Banks, Paul, and Hugh Macdonald. Foreword to *New Edition of the Complete Works*, vol. 17, *Harold en Italie*, by Hector Berlioz, edited by Paul Banks and Hugh Macdonald, viii–xv. Kassel: Bärenreiter, 2001.

Barker, John W. *The Pro Arte Quartet: A Century of Musical Adventure on Two Continents*. Rochester, NY: University of Rochester Press, 2017.

Bartók, Béla. *Viola Concerto: Facsimile Edition of the Autograph Draft.* Homosassa, FL: Bartók Records, 1995.

Bartók, Béla, Jr. "Béla Bartók's Diseases." *Studia Musicologica Academiae Scientiarum Hungaricae* 23, nos. 1–4 (1981): 427–41.

Bartók, Peter. "Correcting Printed Editions of Béla Bartók's Viola Concerto and Other Compositions." In *Bartók Perspectives: Man, Composer, and Ethnomusicologist,* edited by Elliott Antokoletz, Victoria Fischer, and Benjamin Suchoff, 245–59. Oxford: Oxford University Press, 2000.

"Bartók's Finale." *Newsweek* 34, no. 24 (December 12, 1949): 80.

Beck, Georges. *Darius Milhaud: Etude suivie du Catalogue chronologique complet de son oeuvre.* Paris: Heugel, 1949.

Behr, Johannes. Preface to *Sonaten Opus 120 für Klarinette und Klavier, Fassung für Viola,* by Johannes Brahms, edited by Egon Voss and Johannes Behr, v–vi. Munich: Henle, 2013.

Bellman, Jonathan. *The Style Hongrois in the Music of Western Europe.* Boston: Northeastern University Press, 1993.

"Benjamin Britten." In *British Composers in Interview,* by Murray Schafer, 113–24. London: Faber and Faber, 1963.

Bentoiu, Pascal. *Masterworks of George Enescu: A Detailed Analysis.* Translated by Lory Wallfisch. Lanham, MD: Scarecrow, 2010.

Berkshire Festivals of Chamber Music: 1918–1938. Pittsfield, MA: Eagle Printing & Binding, [1938].

Berlioz, H. "Concert de M. Berlioz au Théatre-Italien." *Revue et Gazette musicale de Paris* 11, no. 19 (May 12, 1844): 167–69.

Berlioz, Hector. *Autobiography of Hector Berlioz, Member of the Institute of France: From 1803 to 1865, Comprising His Travels in Italy, Germany, Russia, and England.* 2 vols. Translated by Rachel Scott Russell Holmes and Eleanor Holmes. London: Macmillan, 1884.

Berlioz, Hector. *Correspondance générale.* Vol. 1, *1803–1832,* edited by Pierre Citron. Paris: Flammarion, 1972.

Berlioz, Hector. *Correspondance générale.* Edited by Pierre Citron. Vol. 2, *1832–1842,* edited by Frédéric Robert. Paris: Flammarion, 1975.

Berlioz, Hector. *Correspondance générale.* Edited by Pierre Citron. Vol. 4, *1851–1855,* edited by Pierre Citron, Yves Gérard, and Hugh J. Macdonald. Paris: Flammarion, 1983.

Berlioz, Hector. *The Memoirs of Hector Berlioz.* Translated and edited by David Cairns. New York: Alfred A. Knopf, 2002.

Besseler, Heinrich. "Zur Chronologie der Konzerte Joh. Seb. Bachs." In *Festschrift Max Schneider: Zum achtzigsten Geburstage,* edited by Walther Vetter, 115–28. Leipzig: Deutscher Verlag für Musik, 1955.

Beyer, Franz. [Introduction] to *Konzert in G-dur für Viola und Orchester,* by Georg Philipp Telemann, edited by Franz Beyer, [i]. Berg am Irchel, Switzerland: Amadeus, 1974. Piano reduction.

Beyer, Franz. *Kadenzen zu Viola-Konzerten von Stamitz, Zelter und Hoffmeister.* Adliswil, Switzerland: Kunzelmann, [1991], © 1971.

Biancolli, Louis. "*Sinfonia Concertante* for Violin, Viola, and Orchestra in E Flat Major (K. 364)." In *The Mozart Handbook: A Guide to the Man and His Music,* compiled and edited by Louis Biancolli, 439–42. Cleveland: World Publishing, 1954.

Bloch, Ernest. *Ernest Bloch (1880–1959): Sa vie et sa pensée suivi du catalogue de l'œuvre.* Edited by Joseph Lewinski and Emmanuelle Dijon. Vol. 4, *Le Havre de Paix en Oregon (1939–1959).* Geneva: Slatkine, 2005.

Blom, Eric. *Mozart.* New York: Pellegrini and Cudahy, 1949.

Bloom, Peter. *The Life of Berlioz.* Cambridge: Cambridge University Press, 1998.

Bloom, Peter. "Recio [Récio], Marie." In *The Cambridge Berlioz Encyclopedia*, edited by Julian Rushton, 271–72. Cambridge: Cambridge University Press, 2018.

Blyth, Alan, ed. *Remembering Britten.* London: Hutchinson, 1981.

Boatwright, Howard. "Quincy Porter." *Bulletin of American Composers Alliance* 6, no. 3 (1957): 2–9.

Boatwright, Howard. "Quincy Porter (1897–1966)." *Perspectives of New Music* 5, no. 2 (Spring–Summer 1967): 162–65.

Boisdeffre, René de. *Trois pièces pour clarinette (en la) ou alto avec accompagnement de piano, op. 40.* Paris: J. Hamelle, [1888].

Borowski, Felix. Program note to *Concerto No. 6, B Flat Major,* by Johann Sebastian Bach. Chicago Symphony Orchestra, Thirty-Second Season, Sixteenth Program, January 26 and 27, 1923, 5–7.

Boulanger, Nadia. *Nadia Boulanger and the Stravinskys: A Selected Correspondence.* Edited by Kimberly A. Francis. Rochester, NY: University of Rochester Press, 2018.

Boyd, Malcolm. *Bach: The Brandenburg Concertos.* Cambridge: Cambridge University Press, 1993.

Brahms, Johannes. *Johannes Brahms Briefe an P. J. Simrock und Fritz Simrock.* 4 vols. Edited by Max Kalbeck. [Tutzing]: Hans Schneider, 1974.

Brahms, Johannes. *Johannes Brahms im Briefwechsel mit Joseph Joachim.* 2 vols. Edited by Andreas Moser. Berlin: Deutschen Brahms-Gesellschaft, 1908.

Brahms, Johannes. *Neue Ausgabe sämtlicher Werke.* Serie II: *Kammermusik,* vol. 9, *Violoncello- und Klarinettensonaten,* edited by Egon Voss and Johannes Behr. Munich: Henle, 2010.

Braun, Rachel Heimovics. "Ernest Bloch and His Chicago Jewish Colleagues." *Chicago Jewish History* 35, no. 2 (Spring 2011): 4–7.

Brin, David M. "Sonata in C Minor for Viola and Piano: A Neglected Work by a Master Composer." *Strings* 5, no. 6 (May/June 1991): 28–31.

Britten, Benjamin. *Letters from a Life: The Selected Letters of Benjamin Britten, 1913–1976.* Vol. 3, *1946–1951,* edited by Donald Mitchell, Philip Reed, and Mervyn Cooke. Berkeley: University of California Press, 2004.

Britten, Benjamin. *Letters from a Life: The Selected Letters of Benjamin Britten, 1913–1976.* Vol. 5, *1958–1965,* edited by Philip Reed and Mervyn Cooke. Woodbridge, UK: Boydell Press, 2010.

Britten, Benjamin. *Letters from a Life: The Selected Letters of Benjamin Britten, 1913–1976.* Vol. 6, *1966–1976,* edited by Philip Reed and Mervyn Cooke. Woodbridge, UK: Boydell Press, 2012.

Brook, Barry S. *The Breitkopf Thematic Catalogue: The Six Parts and Sixteen Supplements, 1762–1787.* New York: Dover, 1966.

Brook, Donald. "York Bowen." In *Composers' Gallery: Biographical Sketches of Contemporary Composers,* 35–37. London: Rockliff, 1946.

Brown, Clive. Preface to *Sonaten in f und Es für Viola und Klavier, op. 120,* by Johannes Brahms, edited by Clive Brown and Neal Peres Da Costa, iii–ix. Kassel: Bärenreiter, 2016.

Brown, Malcolm Hamrick, ed. *A Shostakovich Casebook*. Bloomington: Indiana University Press, 2004.

Brown, Thomas Alan. *The Aesthetics of Robert Schumann*. New York: Philosophical Library, 1968.

Browning, James. "The American Music Center." *Notes*, 2nd ser., 21, no. 4 (Autumn 1964): 511–12.

Bruhn, Siglind. *Hindemiths große Instrumentalwerke*. Waldkirch, Germany: Edition Gorz, 2012.

Burt, Peter. *The Music of Tōru Takemitsu*. Cambridge: Cambridge University Press, 2001.

Butler, Gregory G. "J. S. Bach's Reception of Tomaso Albinoni's Mature Concertos." In *Bach Studies 2*, edited by Daniel R. Melamed, 20–46. Cambridge: Cambridge University Press, 1995.

Bynog, David M. "A Catalogue of Cadenzas for Carl Stamitz's Concerto in D Major for Viola and Orchestra, 1900–2015." *Journal of the American Viola Society* 34, online issue (2018): 18–39.

Bynog, David M. "Cecil Forsyth: The Forgotten Composer?" *Journal of the American Viola Society* 24, no. 1 (Spring 2008): 13–18.

Bynog, David M. "The Vocal Music of Cecil Forsyth." *British Music* 30 (2008): 6–15.

Cahn, Peter. Einleitung to *Sämtliche Werke*, vol. 5, no. 6, *Streicherkammermusik III*, by Paul Hindemith, edited by Peter Cahn, ix–xv. Mainz: B. Schott's Söhne, 1976.

Cairns, David. *Berlioz*. [Vol. 1], *1803–1832: The Making of an Artist*. London: André Deutsch, 1989.

Campbell, Stuart, ed. and trans. *Russians on Russian Music, 1880–1917: An Anthology*. Cambridge: Cambridge University Press, 2003.

Canarina, John. *Pierre Monteux, maître*. Pompton Plains, NJ: Amadeus, 2003.

Caplin, William E. *Classical Form: A Theory of Formal Functions for the Instrumental Music of Haydn, Mozart, and Beethoven*. Oxford: Oxford University Press, 1998.

Carner, Mosco. "Béla Bartók (1881–1945)." In *The Concerto*, edited by Ralph Hill, 327–56. Westport, CT: Greenwood, 1978.

Carpenter, Humphrey. *Benjamin Britten: A Biography*. New York: Charles Scribner's Sons, 1992.

Casadesus, Henri. "Handel concerto en si mineur pour alto avec accompagnement d'orchestre." *Notes*, no. 1 (July 1934): 9.

Casadesus, Jean-Claude. *La partition d'une vie*. Paris: Écriture, 2012.

Casella, Alfredo. *Music in My Time*. Translated and edited by Spencer Norton. Norman: University of Oklahoma Press, 1955.

Charney, Noah. *The Art of Forgery: The Minds, Motives, and Methods of Master Forgers*. London: Phaidon, 2015.

Cheng, Christine. "On Approaching a Performance of Paul Hindemith's *Der Schwanendreher*." Master's thesis, University of Queensland, 2016.

Chicago Symphony Orchestra, Fourteenth Program, January 1 and 2, 1953.

Clapham, John. "Martinů's Instrumental Style." *Music Review* 24, no. 2 (May 1963): 158–67.

Clarke, Rebecca. Diaries (1919–1933). 3 vols., unpublished. Copyright © 2004, Christopher Johnson. Reproduced by permission.

Clarke, Rebecca. "I Had a Father Too, or The Mustard Spoon." Unpublished manuscript, n.d. [c. 1967–1977]. Copyright © 2004, Christopher Johnson. Reproduced by permission.

Clarke, Rebecca. Program note to *Viola Sonata*, by Rebecca Clarke. Toby Appel (viola) and Andrew Willis (piano) recital, April 2, 1977. *Lincoln Center for the Performing Arts Stagebill* 4, no. 8 (April 1977): [31].

"Classical Records . . . for Week Ending January 10." *Billboard* (January 17, 1953): 50.

Clive, Peter. *Brahms and His World: A Biographical Dictionary*. Lanham, MD: Scarecrow, 2006.

Cobbett, Walter Wilson, comp. and ed. *Cobbett's Cyclopedic Survey of Chamber Music*. 2nd ed., with supplemental material edited by Colin Mason. 3 vols. London: Oxford University Press, 1963.

Codignola, Arturo. *Paganini intimo*. Genoa: Edito a Cura del Municipio, 1935.

Cohen, Alex, and Suzanne Bloch. "Ernest Bloch—A Biography." In *Ernest Bloch: Creative Spirit; A Program Source Book*, prepared by Suzanne Bloch with Irene Heskes, 3–8. New York: Jewish Music Council of the National Jewish Welfare Board, 1976.

Collaer, Paul. *Darius Milhaud*. Translated and edited by Jane Hohfeld Galante. San Francisco: San Francisco Press, 1988.

"Comments and Opinions: Opera and Two Concerts." *Musical Standard* 23, no. 595 (May 27, 1905): 319.

The Complete Programme Book, The Third Aldeburgh Festival of Music and the Arts, June 17–25, 1950.

The Complete Programme Book, The Fifth Aldeburgh Festival of Music and the Arts, June 14–22, 1952.

"Les Concours du Conservatoire: Alto." *Le Ménestrel* 74, no. 28 (July 11, 1908): 219.

Cone, Edward T. "Inside the Saint's Head: The Music of Berlioz." In *Music: A View from Delft; Selected Essays*, edited by Robert P. Morgan, 217–48. Chicago: University of Chicago Press, 1989.

Conitz, Aaron Daniel. "(Re)Examining Narratives: Personal Style and the Viola Works of Quincy Porter (1897–1966)." DMA thesis, Rice University, 2019.

"Contingencies." *Sackbut* 1, no. 3 (July 1920): 104–9.

Cooper, David. *Béla Bartók*. New Haven, CT: Yale University Press, 2015.

Cope, David. Review of *Rhapsody-Concerto*, by Bohuslav Martinů. *Notes*, 2nd ser., 36, no. 3 (March 1980): 744–45.

Cornaz, Marie. Preface to *Sonate B-dur Opus 36 für Klavier und Viola*, by Henry Vieuxtemps, edited by Peter Jost, iv–v. Munich: Henle, 2013.

"Correspondances: Anvers." *Le Guide musical* 58, no. 2 (January 14, 1912): 36.

Courcy, G. I. C. de. *Paganini: The Genoese*. 2 vols. New York: Da Capo, 1977.

Craggs, Stewart R. *William Walton: A Catalogue*. 3rd ed. Oxford: Oxford University Press, 2015.

C[raig], D[avid] M[illar]. Descriptive note to *Concerto for Viola and Orchestra*, by William Walton. Promenade Concerts, British Composers Concert, October 3, 1929, [17–18].

Cross, Jonathan. *Igor Stravinsky*. London: Reaktion, 2015.

Crump, Michael. *Martinů and the Symphony*. [London]: Toccata, 2010.

Dalton, David. *Playing the Viola: Conversations with William Primrose*. Oxford: Oxford University Press, 1988.

Danuser, Hermann. "Symphonisches Subjekt und Form in Berlioz' Harold en Italie." *Melos/NZ* 3, no. 3 (May/June 1977): 203–12.

Daverio, John. *Robert Schumann: Herald of a "New Poetic Age."* New York: Oxford University Press, 1997.

David, Hans T., and Arthur Mendel, eds. *The Bach Reader: A Life of Johann Sebastian Bach in Letters and Documents*. New York: W. W. Norton, 1945.

Davis, Hazel. "Lawrence Power." *Strad* 118, no. 1405 (May 2007): 24–30.

Davis, Richard Beattie. *The Beauty of Belaieff*. 2nd ed. Bedford, England: G-Clef, 2009.

Day, James. *Vaughan Williams*. 3rd ed. Oxford: Oxford University Press, 1998.

DeBolt, Katharine Gerson. "Information and Imagination as Sources of Interpretation: The Performer's Procedures Applied to Telemann's Viola Concerto in G Major." MA Thesis, Ohio State University, 1965.

Dehn, S. W. Preface to *Sixième Concerto pour deux Altos, deux Violes da gamba, avec Violoncelle et Basse*, by Jean Sebastien Bach, edited by S. W. Dehn, 3. Leipzig: Au Bureau de Musique de C. F. Peters, [1852].

Desbruslais, Simon. *The Music and Music Theory of Paul Hindemith*. Woodbridge, UK: Boydell Press, 2018.

Dickinson, A. E. F. *Vaughan Williams*. London: Faber and Faber, 1963.

Dickinson, Emily. *Poems*. Second series. Edited by T. W. Higginson and Mabel Loomis Todd. Boston: Roberts Brothers, 1891.

"Did You Hear That?: How to Become a Composer." *Listener* 36, no. 930 (November 7, 1946): 624.

Diergarten, Felix. "Sonate c-moll für Viola und Klavier, MWV Q 14." In *Felix Mendelssohn Bartholdy: Interpretationen seiner Werke*, vol. 1, edited by Matthias Geuting, 125–28. Laaber, Germany: Laaber-Verlag, 2016.

Dinerchtein, Viacheslav. "Shostakovich's Viola Sonata: A Historical Survey." DMA thesis, Northwestern University, 2008.

Dmitri Shostakovich [Work List]. 2nd ed. Hamburg: Sikorski Musikverlage, 2011, updated 2014. https://www.sikorski.de/336/en/shostakovich_dmitri.html.

Doctor, Jennifer. *The BBC and Ultra-Modern Music, 1922–1936: Shaping a Nation's Tastes*. Cambridge: Cambridge University Press, 1999.

Doktor, Paul. [Preface] to *Suite für Viola Solo*, by Adolf Busch, 2. Winterthur: Amadeus, 1980.

Downes, Olin. "Ernest Bloch, the Swiss Composer, on the Influence of Race in Composition." *Musical Observer* 15, no. 3 (March 1917): 11–12.

Downs, Philip G. *Classical Music: The Era of Haydn, Mozart, and Beethoven*. New York: W. W. Norton, 1992.

Drummond, Pippa. *The German Concerto: Five Eighteenth-Century Studies*. Oxford: Clarendon Press, 1980.

Drüner, Ulrich. "Glanz und Elend eines Musikers der Empfindsamkeit: Carl Stamitz zum 250. Geburstag." *Das Orchester* 43, no. 12 (1995): 16–23.

Drüner, Ulrich. [Preface] to *Concerto in D-dur für Viola und Orchester, op. 1*, by Carl Stamitz, edited by Ulrich Drüner, [i]. Winterthur: Amadeus, 1995. Score.

Drüner, Ulrich. [Preface] to *Konzert für Viola und Orchester D dur*, by Franz Anton Hoffmeister, edited by Ulrich Drüner, [i–ii]. Adliswil, Switzerland: Kunzelmann, 1982. Score.

Druzhinin, Fedor. *Memoirs: Pages from the Life and Works*. Edited by Elena Skripka. Translated by Emily Finer. Moscow: Museum Graeco-Latinum, 2015.

Dumanowski, Jacek. *Sonaty altówkowe Carla Stamitza, Johanna Baptisty Vanhala i Johanna Nepomuka Hummla: Studium klasycznej stylistyki wykonawczej*. Kraków: Akademia Muzyczna w Krakowie, 2013.

D[unhill], T[homas] F. "Obituary: Cecil Forsyth." *RCM Magazine* 38, no. 2 (June 1942): 65.

Edgewood Convent Annals II. Edgewood College Archives, Madison, WI.

Egremont, Max. *Siegfried Sassoon: A Biography*. London: Picador, 2005.

[Eisel, Johann Philipp]. *Musicus Autodidaktos, Oder Der sich selbst informirende Musicus* […]. Erfurt: Johann Michael Funcken, 1738.

Eisen, Cliff, and Stanley Sadie. *The New Grove Mozart.* London: Macmillan, 2002.

Elwell, Herbert. "American Composers, XXIV: Quincy Porter." *Modern Music* 23, no. 1 (Winter 1946): 20–26.

Engelstoft, Povl, and Svend Dahl, eds. *Dansk biografisk Leksikon.* 27 vols. Copenhagen: J. H. Schultz, 1933–1944.

Erdélyi, Csaba. Foreword to *Viola Concerto,* by Béla Bartók, critical restoration and orchestration by Csaba Erdélyi, iii–v. Wellington, NZ: Promethean Editions, 2004. Score.

Erk, Ludwig. *Erk's Deutscher Liederschatz: Eine Auswahl der beliebtesten Volks-, Vaterlands-, Soldaten-, Jäger-, und Studenten-Lieder für eine Singstimme mit Pianofortebegleitung.* 2 vols. Leipzig: C. F. Peters, [1880s].

Ernest Bloch collection, ARCHIVES BLOCH 1, Music Library, University of California, Berkeley.

Ervin, Major. *Fejezetek a magyar zene történetéből: Válogatott tanulmányok.* Edited by Bónis Ferenc. Budapest: Zeneműkiadó, 1967.

Evans, Edwin. Analytical note to *Suite for Viola and Orchestra,* by Ralph Vaughan Williams. Courtauld-Sargent Concerts (6th Series), November 12 and 13, 1934, [16–17].

E[vans], E[dwin]. Analytical program note to *Concerto for Viola and Orchestra,* by William Walton. The Royal Philharmonic Society (124th Season, Ninth Concert, Series A), February 27, 1936, 14–21.

Evans, Edwin. *Handbook to the Chamber & Orchestral Music of Johannes Brahms.* Vol. 2, *Second Series Op. 68 to the End.* London: William Reeves, 1935.

Evans, Peter. *The Music of Benjamin Britten.* Minneapolis: University of Minnesota Press, 1979.

Everett, William E. "Ralph Vaughan Williams's Suite for Viola and Orchestra." *Journal of the American Viola Society* 13, no. 2 (1997): 9–19.

Fay, Laurel E. *Shostakovich: A Life.* Oxford: Oxford University Press, 2000.

Fay, Laurel E. "Shostakovich versus Volkov: Whose *Testimony*? (1980)." In *A Shostakovich Casebook,* edited by Malcolm Hamrick Brown, 11–21. Bloomington: Indiana University Press, 2004.

Fay, Laurel Elizabeth. "The Last Quartets of Dmitrii Shostakovich: A Stylistic Investigation." PhD diss., Cornell University, 1978.

Festival Programme Book, Thirty-Seventh Aldeburgh Festival of Music and the Arts, June 8–24, 1984.

"Feuilleton." *Neue Zeitschrift für Musik* 18, no. 31 (April 17, 1843): 126.

Fifield, Christopher. *Max Bruch: His Life and Works.* London: Victor Gollancz, 1988.

Filmer, Andrew. Introduction to *Concerto for Two Violettas, TWV 52:G3,* by Georg Philipp Telemann, edited by Andrew Filmer and David M. Bynog, 1–13. [Dallas, TX]: American Viola Society, 2013.

Fischer, Wilfried. "Hat Bach ein Bratschenkonzert geschrieben?: Neue Überlegungen zur Vorlage von BMV [sic] 1053, 169 und 49." In *Bericht über das 1. Dortmunder Bach-Symposion 1996,* edited by Martin Geck and Werner Breig, 249–56. Witten, Germany: Klangfarben Musikverlag, 1997.

Forster, E. M. "The Abinger Pageant." In *Abinger Harvest,* 337–51. London: Edward Arnold, 1936.

Forsyth, Cecil. *Orchestration.* London: Macmillan, 1914.

Framery, [Nicolas Etienne], and [Pierre-Louis] Ginguené, eds. *Encyclopedie méthodique: Musique.* Vol. 1. Paris: Panckoucke, 1791.

Frisch, Walter. "Reger's Bach and Historicist Modernism." *19th Century Music* 25, nos. 2–3 (Fall/Spring 2001–2002): 296–312.

Fuchs, Lillian. "In Reverence to the Viola." *American String Teacher* 29, no. 2 (Spring 1979): 5.

Fuller, Donald. "Forecast and Review: Russian and American Season, 1945." *Modern Music* 22, no. 4 (May–June 1945): 254–58.

Ganina, M. *Aleksandr Konstantinovich Glazunov: Zhizn' i tvorchestvo.* Leningrad: Gosudarstvennoe muzykal'noe izdatel'stvo, 1961.

Gatens, [William J.]. Review of *Bach: Apocryphal Cantatas II: 15, 141, 142, 160,* with I Febiarmonici and the Alsfeld Vocal Ensemble, Wolfgang Helbich (conductor), cpo 999985. *American Record Guide* 67, no. 6 (November/December 2004): 53.

Gavoty, Bernard. *Les Souvenirs de Georges Enesco.* Bucharest: Curtea Veche, 2005.

Gavoty, Bernard. *Yehudi Menuhin and Georges Enesco.* Geneva: René Kister, 1955.

Geck, Martin. "Gattungstraditionen und Altersschichten in den Brandenburgischen Konzerten." *Die Musikforschung* 23, no. 2 (April/June 1970): 139–52.

Geck, Martin. *Robert Schumann: The Life and Work of a Romantic Composer.* Translated by Stewart Spencer. Chicago: University of Chicago Press, 2013.

Gerber, Ernst Ludwig. *Historisch-biographisches Lexicon der Tonkünstler [. . .].* 2 vols. Leipzig: Johann Gottlob Immanuel Breitkopf, 1790–1792.

Gerber, Ernst Ludwig. *Neues historisch-biographisches Lexikon der Tonkünstler [. . .].* 4 vols. Leipzig: A. Kühnel, 1812–1814.

Gerling, Daphne Cristina Capparelli. "Connecting Histories: Identity and Exoticism in Ernest Bloch, Rebecca Clarke, and Paul Hindemith's Viola Works of 1919." DMA thesis, Rice University, 2007.

Gilman, Lawrence. "Notes on the Program." Tenth Pair of Concerts, Twenty-Seventh Season, The Philadelphia Orchestra, December 10 and 11, 1926, 459–73.

Gilman, Lawrence. Program note to *Der Schwanendreher: Concerto on Old Folk-Melodies, for Viola and Small Orchestra,* by Paul Hindemith. The Philharmonic-Symphony Society of New York (Ninety-Fifth Season, 3314th and 3315th Concerts), April 15 and 16, 1937, [4–6].

Ginsburg, L. *Vieuxtemps.* Edited by Herbert R. Axelrod. Translated by I. Levin. Neptune City, NJ: Paganiniana, 1984.

Giuranna, Bruno. "Brahms' 'Viola' Sonata in E Flat." *Strad* 104, no. 1238 (June 1993): 552–57.

Glazunov, A. K. *Pis'ma, stat'i, vospominaniia: Izbrannoe.* Compiled by M. A. Ganina. Moscow: Gos. muzykal'noe izd-vo, 1958.

Glebov, Igor [Boris Vladimirovich Asaf'yev]. "Pathways into the Future." *Melos* 2 (1918): 50–96.

Goldstein, Elias. " 'J. S. Bach Viola Concerto in E Flat Major': A Reconstruction of BWV 169, 49, and 1053; Merits and Shortcomings." DMA diss., University of Wisconsin–Madison, 2011.

Green, Phoebe. "The Influence of Nature on Two Works for the Viola by Toru Takemitsu and Ross Edwards." Master's thesis, University of Queensland, 2010.

Grierson, Mary. *Donald Francis Tovey: A Biography Based on Letters.* London: Oxford University Press, 1952.

Griffin, Judson. "A Guide to American Viola Music." DMA thesis, The Juilliard School, 1977.

Griffiths, Paul. *Bartók.* London: J. M. Dent & Sons, 1984.

Griffiths, Paul. *Stravinsky.* New York: Schirmer, 1992.

Grimm, Jacob Ludwig Karl, and Wilhelm Karl Grimm. "The Hen-Roost." In *The Complete Illustrated Works of the Brothers Grimm*, 698–99. London: Chancellor, 1984.

Hall, Willard Kent. "Quincy Porter: His Life and Contributions as a Composer and Educator (1897–1966)." DMA thesis, University of Missouri–Kansas City, 1970.

Haney, Joel Christian. "The Emergence of a Postwar Musical Outlook: Hindemith's 'Hard-Edged Simplicity,' 1919–1922." PhD diss., Yale University, 2006.

Hansen, Kelly Dean. "Clarinet (or Viola) Sonata No. 2 in E-Flat Major, Op. 120, No. 2." *Listening Guides to the Works of Johannes Brahms.* http://www.kellydeanhansen.com/opus120-2.html.

Hanslick, Eduard. *Geschichte des Concertwesens in Wien.* Vol. 1. Vienna: Wilhelm Braumüller, 1869.

"Hanslick on Brahms's Chamber Music with Clarinet." Translated by John Daverio. *American Brahms Society Newsletter* 13, no. 1 (Spring 1995): 5–7.

Hardisty, Nicholas. "Studies of Vocality in the Music of Max Bruch: Instrumental Recitative." In *Max Bruch: Neue Perspektiven auf Leben und Werk*, edited by Fabian Kolb, 161–82. Kassel: Merseburger, 2016.

Harrison, Daniel. "Max Reger's Motivic Technique: Harmonic Innovations at the Borders of Atonality." *Journal of Music Theory* 35, nos. 1/2 (Spring–Fall 1991): 61–92.

Haug-Freienstein, Wiltrud. Preface to *Märchenbilder für Klavier und Viola Opus 113*, by Robert Schumann, edited by Wiltrud Haug-Freienstein, iv–v. Munich: Henle, 2000.

Hewitt, James Robert. "The Tropes of Self in the Poetry of Alfred de Musset." PhD diss., New York University, 1973.

Hilse, Walter Bruno. "Factors Making for Coherence in the Works of Paul Hindemith, 1919–1926." PhD diss., Columbia University, 1971.

Hilse, Walter Bruno. "Hindemith and Debussy." *Hindemith-Jahrbuch* 2 (1972): 48–90.

Hindemith, Paul. *A Composer's World: Horizons and Limitations.* Garden City, NY: Anchor Books, 1961.

Hindemith, Paul. Note to *Sonata for Viola and Piano, Opus 11, No. 4*, 2. New York: Associated Music Publishers, 1922.

Hindemith, Paul. [Preface] to *Der Schwanendreher: Konzert nach alten Volksliedern für Bratsche und kleines Orchester.* Mainz: B. Schott's Söhne, 1936, [i]. Score.

Hindemith, Paul. *Sämtliche Werke.* Series III, vol. 4, *Bratschenkonzerte*, edited by Hans Kohlhase. Mainz: Schott, 1997.

Hindemith, Paul. *Selected Letters of Paul Hindemith.* Edited and translated by Geoffrey Skelton. New Haven, CT: Yale University Press, 1995.

Hindemith, Paul. *Unterweisung im Tonsatz: Theoretischer Teil.* Mainz: B. Schott's Söhne, 1937.

Hindemith, Paul. Verzeichnis aller fertigen Kompositionen, 1913–1938. Unpublished manuscript.

"Hindemith Gives Germans New Outlook on Music." *Information Bulletin*, no. 157 (March 22, 1949): 11–12, 23.

Hinton, Stephen. "Aspects of Hindemith's Neue Sachlichkeit." *Hindemith-Jahrbuch* 14 (1985): 22–80.

Hirschmann, Wolfgang. Preface to *Konzert in G-Dur für Viola, Streicher und Basso continuo, TWV 51:G9*, by [Georg Philipp] Telemann, edited by Wolfgang Hirschmann, vii–x. Kassel: Bärenreiter, 2002. Score.

Hirschmann, Wolfgang. "Telemanns Konzertschaffen im Beziehungsfeld von Quellenforschung—Edition—Interpretation." In *Historische Aufführungspraxis im heutigen Musikleben: Konferenzbericht der XVII. Wissenschaftlichen Arbeitstagung Michaelstein, 8.–11. Juni 1989*, vol. 1, edited by Eitelfriedrich Thom and Frieder Zschoch, 87–96. Michaelstein, Germany: Institut für Aufführungspraxis-Kultur- und Forschungsstätte Michaelstein, 1990.

Ho, Allan B., and Dmitry Feofanov. *Shostakovich Reconsidered*. [London]: Toccata, 1998.

Hofmann, Renate, and Kurt Hofmann. *Johannes Brahms: Zeittafel zu Leben und Werk*. Tutzing: Hans Schneider, 1983.

Holoman, D. Kern. *Berlioz*. Cambridge, MA: Harvard University Press, 1989.

Holoman, D. Kern. "Conducting (1). Berlioz Conducting His Own Works." In *The Cambridge Berlioz Encyclopedia*, edited by Julian Rushton, 79. Cambridge: Cambridge University Press, 2018.

Howes, Frank. *The Music of Ralph Vaughan Williams*. London: Oxford University Press, 1954.

Howes, Frank. *The Music of William Walton*. 2nd ed. London: Oxford University Press, 1974.

Hulme, Derek C. *Dmitri Shostakovich Catalogue: The First Hundred Years and Beyond*. 4th ed. Lanham, MD: Scarecrow, 2010.

Hutchings, Arthur. *The Baroque Concerto*. Rev. ed. New York: Charles Scribner's Sons, 1979.

Imai, Nobuko. "Tōru Takemitsu's *A Bird came down the Walk*." *Strad* 124, no. 1477 (May 2013): 86–89.

"II. Instrumentalmusik." *Allgemeine musikalische Zeitung* 10, no. 31 (April 27, 1808): cols. 490–96.

Jacob, Gordon. "[Remembrance of Ralph Vaughan Williams]." *RCM Magazine* 55, no. 1 (February 1959): 31–32.

Jacobs, Arthur. *Henry J. Wood: Maker of the Proms*. London: Methuen, 1994.

Jähns, Friedr[ich] Wilh[elm]. *Carl Maria von Weber in seinen Werken: Chronologisch-thematisches Verzeichnis seiner sämmtlichen Compositionen* [. . .]. Berlin-Lichterfelde: Robert Lienau, 1967. First published 1871 by Verlag der Schlesinger'schen Buch- und Musikhandlung, 1871 (Berlin).

Jakubov, Manashir. "A Bridge over the Past into the Future." Translated by David Babcock. In *Sonate für Viola und Klavier, op. 147*, by Dmitri Schostakowitsch, 5–6. Facsimile edition. [Hamburg]: Sikorski, n.d. [c. 2001].

James, Dianne, and Allan Badley. Foreword to *Viola Concerto in B♭*, by Franz Anton Hoffmeister, iii–iv. Edited by Allan Badley. Wellington, NZ: Artaria, 2002.

Jappe, Michael, and Dorothea Jappe. *Viola Bibliographie: Das Repertoire für die historische Bratsche von 1649 bis nach 1800*. Winterthur: Amadeus, 1999.

Johnson, Christopher. Introduction to *Trio: For Piano, Violin, and Cello*, by Rebecca Clarke, v–vii. New York: Da Capo, 1980.

Johnson, H. Earle. *Symphony Hall, Boston*. Boston: Little, Brown, 1950.

Johnson, Leslie Faye. "The Shostakovich Viola Sonata: An Analytical Performer's Guide." DMA diss., University of Washington, 1991.

Kaczmarczyk, Adrienne, and Eszter Mikusi. Preface to *Neue Ausgabe sämtlicher Werke*, supplement no. 9, *Harold en Italie (Berlioz) und andere Werke*, by Franz Liszt, edited by Adrienne Kaczmarczyk and Eszter Mikusi, translated by Lorna Dunbar, xxxii–xlix. Budapest: Editio Musica Budapest, 2009.

Keefe, Simon P., ed. *The Cambridge Companion to the Concerto*. Cambridge: Cambridge University Press, 2005.

Kemp, Ian. *Hindemith*. London: Oxford University Press, 1970.

Kemp, Ian. "Some Thoughts on Hindemith's Viola Concertos." *Hindemith-Jahrbuch* 35 (2006): 68–117.

Kennedy, Michael. *Britten*. Oxford: Oxford University Press, 2001.

Kennedy, Michael. *Portrait of Walton*. Oxford: Oxford University Press, 1990.

Kennedy, Michael. *The Works of Ralph Vaughan Williams*. London: Oxford University Press, 1964.

King, A. Hyatt. *Mozart Wind and String Concertos*. BBC Music Guides. London: British Broadcasting Corporation, 1978.

Kloiber, Rudolf. *Handbuch des Instrumentalkonzerts*. Vol. 1, *Vom Barock bis zur Klassik*. Wiesbaden: Breitkopf & Härtel, 1972.

Knapp, Alexander. "Ernest Bloch's *Suite Hébraïque* and *Meditation and Processional*: Historical Overview and Analysis of Traditional Musical Materials." *Journal of the American Viola Society* 33, no. 2 (Fall 2017): 19–33.

Knapp, Alexander. "From Geneva to New York: Radical Changes in Ernest Bloch's View of Himself as a 'Jewish Composer' during His Twenties and Thirties." In *Ernest Bloch Studies*, edited by Alexander Knapp and Norman Solomon, 12–19. Cambridge: Cambridge University Press, 2016.

Knapp, Alexander. "The Jewishness of Bloch: Subconscious or Conscious?" *Proceedings of the Royal Musical Association* 97 (1970–1971): 99–112.

Koch, Armin. "Kritischer Bericht: Märchenbilder. Four Pieces for Piano and Viola (*Ad Libitum* Violin), Op. 113." In Schumann, *Werke für verschiedene Instrumente und Klavier*, 329–71.

Koch, Heinrich Christoph. *Versuch einer Anleitung zur Composition*. Vol. 3. Leipzig: Böhme, 1793.

Köchel, Ludwig Ritter von. *Chronologisch-thematisches Verzeichnis sämtlicher Tonwerke Wolfgang Amade Mozarts: Nebst Angabe der verlorengegangenen, angefangenen, übertragenen, zweifelhaften und unterschobenen Kompositionen*. 6th ed., edited by Alfred Einstein. Leipzig: VEB Breitkopf & Härtel, 1969.

Kohlhase, Hans. "Paul Hindemiths Bratschenkonzert "Der Schwanendreher."" In *2. Viola-Symposium 1990: Dokumentation*, edited by Rolf Fritsch, 47–84. Trossingen, Germany: Bundesakademie für musikalische Jugendbildung, 1991.

Koozin, Timothy. Review of *A Bird came down the Walk for Viola Accompanied by Piano*, by Toru Takemitsu. *Notes*, 2nd ser., 54, no. 1 (September 1997): 278–80.

Kopitz, Klaus Martin, and Torsten Oltrogge. "Ein Dichter namens Louis du Rieux und Schumanns 'Märchenbilder' op. 113." *Denkströme: Journal der Sächsischen Akademie der Wissenschaften zu Leipzig* 11 (2013): 112–40. http://www.denkstroeme.de/heft-11/s_112-140_kopitz-oltrogge.

Kotlyarov, B. *Enesco: His Life and Times*. Translated by B. Kotlyarov and E. D. Pedchenko. Neptune City, NJ: Paganiniana, 1984.

Kratochvíl, Jirka, and Michael Beckerman. "A Talk around Martinů." In *Martinů's Mysterious Accident: Essays in Honor of Michael Henderson*, edited by Michael Beckerman, 155–88. Hillsdale, NY: Pendragon, 2007.

Krautwurst, Franz. "Felix Mendelssohn Bartholdy als Bratschist." In *Gedenkschrift Hermann Beck*, edited by Hermann Dechant and Wolfgang Sieber, 151–60. Laaber, Germany: Laaber-Verlag, 1982.

Kroll, Mark. *Johann Nepomuk Hummel: A Musician's Life and World*. Lanham, MD: Scarecrow, 2007.

Kufferath, Maurice. *Henri Vieuxtemps: Sa vie et son oeuvre*. Brussels: J. Rozez, 1882.

Küntzel, Hans. *Brahms in Göttingen: Mit Erinnerungen von Agathe Schütte, geb. von Siebold*. Göttingen: Edition Herodot, 1985.

"Kurze Anzeigen: Sonate pour le Pianoforte, av. accomp. d'Alto ou (de) Violon, comp. par J. N. Hummel. Oeuvr. 19. Leipzig, chez Peters. (Pr. 20 Gr.)." *Allgemeine musikalische Zeitung* 20, no. 31 (August 5, 1818): cols. 563–64.

"Kurze Anzeigen: Trois Sonates p. le Pianoforte, ded. à M. la Pr. roy. de Danemark, p. Jean Nep. Hummel. Oeuv. 3 [*sic*]. Bey Ebend. (3 Fl. 30 Xr.)." *Allgemeine musikalische Zeitung* 1, no. 10 (December 5, 1798): cols. 157–58.

Kushner, David Z. *The Ernest Bloch Companion*. Westport, CT: Greenwood, 2002.

Küster, Konrad. *Mozart: A Musical Biography*. Translated by Mary Whittall. Oxford: Clarendon Press, 1996.

[Laborde, Jean-Benjamin]. *Essai sur la musique ancienne et moderne*. 4 vols. Paris: Pierres, 1780.

Lainé, Frédéric. *L'alto: Histoire, facture, interprètes, répertoire, pédagogie*. Bressuire, France: Anne Fuzeau, 2010.

Laki, Peter. "Violin Works and the Viola Concerto." In *The Cambridge Companion to Bartók*, edited by Amanda Bayley, 133–50. Cambridge: Cambridge University Press, 2001.

Landon, H. C. Robbins. "The Concertos: (2) Their Musical Origin and Development." In *The Mozart Companion*, edited by H. C. Robbins Landon and Donald Mitchell, 234–82. New York: W. W. Norton, 1956.

Langford, Jeffrey. "The Symphonies." In *The Cambridge Companion to Berlioz*, edited by Peter Bloom, 53–68. Cambridge: Cambridge University Press, 2000.

Lansdown, Louise. "Paul Hindemith's *Der Schwanendreher*: A Biographical Landmark." *Journal of the American Viola Society* 28, no. 2 (Fall 2012): 33–51.

Large, Brian. *Martinů*. New York: Holmes & Meier, 1976.

Larsen, J. P. "Some Observations on the Development and Characteristics of Vienna Classical Instrumental Music." *Studia Musicologica Academiae Scientiarum Hungaricae* 9, nos. 1–2 (1967): 115–39.

Lawrence, Vera Brodsky. *Strong on Music: The New York Music Scene in the Days of George Templeton Strong, 1836–1875*. Vol. 1, *Resonances: 1836–1850*. New York: Oxford University Press, 1988.

Lebermann, Walter. "Apokryph, Plagiat, Korruptel oder Falsifikat?" *Die Musikforschung* 20, no. 4 (October/December 1967): 413 25.

Ledbetter, David. "Instrumental Chamber and Ensemble Music." In *The Routledge Research Companion to Johann Sebastian Bach*, edited by Robin A. Leaver, 317–57. London: Routledge, 2017.

Ledebur, Carl Freiherrn von. *Tonkünstler-Lexicon Berlin's von den ältesten Zeiten bis auf die Gegenwart*. Berlin: Ludwig Rauh, 1861.

Lendvai, Ernő. *Béla Bartók: An Analysis of His Music*. Revised reprint ed. London: Kahn & Averill, 1979.

"Lillian Fuchs." In *The Way They Play: Book 2*, by Samuel Applebaum and Sada Applebaum, 208–23. Neptune City, NJ: Paganiniana, 1973.

Lindner, Adalbert. *Max Reger: Ein Bild seines Jugendlebens und künstlerischen Werdens*. Stuttgart: J. Engelhorns Nachf., 1922.

Litzmann, Berthold. *Clara Schumann: An Artist's Life*. Translated by Grace E. Hadow. 2 vols. London: Macmillan, 1913.

Lloyd, Stephen. *William Walton: Muse of Fire*. Woodbridge, UK: Boydell Press, 2001.

Lloyd-Jones, David. "Violin and Cello Concertos *(Vol. 11)*." In *The William Walton Reader: The Genesis, Performance, and Publication of His Works*, edited by David Lloyd-Jones, 158–70. Oxford: Oxford University Press, 2018.

Loft, Abram. Review of *Suite Hébraique for Viola (or Violin) and Piano*, by Ernest Bloch. *Notes*, 2nd ser., 11, no. 2 (March 1954): 273.

"London Concerts: Viola Recital." *Musical Times* 46, no. 748 (June 1, 1905): 403–4.

Lotz, Wilhelm, and Heinrich Walther. "Die Gießener Musikgeschichte." In *Giessen, 1248–1948: Siebenhundert Jahre Gießen in Wort und Bild*, 84–87. Giessen, Germany: Brühlsche Universitätsdruckerei Gießen, 1948.

MacDonald, Calum. [Introduction] to *Trio for Violin, Violoncello and Piano*, by Rebecca Clarke, [i]. London: Winthrop Rogers, 1994.

Macdonald, Hugh. *Berlioz*. London: J. M. Dent & Sons, 1982.

Macdonald, Hugh. Foreword to *Harold en Italie: Symphonie en 4 parties avec un alto principal*, by [Hector] Berlioz, piano reduction by Hugh Macdonald, iii. Kassel: Bärenreiter, 2001. Piano reduction.

MacDonald, Malcolm. *Brahms*. New York: Schirmer, 1990.

MacDonald, Malcolm. "'I Took a Simple Little Theme and Developed It': Shostakovich's String Concertos and Sonatas." In *The Cambridge Companion to Shostakovich*, edited by Pauline Fairclough and David Fanning, 115–43. Cambridge: Cambridge University Press, 2008.

Magidoff, Robert. *Yehudi Menuhin: The Story of the Man and the Musician*. 2nd ed. London: Robert Hale, 1973.

Mahling, Christoph-Hellmut. Foreword to *Neue Ausgabe sämtlicher Werke*, Serie V, *Konzerte*, Werkgruppe 14, *Konzerte für ein oder mehrere Streich-, Blas- und Zupfinstrumente und Orchester*, vol. 2, *Concertone, Sinfonia concertante*, by Wolfgang Amadeus Mozart, edited by Christoph-Hellmut Mahling, vii–xiv. Leipzig: VEB Deutscher Verlag für Musik, 1975.

Maine, Basil. *Twang with Our Music*. London: Epworth, 1957.

Malcolm, Noel. *George Enescu: His Life and Music*. [London]: Toccata, 1990.

Malcolm, Noel. "The Universality of George Enescu." In *Celebrating George Enescu: A Symposium*, 21–32. Washington, DC: Education for Peace, 1997.

Marissen, Michael. *The Social and Religious Designs of J. S. Bach's Brandenburg Concertos*. Princeton, NJ: Princeton University Press, 1995.

Martinson, Kenneth. "The Music for Viola of Milhaud." *Journal of the American Viola Society* 15, no. 1 (1999): 27–33.

Martinů, Bohuslav. Descriptive note to *Symphony No. 1*, by Bohuslav Martinů. *Concert Bulletin of the Boston Symphony Orchestra* (Sixty-Second Season, Sixth Programme), November 13 and 14, 1942, 228–38.

Martinů, Bohuslav. *Domov, hudba a svět: Deníky, zápisníky, úvahy a články*. Prague: Státní Hudební, 1966.

Martinů, Bohuslav. *Reminiscences*. Polička: Popelka, 1945.

Mason, Daniel Gregory. *The Chamber Music of Brahms*. Reprint ed. Ann Arbor, MI: Edwards Brothers, 1950.

Massip, Catherine. "Bibliothèque du Conservatoire." In *The Cambridge Berlioz Encyclopedia*, edited by Julian Rushton, 55–56. Cambridge: Cambridge University Press, 2018.

Maurice, Donald. *Bartók's Viola Concerto: The Remarkable Story of His Swansong*. Oxford: Oxford University Press, 2004.

McInnes, Donald. "Berlioz's *Harold in Italy*." *Strad* 123, no. 1469 (September 2012): 84–87.

McN[aught], [William]. "London Concerts: Courtauld-Sargent Concert." *Musical Times* 75, no. 1102 (December 1934): 1128.

McVeigh, Simon. "Concerto of the Individual." In *The Cambridge History of Eighteenth-Century Music*, edited by Simon P. Keefe, 583–612. Cambridge: Cambridge University Press, 2005.

McVeigh, Simon, and Jehoash Hirshberg. *The Italian Solo Concerto, 1700–1760: Rhetorical Strategies and Style History*. Woodbridge, UK: Boydell Press, 2004.

Menuhin, Yehudi. *Unfinished Journey*. New York: Alfred A. Knopf, 1977.

Mercer-Taylor, Peter. *The Life of Mendelssohn*. Cambridge: Cambridge University Press, 2000.

Meyer, Clemens, ed. *Sammlung auserlesener und seltener Werke (aus d. 18. Jahrhundert) für Viola und Clavier*. 2 vols. Leipzig: J. Rieter-Biedermann, 1900.

Michael, Julie. "Zen in the Art of Viola Playing: Takemitsu's *A Bird came down the Walk*." *Journal of the American Viola Society* 30, no. 1 (Spring 2014): 29–38.

Milburn, Dwayne Steven. "The Use of Quotation in *Sonata for Viola and Piano* and *Symphony No. 15* as Examples of Late Style in Shostakovich." PhD diss., University of California, Los Angeles, 2009.

Milhaud, Darius. *Notes without Music: An Autobiography*. Translated by Donald Evans. Edited by Rollo H. Myers. New York: Alfred A. Knopf, 1953.

"Monday Popular Concerts." *Players* 3, no. 57 (January 26, 1861): 235.

Mozart, Wolfgang Amadeus. *Mozart's Letters, Mozart's Life: Selected Letters*. Edited and translated by Robert Spaethling. New York: W. W. Norton, 2000.

"Mr. York Bowen." *Musical Herald*, no. 769 (April 1, 1912): 99–101.

Mundy, Simon. *Alexander Glazunov: Russia's Great Musical Conciliator*. London: Thames, 1987.

Musgrave, Michael. *The Life of Schumann*. Cambridge: Cambridge University Press, 2011.

Musgrave, Michael. *The Music of Brahms*. London: Routledge & Kegan Paul, 1985.

Musicale Program, The Covenant Club, March 3, 1952.

"Musikalien-Anzeige." *Kurpfalzbaierischer Münchner Anzeiger*, no. 40 (October 7, 1801): [7].

Musikalischer Almanach auf das Jahr 1782. Alethinopel: self-pub, 1782.

"Nachrichten: Berlin. Uebersicht des April." *Allgemeine musikalische Zeitung* 25, no. 21 (May 1823): cols. 337–39.

Neumeyer, David. *The Music of Paul Hindemith*. New Haven, CT: Yale University Press, 1986.

Newman, Michael. Review of *Cadenza for Solo Viola*, by Krzysztof Penderecki. *Strad* 99, no. 1182 (October 1988): 817.

Newman, William S. *The Sonata in the Baroque Era*. Chapel Hill: University of North Carolina Press, 1959.

Nichols, Roger. *Conversations with Madeleine Milhaud*. London: Faber and Faber, 1996.

Noss, Luther. *Paul Hindemith in the United States*. Urbana: University of Illinois Press, 1989.

Note to *Suite for Viola and Orchestra (Pianoforte)*, by R. Vaughan Williams. 3 vols., [i]. London: Oxford University Press, 1936. Piano reduction.

"Notizen: St. Petersburg." *Allgemeine Wiener Musik-Zeitung* 8, no. 42 (April 6, 1848): 168.

"Nouvelles." *Gazette musicale de Paris* 1, no. 4 (January 26, 1834): 34.

Novello, Vincent, and Mary Novello. *A Mozart Pilgrimage: Being the Travel Diaries of Vincent & Mary Novello in the Year 1829.* Translated and compiled by Nerina Medici di Marignano. Edited by Rosemary Hughes. London: Novello, 1955.

"The Official Denunciation of Shostakovich's *Lady Macbeth of Mtsensk District.*" In *Epic Revisionism: Russian History and Literature as Stalinist Propaganda,* edited by Kevin M. F. Platt and David Brandenberger, 135–39. Madison: University of Wisconsin Press, 2006.

Olkhovsky, Andrey. *Music under the Soviets: The Agony of an Art.* New York: Frederick A. Praeger, 1955.

Oppelt, Robert Lloyd. "A Study of Contemporary American Viola Solos." DMA diss., University of Rochester, 1956.

Orga, Ates. "Penderecki: Composer of Martyrdom." *Music and Musicians* 18, no. 1 (September 1969): 34–38, 76.

Ottaway, Hugh. "English Orchestral," review of *Suite for Viola and Small Orchestra,* by Ralph Vaughan Williams. *Musical Times* 107, no. 1482 (August 1966): 708.

"Panel Discussion: The Bartók Viola Concerto; From the 1997 International Viola Congress in Austin, Texas." *Journal of the American Viola Society* 14, no. 1 (1998): 15–49.

Patorni-Casadesus, Régina. *Souvenirs d'une claveciniste: Ma famille Casadesus.* Paris: La Ruche Ouvriere, 1962.

Paulu, Norman, and Catherine Paulu. "Germain Prévost: A Reminiscence of the Pro Arte Quartet." WHA radio broadcast.

Paynter, Mary. *Phoenix from the Fire: A History of Edgewood College.* Madison, WI: Edgewood College, 2002.

Penderecki, Krzysztof. *Cadenza per viola sola: Fassung für Violine solo.* Arranged by Christiane Edinger. Mainz: B. Schott's Söhne, 1989.

Penderecki, Krzysztof. *Labyrinth of Time: Five Addresses for the End of the Millennium.* Edited by Ray Robinson. Translated by William Brand. Chapel Hill, NC: Hinshaw Music, 1998.

Penderecki, Krzysztof. "The Tree Inside." In Penderecki, *Labyrinth of Time,* 15–19. Chapel Hill, NC: Hinshaw Music, 1998.

Penderecki, Krzysztof, and Ray Robinson. "Krzysztof Penderecki's 'Labyrinth of Time': Conversations at the End of the Millennium." In Penderecki, *Labyrinth of Time,* 71–91. Chapel Hill, NC: Hinshaw Music, 1998.

"Peter Schidlof." In *Remembering Britten,* edited by Alan Blyth, 47–49. London: Hutchinson, 1981.

Pethő, Csilla. "*Style Hongrois.* Hungarian Elements in the Works of Haydn, Beethoven, Weber and Schubert." *Studia Musicologica Academiae Scientiarum Hungaricae* 41, nos. 1–3 (2000): 199–284.

Petzoldt, Richard. *Georg Philipp Telemann.* Translated by Horace Fitzpatrick. New York: Oxford University Press, 1974.

P[eyser], H[erbert] F. "Gifted Artists Join in Unique Recital." *Musical America* 27, no. 17 (February 23, 1918): 10.

Ponder, Michael. "Rebecca Clarke." *Journal of the British Music Society* 5 (1983): 82–88.

Popp, Susanne, ed. *Thematisch-chronologisches Verzeichnis der Werke Max Regers und ihrer Quellen: Reger-Werk-Verzeichnis (RWV).* 2 vols. Munich: Henle, 2010.

Popp, Susanne, and Susanne Shigihara. *Max Reger: At the Turning Point to Modernism.* Bonn: Bouvier, 1988.

Potter, Tully. "Max Reger Explores the Alto Clef." *Mitteilungen* [Internationale Max-Reger-Gesellschaft], no. 16 (2008): 29–31.

Powell, Neil. *Benjamin Britten: A Life for Music.* London: Hutchinson, 2013.

[Preface] to *Concerto for Viola and Orchestra*, by William Walton, [1]. Oxford: Oxford University Press, [1964], © 1930. Piano reduction.

Primrose, William. *Walk on the North Side: Memoirs of a Violist.* Provo, UT: Brigham Young University Press, 1978.

Prout, Ebenezer. *Applied Forms: A Sequel to* Musical Form. London: Augener, 1895.

Rabl, Walter. *Quartett (Es dur) für Pianoforte, Violine, Clarinette (oder Bratsche) und Violoncell, op. 1.* Berlin: Simrock, 1897.

Raby, Peter. "Smithson, Harriet ('Henriette') Constance." In *The Cambridge Berlioz Encyclopedia*, edited by Julian Rushton, 310–11. Cambridge: Cambridge University Press, 2018.

Radoux, J. T. *Henry Vieuxtemps: His Life and Works.* Translated by Samuel Wolf. Linthicum Heights, MD: Swand, 1983.

Rafael, Ruth. "Ernest Bloch at the San Francisco Conservatory of Music." *Western States Jewish Historical Quarterly* 9, no. 3 (April 1977): 195–215.

Ramey, Corinne. "Bach's Baroque Gem Offers (Grateful) Violists the Spotlight." *Strings* 27, no. 6 (January 2013): 29–30.

Rampe, Siegbert, and Dominik Sackmann, eds. *Bachs Orchestermusik: Entstehung, Klangwelt, Interpretation; Ein Handbuch.* Kassel: Bärenreiter, 2000.

Rapoport, Erez. *Mendelssohn's Instrumental Music: Structure and Style.* Hillsdale, NY: Pendragon, 2012.

Ratner, Leonard G. *Classic Music: Expression, Form, and Style.* Paperback ed. New York: Schirmer, 1985.

Reed, Philip. Introduction to *Letters from a Life: The Selected Letters of Benjamin Britten, 1913–1976*, vol. 4, *1952–1957*, edited by Philip Reed, Mervyn Cooke, and Donald Mitchell, 1–14. Woodbridge, UK: Boydell Press, 2008.

Reger, Max. *Max Reger: Briefe an Karl Straube.* Edited by Susanne Popp. Bonn: Ferd. Dümmlers, 1986.

Reger, Max. *Sämtliche Werke.* Vol. 24, *Werke für Streicher: I*, edited by Hermann Grabner. Wiesbaden: Breitkopf & Härtel, 1957.

Reger, Max. "[Was ist mir Johann Sebastian Bach und was bedeutet er für unsere Zeit?]." *Die Musik* 5, no. 1 (October 1905): 74.

Reich, Willi. "Paul Hindemith." *Musical Quarterly* 17, no. 4 (October 1931): 486–96.

Reiter, Erica Amelia. "Krzysztof Penderecki's Cadenza for Viola Solo as a Derivative of the Concerto for Viola and Orchestra: A Numerical Analysis and a Performer's Guide." DMA thesis, University of Arizona, 1997.

"Reviews: 'Elegie'—for Alto, Violin, or Violoncello, with Accompaniment for the Pianoforte. By H. Vieuxtemps, Op. 30, Ewer & Co." *Musical World* 32, no. 26 (July 1, 1854): 439.

"Reviews: 'Elégie,' pour alto, ou violoncelle, ou violon, avec accompagnement de piano—par H. Vieuxtemps, Op. 30 (Ewer & Co.)." *Musical World* 37, no. 26 (June 25, 1859): 403.

Reynolds, Roger, and Toru Takemitsu. "Roger Reynolds and Toru Takemitsu: A Conversation." *Musical Quarterly* 80, no. 1 (Spring 1996): 61–76.

Rice, John A. "The Musical Bee: References to Mozart and Cherubini in Hummel's 'New Year' Concerto." *Music & Letters* 77, no. 3 (August 1996): 401–24.

Riley, Maurice W. *The History of the Viola*. 2 vols. Ann Arbor, MI: Braun-Brumfield, 1980–1991.

Riley, Maurice W. "Scordatura for the Viola." Chap. 9 in *The History of the Viola*, vol. 2. Ann Arbor, MI: Braun-Brumfield, 1991.

Rimsky-Korsakoff, Nikolay Andreyevich. *My Musical Life*. Edited by Carl van Vechten. Translated by Judah A. Joffe. 2nd ed., rev. New York: Alfred A. Knopf, 1928.

Robinson, Ray. *Krzysztof Penderecki: A Guide to His Works*. Princeton, NJ: Prestige, 1983.

Roger, Juliusz. *Pieśni ludu polskiego w Górnym Szląsku z muzyką*. Wrocław: H. Skutsch, 1863.

Rolf, Ares. *J. S. Bach: Das sechste Brandenburgische Konzert; Besetzung, Analyse, Entstehung*. Dortmund, Germany: Klangfarben Musikverlag, 2002.

Rood, Louise. "Quincy Porter: Suite for Solo Viola." *Repertoire* 1, no. 2 (November 1951): 110–11.

Rood, Louise. "The Viola as Solo Instrument." MA thesis, Smith College, 1942.

Rood, Louise. "A Welcome Viola Concerto." *Repertoire* 1, no. 1 (October 1951): 47–49.

Rooney, Dennis. "Traditional Values." *Strad* 96, no. 1149 (January 1986): 676–78.

Rosen, Charles. *The Classical Style: Haydn, Mozart, Beethoven*. New York: W. W. Norton, 1972.

Rosenberg, Donald. *The Cleveland Orchestra Story: "Second to None."* Cleveland: Gray & Company, 2000.

Rosenfeld, Paul. *Musical Portraits: Interpretations of Twenty Modern Composers*. New York: Harcourt, Brace, 1920.

Rosselli, John. *The Life of Mozart*. Cambridge: Cambridge University Press, 1998.

Rubbra, Edmund. "The Later Vaughan Williams." *Music & Letters* 18, no. 1 (January 1937): 1–8.

Rushton, Julian. *The Music of Berlioz*. Oxford: Oxford University Press, 2001.

Rushton, Julian. *The Musical Language of Berlioz*. Cambridge: Cambridge University Press, 1983.

Rushton, Julian, ed. *The Cambridge Berlioz Encyclopedia*. Cambridge: Cambridge University Press, 2018.

Rybka, F. James. *Bohuslav Martinů: The Compulsion to Compose*. Lanham, MD: Scarecrow, 2011.

Sachs, Joel. *Kapellmeister Hummel in England and France*. Detroit Monographs in Musicology 6. Detroit: Information Coordinators, 1977.

Sadie, Stanley. *Handel Concertos*. BBC Music Guides. Seattle: University of Washington Press, 1972.

Šafránek, Miloš. *Bohuslav Martinů: His Life and Works*. Translated by Roberta Finlayson-Samsourová. London: Allan Wingate, 1962.

Šafránek, Miloš. *Bohuslav Martinů: The Man and His Music*. Translated by Božena Linhartová. New York: Alfred A. Knopf, 1944.

Saleski, Gdal. *Famous Musicians of Jewish Origin*. New York: Bloch, 1949.

Sárosi, Bálint. *Gypsy Music*. Translated by Fred Macnicol. Budapest: Corvina, 1978.

Saunders, William. *Weber*. London: J. M. Dent and Sons, 1940. Reprint, New York: Da Capo, 1970.

Saylor, Eric. *English Pastoral Music: From Arcadia to Utopia, 1900–1955*. Urbana: University of Illinois Press, 2017.

Schader, Luitgard. "Hindemiths Skizzenbücher Nr. 1 bis 41: Entstehungszusammenhang und Inhalt einer Quellengruppe." *Hindemith-Jahrbuch* 30 (2001): 203–55.

Schafer, Murray. *British Composers in Interview*. London: Faber and Faber, 1963.

Schleuning, Peter. "Bachs sechstes *Brandenburgisches Konzert*—eine Pastorale." In *Bachs Orchesterwerke: Bericht über das 1. Dortmunder Bach-Symposion 1996*, edited by Martin Geck and Werner Breig, 203–21. Witten, Germany: Klangfarben Musikverlag, 1997.

Schmusch, Rainer. "Prix de Rome (1)." Translated by Louisa Tsougaraki. In *The Cambridge Berlioz Encyclopedia*, edited by Julian Rushton, 262–63. Cambridge: Cambridge University Press, 2018.

Schneider, David E. "Contrasts and Common Concerns in the Concerto, 1900–1945." In *Cambridge Companion to the Concerto*, edited by Simon P. Keefe, 139–60. Cambridge: Cambridge University Press, 2005.

Schrader, Bruno. "Musikbrief: Aus Berlin." *Neue Zeitschrift für Musik* 84, no. 11 (March 15, 1917): 89–90.

Schubart, Christ[ian] Fried[rich] Dan[iel]. *Ideen zu einer Ästhetik der Tonkunst*. Edited by Ludwig Schubart. Vienna: Bey J. V. Degen, 1806.

Schubert, Giselher. Preface to *Der Schwanendreher: Concerto after Old Folksongs for Viola and Small Orchestra*, by Paul Hindemith, iii–ix. Translated by Penelope Souster. London: Ernst Eulenburg, 1985. Miniature score.

Schubert, Giselher. "Vorgeschichte und Entstehung der *Unterweisung im Tonsatz. Theoretischer Teil.*" *Hindemith-Jahrbuch* 9 (1980): 16–64.

Schumann, Robert. *Märchenbilder für Viola (Violine) und Klavier, opus 113*. Edited by Armin Koch. Mainz: Schott, 2018.

Schumann, Robert. *Neue Ausgabe sämtlicher Werke*. Serie II, *Kammermusik*, Werkgruppe 3, *Werke für verschiedene Instrumente und Klavier*. Edited by Michael Beiche, Tirza Cremer, Ute Scholz, Matthias Wendt, Armin Koch, and Elisa Novara. Mainz: Schott, 2015.

Schumann, Robert. *Tagebücher*. Vol. 3, pt. 2, *Haushaltbücher, 1847–1847 [sic]*, edited by Gerd Nauhaus. Leipzig: VEB Deutscher, 1982.

Schumann, Robert. "Zweiter Quartett-Morgen." *Neue Zeitschrift für Musik* 8, no. 49 (June 19, 1838): 193–95.

Schwandt, Christoph. *Carl Maria von Weber in seiner Zeit: Eine Biografie*. Mainz: Schott, 2014.

Schwarz, Boris. *Great Masters of the Violin: From Corelli and Vivaldi to Stern, Zukerman and Perlman*. New York: Simon & Schuster, 1983.

Schwarz, Boris. *Music and Musical Life in Soviet Russia*. Enlarged edition. Bloomington: Indiana University Press, 1983.

Schwinger, Wolfram. *Krzysztof Penderecki: His Life and Work*. Translated by William Mann. London: Schott, 1989.

Scott, Heather K. "Living in Alto Clef: 11 Top Players Pick the Best Loved, and Most Overlooked, Viola Works of All Time." *Strings* 22, no. 5 (December 2007): 61–68.

Scott, Walter. *The Abbot*. Edited by Christopher Johnson. Edinburgh: Edinburgh University Press, 2000.

"Second concert de M. Berlioz." *Gazette musicale de Paris* 1, no. 49 (December 7, 1834): 394–95.

Serly, Tibor. "A Belated Account of the Reconstruction of a 20th Century Masterpiece." *College Music Symposium* 15 (Spring 1975): 7–25.

Sharp, Cecil J. Introduction to *English Folk Songs from the Southern Appalachians*, collected by Olive Dame Campbell and Cecil J. Sharp, iii–xxxiii. New York: G. P. Putnam's Sons, 1917.

Shaver-Gleason, Linda. "Felix Mendelssohn: Violist." *Journal of the American Viola Society* 27, no. 2 (Fall 2011): 19–27.

Shore, Bernard. *Sixteen Symphonies*. London: Longmans, Green, 1949.

Sills, David. "Benjamin Britten's *Lachrymae*: An Analysis for Performers." *Journal of the American Viola Society* 13, no. 3 (1997): 17–34.

Sills, David. "The Viola Music of Lillian Fuchs." *American String Teacher* 35, no. 2 (Spring 1985): 59–61.

Sills, David L. Review of *Concerto per viola ed orchestra* and *Cadenza per viola solo*, by Krzysztof Penderecki. *Notes*, 2nd ser., 46, no. 1 (September 1989): 230–31.

Silverthorne, Paul. "Brahms Viola Sonata Op. 120 No. 2." *Strad* 127, no. 1518 (October 2016): 69–78.

Singer, Isidore, ed. *The Jewish Encyclopedia*. 12 vols. New York: Funk and Wagnalls, 1901–1906.

"Sir Michael Tippett." In *Remembering Britten*, edited by Alan Blyth, 62–71. London: Hutchinson, 1981.

"Sir Peter Pears." In *Remembering Britten*, edited by Alan Blyth, 17–23. London: Hutchinson, 1981.

"Sir William Walton Talks to John Warrack." *Listener* 80, no. 2054 (August 8, 1968): 176–78.

"Sir William Walton's 70th Birthday: All Week, BBC2 and Radio 3." *Radio Times* 194, no. 2524 (March 23, 1972): 15.

Sitwell, Osbert. *Laughter in the Next Room*. Boston: Little, Brown, 1948.

Skelton, Geoffrey. *Paul Hindemith: The Man behind the Music*. London: Victor Gollancz, 1975.

Smith, George H. L. Historical and analytical note to *Rhapsody-Concerto for Viola and Orchestra*, by Bohuslav Martinu. The Cleveland Orchestra (Fifteenth Program), February 19 and 21, 1953, 459–62.

Smith, Peter H. "*Hausmusik* for Cognoscenti: Some Formal Characteristics of Schumann's Late-Period Character Pieces for Instrumental Ensemble." *Music Theory Spectrum* 37, no. 1 (Spring 2015): 51–70.

Sokolov, Ivan. "Moving towards an Understanding of Shostakovich's Viola Sonata." Translated by Elizabeth Wilson. In *Contemplating Shostakovich: Life, Music and Film*, edited by Alexander Ivashkin and Andrew Kirkman, 79–94. Burlington, VT: Ashgate, 2012.

Sorabji, Kaikhosru Shapurji. *Mi Contra Fa: The Immoralisings of a Machiavellian Musician*. London: Porcupine, 1947.

Stamic, Karel. *Koncert D-dur nr 1 na altówkę i orkiestrę*. Edited by Janusz Zathey and Jerzy Kosmala. [3rd ed.] Kraków: Polskie Wydawnictwo Muzyczne, 1979. Piano reduction.

Stamitz, Carlo. *Six Duo Pour un Violon et un Alto, Oeuvre X*. Paris: Heina, [c. 1773].

Stamitz, K[arl]. *Kontsert dlia al'ta s orkestrom*. Edited by Vadim Borisovsky. Moscow: Muzgiz, 1962. Piano reduction.

Stamitz, Karl. *Konzert in D Dur für Viola und Klavier, Op. 1*. Edited by Paul Klengel. Leipzig: Breitkopf & Härtel, 1932. Piano reduction.

Steblin, Rita. *A History of Key Characteristics in the Eighteenth and Early Nineteenth Centuries*. 2nd ed. Rochester, NY: University of Rochester Press, 2002.

Stevens, Halsey. *The Life and Music of Béla Bartók*. New York: Oxford University Press, 1953.

Stowell, Robin. *The Early Violin and Viola: A Practical Guide*. Cambridge: Cambridge University Press, 2001.

Straeten, E. van der. *The History of the Violin: Its Ancestors and Collateral Instruments from Earliest Times*. 2 vols. New York: Da Capo, 1968.

Straeten, E. van der. "The Viola: Part IV; Noted Players of the Viola and Viole D'amour." *Strad* 24, no. 280 (August 1913): 133–34.

Straube, Karl. *Karl Straube: Briefe eines Thomaskantors.* Edited by Wilibald Gurlitt and Hans-Olaf Hudemann. Stuttgart: K. F. Koehler, 1952.

Strauss, Virginia Rose Fattaruso. "The Stylistic Use of the Violin in Selected Works by Stravinsky." DMA treatise, University of Texas at Austin, 1980.

Stravinsky, Igor. *An Autobiography.* New York: M. & J. Steuer, 1958.

Stravinsky, Igor. *Élégie for Viola or Violin Unaccompanied.* New York: Chappell, 1945.

Sweeting, Elizabeth. "The First Festival and Its Background: 1948." In *Time & Concord: Aldeburgh Festival Recollections,* compiled and edited by Jenni Wake-Walker, 1–2. Saxmundham, UK: Autograph Books, 1997.

Takemitsu, Asaka. *A Memoir of Tōru Takemitsu.* Translated by Tomoko Isshiki with David Pacun and Mitsuko Ono. Bloomington, IN: iUniverse, 2010.

Takemitsu, Toru. *Confronting Silence: Selected Writings.* Translated and edited by Yoshiko Kakudo and Glenn Glasow. Berkeley, CA: Fallen Leaf, 1995.

Takemitsu, Tōru. "Contemporary Music in Japan." *Perspectives of New Music* 27, no. 2 (Summer 1989): 198–204.

Takemitsu, Toru. "Dream and Number." In Takemitsu, *Confronting Silence,* 97–126. Berkeley, CA: Fallen Leaf, 1995.

Takemitsu, Toru. "Mirror and Egg: 2. The Garden of Music." In Takemitsu, *Confronting Silence,* 95–96. Berkeley, CA: Fallen Leaf, 1995.

Takemitsu, Toru. "Notes on *November Steps.*" In Takemitsu, *Confronting Silence,* 83–90. Berkeley, CA: Fallen Leaf, 1995.

Talbot, Michael. "The Italian Concerto in the Late Seventeenth and Early Eighteenth Centuries." In *Cambridge Companion to the Concerto,* edited by Simon P. Keefe, 35–52. Cambridge: Cambridge University Press, 2005.

Talbot, Michael. "Purpose and Peculiarities of the *Brandenburg Concertos.*" In *Bach und die Stile: Bericht über das 2. Dortmunder Bach-Symposion 1998,* edited by Martin Geck and Klaus Hofmann, 255–89. Dortmund, Germany: Klangfarben Musikverlag, 1999.

Tari, Lujza. "Unterhaltungsmusik als Quelle für das 'Ungarische' im 'Andante e Rondo Ungarese' op. 35 von Carl Maria von Weber." In *Kulturelle Identität durch Musik?: Das Burgenland und seine Nachbarn,* edited by Klaus Aringer, Ulrike Aringer-Grau, and Bernhard Habla, 83 93. Vienna: Kliment, 2009.

Tatlow, Ruth. *Bach's Numbers: Compositional Proportion and Significance.* Cambridge: Cambridge University Press, 2015.

Taylor, Benedict. *Mendelssohn, Time and Memory: The Romantic Conception of Cyclic Form.* Cambridge: Cambridge University Press, 2011.

Taylor, Ronald. *Robert Schumann: His Life and Work.* New York: Universe, 1982.

Terry, C. Sanford. "Baron Bach." *Music & Letters* 12, no. 2 (April 1931): 130–39.

Tertis, Lionel. *Cinderella No More.* London: Peter Nevill, 1953.

Tertis, Lionel. *My Viola and I: A Complete Autobiography.* London: Paul Elek, 1974.

Thayer, Alexander Wheelock. *Thayer's Life of Beethoven.* Revised and edited by Elliot Forbes. 2 vols. Princeton, NJ: Princeton University Press, 1967.

T[ilmouth], M[ichael]. Review of *Rhapsody-Concerto,* by Bohuslav Martinů. *Music & Letters* 54, no. 4 (October 1973): 520.

Todd, R. Larry. "The Chamber Music of Mendelssohn." In *Nineteenth-Century Chamber Music,* edited by Stephen E. Hefling, 170–207. New York: Schirmer Books, 1998.

Todd, R. Larry. *Mendelssohn: A Life in Music.* Oxford: Oxford University Press, 2003.

Todd, R. Larry. *Mendelssohn's Musical Education: A Study and Edition of His Exercises in Composition*. Cambridge: Cambridge University Press, 1983.

Tovey, Donald Francis. "Berlioz: 'Harold in Italy', Symphony with Viola Obbligato, op. 16." In *Essays in Musical Analysis*, vol. 4, *Illustrative Music*, 74–82. London: Oxford University Press, 1948.

Tovey, Donald Francis. *Essays in Musical Analysis*. Vol. 3, *Concertos*. London: Oxford University Press, 1948.

Trygstad, Alexander. "Ritornello Form and the Dynamics of Performance in Telemann's Viola Concerto in G Major." *Journal of the American Viola Society* 31, no. 2 (Fall 2015): 11–25.

Tunbridge, Laura. *Schumann's Late Style*. Cambridge: Cambridge University Press, 2007.

Tyrrell, John. *Czech Opera*. Cambridge: Cambridge University Press, 1988.

Vaughan Williams, Ralph. "British Music." Chap. 8 in *Vaughan Williams on Music*, ed. David Manning. Oxford: Oxford University Press, 2008.

Vaughan Williams, Ralph. "A Musical Autobiography." In *National Music: And Other Essays*, 177–94. London: Oxford University Press, 1963.

Vaughan Williams, Ursula. *R. V. W.: A Biography of Ralph Vaughan Williams*. London: Oxford University Press, 1964.

Veinus, Abraham. "George Frederick Handel: Concerto for Viola and Orchestra in B Minor." In *Victor Book of Concertos*, 187. New York: Simon and Schuster, 1948.

Venturini, Donald J. *Alexander Glazounov: His Life and Works*. Delphos, OH: Aero Printing, 1992.

"Vermischtes: Literarische Notizen." *Neue Zeitschrift für Musik* 8, no. 19 (March 6, 1838): 76.

Vieuxtemps, Henry. "The Autobiography of Henry Vieuxtemps." In J. T. Radoux, *Vieuxtemps: His Life and Works*, 60–69. Linthicum Heights, MD: Swand, 1983.

Vitercik, Greg. *The Early Works of Felix Mendelssohn: A Study in the Romantic Sonata Style*. Philadelphia: Gordon and Breach, 1992.

Vogel, Oliver. "*Harold en Italie*." Translated by Gillian Andrews. In *The Cambridge Berlioz Encyclopedia*, edited by Julian Rushton, 154–57. Cambridge: Cambridge University Press, 2018.

Volkov, Simon, ed. *Testimony: The Memoirs of Dmitri Shostakovich*. Translated by Antonina W. Bouis. New York: Harper & Row, 1979.

Wallfisch, Lory. Translator's preface to *Masterworks of George Enescu: A Detailed Analysis*, by Pascal Bentoiu, vii–viii. Translated by Lory Wallfisch. Lanham, MD: Scarecrow, 2010.

Walsh, Stephen. *Stravinsky: A Creative Spring; Russia and France, 1882–1934*. New York: Alfred A. Knopf, 1999.

Walsh, Stephen. *Stravinsky: The Second Exile; France and America, 1934–1971*. New York: Alfred A. Knopf, 2006.

Walton, Susana. *William Walton: Behind the Façade*. Oxford: Oxford University Press, 1988.

Walton, William. *The Selected Letters of William Walton*. Edited by Malcolm Hayes. London: Faber and Faber, 2002.

Walton, William. *William Walton Edition*. Vol. 12, *Concerto for Viola and Orchestra*, edited by Christopher Wellington. Oxford: Oxford University Press, 2002.

Warrack, John. *Carl Maria von Weber*. 2nd ed. Cambridge: Cambridge University Press, 1976.

Wasielewski, Wilh. Josef v. *Robert Schumann: Eine Biographie*. Edited by Waldemar v. Wasielewski. Leipzig: Breitkopf und Härtel, 1906.

Wasielwski, [Wilhelm Joseph] von. *Life of Robert Schumann*. Translated by A. L. Alger. Boston: Oliver Ditson, 1871.

Watson, Monica. *York Bowen: A Centenary Tribute*. London: Thames, 1984.

Weaver, Andrew H. "Crafting the Fairy Tales: Schumann's Autograph Manuscript of *Märchenbilder*, Op. 113." *Journal of the American Viola Society* 34, no. 1 (Spring 2018): 33–45.

Weber, Max Maria von. *Carl Maria von Weber: The Life of an Artist*. Translated by J. Palgrave Simpson. 2 vols. London: Chapman and Hall, 1865.

Weinmann, Alexander. *Johann Traeg: Die Musikalienverzeichnisse von 1799 und 1804 (Handschriften und Sortiment)*. Vol. 1. Vienna: Universal Edition, 1973.

Weinmann, Alexander. *Die Wiener Verlagswerke von Franz Anton Hoffmeister*. Vienna: Universal Edition, 1964.

Wellington, Christopher. "Preface." In William Walton, *William Walton Edition*, vol. 12, *Concerto for Viola and Orchestra*, v–xi. Oxford: Oxford University Press, 2002.

Wellington, Christopher. "Sources." In William Walton, *William Walton Edition*, vol. 12, *Concerto for Viola and Orchestra*, xii–xiii. Oxford: Oxford University Press, 2002.

Wellington, Christopher. "Textual Notes." In William Walton, *William Walton Edition*, vol. 12, *Concerto for Viola and Orchestra*, xiv–xx. Oxford: Oxford University Press, 2002.

Whang, Daejin. "Observations of Paul Hindemith's Approach to Form and Tonal Language: The Three Sonatas for Viola and Piano." DMA diss., The Hartt School, University of Hartford, 2005.

White, Chappell. *From Vivaldi to Viotti: A History of the Early Classical Violin Concerto*. Philadelphia: Gordon and Breach, 1992.

White, Eric Walter. *Stravinsky: The Composer and His Works*. 2nd ed., paperback. Berkeley: University of California Press, 1984.

White, John. "The Viola Music of York Bowen." In *An Anthology of British Viola Players*, compiled and edited by John White, 19–21. Colne, UK: Comus, 1997.

White, John, comp. and ed. *An Anthology of British Viola Players*. Colne, UK: Comus, 1997.

Wiéner, Jean. *Allegro Appassionato*. Paris: Pierre Belfond, 1978.

"William Walton." In *British Composers in Interview*, by Murray Schafer, 73–82. London: Faber and Faber, 1963.

Williams, Amédée Daryl. *Lillian Fuchs: First Lady of the Viola*. 2nd rev. ed. New York: iUniverse, 2004.

Williams, Peter. *Bach: A Musical Biography*. Cambridge: Cambridge University Press, 2016.

Wilson, Elizabeth. *Shostakovich: A Life Remembered*. Princeton, NJ: Princeton University Press, 1994.

Wingfield, Paul, and Julian Horton. "Norm and Deformation in Mendelssohn's Sonata Forms." In *Mendelssohn Perspectives*, edited by Nicole Grimes and Angela R. Mace, 83–112. Farnham, UK: Ashgate, 2012.

Wojatycka, Anna. "Śląski motyw w 'Andante e rondo ungarese' Karola Marii Webera." *Prace Archiwum Śląskiej Kultury Muzycznej przy Bibliotece Głównej Akademii Muzycznej w Katowicach*, no. 8 (1979): 65–71.

Wolff, Christoph. *Johann Sebastian Bach: The Learned Musician*. New York: W. W. Norton, 2000.

Wolff, Christoph, Walter Emery, Richard Jones, Eugene Helm, Ernest Warburton, and Ellwood S. Derr. *The New Grove Bach Family*. New York: W. W. Norton, 1983.

Woodward, Ann M. "Observations on the Status, Instruments, and Solo Repertoire of Violists in the Classical Period." *Journal of the Violin Society of America* 9, no. 2 (1988): 81–104.

Woolley, Scott. "Milton Preves: A Remarkable Musical Career." *Journal of the American Viola Society* 5, no. 1 (Spring 1989): 9–13.

"The Works of William Walton in the Oxford Catalogue." The Royal Philharmonic Society (Hundred and Nineteenth Season, Eighth Concert), March 26, 1931, 6

Yearsley, David. "The Concerto in Northern Europe to c. 1770." In *Cambridge Companion to the Concerto*, edited by Simon P. Keefe, 53–69. Cambridge: Cambridge University Press, 2005.

Young, Percy M. *Vaughan Williams.* London: Dobson, 1953.

Ysaÿe, Eugène. *Henri Vieuxtemps: Mon maître.* Les cahiers Ysaÿe, no. 1. Brussels: Éditions Ysaÿe, 1968.

Yuzefovich, Victor. "Posledneye sochineniye Shostakovicha." ["Shostakovich's Last Work."] *Muzykal'naia zhizn'*, no. 21 (November 1975): 4–5.

Zaslav, Bernard. *The Viola in My Life: An Alto Rhapsody.* Palo Alto, CA: Science & Behavior Books, 2011.

Zelter, Carl Friedrich. *Carl Friedrich Zelters Darstellungen seines Lebens.* Edited by Johann-Wolfgang Schottländer. Weimar: Verlag der Goethe-Gesellschaft, 1931.

Zohn, Steven. *Music for a Mixed Taste: Style, Genre, and Meaning in Telemann's Instrumental Works.* Oxford: Oxford University Press, 2008.

"Zum zweiten Kammermusikfest in Donaueschingen: Paul Hindemith." *Neue Musik-Zeitung* 43, no. 20 (1922): 329.

Discography

Bezrukov, Georgii (viola). *Sonaty dlia al'ta i fortepiano.* With Anatolii Spivak (piano). Melodiia D 023785/023786, 1968, 33-1/3 rpm.

Bloch, Ernest. *Five Jewish Pieces.* With Milton Preves (viola) and Helene Brahm (piano). Covenant Club of Illinois E2-CL-3628–3629, [1952], 33-1/3 rpm.

Carpenter, David Aaron (viola). Overture to *Béatrice et Bénédict*, op. 27 and *Harold in Italy*, op. 16, by Hector Berlioz and *Sonata per la Gran Viola e Orchestra*, op. 35, by Nicolò Paganini. With the Helsinki Philharmonic Orchestra, conducted by Vladimir Ashkenazy. Ondine ODE 1188-2, 2011, compact disc.

Erdélyi Csaba (viola). *Viola Concerto (The Erdélyi Restoration and Orchestration 2001),* by Béla Bartók and *Harold en Italie*, by Hector Berlioz. With the New Zealand Symphony Orchestra, conducted by Marc Taddei. Concordance CCD03, 2002, compact disc.

Handel, [G. F.]. *Concerto in B Minor for Viola and Chamber Orchestra.* Arranged by [Henri] Casadesus. With William Primrose (viola) and unidentified chamber orchestra, conducted by Walter Goehr. Columbia 68975D–S68977D, 1937, 78 rpm.

Imai, Nobuko (viola). *A Bird came down the Walk: Original Works for Viola and Piano.* With Roland Pöntinen (piano). BIS CD-829, 1997, compact disc.

Kashkashian, Kim (viola). *Elegies.* With Robert Levin (piano). ECM 1316, 1986, compact disc.

Krieg, Else (violin and viola). *Romantic Recital.* With Frédéric Meinders (piano). Young Artists YA 1021, 1980, 33-1/3 rpm.

Myers, Roger (viola). *Fantasy and Farewell: Music for Viola and Orchestra.* With London Symphony Orchestra, conducted by Michael Francis. Delos DE 3441, 2013, compact disc.

Nelson, Eliesha (viola). *Quincy Porter: Complete Viola Works*. With John McLaughlin Williams (violin, piano, harpsichord, and conductor), Douglas Rioth (harp), and Northwest Sinfonia. Dorian Sono Luminus DSL-90911, 2009, compact disc.

Penderecki, Krzysztof. *Concerto for Viola and Orchestra / Symphony No. 2*. With Grigori Zhislin (viola) and the Leningrad Philharmonia Orchestra, conducted by Krzysztof Penderecki. Melodiia C10 23281 002, © 1985, 33-1/3 rpm.

Porter, Quincy. *Suite for Viola Alone*. With Quincy Porter (viola). New Music Recordings 1512, 1939, 78 rpm.

Power, Lawrence (viola). *Viola Concertos*, by William Walton and Edmund Rubbra. With BBC Scottish Symphony Orchestra, conducted by Ilan Volkov. Hyperion CDA67587, 2007, compact disc.

The Recorded Viola. Vol. 2. Pearl GEMM CDS 9149, 1995, 2 compact discs.

Smith, Erik. Liner notes to *Six "Brandenburg Concertos,"* by Johann Sebastian Bach. With Academy of St. Martin-in-the-Fields, Neville Marriner (director). Philips 6880 004–005, 33-1/3 rpm.

Stamitz, Karl. *Concerto in D Major for Viola and Orchestra, Op. 1; Sinfonia concertante for Violin and Viola with Orchestra*. With Ernst Wallfisch (viola); Susanne Lautenbacher (violin); Württemberg Chamber Orchestra, Heilbronn, conducted by Jörg Faerber; and Stuttgart Soloists. Turnabout TV 34221, [1968], 33-1/3 rpm.

Index